DATE DUE

OCT 2 3 1995	
NOV 2 0 1995	

CURRENT RESEARCH IN FILM:
Audiences, Economics, and Law

Volume 2

Bruce A. Austin, *Editor*
Rochester Institute of Technology

Ablex Publishing Corporation
Norwood, New Jersey 07648

ISBN: 0–89391–315–4   ISSN: 0748–8580

Ablex Publishing Corporation
355 Chestnut Street
Norwood, New Jersey 07648

CONTENTS

About the Contributors

Bruce A. Austin is an Associate Professor in the College of Liberal Arts, Rochester Institute of Technology.

Clifford Christians is a Research Associate Professor in the College of Communications at the University of Illinois-Urbana.

Thomas Doherty teaches in the College of Basic Studies at Boston University. His reviews of film and popular culture have appeared in *Film Quarterly* and *TV Guide*. He is currently at work on a book on exploitation filmmaking.

Gary Edgerton is an Associate Professor and Chair of the Communication Department at Goucher College. He has previously taught in the area of Radio–Television–Film at Bowling Green State University and the University of Massachusetts.

Garth S. Jowett is Director of the School of Communication at the University of Houston.

Steven Knapp is instructor in film, Department of Speech and Drama, Mercer University, Macon, Georgia. He has a master's degree in journalism from the University of Georgia.

Steve Lipkin is an Assistant Professor of Communication Arts and Sciences at Western Michigan University, where he teaches film studies and film and video production.

Gina Marchetti spent a year in Paris, France doing post-doctoral research in film theory and Asian cinema studies after completing her doctorate at Northwestern University. She teaches in the Department of Theater and Communication at the University of New Hampshire. Her articles have appeared in *Film Reader, Millennium Film Journal* and *Jump Cut,* where she is also a member of the editorial staff.

Richard Alan Nelson is Associate Professor of Communication and Associate Director of the International Telecommunications Research Institute in the School of Communication, University of Houston-University Park. He is the author of the two-volume *Florida and the American Motion Picture Industry, 1898–1980* (New York and London: Garland Publishing, 1983) and *Propaganda: A Reference Guide* (Westport, CT: Greenwood Publishing, 1986).

Martin F. Norden is an Associate Professor of Communication Studies at the University of Massachusetts/Amherst. He has published numerous articles and reviews on film and television in such journals as *Journal of Film and Video, Journal of Communication, Film and History,* and *Quarterly Review of Film Studies.* He is the coauthor of *Movies: A Language in Light* (Prentice-Hall, 1984).

Manjunath Pendakur is Assistant Professor in the Department of Radio-Television-Film at Northwestern University in Evanston, Illinois. He teaches a number of courses including International Communication, Political Economy of Media, and Third World Cinema. His publications include "The New International-al Information Order After the MacBride Commission Report" in *Media, Culture and Society*, 1983 and "United States-Canada Relations: Cultural Dependence and Conflict" in Vincent Mosco and Janet Wasko (Eds.), *Changing Patterns of Communications Control*, vol. 2, Ablex Publishing Corporation, forthcoming. Prof. Pendakur is currently researching U.S. film industry's policies in a comparative context in South Asia.

Calvin Pryluck is a Professor in the Department of Radio-Television-Film at Temple University. He has previously written on itinerant movie shows, the Big Studio era, documentary ethics, and film theory. The article presented here is part of a larger study of the industrialization of entertainment.

Kim Rotzoll is a Professor in the College of Communications at the University of Illinois-Urbana.

Cathy Schwichtenberg is an Instructor in the Department of Communication at Florida Atlantic University. Her articles have appeared in *Jump Cut, Enclitic, Sub-Stance, Central States Speech Journal,* and *Media, Culture and Society*. She is currently writing her dissertation on a social theory of television.

Barry L. Sherman is Assistant Professor of Telecommunication, Henry W. Grady School of Journalism and Mass Communication, University of Georgia. He earned the Ph.D. in speech commnication-broadcasting from the Pennsylvania State University.

Kim Wolfson is a ComputerLand marketing representative and a doctoral candidate in Communication Studies at the University of Massachusetts/Amherst.

Foreword

Volume 2 of *Current Research in Film* presents 13 original articles. As was the case for Volume 1, a wide range of topics and issues is addressed. Still, an underlying continuity among the chapters is easy to discern. In fact, the thematic and conceptual links among these 13 articles provoked some difficulty—or at least a good deal of mind-changing—when it was time to arrange Volume 2's contents.

I am pleased to report that the number of high-quality manuscripts submitted for review to *CRF* continues to increase. And, as is common practice in other publications, *CRF* has sought editorial advice and input from several scholars. The time, energy, and effort of these individuals has helped to improve and refine the work of *CRF* contributors and, as a result, *Current Research in Film* as a whole. Acknowledgement of and appreciation for their generous assistance is warmly extended to Joseph R. Dominick, Robert E. Golden, Thomas F. Gordon, Thomas Guback, John Jacobi, Christopher H. Sterling, Paul G. Ventura, and Janet Wasko.

At the time of this writing, Volume 3 of *Current Research in Film* is beginning to take shape. Again, I wish to extend an invitation to scholars whose research fits within the editorial scope of *CRF* to submit their manuscripts. Reader reaction is, of course, welcomed.

Bruce A. Austin
Rochester, New York
December, 1984

1

From Entertainment To Social Force: The Discovery of the Motion Picture 1918–1945

Garth S. Jowett

We do not really know what the final effects are when a new form of communication is introduced into a society. Since the beginning of human history mankind has adjusted to the advent of new ways of transferring and storing information, and these different forms of communication have each, in their own particular ways, made a significant contribution to the tapestry of human progress. Thus the shift from an oral society to a scriptural society made possible a whole new series of human behaviors related to information storage and retrieval (23, 27) while the advent of printing in the mid-fifteenth century enhanced the study of science, encouraged the breakdown of feudalism, and undermined the power of the Catholic Church (17). These macroshifts, while widely acknowledged as historical fact, are not clearly understood, and historians have never really come to grips with the importance of changes in the modes of communication as major factors in social and cultural change.

What we lack are the more particularistic examinations of the impact caused by the introduction of a new form of communication into an existing social and cultural system. This is especially and anomalously true of modern media systems, where the major research emphasis continues to lie in obtaining audience information which will enhance the marketability for advertising purposes. But communications media have a much more fundamental historical significance, for they have an immutable influence on the structure of the society that accepts and uses them (35, 37). The Canadian economic historian and communications philosopher Harold Innis, in his difficult book *The Bias of Communication* (34, p.4), noted that "inventions in communication compel realignments in the monopoly or the oli-

gopoly of knowledge.'' Innis' best interpretor, James W. Carey, illuminates this
concept:

> The explanation for this historical fact Innis derived from a conception of society
> based upon a model of competition appropriated from economics and extended to all
> social institutions. And in this competitive model, competition for new means of
> communications was a principal axis of the competitive struggle. Innis argued that
> the available media of communication influence very strongly the forms of social or-
> ganization that are possible. The media thus influence the kinds of human associa-
> tions that can develop in any period (7, p.273).

Yet few histories of communication systems utilize the rich tapestry left for us
to ponder in the work of Innis and his chief disciple, Marshall McLuhan. Both
Innis and McLuhan require a close reading before one can reap any intellectual
benefits from the dense, often frustrating, prose, studded with obscure aphorisms
and brilliant juxtapositions. But the ultimate rewards are sufficient to shape an entire academic career and certainly contain enough suggestions for paths of research
to keep one busy for a lifetime.

The work of McLuhan has particularly suffered from both over- and misinter-
pretation, and his contribution to the study of communications history has been ob-
scured as a result. Yet few historians and media scholars can fail to be intrigued by
the underlying thrust in all of his work, that the meaning and effect of any communications innovation is to be found in the way it structures thought and perception
(41, 42). Thus, for McLuhan, the introduction of a new form of communication or
information transferring capability, will drastically alter what he calls the ''sense
ratio'' of that society (basically, the way in which the society perceives itself by
utilizing the various communications media available to it). If the existing ratio is
disturbed by the introduction of what McLuhan calls a new ''extension'' of the human senses, such as the motion picture with its overwhelming emphasis on the visual, this will necessitate a readjustment and will ultimately require some form of
social and cultural accommodation. This accommodation can take various forms
but usually involves a process of defining the medium's utility to the society and
establishing its institutional structure (private industry, governmental control,
etc.), and often leads to the imposition of a specific regulatory mechanism to ensure a degree of social control.

The work of these two Canadian scholars, and others who have developed similar perspectives on the role of communication systems as agents of historical
change, such as Walter Ong (46), Jack Goody (23), Elizabeth Eisenstein (17),
Colin Cherry (10), Eric Havelock (27), Michael T. Clanchy (11), Thomas Carney
(9), and most recently, Harvey J. Graff (24), must be considered when dealing
with the complex issue of the history of communication. These scholars and others
have begun to point the way towards an understanding of the historical role of
communication systems in changing and shaping societies and their cultures. Such
an understanding will provide a reassessment of the significance of individual

forms of communication which will go a long way to correcting the obvious lacuna which now exists in historical scholarship concerning the role of communication systems.

As a contribution to the specialized studies mentioned earlier, this article will deal with a specific aspect of motion picture history as a modest contribution to our reevaluation of the role of communication systems as significant factors in social and cultural change. Despite the enormous number of books and articles published on motion pictures in the last eighty years, few examine in any real or meaningful sense the ways in which the advent of this popular communications medium contributed to changes in twentieth century society and culture. Only in very recent years have a number of serious historical works examined this issue in a systematic way; and, while the end results may not always be entirely satisfactory, the position of the motion picture as a significant factor in the shaping of twentieth century culture is widely acknowledged (36, 55). Historians are now much more intellectually secure when discussing the role that such entertainment forms have played in the march of human culture.

THE RESPONSE:
THE MOTION PICTURE AS CULTURAL INTRUSION

The motion picture occupies a unique place in the history of modern society, for it was the first of the major international forms of mass communication. Books, magazines, and newspapers could all command fairly large audiences but only the movies could claim world-wide audiences of hundreds of millions in the period before the introduction of radio and television. In addition, it was exactly because they were the first medium of communication to garner such large audiences that motion pictures were feared by those who evinced concern for the unbridled effects of such a potentially powerful means of persuasion. The reponse to the motion picture was a harbinger of responses to the other forms of communication introduced in the twentieth century. In may ways, these often irrational responses to the "threat" of the movies also reflected the increasing concern for the emergence of an international "mass society" so greatly feared by those concerned with the preservation of a more elite and nationalistic culture.

While there is a vast literature on all aspects of the history of motion pictures, this article concentrates on that segment which reveals the hopes and fears, the concerns and paeans, and the types of social control mechanisms and accommodation processes which were implemented as a result of the introduction of this communications-entertainment medium. The use of such material might be considered as being unfairly selective: after all, millions of people enjoyed the movies every day without undue concern for their health or their moral well-being, and without the trepidation of being "influenced." Where is their side of the story? There is a reality to such accusations in the purest scholarly sense but it is equally true to point out that these millions of eager movie patrons did not formulate the policies which ultimately affected the product that illuminated their neighborhood screens. These policies were made and promulgated instead by a select group of men and women sometimes elected by a democratic process, but more often than not appointed—or worst of all, self-appointed—to act as guardians of the public morality. Such actions were seldom based upon any real knowledge or understanding of the "influence" of the movies, but upon perception of that influence. Whether these perceptions were right or wrong is not important; what was important is that they were used as the basis for calling for control mechanisms, establishing international agreements, and passing laws which affected the flow of information between the creators (the studios) and the receivers (the public).

It was the vehemence of this response (especially the negative perspective), the wide range of sources from which it emanated, and its' longevity which captures the interest of social and cultural historians. It was for this reason that the motion picture was the most "unexpected" cultural phenomenon of the first half of the twentieth century. There had been previous acrimonious debates about the role of entertainment in society, and society's watchdogs were on constant alert to signal the dangers for the uninitiated to be found in such diversions as the "penny dreadful," pool rooms, dance halls, and even roller-skating rinks (15). Every amusement had its detractors, but the advent of the motion picture on the national and international scene elevated such protests and concerns to a much wider arena of discourse. No one had expected this when the first peep shows began, innocuously enough, in grubby storefronts in the early 1890s; but just ten years later the battle lines were already firmly drawn as the existence of the medium seemed to symbolize for many a genuine threat to their hopes and aspirations for an orderly progression of the twentieth century.

The motion picture is so much an integral part of modern life, so much an automatic feature of the current entertainment world, that it is hard to conceive of the period in the past when "movies" were the subject of such intense debate— sometimes at the highest levels of international diplomacy—concerning their perceived role as a major agent of social and cultural change. Yet there was such a time. The ubiquity of television in today's world—replete with communication satellites, inexpensive receiving antennae, microwave links, multichannel coaxial cables, and the incredible array of technological hardware which makes it possible for more than half the world's population to simultaneously view a soccer match— has obliterated from historical consideration the fact that in the first half of this century the motion picture attained a level of mass popularity only dreamed of by great conquerors of the past. What Ghengis Khan and Napolean had failed to achieve was now attained by a little man wearing a bowler hat, baggy pants, and carrying a cane.

The humble origins of the movies have been widely chronicled and, while many accounts are overly sentimental and often inaccurate, the development from peep-show device to the full-fledged "dream-palace" is universally understood (35, 56). What has not been chronicled by historicans as part of the mainstream of social and cultural history are the difficulties experienced by the new form of entertainment in the years before the introduction of television. Although the motion picture may be thought of today as a glamorous, sometimes seedy, and declining form of mass entertainment, in the period before 1947 the movies were often a fulcrum point around which the very culture of nations seemed to revolve. The motion picture was not just another popular culture diversion (although it filled that role admirably); it was also a creator of dreams, a shaper of thoughts, and a model for behavior. In every country, those people who historian Henry May has so aptly called the "custodians of culture" were aware of the motion picture's enormous potential side influences, and were very cautious in their assessment of the medium's role in society. The reason for this fear was becoming obvious, for as May notes: "Because it dealt, or might have dealt, with ideas, the moving picture was alarming in a special way" (40, p.335).

There is a special irony in the consideration of the motion picture as a potent purveyor of ideas, for this was clearly the motivating factor in the very important U.S. Supreme Court decision in 1915 that movies were not to be accorded the free speech rights guaranteed under the First Amendment. In the case *Mutual Film Corp.* v. *Ohio,* Justice McKenna, speaking for the unanimous Court, noted:

> The exhibition of motion pictures is a business pure and simple, originated and conducted for profit like other spectacles, not to be regarded, nor intended to be regarded . . . as part of the press of the country or as organs of public opinion. They are mere representations of events, of ideas and sentiments published or known; vivid, useful, and entertaining, no doubt, but . . . capable of evil, having power for it, the greater because of their attractiveness and manner of exhibition (43, p.244).

There is an irony in the Court's decision, for by 1915 the motion picture had clearly demonstrated that it was a powerful purveyor of ideas in the right circumstances, and yet the Court considered the medium to be a "mere representation of events" and therefore was not willing to grant the medium the same rights as other public information sources. At the same time, the Court feared the "power" of the medium to convey "evil" ideas. McKenna's arguments are thus both tautological and convoluted in his attempt to justify the Court's decision to allow the rather unprecedented step of systematic legal prior censorship of an American social institution. The Court was obviously reflecting an opinion echoed in some elitist quarters of American society, and was not in any mood to grant unrestricted freedom to a medium of communication that had already demonstrated its ability to vividly convey ideas to an increasingly eager public, while at the same time the Court denied the movies' role as a means of communication! (8, 36, 49).

The *Mutual* decision had a profound effect upon the film industry, and played a significant role in shaping the relationship between the medium and the local community, for it was construed to mean that motion picture censorship was permissable under the Constitution, and many state courts would uphold similar censorship laws on these grounds. Thus the unprecedented issue of legalized prior censorship, so obviously against the spirit of the First Amendment, was provided with an aura of judicial respectability. It also clearly signaled that there was some intangible quality associated with this new form of entertainment that demanded close surveillance from those responsible for the public's welfare. The result was that for whatever reasons, real or imagined, the motion picture was subjected to a form of systematic legal restriction unknown since before the War of Independence, and never again used on any form of mass communication. It is for this reason that we can consider the motion picture to be "unexpected" in its far-reaching impact, both as an entertainment-information medium, and as a source for social and cultural concern.

This interest in investigating and monitoring the role and influence of the motion picture began very soon after its introduction, and even before the *Mutual* decision. As early as 1909, as a result of an attempt by the mayor to close all motion picture theaters in New York, a local civic organization—The People's Institute—was persuaded by the city's film exhibitors to organize an advisory committee to evaluate and preview films prior to their exhibition thus creating the first of the industry's self-regulatory mechanisms as an alternative to official censorship (19). In 1914 a bill was introduced in both the Senate and House of Representatives to create a Federal Motion Picture Commission. This proposed bill would have authorized the President to appoint five persons to a Federal Motion Picture Commission with the authority to license all motion pictures entering interstate commerce, and bar all objectionable films judged immoral, indecent, obscene, or depicting a prize fight or bullfight (63). In his testimony at the hearings on this bill, the editor of the trade journal, *Motion Picture Story Magazine*, articulated the dimensions of the issue caused by the introduction of the movies:

> There is, perhaps, no question before the public so important and perplexing as the censorship question. In every country, in every State in the Union, and in almost every city and hamlet, the subject is pressing for societies have demanded it, newspapers and magazines have expressed opinions for and against it, the police authorities have been urged to adopt it, while the film manufacturers, exhibitors, and the amusement world are apparently divided on the subject (63, p. 12).

While the 1914 bill to establish Federal censorship control over the motion picture failed, in 1916 another attempt was made. While this piece of legislation also failed, this continuous legislative concern was a clear indication that the medium was apparently too powerful to ignore. (It is interesting to note that, in 1927, the radio industry was subjected to control under the newly established Federal Radio Commission, but the authority of the FRC was limited to "technical" matters, and it had no legislative power to censor broadcasts).

The motion picture industry was surprisingly restrained in its response to the *Mutual* decision, perhaps because the owners of the studios did not want to call attention to themselves in a highly public fashion, but also because there seemed to be some sentiment in favor of one form of federal censorship in preference to a myriad of state and local censorship bodies, each requiring specific and costly re-editing. The motion picture industry did not have an effective centralized industry organization at this time; in fact, quite the opposite was true, as the businessmen who had founded the studios were engaged in some very destructive competitive practices in the period before 1921 (57). Under these circumstances, a construct-ive unified response was impossible, and thus the inexorable march toward state and local censorship continued.

There were similar concerns in Great Britain, and in an effort to avoid the con-fusion and disruption of business caused by the activities of numerous local au-thorities acting as moral guardians, the motion picture industry approached the Home Office in 1912 to create a Board of Film Censors. When the government eventually refused to become officially involved, an independent board was cre-ated which had tacit government approval. A key document in shaping the British perspective on social control of the motion picture was the Report by the National Council of Public Morals on the Cinema. This document provided a well-reasoned assessment of the medium's social and cultural role and potential, and indicated a clear understanding that the motion picture was not merely an entertaining and in-nocuous diversion. The Report noted:

> It may be doubted if there is even yet sufficient realization of the strong and perma-nent grip which the picture palace has taken upon the people of this country . . . the lure of the pictures is universal . . . In the course of our inquiry we have been much impressed by the evidence brought before us that moving pictures are having a pro-found influence upon the mental and moral outlook of millions of our young people—an influence the more subtle in that it is subconsciously exercised—and we leave our labours with the deep conviction that no social problem of the day demands more earnest attention (50, p. xxi).

Throughout the world, wherever commercial films were shown, the question of motion picture control, either through formal censorship laws or regulations, or by means of industry self-regulatory measures was an important issue. In most cases, not having to deal with the legalities created by the unique American constitutional protection of free speech, governments enacted official censorship laws; India, as one example, passed the Cinematograph Act in 1918; the Province of Ontario, Canada passed the Theatres and Cinematographs Act in 1911 and the other Cana-dian provinces quickly followed with their own laws; in Australia, where the vari-ous states had their own regulations which were used to control the content of films, and which were jealously protected from federal intervention, Tasmania had the first formal film censorship statutes introduced in 1917; while in France, the Ministry of the Interior, by using the powers of the local authorities throughout the country, was controlling the exhibition of certain films as early as 1909, and this system was formalized by a centralized Censorship Decree in 1919 (26, 33). These are but a few examples of how the motion picture as a new social and cultural force elicited the enactment of specific laws and regulations from very suspicious governments anxious to control its potential influence.

MASS SOCIETY AND THE MOTION PICTURE

From a historical perspective, the amount of time and effort—often at the highest diplomatic levels—devoted to the questions raised by the motion picture is quite remarkable. What had started out as a rather innocent entertainment novelty had by the mid 1920s become a source of international tension, with many nations expressing concern for the very survival of their indigenous cultures. The motion picture had become so powerful an entertainer that its perceived persuasive capabilities were given credence for precipitating all sorts of unwelcomed events, from a rise in the crime rate to the destruction of national identities. Movie stars became international celebrities and were far more recognizable than the most famous politicans of the period; they were certainly capable of attracting larger crowds when they appeared in public. The motion picture symbolized for many, in the most obvious way possible, that the new communications media of the twentieth century—movies and radio—were creating an international "mass culture" which transcended any political attempts to curb their acceptance and persuasiveness. In the period before the introduction of sound, movies were far more internationally pervasive than radio because they were not hampered by the language problem. In particular, the American motion picture industry represented, in a way in which military strength could never hope to achieve, the "Americanization" of world culture (61, 62).

The media of communication were inextricably linked with the sociological concept of "mass society"; a concept which was much discussed by European intellectuals and which negatively colored much of their elite perspective on the potential dangers inherent in the new communication and entertainment forms. The most clearly articulated description of the shift from "traditional" forms of social organization to the "modern" is that found in Ferdinand Tonnies influential work *Gemeinschaft and Gesellschaft* (1887). This work, which can roughly be translated to mean "Community and Association," dealt with the historical shift from primitive preindustrial societies to modern industrial and technological societies, and was the forerunner of several major sociological treatises on the same theme of the significance of this historical shift in social organization (16, 60, 64). Leon Bramson in his excellent review of this subject, *The Politicial Context of Sociology,* notes that European sociological pessimism on the subject of "mass society" stems from the nineteenth century notion of the breakdown of the traditional community. Thus nineteenth century sociology had a preoccupation with "social disorganization" and "social disintegration" caused by the emergence of large-scale society, increasingly industrialized and concentrated in urban centers. The end result is that:

This perspective of nineteenth century sociology is recapitulated in the twentieth century theory of mass society, particularly in its view of the past. By contrast with the anarchic individualism of life in the cities, the impersonality of social relationships, the peculiar mental qualities fostered by urban life with its emphasis on money and abstraction, theorists of mass society idealized the social aspects of the traditional society of the later middle ages (5, p.32).

One can find a strong residual influence of the notion of the dangers of mass society in the works of such important twentieth century intellectuals as Erich Fromm (21), Hannah Arendt (2), and Jose Ortega y Gasset (47). Even the poet T.S. Eliot's work owed much to the suggestion that we were all becoming part of an amorphous mass society (18). The perceived role of the emerging communications media in this process was crucial, for they were seen as being central to the fostering of a type of cultural blandness which satisfied public tastes at the lowest possible level, and therefore thwarted mankind from achieving its full creative potential. The media were often described as offering messages with fluid values to an audience which was treated as homogeneous, faceless, and low in intelligence. Further, from the perspective of the socialist and communist thinkers whose ideas were just beginning to gain some credence, the mass media in Western society were essentially the handmaidens of the capitalist system, lulling the populace into a politcal lethargy which prevented them from realizing their true plight (44). The dominance of the negative concept of mass society in intellectual circles in the first part of the twentieth century was a salient factor in shaping the attitudes and subsequent political and social actions which overtook the film industry. The motion picture, more than any other form of communication in this period, was thought to be able to elicit the type of universal "collective behavior" (another emerging sociological concept at this time) which gave cause for alarm.

THE MOTION PICTURE AS AN AGENT OF CHANGE

What fundamental changes did the motion picture precipitate? Was there an actual shift in the nature of human perception in terms of Marshal McLuhan's suggestion that the advent of a new form of communication would bring about the alteration in the "sense ratio" of a society? The evidence is not clear enough to provide definitive answers; however, we can reasonably speculate that the introduction of the motion picture created a sufficient alteration in the social and cultural framework to warrant serious social and political concerns. Why else would communities, cities, states, and nations give so much attention to the "problem of the movies"? Such responses are to people's perceptions of "what is"; scientific, verifiable accuracy seldom matters in the face of stated concern and political reality. What does matter is the *perception* of reality, and all responses—social, cultural, and regulatory—are made on this basis. In that the motion picture's very existence demanded that forms of social control be instituted, it did have a profound effect on how societies received information.

The most obvious attribute of the motion picture was its very pictorial nature; audiences could learn to understand the narrative with a modicum of initial confusion. (It is quite true that the first audiences did duck their heads when trains pulled into stations, or when pies were thrown; but they quickly learned that the action on the screen was a one-dimensional reproduction—this did not, however, diminish the actual excitement of the narrative.) The simple pictorial was far easier to understand than the written word, and thus the movies were more accessible to a wider range of people—literacy did not really matter, for captions were often extraneous to the action. Thus children, in particular, were attracted to an exciting narrative which required no literacy skills, and which provided action specifically of the type most calculated to appeal to them. The motion picture therefore did provide for many individuals a new, easier way to view the world; but a world shaped by the hands of those creating the films, which, more often than not, bore little resemblance to the reality of the humdrum, everyday lives of the audience. (It is no accident that many of the arguments made by critics of television content deal with precisely this issue of the medium's unreal view of the world, and the ills created by such distortions (21).)

It was this aspect of escapism, presented in a novel, easy-to-master fashion which ensured the popularity of the new medium, together with the low cost for audience accessibility. It was this desire to escape into the content of the films, as well as use of the medium as a means of escaping the everyday world, evidenced by young and old alike, which alarmed critics. The movies were often compared to a form of addiction, to which individuals were drawn like moths to the destructive flame. One famous example is the great reformer Jane Addams, who devoted an entire chapter to "The House of Dreams" in her 1909 book, *The Spirit of Youth and City Streets* in an attempt to encourage a wider range of recreational alternatives to the ubiquitous habit of movie-going. Her concern centered around the fact that " 'going to the show' for thousands of young people in every industrial city is the only place where they can satisfy that craving for a conception of life higher than that which the actual world offers them . . . The theater becomes to them a 'veritable house of dreams' infinitely more real than the noisy streets and the crowded factories" (1, pp.75–76).

There was an added dimension to this issue: the motion picture's perceived ability to bypass or negate the traditional, accepted socializing institutions such as the family, the school, and the church, and to establish direct contact with its audience. Children and adults alike were actually learning things at the movies, and, it was claimed, much of this information was at best erroneous, or at worst contrary to the prevailing values of the community. School teachers were perhaps in the most unenviable position of all, having to compete with the excitement of the movies as a means of dispensing knowledge. In 1923, the chairman of the National Education Association, Mr. L. N. Hines, in a report to his constituency warned that:

The daily work of the schools in all village and urban communities is affected by what goes on at the movie house. Over much seeing [sic] of the inanities and absurdities of the movie seems to be developing the so-called "movie-mind." School is a rather slow place to millions of our youngsters. The whole situation affects the work of the school, creates a demand for visual education, and at the same time tends to make that demand one for the vulgarities of the commercial film (30, p. 532).

The shift in the information base afforded by the motion picture was becoming quite obvious in the classroom and, as one exasperated teacher wrote in 1923: "In a recent intelligence and current knowledge test given to them [children in her classroom] one hundred percent of these children could name ten or more moving-picture actors and actresses, while [only] five percent could name ten names to be selected from President, Vice-President, Cabinet Member, Supreme Court Justice . . . [etc. etc.]" (48). The editor of *Educational Screen,* a publication created to assist in the use of films in the classrooms of the United States, suggested that "it is of vital importance today that teachers should reckon with the theatrical movie as a definite competitor and frequently a dangerous opponent, of what they are trying to accomplish in the classroom" (25, p. 122).

It was not only education that was affected by the creation of an alternate source of information, for the complaints from organized religion, social workers, and law enforcers echoed the belief that much of the content of motion pictures was antisocial and provided an opportunity for adolescents and adults to acquire a more intimate knowledge of undesirable sexual or criminal behavior. These complaints had begun with the introduction of the medium in the 1890s, and continue unabated until the present day. These early criticisms were usually based upon personal observation or experiences; sometimes teachers obtained crude measurements of attendance or conduct by administering questionnaires to students in the classroom (35, pp.45–46). There were many complaints about movie influence from social workers, and even psychiatrists or other doctors, based upon cases they were familiar with, and often these individual incidents were generalized and ascribed to the entire population. As an example, in 1915, William Healy—the pioneer in the study of juvenile delinquency—included several case studies in his book *The Individual Delinquent* concerning children who, he alleged, had been "influenced" by the movies into committing criminal acts (29, pp. 307-308). (Interestingly, in later editions of this book, he repudiated his earlier stance on the movie influence issue.)

This is what made the period under consideration unique, for after 1918 there was a very sincere attempt made to provide social scientific support for these charges. Whereas before rhetoric had been sufficient to arouse public opinion, now the growth of the social sciences and the development of sophisticated research techniques necessitated that more empirical studies be undertaken to examine the extent of motion picture influence (51). The increasing awareness of the role of the mass media in shaping the attitudes and perceptions of the populations of modern societies made the subject of media influence a natural area of investigation for the social sciences in the period after 1918. Their highly publicized role in propaganda activities during the First World War had focussed attention on the potential of the mass media to forge and shape public opinion. As George Creel, the former chairman of the Committee on Public Information, later stated in his confessional book, *How We Advertised America:* "The printed word, the spoken word, the motion picture, the telegraph, the cable, the wireless, the poster, the signboard—all were used in our campaign to make our own people and all other peoples understand the causes that compelled America to take arms" (12, p. 5).

One overarching intellectual problem was the strength of the prevailing theories of *instinct* psychology, which stressed the uniform psychological nature of humans, and the notion that each member of the mass audience reacted uniformly to uncontrolled inner urges when exposed to a stimulus. This theory, variously called the "stimulus-response theory" or sometimes "the hypodermic-syringe model," left the impression that the public " could be swayed and influenced by those in possession of the media, especially with the use of emotional appeals" (14, p. 163). It was the enormous interest in this subject in the 1920s and 1930s which caused social scientists to turn their skills to understanding the nature of communication and, by using increasingly sophisticated empirical methods, they were able to come to a gradual awareness of the "differential impact" of a particular communication content on the heterogeneous audience (14, pp.184–190; 6).

The motion picture presented an ideal target for such empirical research because of the intense debate which always seemed to rage on the issue of motion picture influence. In 1928 our understanding of the subject was greatly enhanced when the Payne Fund provided $200,000 to the Motion Picture Research Council to carry out a nation-wide study to determine the degrees of influence and effect of films upon children and adolescents. These reports, known today as the Payne Fund Studies, were carried out by a group of social scientists—psychologists, sociologists, and educators—over the four-year period from 1929 to 1933. The first volume appeared in 1933, and with the other ten volumes which followed in the next two years, these studies still constitute the most concentrated series of examinations ever undertaken of the motion picture.

There were many attempts to utilize the findings of these reports to secure tighter control and censorship over movie content, but these were ultimately unsuccessful. In particular, the early publication of the popularized version of the findings of the various studies by Henry James Forman in his specially commissioned book, *Our Movie-Made Children,* was a blatant ploy to arouse fervor for yet another effort to establish some sort of national film censorship commission (20). The studies were widely quoted in all types of media and formed the platform for the launching of many critical essays on the state of the motion picture industry. It was unfortunate that precisely at this time the industry was beginning to feel the effects of the Depression and, still suffering from the cost of the introduction of sound into the studios and theaters, the film industry had resorted to a particularly excessive concentration on films with "adult" themes, mostly sexual and violent in nature in order to boost attendance. The Payne Fund Studies were just the grist that critics of the industry needed for their mill, which now ground out an unending series of attacks on the "morals of the movies."

The results of the Studies presented a reasonably accurate account of the extent of motion picture usage and influence in the lives of the American people, revealing that movies were widely attended, with average weekly audiences conservatively estimated at 77 million in 1929. Of these, about 28 million were under twenty-one; 11 million were under fourteen; and 6 million were seven years old or less. It was estimated that in congested urban areas, the percentage of children attending was much higher (13, p.73). The results also confirmed that under the right circumstances, the movies were indeed an important source of information and a potent force in the creation of ideas and concepts. In his seminal and controversial study, *Movies and Conduct,* social psychologist Herbert Blumer concluded that movies were highly influential:

> For to many the pictures are authentic portrayals of life, from which they draw patterns of behavior, stimulation to overt conduct, content for a vigorous life of imagination, and ideas of reality. They are not merely a device for surcease; they are a form of stimulation . .motion pictures are a genuine educational institution . . . in the truer sense of actually introducing him [the student] to and acquainting him with a type of life which has immediate, practical and monotonous significance (3, pp. 196–197).

In the end, after the rhetoric and attendant publicity surrounding their publication had died down, the Payne Fund Studies symbolized the culmination of the long struggle to understand the nature of this new force in society, and, in a more pragmatic political sense, provided ammunition to make the motion picture industry more responsive to calls for a greater degree of social responsibility. It was no accident that the combined forces of the Catholic Legion of Decency, The Hays Office (the industry "front office"), and the findings of the Payne Fund Studies led to the introduction of the first effective industry self-regulatory code in July, 1934 (35, pp. 246–256). From that time on, to the late 1960s, the American motion picture industry was essentially under a Catholic hegemony, with movie content supposedly adhering to the mores of what the industry preferred to call the basic Judeo-Christian tenets (53).

THE MOTION PICTURE AND INTERNATIONAL CONCERN

The concern over the motion picture as an unknown and uncontrolled cultural and social force was not confined to the United States. In 1921, the English journalist Arthur Weigall summarized many of these fears when he wrote:

To the remotest towns of England, as to those of America and other countries, these films penetrate, carrying with them this mild but ultimately dangerous poison; and gradually the world, from end to end, is being trained to see life as it is seen by a certain group of kinema producers and writers congregated in a corner of the United States. The world is being Americanized by the photoplay; but the trouble is that this Americanization does not represent the best element of that nation, or even the most popular . . . (65, p. 688).

The international dominance of the American film industry in the period after 1918 was difficult to deny, for the Hollywood studios—unhampered by the ravages of war—were able to fill the void created by the financially strapped European studios. Originating as an industry more than as an art form, the Hollywood studios had also mastered the technique of making films with mass universal appeal which transcended international borders. The result was that American film stars became international celebrities, and the ''Americansim'' fostered in the Hollywood product became a symbol for the new international mass-mediated popular culture which emerged in the 1920s.

In the prewar period the French and German motion picture industries had actually led the world production, but by 1924 American films represented ''about seventy-five per cent of the motion pictures shown day in and day out the world over'' (45, p.101). When C.J. North, Chief, Motion Picture Section, U.S. Department of Commerce made the above assessment, he did so not only with a great deal of national pride, but also as a loving embodiment of the U.S. Government's commitment to the overseas marketing of motion pictures. He further estimated that the gross revenues accruing from foreign trade in 1925 was over $50,000,000 and that thirty percent of the gross revenues to the industry from all sources came from foreign trade. Clearly there was a vital need to maintain this source of revenue in the face of increasingly hostile reactions to the enormous, and now threatening, presence of American films in foreign countries.

To combat the ''American movie problem'' European countries devised a variety of political and economic schemes. Germany, on January 1, 1925, established the *Kontingent* system, which required a producer importing a foreign film to also subsidize the production of a German film. This law reduced the percentage of American films on German screens from sixty in 1925 to forty-five in 1928 (59 pp. 307–315). The German law was widely imitated with varying degrees of success throughout Europe, depending on the strength of the local film-producing industry and its political clout. In Britain, after 1927, exhibitors were required to reserve a certain portion of their screen time for British pictures, the portion increasing from year to year. Fearing a dilution of the ''British way of life,'' many countries in the British Empire agitated for a similar quota system (39).

It was in France, however, that the most virulent attacks on the American motion picture took place starting in the late 1920s. The French were particularly upset, not only by the growing economic domination of the United States in

Europe, but also on an issue of national pride. Certain French intellectuals felt that Hollywood had misued the French invention of the motion picture apparatus for strictly commercial ends. Even if the Lumiere brothers had been the sole inventors of the movie camera and projector, which they were not, the French could not have claimed to have developed that peculiar intangible magic of Hollywood, which proved to be such a potent salesman for American material culture and ideas. Each movie bore the unmistakable mark of Americanism, from clothes and speech patterns (even in translation!), to the casual use of automobiles and the quintessential American characters of the "blond bombshell" or the cowboy. These were all seen as threats to French culture, and considered to be far more potent and damaging than the more blatant propaganda activities of the recently concluded war (58).

The litany of French complaints was lengthy, and, all to often, quite justifiable. The objections to American films included the theft of popular French stars and directors by the Hollywood studios, the homogenization of French lifestyles, the replacement of Paris by Hollywood as the world fashion center, the deliberate promotion of American products in American films, the potential destruction of the French language, and perhaps most annoying of all, the discovery that American movies often spread stereotyped views of French life (58, pp.755–756). The American film industry had never really been concerned abouts its cavalier portrayal of history, a problem often alluded to by U.S. educators; now the proud, history-conscious Europeans found themselves the unwilling subjects of "the Hollywood version." Edouard Herriot, the French cabinet minister under whose control motion pictures fell, noted that in American films "our European folk tradition, as well as the history of our continent, is translated by some honorable citizens of Los Angeles. Joan of Arc might be played by a young Californian, and a native of Illinois with the features of his region might appear as Napoleon" (58, p. 757).

By an executive decree of February 28, 1928, the French government declared in substance that no motion pictures were to be imported into France or shown throughout the nation unless approved by the Minister of Public Instructions and Fine Arts, and an advisory committee of 32 members designated by him (54, p. 131). The real thrust behind this dramatic political and economic action was to force the reciprocal exhibition of French motion pictures in other countries, particularly the United States. (Americans had never shown any consistent interest in foreign films after the First World War, and distributors considered them to be a liability.) The "Czar" of the American motion picture industry, Will Hays, president of the Motion Picture Producers and Distributors of America, was quickly dispatched to France, where he personally consulted with M. Herriot to present the American industry's objection to any such legislation. Hays made a point of involving the U.S. Consulate, for as he noted: "I always maintained that the film industry could not successfully carry on a contest with a foreign government"

(28, p. 404). Hollywood eventually had its way, and by 1933 the sounds and fury emanating from Nazi Germany were seen as a greater threat by French intellectuals than American films.

The international interest in motion pictures both as a deliberate educational tool and the more controversial problem of cultural domination became centered in the League of Nations after 1926. In September of that year the International Committee on Intellectual Cooperation of the League of Nations held an International Motion Picture Congress in Paris. There were 435 delegates representing 31 countries, and 16 governments sent official delegates to the Congress. However, the American film industry was dramatically conspicuous by its absence, claiming through the MPPDA offices that the time was not right, and therefore no official delegates were to be sent (55, pp.147–166). Like many of the League of Nations Congresses, this one generated a wide range of resolutions, from author's rights to international trade, but without the American industry present there was no way to implement or enforce any of them.

The most significant of the League's motion picture achievements was the creation of the International Institute of Educational Cinematography. In its nine-year existence (1928–1937), the IIEC produced an enormous volume of material related to almost every facet of motion pictures. In particular the publication of the Institute's periodical, first called the *International Review of Educational Cinematography* and later *Intercine* was a highwater mark in the history of international concern over motion picture influence (26, pp. 200–202). When Italy withdrew from the League following the invasion of Ethiopia, the Institute—which was based in Rome—unfortunately closed down, and efforts to find another location for it were ended by the collapse of the League itself.

The League's various committees and commissions from time to time indicated their specific interest in films, and this resulted in the publication of several reports of substantial historical interest, and bearing directly on the international concern surrounding the medium. The most significant of these was the report *The Recreational Cinema and the Young,* prepared by the Advisory Committee on Social Questions in 1938 (38). Considering that the motion picture had been introduced forty-two years earlier, it is perhaps with a degree of frustration that this report noted: "The cinema has become in a short time one of the most popular forms of indoor entertainment, and it is not surprising that many of the problems which have arisen have not yet been finally or satisfactorily solved" (38, p.1). Nor were they likely to be resolved. The motion picture was by now too large a subject to deal with in neat, easy-to-define categories. The Report itself provided a detailed summary of the role of the motion picture in the lives of children world-wide, noting that in most industrialized countries, the movies were among the major recreational pursuits of those under seventeen, and called for greater international cooperation in using the medium as a positive educational force.

It is somewhat ironic that these interwar-year pleas for the use of motion pictures to promote peace achieved very few positive results, whereas the onset of

World War Two provided the medium with perhaps its greatest triumphs. While the Hollywood film industry was very slow to harness its considerable powers of persuasion against the Fascist menace—waiting until almost 1939 to make the first anti-Nazi film, *Confessions of a Nazi Spy*—when unleashed it became a major factor in the propaganda war then taking place on the global screen. But it did so without having to resort to the blatant and therefore ineffective propaganda tactics of the totalitarian regimes. Hollywood was far more effective by just being "Hollywood," and by continuing to export, when possible, the American way of life to millions in other countries (35, pp. 293–332; 53).

The American government made substantial use of film as a means of educating both civilian populations and for training purposes, and the talents of the Hollywood industry were utilized extensively in both of these endeavors. Not only were the studios asked to include morale-building messages in their nonwar films, but those films which dealt with the war played an important role in "explaining" the nature of the fight against the enemy. In the production of Frank Capra's "Why We Fight" series for the army, commerce and government combined forces to produce what were ostensibly training films, but they had greater impact in civilian showings than as required viewings for soldiers (4). The films themselves were the subject of an extensive series of experiments in sociopsychological research, which ultimately gave us clearer insight into the limitations of media influence. In summary, the research tended to discount the "mass" impact of such propaganda films, but indicated that there were many factors to be considered before "effects" could be measured (32).

By the end of the 1940s the movies reigned supreme as the great world-wide entertainment, and the American industry had maintained its international domination even in the face of the state supported industries of Germany and Italy. The question of what changes the motion picture's inroduction into society had caused could now be answered, for the results were there for any who took the trouble to look. Some of the changes were so obvious that their historical significance has been all but ignored.

The "Americanization" of world culture through the movies goes far beyond mere rhetoric, and the reality of this issue needs more careful attention from historians and other scholars. But there are many other equally important aspects of the motion picture's contribution that are worthy of more systematic research. Consider the effect or influence on the choice of reading matter; on furniture and fashion; on architecture and interior design; on song and gesture; on racial and ethnic stereotypes; on perceptions of history; and perhaps most difficult of all to assess, on morals, values, and mores.

In a more universal sense the motion picture did bring rural and urban ideology and values closer, creating a more uniform national culture and helping to dissolve the isolationism of nonurban life in the period before television. They also provided significant role models, in the absence of any formalized socialization process, for how the sexes should behave toward each other, and they reshaped our attitudes toward marriage and divorce. The motion picture industry refused to officially admit that it was capable of doing all this, for to do so would leave it vulnerable to attack on other issues, particularly regarding the influence of sexual and violent content. But the role of the motion picture as a major socializing factor in modern life has been ensured by the continued interest in the subject, and as we learn more, the extent of the medium's influence on our personal lives seems to widen. As John Clellon Holmes has noted: "The movies of the 1930s constitute, for my generation, nothing less than a kind of Jungian collective unsconsciousness, a decade of coming attractions out of which some of the truths of our maturity have been formed" (31, p.51).

The international extent of Hollywood's influence, and the specific interest in the lifestyle of the Hollywood community in the period 1930-1940, can be gauged from the fact that there were "almost four hundred newspapermen, columnists, and feature writers (including a correspondent for the Vatican) assigned fulltime to Hollywood. Only Washington . . . and New York . . . possess[ed] larger press corps" (52, p. 7). The enormous amount of information both from and about the motion picture industry left an indelible impression on all our minds. In the long run the medium was a truly "unexpected" influence which caused a series of major social, cultural, and political adjustments which inextricably altered the shape of the twentieth century and the way in which we perceive the world around us.

REFERENCES

1. Addams, Jane. *The Spirit of Youth and City Streets.* New York: Macmillan Company, 1909.
2. Arendt, Hannah. *Origins of Totalitarianism.* New York: Harcourt, Brace and World, 1951.
3. Blumer, Herbert. *Movies and Conduct.* New York: Macmillan Company, 1933.
4. Bohn, Thomas. *An Historical and Descriptive Analysis of the "Why We Fight" Series.* New York: Arno Press, 1977.
5. Bramson, Leon. *The Political Context of Sociology.* Princeton, NJ: Princeton University Press, 1961.
6. Brown, Roger L. "Approaches to the Historical Development of Mass Media Studies," pp. 41–57. In Jeremy Tunstall (Ed.), *Media Sociology,* Urbana: University of Illinois Press, 1970.
7. Carey, James W. "Harold Adams Innis and Marshall McLuhan." In Raymond Rosenthal (Ed.), *McLuhan: Pro and Con.* Baltimore: Penguin Books, 1969.
8. Carmen, Ira H. *Movies, Censorship and the Law.* Ann Arbor: University of Michigan Press, 1966.
9. Carney, Thomas. *From Fable to Cable.* Winnipeg: The Natural Resource Institute, University of Manitoba, 1975.
10. Cherry, Colin. *World Communication, Threat or Promise.* New York: Wiley-Interscience, 1971.
11. Clanchy, Michael T. *From Memory to Written Record, England, 1066–1307.* Cambridge, MA: Harvard University Press, 1979.
12. Creel, George. *How We Advertised America.* New York: Harper and Brothers, 1920.
13. Dale, Edgar. *Children's Attendance at Motion Pictures.* New York: Macmillan Company, 1935.
14. De Fleur, Melvin L. and Sandra Ball-Rokeach. *Theories of Mass Communication.* New York: Longman, 1982.

15. Dulles, Foster Rhea. *A History of Recreation: America Learns to Play*. New York: Appleton-Century-Crofts, 1965

16. Durkheim, Emile. *The Division of Labour in Society*. Glencoe: The Free Press, 1949.

17. Eisenstein, Elizabeth L. *The Printing Press as an Agent of Change*. Cambridge: Cambridge University Press, 1979.

18. Eliot, T.S. *Notes Toward a Definition of Culture*. New York: Harcourt, Brace, 1949.

19. Feldman, Charles M. *The National Board of Censorship (Review) of Motion Pictures, 1909–1922*. New York: Arno Press, 1977.

20. Forman, Henry James. *Our Movie-Made Children*. New York: Macmillan Company, 1933.

21. Fromm, Erich. *Escape From Freedom*. London: Routledge, Kegan Paul, 1943.

22. Gerbner, George and Larry Gross. "Living With Television: The Violence Profile." *Journal of Communication* 26 (2), Spring 1976, pp. 173–199.

23. Goody, Jack, (Ed.). *Literacy in Traditional Societies*. Cambridge: Cambridge University Press, 1968.

24. Graff, Harvey J. "The Legacies of Literacy." *Journal of Communication* 32 (1), Winter 1982, pp. 12–26.

25. Greene, Nelson L. "Motion Pictures in the Classroom." *Annals of the American Academy of Political and Social Science*, no. 128, November 1926, pp. 122–130.

26. Harley, John Eugene. *World-Wide Influences of the Cinema*. Los Angeles: University of Southern California Press, 1940.

27. Havelock, Eric. *Preface to Plato*. Cambridge, MA: Harvard University Press, 1963.

28. Hays, Will H. *The Memoirs of Will H. Hays*. Garden City, NY: Doubleday & Company, 1955.

29. Healey, William. *The Individual Delinquent*. Boston: Little, Brown and Co., 1915.

30. Hines, L. N. In *Proceedings of the National Education Association Annual Meeting, 1923*, p. 23.

31. Holmes, John Clellon. "15c Before 6:00 p.m.: The Wonderful Movies of 'The Thirties.' " *Harper's*, December 1965, pp. 51–55.

32. Hovland, Carl I., A.A. Lumsdaine, and F.D. Sheffield. *Experiments in Mass Communication*. New York: John Wiley and Sons, 1965.

33. Hunnings, Neville March. *Film Censors and the Law*. London: George Allen & Unwin Ltd., 1967.

34. Innis, Harold Adams. *The Bias of Communication*. Toronto: University of Toronto Press, 1968.

35. Jowett, Garth S. *Film: The Democratic Art*. Boston: Little, Brown and Company, 1976.

36. Jowett, Garth S. "Giving Them What They Want: Movie Audience Research Before 1950," In Bruce A. Austin (Ed.), pp. 19–35. *Current Research in Film*, vol. 1, Norwood, NJ: Albex Publishing, 1985.

37. Katzman, N. "The Impact of Communication Technology: Promises and Prospects," pp. 47–59. *Journal of Communication* 24 (4), Fall 1974.

38. League of Nations publication C 256. M.152, 1938. IV. 31 pages.

39. Low, Rachel. *The History of the British Film, 1918–1929*. London: George Allen & Unwin Ltd., 1971.

40. May, Henry F. *The End of American Innocence*. New York: Alfred A. Knopf, 1959.

41. McLuhan, H. Marshall. *The Gutenberg Galaxy*. Toronto: University of Toronto Press, 1962.

42. McLuhan, H. Marshall. *Understanding Media*. New York: McGraw-Hill, 1964.

43. Mutual Film Corp. v. Ohio Indus'l. Comm. 236 U.S. 230. U.S. Supreme Ct. 1915.

44. Nordenstreng, Kaarle and Herbert I. Schiller (Eds.). *National Sovereignty and International Communication*. Norwood, NJ: Albex Publishing, 1979.

45. North, C.J. "Our Foreign Trade in Motion Pictures." *Annals of the American Academy of Political and Social Science*, no. 128, November 1926, pp. 100–108.

46. Ong, Walter J. *The Presence of the Word*. New York: Simon and Schuster, 1970.

47. Ortega y Gasset, Jose. *The Revolt of the Masses*. New York: W.W. Norton & Company, Inc., 1932.

48. Letter in *Outlook,* May 16, 1923, pp. 882–883.
49. Randall, Richard S. *Censorship of the Movies.* Madison: University of Wisconsin Press, 1968.
50. Report of the Commission, National Council of Public Morals. *The Cinema: Its Present and Future Possibilities.* London: Williams and Norgate, 1917.
51. Ross, Dorothy. "The Development of the Social Sciences." In Alexandra Oleson and John Voss (Eds.), *The Organization of Knowledge in Modern America, 1860–1920.* Baltimore: John Hopkins University Press, 1979.
52. Rosten, Leo C. *Hollywood: The Movie Colony, The Movie Makers.* New York: Harcourt, Brace and Company, 1941.
53. Sargent, John A. "Self-Regulation: The Motion Picture Production Code, 1930–1961." Ph.D. Dissertation, University of Michigan, 1963.
54. Schindler, Colin. *Hollywood Goes to War.* London: Routledge & Kegan Paul, 1979.
55. Seabury, William Marston. *Motion Picture Problems: The Cinema and The League of Nations.* New York: The Avondale Press, 1929.
56. Sklar, Robert. *Movie-Made America.* New York: Random House, 1975.
57. Staiger, Janet. "Combination and Litigation: Structures of U.S. Film Distribution, 1896–1917," pp. 41–72. *Cinema Journal* 23 (2) Winter 1984.
58. Straus, David. "The Rise of Anti-Americanism in France: French Intellectuals and the American Film Industry, 1927–1932," pp. 754–759. *Journal of Popular Culture* 10 (4), Spring 1977.
59. Strauss, William V. "Foreign Distribution of American Foreign Motion Pictures," pp. 307–315. *Harvard Business Review* 8, 1930.
60. Tönnies, Ferdinand. *Community and Society.* New York: Harper & Row, 1963.
61. Tunstall, Jeremy. *The Media are American.* New York: Columbia University Press, 1977.
62. Tunstall, Jeremy. *Media Made in California: Hollywood Politics and the News.* New York: Oxford University Press, 1981.
63. U.S. Congress, House, Committee on Education, Motion Picture Commission. *Hearings Before the Committee on Education on Bills to Establish a Federal Motion Picture Commission,* 63 Cong., 2nd sess., 1914.
64. Weber, Max. *Essays in Sociology.* London: Routledge and Kegan Paul, 1957.
65. Weigall, Arthur. "The Influence of the Kinematograph upon National Life." *Nineteenth Century,* April 1921, pp. 661–672.

2

Cultural Influences on Film Interpretation among Chinese and American Students

Martin F. Norden and Kim Wolfson

One of the hazards of showing a foreign film to a domestic audience is the strong probability that the audience will misinterpret the intended meaning behind some of the film's messages. Many films contain considerable information accessible only to those audiences having some familiarity with the cultures out of which the films come. Yet despite the obviousness of these observations, they have received minimal scholarly attention, particularly attention of an empirical nature. As a partial means of rectifying this situation, this article presents the results of an empirical study which focuses directly on the issue of differing film interpretations between two cultures: the reactions of Americans and Chinese to a single topic—interpersonal conflict—as depicted in a documentary film by Frederick Wiseman. In addition to discussing the rationale, method, and results of this study, we plan to relate them to larger theoretical issues pertaining to culture-bound interpretations of films.

AUDIENCE RESPONSE TO FILM MESSAGE LEVELS

We recognize at the outset that some leading contributors to varying film interpretations among cultures are differences in prints of the same film related to the vagaries of subtitling and dubbing. Beyond such obvious differences, however, looms a more complex problem which is really at the heart of the current study: cultural differences in general, which, among other functions, help shape the varying ways that humans interpret films. Perhaps the greatest cultural differences in film interpretation arise during the viewing of those moments in films that semioticians such as Metz (14) have labeled "paradigmatic." The semioticians have argued that the messages in a given film are organized along two axes: the syntagmatic and the paradigmatic. The syntagmatic axis refers primarily to the linear, causal, horizontal movement of a film: in short, its storytelling dimension. On this level of message-perception, cultural differences in interpretation may be minimal, if still very much present. For example, Western audiences can easily grasp and follow the narrative of Akira Kurosawa's *Seven Samurai* (1954), though some subtleties are doubtless missed by those not intimately acquainted with Japanese culture. More substantial differences emerge, however, with regard to perception of messages on the paradigmatic axis, which is concerned with associative, connotative, vertical messages. During such moments within a film, viewers often have to draw on some outside frame of reference to construct meaning. In other words, viewers have to move beyond the immediate world of the film story to some other reference point to make reasonably full sense out of these moments. An example may be drawn from John Ford's *Young Mr. Lincoln* (1939), which focuses on the pre-Civil War life and times of the title character. At one point in the film, and well before the Civil War, Lincoln (Henry Fonda) plays "Dixie" on a jew's harp while riding a horse. To experience the obvious (and paradigmatic) irony of this scene, viewers have to move beyond the film to an outside frame of reference: their knowledge of Lincoln's role in America's Civil War. Viewers lacking this particular frame of reference would either interpret this moment as merely an embroidering of the narrative of the film or perhaps attach some idiosyncratic meaning to it.

Another example may be taken from the British film *The Wicker Man* (1974) by Anthony Schaffer and Robin Hardy, which, in the guise of a mystery, explores pagan rituals on a small island off the coast of Scotland. At one point in the film, a police sergeant from the Scottish mainland (Edward Woodward) is dozing in his hotel room but awakens with a start to find a severed human hand placed near his bed, its fingers set afire. To those unfamiliar with paganism in that part of the world, the scene is meaningless except for the transient shock effect it creates. To the cognoscenti, however, this scene has another message: according to pagan beliefs, the amputated hand of a criminal set afire in a room is supposed to have the effect of keeping the room's occupants in a trance.

AN EMPIRICAL APPROACH TO BICULTURAL FILM INTERPRETATION

Anecdotal and hypothetical examples such as these, which are clear-cut and obvious, can only go so far in helping to identify and explain cultural differences in the interpretations of films. In the remainder of this article, we will explore this issue through empirical means. Before we proceed, however, we do wish to acknowledge our awareness that some resistance to an empirical approach within the area of film study exists, inasmuch as the field is still largely dominated by humanists concerned primarily with aesthetics, criticism, and other issues related to the concept of film as art. We anticipate a major question posed by humanist film scholars: what will such a study tell us that we don't know intuitively already—that people from different cultures may interpret the same film differently?

This question, and it is an entirely legitimate one, may be answered thusly: in addition to discussing in specific detail the nature of these differences, we will move beyond such elementary issues to explore a theoretical framework that attempts to explain the processes that allow for cultural differences to occur. In other words, we will attempt to explain the sources which contribute to the emergence and development of such differences. Mindful of the growing interest in phenomenological and other audience-oriented approaches to the film field, we believe the present study will be valuable to both humanists concerned with the interpretation and criticism of the medium from multiple perspectives, and social scientists interested in the ways that film as the product of psycho-socio-cultural forces communicates information.

SURVEY OF LITERATURE

Anyone who studies film will not find surprising the shortage of cross-cultural film audience studies, both experimental and survey-oriented. Among the few extant studies are Dronberger's (7) examination of varying reactions of midwestern American college students to a group of foreign films, and a *Film Comment* article (3) reporting the results of surveys conducted by the U.S. Information Agency in Japan and several Western European nations, part of which deals with attitudes toward U.S. films. Carter and Sepulveda (5) interviewed 452 Santiagans in early 1963 and learned that U.S. and Canadian films were the most popular in Chile, with 56 percent of the respondents believing that films accurately reflect everyday life in the countries from which they were exported. Gans (8) surveyed 80 British adults and adolescents and discovered that younger, working-class audiences in particular were attracted to Hollywood films, which often depict people from working-class backgrounds seeking middle-class life styles. Paletz *et al.* (16) examined the influence of Peter Brook's British film *Tell Me Lies* (1967), which opposed American involvement in Viet Nam, on a group of Americans who also opposed the war. The authors discovered that although the vast majority of the viewers shared the film's antiwar orientation, the film did not, in most cases, reinforce viewers' attitudes. The film's foreignness, along with other factors (e.g., the film's hectoring tone, its lack of constructive arguments) were judged the major elements contributing to what the authors termed a boomerang effect.

These scattered and somewhat dated writings provided an insufficient structure on which to build our study, so we turned to the sizable body of literature that deals with cultural differences between Americans and East Asians—two extremely broad but distinct cultures—in general, and used that as our point of departure en route to gauging the reactions of Americans and Chinese to selected moments from a film.

There is indeed no dearth of studies which illustrate cultural differences between Americans and East Asians. For instance, Barnlund (4) discovered that Japanese were more cautious, tentative, agreeable, reserved, modest, and hesitant to criticize than Americans, and that Japanese preferred to react passively, such as remaining silent, when forced to deal with threatening situations. Yoshikawa (19) underscored these observations in his own study which suggested that Japanese were more harmonious, humble, timid in the presence of others who hold high social or occupational status, and mistrustful of verbose, articulate people than were Americans. Huang and Harris (10) learned that Chinese displayed a high degree of deference and respect for others of higher status, while Americans were more affected by their perceptions of others' competence. Chu (6) learned that American children were more autonomous in various social environments than Chinese children, who were more conforming in their behavior. Kang and Pearce (12) found that communication "logic" differed in American and Korean cultures, while Wolfson and Pearce (18) arrived at a similar conclusion after comparing American and Chinese responses to the issue of self-disclosure: the cultures differed with respect to the meanings they ascribed to self-disclosure and to the ways these meanings were linked to subsequent interpersonal communicative acts.

Of course, differences exist among and within Japanese, Chinese, Korean, and other East Asian cultures; indeed, it is certainly arguable that the generic term "East Asian" is reductionistic when used within the context of communication and behavior. For example, Klopf and Cambra (13) found that Koreans were more outgoing, talkative, and aggressive than Japanese, while Heiliger (9) has underscored basic differences between the traditional Chinese personality and its communist Chinese counterpart. Yet the East Asian cultures share a broad heritage strongly influenced by the Shinto, Buddist, Taoist, and Confucian traditions, all of which stress the importance of social harmony, caution, and submissiveness. Even the communist Chinese structure of behavior patterns is based solidly on the deep-rooted Confucian tradition of the region, according to Heiliger (9). As suggested by Ahn Toupin (1), the East Asian cultures share certain norms, such as deference to others, verbal devaluation of self and family, absence of verbal aggression, absence of direct expression of feelings, avoidance of confrontation, and lack of assertiveness. For purposes of this study, we have used these general qualities, which are fundamentally different from those of American culture, to characterize the Chinese culture.

METHODS

With such a wealth of information on the general issue of intercultural communication, we decided to use a film-mediated topic linked to this area. We chose "interpersonal conflict," since it seemed clear, judging from the intercultural literature, that we would encounter distinct differences in the ways that Chinese and Americans would interpret and respond to it.

Our next step was to procure a film that embodied at least one clear-cut example of verbal conflict between two people and at least one example of a relatively benign or neutral conversation between two people. We chose Frederick Wiseman's 1968 documentary film *High School,* primarily because of its availability and because it had several examples of precisely the type of interactions we were looking for in relatively discrete segments. *High School,* which deals with the daily routine of students and teachers at a Philadelphia high school, eschews the use of narration in its presentation of nonprofessional performers engaging primarily in spontaneous activities. We recorded on videotape six brief (approximately two-minute) segments of *High School* depicting dyadic interactions, and a panel of four judges rated the degree of conflict of each segment with a six-item Likert-type conflict scale. Based on the judges' ratings, we chose two segments for use in our study: a "high-conflict" episode consisting of a heated argument between a teacher and a student regarding the latter's refusal to attend gym class, and a "low-conflict" episode depicting a calm conversation between a student and a teacher concerning the student's plans for college.

Sample

A total of 60 subjects participated in the study. The American subjects were volunteers drawn from several small-group communication courses at a large northeastern university, while the Chinese subjects were volunteers from the Chinese student social organization on the same campus. Chinese subjects were categorized as such if they were of Chinese ethnic ancestry and raised in a Chinese country, while Americans were so designated if they were raised in the United States and were not of Asian ethnic ancestry. The 60 subjects included 30 Chinese and 30 Americans, and ranged in age from 18 to 33 with an average age of 22.5. The average ages for Americans and Chinese were 20.5 and 24.6, respectively. Seventeen of the Americans and 14 of the Chinese were female.

Instrument

The questionnaire consisted of three short sections, the first of which dealt with demographic information (age, sex, race, and country raised). The second section consisted of ten film sequence descriptions, including such statements as "This is a tense conversation," "These people are having an argument," "These people are friendly toward one another," and so on. This section included four questionnaire items describing the level of conflict, which served both to validate our selection of film sequences—that is, a manipulation check—and to allow comparison of Chinese and American definitions of conflict.

The subjects indicated their level of agreement with each of the descriptive statements, using seven-point scales with response choices ranging from "strongly disagree" to "strongly agree." We chose this type of scale over a semantic differential one (e.g., "very tense" to "very relaxed") because the anchors of the scales use the same basic verb, such as "strongly disagree" to "strongly agree." We assume that the subjects will perceive the anchors as direct opposites. In the semantic differential example above, it is more likely that some subjects would perceive a term other than "relaxed" as the opposite of "tense." Subjects might feel, for example, that "normal" is the polar opposite of "tense."

The final section of the questionnaire represents what we believe is a unique way of measuring the viewers' perceptions of those things that govern their individual behavior, which in turn suggests the impact of culture—among other contexts—on the viewers' interpretations of the film. In short, this last section dealt with "logical force." The concept of logical force is drawn from the Coordinated Management of Meaning (CMM) theory articulated by Pearce and Cronen (17). CMM, a theory of communication firmly rooted in the phenomenological and symbolic-interactionist traditions, posits a reciprocal causal relationship between what people believe—their culture or "social reality"—and the ways they interpret various forms of communication. Logical force refers to the constraints on a person's behavior as perceived by that person. More specifically, it deals with the extent to which the individual feels he or she must perform particular acts because of existing conditions (e.g., a person's self-concept, previously-existing relationships, culture) and/or to bring about certain situations (e.g., to enhance a relationship, to become a certain kind of person). The former subdivision of logical force is called "prefigurative force" while the latter is labeled "practical force." These levels of meaning (e.g., definition of self, culture, etc.) act as contexts for an audience member's interpretation of a film. For example, audiences of different cultural backgrounds would be expected to ascribe different meanings to a given film sequence, which is indeed the very issue under examination here.

To help ensure audience involvement in the film sequence, this section of the questionnaire asked the subjects to pretend they were the high-school student depicted in the film clip, that the conversation continued beyond the sequence's conclusion, and that it was their turn to speak next. Subjects were then requested to indicate what they would say/do (i.e., their next "speech act") in response to the teacher. Eight logical-force statements on the questionnaire were used to measure the degree of influence of various beliefs on the subjects' anticipated behavior as if they were "in the shoes" of the student presented in the film sequence. Seven-point Likert-type scales, with response choices ranging from "strongly disagree" to "strongly agree," were used to measure the degree of logical force. Examples of prefigurative-force statements included "The situation that I find myself in requires me to respond with this particular message" and "It is important to respond with this message because it is required by the kind of relationship I have with the teacher." Examples of practical-force statements included "I very much want to bring about the teacher's next message" and "I would respond in this way in order to have the pattern of conversation go the way I want." (See Table 2 for a complete listing of logical-force statements.)

Procedures

The study used four experimental conditions, consisting of two independent variables: culture (Chinese and American) and level of conflict (high and low). Fifteen subjects were assigned to each condition.

After we distributed the questionnaires, we told the subjects they were participating in an intercultural communication study that dealt with the ways that Americans and Chinese interpret communicative acts as presented in a film. We told them they would be viewing a two-minute videotaped segment from a black-and-white documentary entitled *High School* which depicts a conversation between a high-school student and a teacher. In addition, we described the context of the segment in the same way to all subjects prior to presenting the segment to them.

Data from the questionnaires were analyzed with a two-way analysis of variance procedure. Interaction effects were pinpointed with a Student-Newman-Keuls post hoc analysis.

RESULTS AND DISCUSSION

Sequence Descriptors

Manipulation Check.   Our manipulation check—that is, the four-item conflict scale—revealed that the selection of high- and low-conflict film segments by the panel of judges was appropriate. Significant differences for condition on the

Table 1.   Mean[a] Scores on Film Sequence Descriptors

Sequence Descriptors	$\overline{X}$ Chinese High (n = 15)	$\overline{X}$ American High (n = 15)	$\overline{X}$ Chinese Low (n = 15)	$\overline{X}$ American Low (n = 15)	Conflict Main Effects p	Culture Main Effects p	Interaction Effects p
Harmonious discussion	1.67	1.20	5.00	4.07	.001	.026	
Tense conversation[b]	2.13	1.80	4.33	4.00	.001		
Status similarity	2.53	1.20	3.40	3.73	.001		.048
Informality	4.47	3.27	4.13	3.93			
Proper behavior	2.40	1.73	5.73	4.93	.001	.042	
Argument[b]	2.27	2.87	6.60	5.53	.001		.024
Comfortable conversation	1.40	1.53	5.53	4.13	.001	.067	.028
Agreement	1.93	1.80	5.00	3.80	.001	.088	
Conflict[b]	2.80	1.87	5.67	4.73	.001	.048	
Friendliness	1.53	1.33	5.47	4.20	.001	.049	

[a]Strongly agree = 7; strongly disagree = 1.
[b]Response options were reverse scored (strongly agree = 1; strongly disagree = 7).

conflict scale revealed that the subjects rated high- and low-conflict conditions as significantly different on dimensions of harmony, agreement, argument, and conflict.

Cultural Similarities.   In addition to condition differences on the conflict scale, we found differences for condition on number of other sequence descriptors. Both cultures interpreted the high-conflict film sequence as tenser, less comfortable, and less friendly than the low-conflict sequence. Chinese and American subjects also agreed that the teacher and the student in the high-conflict segment were further apart in social status and less proper in their behavior than their counterparts depicted in the low-conflict segment. Overall, both cultures found the low-conflict conversation generally more pleasant and relaxed. In addition, they viewed the conversants in that sequence as closer in social status and more proper in their behavior when compared with the people in the high-conflict conversation.

Cultural Differences.   A comparison of Americans and Chinese revealed differences for culture on several sequence descriptors. The Chinese students perceived both segments as more harmonious, more agreeable, less conflicting, friendlier, and more comfortable than did American subjects. The difference on the comfort item should be viewed in terms of the interaction effect between culture and condition. That is, Chinese rated only the low-conflict conversation as more comfortable than did Americans. Chinese perceived the teacher and the student as behaving more properly in both sequences as compared with the Americans' responses.

An interaction effect for similarity of status indicated that Americans perceived a significantly greater social status difference between teacher and student in the high-conflict episode than did Chinese. No such cultural difference was found for the low-conflict segment. Finally, culture and condition interacted as well in the argument dimension, as the Chinese subjects rated the low-conflict teacher and student significantly lower on argumentativeness when compared to American responses.

Logical-Force Variables
Four logical-force items showed trends toward significance. All of these items represented practical force: the component of logical force which concerns goal-oriented behavior.

Cultural Similarities.   The linkage between speech act and self-concept showed a significant difference between high- and low-conflict conditions. This suggests that both Chinese and Americans, in the role of the high-school student, felt more obliged to create a good impression on the teacher in the low-conflict conversation than in the high one.

Table 2. Mean[a] Scores on Logical-Force Statements

Logical-Force Statements	$\overline{X}$ Chinese High (n = 15)	$\overline{X}$ American High (n = 15)	$\overline{X}$ Chinese Low (n = 15)	$\overline{X}$ American Low (n = 15)	Conflict Main Effects p	Culture Main Effects p
This statement closely reflects *who I am* and what a person like me must say.	4.40	4.80	5.27	4.87		
The situation that I find myself in requires me to respond with this particular message.	5.67	5.47	5.40	4.73		
It is important to respond with this message because it is required by *the kind of relationship* I have with the teacher.	5.00	4.93	4.53	4.60		
In this situation, I would respond in this way, *no matter what the teacher might say next*.	5.20	4.07	5.13	4.33		0.67
This response would help me create a *good self-image* in this situation.	3.67	4.33	4.33	5.33	.067	.067
I very much want to *bring about* the teacher's next message.	4.33	3.33	4.53	3.93		.099
This response would help me *create a certain kind of relationship* with the teacher.	5.07	4.33	4.80	4.67		
I would respond in this way in order to have the *pattern of conversation go the way I want*.	3.87	4.47	3.87	4.53		

[a]Strongly agree = 7; strongly disagree = 1.
Note: all interaction effects were nonsignificant.

Cultural Differences. We found near-significant differences between Chinese and American responses for three logical-force items. The first, "functional autonomy," refers to a perceived narrow range of responses and a lack of purposiveness, resulting in a decision to act in a particular way no matter what the other person may say/do next. Chinese felt the high-school student would be significantly more functionally autonomous in his or her response to the teacher. In other words, the Chinese believed that the student's responses to the teacher would not be contingent on an anticipated effect, when compared with the Americans.

Another cultural difference was found in the linkage between speech act and self-concept. Americans felt the student would be more compelled to respond to the teacher in a way which would enhance his or her self-image than what Chinese subjects reported.

The third cultural difference concerns the link between the speech act the subjects wrote down and the response they expected from the teacher. In both conditions, the force to respond with an act that would elicit a particular response from the teacher was significantly greater for Chinese subjects.

Definition of Interpersonal Conflict

Across culture, high- and low-conflict conversations were perceived differently. Results from the sequence-descriptor measures indicate that the subjects viewed the low-conflict sequence as generally more pleasant, relaxed, and harmonious than the high-conflict sequence. The subjects also rated the teacher and the student in the low condition as more similar in social status and more proper in their behavior. Subjects as a whole were able to clearly differentiate the levels of conflict and characterize the high- and low-conflict sequences differently on dimensions such as tension, comfort, and similarity of status.

A comparison of conditions also revealed a number of cultural contrasts in defining conflict between people. Compared with Americans, the Chinese subjects seemed to believe that both of the dialogues were generally more positive (e.g., more harmonious, friendlier, more proper with respect to participants' behavior). In light of the intercultural literature reviewed earlier which underscored East Asians' avoidance of conflict, distaste for disagreement, and hesitancy to criticize, we might expect Chinese subjects to define the high-conflict situation as *less* pleasant, appropriate, and so on, than Americans. Despite the statistical difference between Chinese and Americans, however, both groups still rated the high-conflict segment quite negatively (i.e., low on dimensions of friendliness, comfort, appropriateness of behavior). These low ratings, then, tend to diminish the importance of these cultural differences regarding high-conflict sequence description measures.

Two tentative interpretations of the comparatively positive descriptions of high conflict by Chinese subjects might be offered. First, Chinese values seem to dictate relatively passive responses to conflict or threat. Perhaps the value they place on harmony prevents them from "seeing" threatening situations. Americans, on the other hand, tend to react more actively to verbal conflict. American culture legitimizes certain degrees of confrontation, debate, and candid conversation, and hence Americans may be more inclined to pursue argumentative communication. Second, since actions for Chinese appear highly prefigured by their culture, Chinese may believe that Americans follow a certain ritual during high-conflict situations—moments which they themselves would attempt to avoid at all times. Since *High School* is a film made in the United States, the Chinese subjects may have thought something to the effect of "Oh, I've seen this sort of dialogue in other American movies. Arguments are *normal* for Americans."

Responses to Conflict: Logical Force

Only one statistically significant finding indicated cultural similarity: across cultures, subjects felt that the student would be more obliged in the low condition to create a good impression with the teacher. Perhaps the subjects believe that the teacher's helpfulness and the more comfortable "climate" of the low-conflict discussion obligated the student to make a favorable impression with the teacher. Support for this interpretation can be found in the positive descriptions of the low-conflict film sequence by both cultural groups. On the other hand, the high-conflict sequence was defined by subjects as relatively negative. It makes intuitive sense that the possible embarrassment and tension felt by the student would release him/her from an obligation to create a good impression.

Responses to logical force questions suggest cultural differences in the implications conflict may have for further communication. We provide the following explanation of cultural contrasts, based on the three items that reflect trends toward significance (act-to-self concept linkage, act-to-next act linkage, functional autonomy): Chinese subjects apparently believed that the student had a narrow range of choice for responses to the teacher because they thought it necessary for the student to complete a particular pattern of interaction which is dictated by the Chinese culture. That is to say, the Chinese believed essentially that the student *must* say certain things, no matter what results it gets, because both student and teacher must do their "parts" in the tightly "scripted" communication pattern. In order for the student to complete the prefigured pattern, Chinese subjects may have thought that the student needed a particular response from the teacher, and that the teacher would cooperate in completing the pattern. The data indicate that Chinese believed the student had relatively little control over the conversation; his or her actions were guided more by cultural script than by the teacher's behavior. It follows that Chinese subjects placed a higher value on predictability than on control.

The Americans, perceiving a wider range of behavioral options for the student, felt that the student was abler to exert control over the conversation. In contrast to the Chinese, American subjects may have thought that the student opted for spontaneity and choice over certainty. For this reason, the student would be more concerned with creating a favorable impression on the teacher (as evidenced by the high practical force in the act-to-self concept linkage). Because the Americans did not feel that the student's behaviors were as strongly prefigured by cultural norms (as Chinese felt), we might expect that Americans thought that the student was less sure of the way the conversation would proceed. Hence, Americans did not believe that the student anticipated a particular response from the teacher, as supported by the relatively weak association between the act and consequent for American subjects.

CONCLUDING REMARKS

Our interpretations of the data are necessarily tentative, given the limitations of this study. We propose some improvements which might be included in future research studies of this kind, such as those that would address the issue of sample validity, a primary limitation of the current study. The homogeneity of Chinese and American cultures is questionable; it is intuitively obvious, for example, that differences exist between the Southern and Northeastern subcultures of the United States. Certainly such variation exists in Chinese societies as well. Alexander *et al.* (2) noted considerable variation even within a sample of Taiwanese subjects. Careful consideration of sample homogeneity, along with a large number of subjects (at 60, ours was relatively small), should increase the population validity of the sample.

Another variable which may have confounded our results is the degree of acculturation of the Chinese subjects into the American culture. We circumvented the potential problems of subtitling and dubbing by asking Chinese people who have lived in the United States for several years to participate in our study, but testing them may have yielded different results than testing Chinese within the context of their native countries.

Language differences obviously need to be considered in future film studies dealing with international differences in interpretation. Since our film was American-made and the questionnaire written in English, we expect that some Chinese subjects may have had trouble understanding several of the questions we asked and/or portions of the dialogue in the film. Translating the questionnaire into Chinese would solve the former problem, but the latter issue may forever prove problematic because of the message variations inherent in dubbed and subtitled films.

The film segments that we chose to use in this study are limited in ways other than noted above. Despite our successful selection of high- and low-conflict sequences, they varied on dimensions other than conflict. Consistency was a high priority in our selection of film segments (e.g, both involved a teacher and a student, each segment lasted about two minutes, and, of course, the segments were taken from the same film), but they unavoidably varied with respect to the topic of conversation, setting, and sex of the people depicted.

Despite these limitations, the differences that we uncovered between Chinese and American interpretations of segments from *High School* may be viewed as manifestations of disparate ''logics'' for behavior in Chinese and American cultures. The differences provide support for that portion of the Coordinated Management of Meaning theory that suggests culture exerts influence on people's structuring of reality—in this case, interpreting a film sequence.

As to the relationship between our findings and the paradigmatic/syntagmatic issue raised earlier, we find we must tread with caution since our subjects did not view *High School* in its entirety. Even though they viewed the sequences ''out of context,'' we can still discuss to some degree their reactions to the paradigmatic messages within the sequences. Regarding the Americans—and particularly the Americans who viewed the high-conflict sequence—we theorize that they drew on at least one of several outside frames of reference: their own experiences in high school and/or their knowledge of American history during the late 1960s and early 1970s, when young people frequently questioned and demonstrated against authority, whether it be in the form of parents, teachers, or various levels of government. In so doing, these subjects were mentally grappling with messages on the film's paradigmatic axis. Semioticians might argue that the Chinese subjects, lacking both the Americans' experiences in domestic high schools and their intimate acquaintance with recent American history, would not perceive these messages. (For example, they might miss altogether Wiseman's criticism of American high school systems and the demi-fascist mentality that has guided them.) Phenomenologists, on the other hand, might posit that the Chinese subjects' responses to the segments, no matter what they might be, are no less valid than the Americans'. Without becoming further embroiled in the semiotic/phenomenological debate, we suggest—assuming one accepts the basic concepts of paradigmatic and syntagmatic messages—that separate cultural groups may interpret messages differently on not only the paradigmatic axis but also the syntagmatic one as well. Bear in mind that the Chinese and the Americans differed with respect to such basic elements of the sequences as harmony, agreeableness, conflict, friendliness, and comfort. Indeed, the Chinese' stress on harmony may have prevented them from even "seeing" conflict, as we suggested earlier. Without belaboring the point further, the results of our study seem to indicate that Americans and Chinese, guided by different sets of cultural norms and values, derived different meanings from the film segments. Their interpretations of the film were colored in large measure by their respective cultural "logics."

Certainly the context of a sequence within a film shapes to some degree the way the sequence will be interpreted. Future film studies that employ empirical means might extend this methodology to measure responses to entire films while at the same time allowing for closeness and precision of film-sequence interpretation. We indeed hope that other researchers will continue to heed the calls issued by Jowett and Linton (11), Norden (15), and others for film studies that utilize both qualitative and empirical methods, since the resulting works would be exploring relatively uncharted territory. Such studies hold out the promise of offering exciting new insights into that elusive topic which intrigues all cinema scholars: the nature of the film-viewing experience.

REFERENCES

1. Ahn Toupin, Elizabeth S.W. "Counseling Asians: Psychotherapy in Context of Racism and Asian-American History." *American Journal of Orthopsychiatry* 50, January 1980, pp. 76-86.

2. Alexander, Alison, Vernon E. Cronen, Kyung-wha Kang, Benny Tsou, and Jane Banks. "Pattern of Topic Sequencing and Information Gain: A Comparative Study of Relationship Development in Chinese and American Cultures." Paper presented at the Speech Communication Association convention, New York City, November 1980.

3. "American Films and Foreign Audiences." *Film Comment* 3, Summer 1965, p. 50.

4. Barnlund, Dean. *Public and Private Self in Japan and the United States*. Tokyo: Simul Press, 1975.

5. Carter, Roy E. and Orlando Sepulveda. "Some Patterns of Mass Media Use in Santiago de Chile." *Journalism Quarterly* 41, Spring 1964, pp. 216-224.

6. Chu, Lily. "The Sensitivity of Chinese and American Children to Social Influences." *Journal of Social Psychology* 109, December 1979, pp. 175-186.

7. Dronberger, Ilse. "Student Attitudes Toward the Foreign Film." *Journal of the University Film Producers Association* 17, 1965, pp. 6-9, 19-22.

8. Gans, Herbert J. "Hollywood Films on the British Screen: An Analysis of the Functions of American Popular Culture Abroad." *Social Problems* 9, 1962, pp. 324-328.

9. Heiliger, Wilhelm S. *Soviet and Chinese Personalities*. Lanham, MD: University Press of America, 1980.

10. Huang, Lily C. and Mary B. Harris. "Conformity in Chinese and Americans: A Field Experiment." *Journal of Cross-Cultural Psychology* 4, 1973, pp. 427-434.

11. Jowett, Garth and James M. Linton. *Movies as Mass Communication*. Beverly Hills, CA: Sage Publications, 1980.

12. Kang, Kyung-wha and W. Barnett Pearce. "Reticence: A Transcultural Analysis." *Communicatiti* 8, 1983, pp. 79-106.

13. Klopf, Donald W. and Ronald E. Cambra. "Communication Apprehension Among College Students in America, Australia, Japan, and Korea." *Journal of Psychology* 102, May 1979, pp. 27-31.

14. Metz, Christian. *Film Language: A Semiotics of the Cinema*. Translated by Michael Taylor. New York: Oxford University Press, 1974.

15. Norden, Martin F. "Toward a Theory of Audience Response to Suspenseful Films." *Journal of the University Film Association* 32, Winter-Spring 1980, pp. 71-77.

16. Paletz, David L., Judith Koon, Elizabeth Whitehead, and Richard B. Hagens. "Selective Exposure: The Potential Boomerang Effect." *Journal of Communication* 22, 1972, pp. 48-53.

17. Pearce, W. Barnett and Vernon E. Cronen. *Communication, Action, and Meaning: The Creation of Social Realities*. New York: Praeger, 1980.

18. Wolfson, Kim and W. Barnett Pearce. "A Cross-Cultural Comparison of the Implications of Self-Disclosure on Conversational Logics." *Communication Quarterly* 31, Summer 1983, pp. 249-256.

19. Yoshikawa, Muneo. "Some Japanese and American Cultural Characteristics," pp. 220-251. In Michael Prosser (Ed.), *The Cultural Dialogue: An Introduction to Inercultural Communication*. Boston: Houghton-Mifflin Co., 1978.

3

Motion Picture Attendance:
A Market Segmentation Approach

Steven Knapp and Barry L. Sherman

Contemporary telecommunications has been characterized by increased audience fragmentation, resulting in a market segmentation approach to programming, sales, and research (5,8). This trend was first visible in radio with the emergence of specialized formats and the targeting of listeners by advertisers based on age group and specific music preferences. The spread of cable has had a similar effect upon television programming. Specialized arts, sports, news, music, and movie channels occupy the satellite transponders and fill the channels of the nation's cable systems. Broadcasting is becoming narrowcasting, and the concept of a mass audience is yielding to the scientific study of audience subgroups and their attitudes, interests, and opinions.

Traditionally, marketing researchers relied on demographic profiles to give them some insight into consumer behavior. However, the dual phenomena of audience fragmentation and media specialization soon rendered demographic data alone inadequate to meet the needs of the telecommunications business.

In the 1960s a new approach, a blend of motivational and personality inventory methodologies, began to gain acceptance among researchers. Variously called lifestyle, activity and attitude, or psychographic research, this new approach quickly sparked the imagination of many who saw it as a more comprehensive method of understanding consumer behavior. During the last twenty years psychographic research has gained wide acceptance as a consumer research tool. Yet there is still considerable confusion over just what it is and how it can be employed.

Psychographic research seeks to define audiences along psychological dimensions by measuring activities, interests, opinions, needs, values, attitudes, and personality traits (19). The utility of such an approach is immediately apparent. Large masses of people can be broken down into dimensions which cluster similar attributes or individuals. In the business world this allows producers to market consumer products more effectively. In academe, the approach enables researchers to discern underlying reasons for otherwise inexplicable behavior. When properly administered, psychographics greatly enhance the ability to understand human behavior. However, significant limitations of the methodology have been noted.

The reliability of psychographics has frequently been questioned. Reliablity problems are a function of instability in measurement, particularly in relation to the dependent variable, typically consumer purchase behavior or media consumption patterns (19). Another problem centers on the validity of psychographic measurements. Are you measuring what you intended to measure or something else altogether? The answer to the validity question is not forthcoming and may never appear. But the emerging psychographic literature, particularly in advertising, has demonstrated that "psychographic variables generally relate to each other, to demographics, and to use of products and media in ways that make perfectly good sense" (19, p. 207). For this reason, despite its drawbacks, psychographic research is a widely used marketing tool. Properly applied, psychographics makes it possible to gain important insights into consumer behavior. As alluded to previously, many executives in the broadcasting field have realized the utility of psychographics in helping them to better understand their various audiences (18).

Unlike their counterparts in broadcasting, however, film executives have been reluctant to adopt a market segmentation approach to their industry. By and large, the film industry maintains an antiquated "blockbuster" mentality and a persistent skepticism about the utility of audience research (11, 14). Box office receipts reported in *Variety* and "head counts" provided by distributors remain the main source of audience information to film industry executives.

Rudimentary demographic data have been utilized to some degree by the industry. For example, it is known that the film audience skews young (typically 12-17 years), and that more men attend films than women (15). Such consumer information has led to a degree of product segmentation and a number of financially successful films have been produced, aimed at specific target audiences. These films include adolescent comedies (such as *Porky's* and *Vacation*), horror (*Halloween* and *Texas Chainsaw Massacre*) and musicals (*Grease, Heavy Metal, Fast Times at Ridgemont High*) geared to the "youth market."

There is growing evidence that the market segmentation approach is gaining a foothold among studio managers. A notable example of a merger between consumer research and film production is Sunn Classic Films, which uses market segmentation studies not only to define the target audience for its films, but also as a tool to select the plot and cast of characters, and to test acceptable resolutions (11).

A recent report documented the beginnings of the use of such marketing techniques at the larger studios (4). It has been reported that Twentieth Century-Fox,

MGM/UA, and Columbia are finding ways to make better (i.e., more profitable) films with the help of various marketing techniques including concept testing and interviewing. While objections to the inclusion of such practices in the creative process are frequent and loud, it appears that psychographic-based research is making inroads into the decision-making process at money-conscious studios.

However, despite this late awakening to the role of consumer research, published findings on the motion picture audience are generally lacking, in particular, behavioral and attitudinal correlates of the adult (age 18 and above) film audience. In this vein, Austin noted that only 104 empirical studies of the motion picture audience had been published since 1960 (3). That situation has not changed appreciably in recent years.

Such research is critical at this time since the traditional movie audience (young males) is declining in the population. At the same time, these same population shifts are making the adult audience one of America's largest and fastest growing demographic groups. Perhaps even more critically, this is the group responsible for the proliferation of the movie theater's main competitors—pay cable and home video recorders (7, 13).

The goal of this exploratory study was to discern psychographic correlates of motion picture attendance among adult moviegoers. The limited body of related research enabled the formulation of a number of tentative expectations about how the movie audience might segment along psychographic dimensions.

Based upon work by Anast (1), who found that some moviegoers seem to have an almost cathartic use for film, it was expected that psychographics might appear which entailed a need for stimulation by proxy. This could be reflected in desires for pleasure-seeking, excitement, and adventure that might not normally be open to the individual. In addition, other findings by Anast suggest that some moviegoers enjoy being nonparticipants, preferring to observe rather than act, much like many sports fans.

Consistent with Olsen's work identifying film-going with feelings of loneliness (16), attitudes and opinions reflecting "social isolation" were anticipated. Such moviegoers might feel that their lives had "settled down." Loneliness, apathy, and conservatism might lead them to a fatalistic view of life where their destiny had already been decided upon.

Finally, demographic correlates of film attendance led to the expectation that film attendance would link to peer affiliation, a concern for personal appearance, and sexual attractiveness.

METHOD

A computer program was utilized to generate a table of 654 four-digit random numbers corresponding to telephone exchanges in use in Athens and Savannah, Georgia. Three hundred eight-three calls were made in Savannah and 271 in Athens to secure 150 completed interviews. Incomplete or unusable calls were due to business, disconnected or inoperative numbers (485), screen-outs based on the age or attendance criteria (8), refusals (6), employment in the film industry (4), and nonresident status (1). Thus the final n for the sample was 150 (57 in Athens, 93 in Savannah). Given restrictions that small samples place upon multivariate statistical procedures, it is important to reiterate the exploratory nature of this study in interpreting the results reported below (12).

The survey instrument was designed to obtain data on the frequency of movie attendance, socioeconomic, attitudinal, and lifestyle characteristics of the sample adults.

The key dependent variable—frequency of motion picture attendance—was operationalized in a manner consistent with ranges utilized by the Motion Picture Association of America (15). Respondents were asked to indicate how many films they had seen during the course of the previous year. Those who had seen more than six films during the course of the preceding year were considered frequent attenders. Those who had attended three to six films were occasional attenders, while individuals who had seen one or two movies during the last year were labeled infrequent attenders.

A total of 64 (43 percent) frequent, 63 occasional (42 percent), and 23 (15 percent) infrequent attenders was interviewed. Respondents' age was coded on a five-point scale based on the following intervals: 18-30, 31-40, 41-50, 51-60, and 61 +. Sex of interviewee was coded by observation. Respondents were asked to indicate the highest grade or year of school they had completed, their marital status, ethnic background, and whether any children were presently living in their household. A final demographic question tapped the family income levels of the interviewees on a five-point scale ranging from under $10,000 to $40,000 and above.

The demographics of the sample were as follows. Sixty percent of respondents were female (n = 92). The median age fell in the 31-40 year range; roughly half of the sample was between 18 and 30 years of age. Forty percent of the sample (n = 59) was single, 52 percent were married (n = 78) and eight percent had been divorced (n = 12). Children were present in 47 percent of the households (n = 70).

The median education level was two years of college, while the modal response (n = 39) was an earned high school diploma. The sample was three quarters white (n = 110). Thirty-two blacks (21 percent) and four Hispanics (3 percent) were interviewed. Income levels reported spanned a wide range, with the median income reported in the $10-20,000 interval.

The bulk of the questionnaire was a replication of a battery of lifestyle, activity, interest, and opinion questions utilized in a prior study of theater and symphony attendance (2). Thirty items addressed general lifestyle interests of the respondents, including their frequency of participation in a range of activities (e.g., traveling and hiking) and their attitudes toward specific issues (including women's rights, the value of education, and the role of the family). Thirty-five items tapped respondents specific leisure lifestyle characteristics including craft and hobby interests, participation in sports, symphony and theater attendance, and their frequency of use of other media. Each leisure-lifestyle item utilized a four-point Likert-type scale in which respondents could strongly disagree, disagree, agree, or strongly agree with a statement to reflect interest in that activity. A full listing of general and specific lifestyle interest is available from the authors.

Data analysis was performed on a Cyber (CDC) mainframe installation, utilizing version 8.3 of Statistical Package for the Social Sciences (17). Frequency and percentage data were computed for all variables. To test relationships between the demographic variables and frequency of attendance, cross-tablulations were performed and the Chi-square statistic was computed.

Psychological characteristics of the sample were obtained by utilizing factor analysis procedures (20). A varimax rotated factor matrix was computed on the set of general lifestyle and leisure-lifestyle characteristics. Consistent with standard techniques used in factor analysis, only factors with eigenvalues greater than 1.0 were used.

Finally, to ferret out the "best predictor" of film attendance, the stepwise multiple regression technique was used with frequency of attendance as the criterion variable. Nominally coded demographic variables were excluded from the regression analysis.

RESULTS

Demographics
Results of the Chi-square tests on the demographic variables replicated prior research associating motion picture attendance with sex, age, and marital status. Frequent attenders were more likely to be young (18-40), single men (see Table 1). No significant differences were observed on education, race, income, and the number of children in the household.

Table 1. Frequency of Film Attendance by Demographic Characteristics

Variable X Attendance	X^2	df	P
Age	6.52	2	.03*
Sex	6.41	2	.04*
Race	6.53	6	.37
Education	2.62	2	.27
Income	3.27	2	.19
Marital Status	14.89	6	.02*
Children in the Household	3.14	2	.20

*$p < .05$

General Lifestyle Characteristics

Factor analysis of the 30 lifestyle items produced four factors accounting for 59.5 percent of the sample variance. These results are summarized in Table 2.

Table 2. Varimax Rotated Factor Matrix of General Lifestyle Characteristics

Items	X̄	SD	Loading
Factor 1: Outward Bound			
Go hiking	1.80	1.00	.72
Go on a picnic	2.28	.89	.66
Friends are college grads	2.67	1.10	.47
Travel by airplane	2.12	.98	.43
Eigenvalue = 3.43			
% Variance = 23.4			
Factor 2: Hedonism/Optimism			
I dread the future	2.01	.88	− .68
I feel attractive to the opposite sex	3.34	1.19	.63
I'll try anything once	2.73	.75	.43
Eigenvalue = 2.14			
% Variance = 14.6			
Factor 3: Cosmopolitanism			
Friends see me for advice	2.72	.81	.60
My greatest achievements are ahead	3.08	1.09	.44
I'd rather live near a big city	2.69	.93	.42
I like to be considered a leader	2.73	.68	.41
Eigenvalue = 1.63			
% Variance = 11.2			
Factor 4: Self-Confidence			
I'll try anything once	2.73	.75	.46
I'm considered good-looking	3.26	1.57	.37
I'd like to travel around the world	3.12	.90	.37
Eigenvalue = 1.50			
% Variance = 10.3			

Factor 1, labeled ''Outward Bound'' was comprised of positive loadings on items broadly related to outdoor activities: adventure, education, travel, leisure-time pursuits, and peer-group allegiance. The outward-bound factor accounted for 23.4 percent of factor variance.

The second factor, ''Hedonism/Optimism'' accounted for 14.6 percent of the variance. This factor consisted of positive loadings on items related to sexual attraction, excitement, willingness "to try anything once," and a prevailing sense of optimism about the future.

"Cosmopolitanism" accounted for an additional 11.2 percent of factor variance. Significant loadings within this factor included a desire to live in an urban environment where it was possible to work toward one's goals and to realize personal achievements. Additional positive loadings indicated that items on this factor related to individuals who saw themselves as community leaders frequently sought by others for advice and support.

The final factor, "Self-confidence" accounted for an additional 10.3 percent of the sample variance. Loadings on this factor included such items as high self-esteem, adventurousness, aggressiveness, and satisfaction in achieving personal and financial goals.

Leisure-Lifestyle Characteristics

The battery of 65 items related to leisure-time interests, activities, and opinions was analyzed utilizing R-type factor analysis. Five factors emerged from the analysis, which together accounted for 54.2 percent of the variance. These results are summarized in Table 3.

Factor 1, accounting for 19.2 percent of the factor variance, can be labeled the "Armchair Athlete." High loadings on nonparticipatory sports-related variables, such as "I frequently go to sports events," "I like to watch sports events on TV" justify this title.

Factor 2, accounting for 14.4 percent of the variance, can be labeled the "Settled" group. Negative loadings on several variables indicate this group of movie-goers will probably not "move in the next five years," that they feel their "greatest achievements" are not ahead of them, and that a college education is "not very important in today's world." Their days seem to follow a definite routine and they like to watch television other than sports events.

Factor 3, accounting for 7.4 percent of factor variance, is comprised of "Adventurers." Similar in make-up to the Hedonist, Adventurers are self-confident, optimistic about the future, and "willing to try anything once." Additionally this group of movie attenders feels attractive to members of the opposite sex.

Factor 4, accounting for 6.8 percent of factor variance, can be labeled "The Sierra Club." This group consisted of positive loadings on such items as "most of my friends are college graduates," "I would like to take a trip around the world," and the enjoyment of picnicking and hiking. A positive loading on airplane travel was also noted in this factor.

Factor 5, accounting for 6.4 percent of factor variance, can be labeled the "Birch Society." This factor linked items related to conservatism and old-fashioned values. A positive loading was observed for "a woman's place is in the home." The factor also included a strongly negative loading for "I feel I will have more money next year."

Table 3.   Varimax Rotated Factor Matrix of Leisure Lifestyle Characteristics

Items	$\overline{X}$	SD	Loading
Factor 1: Armchair Athlete			
I watch sports on TV	3.36	.85	.81
I frequently go to sports events	2.99	.97	.73
I like to attend sports events	2.92	.80	.71
Eigenvalue = 7.12			
% Variance = 54.2			
Factor 2: Settled Group			
I'll probably move in the next 5 years	2.5	1.05	− .81
I know which movies are playing around here	2.68	.74	.50
College is very important	3.30	.74	− .46
My days follow a routine	2.68	.83	.46
My greatest achievements are ahead	3.08	1.09	− .38
Eigenvaue = 5.33			
% Variance = 14.4			
Factor 3: Adventurers			
I'm more confident than others	2.93	.99	.66
I'll try anything once	2.73	.75	.62
I dread the future	2.01	.88	− .36
Eigenvalue = 2.75			
% Variance = 7.4			
Factor 4: Sierra Club			
I frequently go on a picnic	2.28	.89	.71
I frequently go hiking	1.80	1.00	.63
I frequently travel by airplane	2.12	.98	.47
Eigenvalue = 2.53			
% Variance = 6.8			
Factor 5: Birch Society			
I'm somewhat old-fashioned	2.73	.74	.73
I'll probably have more money next year	2.77	1.13	− .59
A woman's place is in the home	2.04	.95	.43
Eigenvalue = 2.53			
% Variance = 6.4			

Predictors of Film Attendance

Results of the regression analysis of frequency of attendance are summarized in Table 4. The best predictor of film attendance (multiple R = .26) was "having many friends interested in movies." Other contributors to the regression equation included interest in hiking, disinterest in radio listening, knowledge of films show-ing in the area, perceived importance of a college education, and the willingness to pay extra for quality television.

DISCUSSION

Results on the demographic items were generally consistent with prior research on the moviegoing public (3,10). Frequent filmgoers tended to be single males be-tween the ages of 18 and 40. However, in the present sample, education, children in the household, income, and race were not associated with frequency of film at-tendance. These results may be due to sampling error or to limited effects size pro-duced by small subsample comparisons. They may also be reflective of contradictions in the literature on the relationship between these variables and the act of motion picture attendance (3).

Results of the multivariate statistical test proved more fruitful. Analysis of gen-eral lifestyle characteristics linked the act of filmgoing to four factors: "Outward Bound," "Hedonism/Optimism," "Cosmopolitanism," and "Self-confi-dence." It appears that the act of filmgoing coincides with a favorable outlook on the future, opinion-leadership, urbanism, and a positive self-image.

Analysis of specific leisure interests associated variability in filmgoing with spectator sports, adventurism, and outdoor pursuits. Another set of items linked filmgoing to feeling settled in one's life and sociopolitical conservatism.

Taken together, these results indicate that the adult film audience is clearly multidimensional. The cluster of "Outward Bound" items suggest that for one subgroup, filmgoing represents an important activity that fits in with their interest

Table 4.   Regression of Frequency of Attendance by Lifestyle Variables

	DF	MS	F	Mult R	R²	P	Constant
Due to regression	9	4.97	7.03	.55	.31	.01	.474
Due to Error	140	.70					
Total	149						

	Beta	F	B
Many friends interested in movies	.27	5.61	.019
Go hiking	.22	10.40	.002
I don't often listen to radio	− .20	4.60	.034
I like to do yard work	− .16	5.69	.018
I know which movies are playing around here	.33	11.07	.001
I dread the future	.23	7.57	.007
College education is important	.29	8.72	.004
Pay extra for quality TV	− .19	7.45	.007
Not feeling you are wasting time	− .13	4.59	.034

in out-of-home experiences. This bodes well for the future of the motion picture theater: this group may be less likely to stay at home to watch movies on a videocassette recorder or home projection system. The cluster of items linking filmgoing to chance-taking and optimism suggests a continued audience for new and unusual film offerings, perhaps in the avant-garde and experimental vein. For these people, filmgoing relates to feelings of sexual attractiveness and the willingness "to try anything once."

The cluster of items related to opinion leadership/cosmopolitanism suggests a sustained audience for film in major urban and suburban areas. This forward-thinking, opinionated, urban filmgoer may have a taste for the "foreign" or "sleeper" films available in urban areas which are unlikely to sustain mass-audience appeal. This group may help account for the well-known disparity in the film industry between the performance of certain films in major cities and their failure in the "hinterlands." Woody Allen's recent films, *Zelig* and *Broadway Danny Rose,* are illustrative of this trend.

The factors emerging from specific leisure interests also point to the existence of key subgroups of the adult moviegoing public. The cluster of items related to spectator sports suggest an audience subgroup that equates filmgoing with "big-time" sports. This group may represent the persistence of the motion picture "fan" in the post-Hollywood era and may be partly responsible for the renaissance of films with a sports theme, including the *Rocky* trilogy, *Raging Bull* and the more recent *Personal Best, Running Brave, The Natural* and *The Slugger's Wife.*

The settled and conservative groups, linked by heavy television viewing, immobility, and a negative view of the future are difficult targets for film producers. These are the people *least* likely to go to a motion picture theater, despite their knowledge of the films in the area. The loadings on these factors directly parallel the findings of Gerbner, associating high television viewing with a fearful, passive, homebody nature (9).

On the other hand, the emergence of the "Adventurer" and "Sierra Club" factors bodes well for motion picture producers. Films with high adventurism and exotic locations are likely to appeal to these groups. This may account for the continued success of action-adventure escapist fare, particularly the super-spy, James Bond genre.

It was not surprising that the best predictor of film attendance was peer interest in films. This is consistent with the literature of film audience research (6). Of more interest were the other predictors which, in combination, accounted for the variance in filmgoing in the sample. Among these were an interest in hiking, disinterest in radio, and knowledge of films in the area.

Interest in hiking is consistent with the "outdoorsy," adventurous orientation of filmgoers described above. That film attendance was inversely related to radio listening is interesting. If this result is replicated, it might suggest that money spent to advertise films on the radio might be put to better use somewhere else. Further, at least for adults, the fact that filmgoing was linked to an awareness of the films in the area underscores the role of promotion in film attendance. Results suggest that the information potential filmgoers need may be met through television and newspaper advertisements and perhaps even billboards in or adjacent to sports stadia.

In sum, the results of the present study clearly argue for a multidimensional market segmentation approach to the study of the motion picture audience. However, several significant limitations of the sample and methodology should be noted.

First, the sample, while randomly generated, is not necessarily representative of the general moviegoing population. It emerged from two Southeastern cities—the site of a major university and a seaport/resort area. Inherent biases in the populations of these two areas may themselves account for the variability observed in the sample irrespective of the act of film attendance.

Second, the analytic methods employed linked clusters of *items,* not *individuals.* Generalizing from attitude-opinion measures (AIO) to individual differences requires considerable subjective decision making on the part of the researchers and has been a consistent limitation of the factor-analytic model (20).

Finally, the self-report measure of film attendance was, by definition, post-hoc. It may not be a valid predictor of *future* film attendance. As other investigators have noted, asking ''what if'' questions of respondents does not typically bear on the likelihood of their carrying through on the behavior (in this case, film attendance) when the situation actually presents itself.

Despite these limitations, the present study represents an exploratory study in the classification of moviegoers by psychographic characteristics. Like radio and television consumption, film attendance is becoming less a ''mass'' activity and more a specialized, fragmented phenomenon.

REFERENCES

1. Anast, Philip. ''Differential Movie Appeals as Correlates of Attendance.'' *Journalism Quarterly* 44, Spring 1967, pp. 86-90.
2. Andreasen, Allen R. and Russell W. Belk. *Audience Development: An Examination of Selected Analysis and Prediction Techniques Applied to Symphony and Theater Attendance in Four Southern Cities.* National Endowment for the Arts, No. 14, 1981.
3. Austin, Bruce A. ''Film Audience Research 1960-1980: An Annotated Bibliography.'' *Journal of Popular Films and Television* 8 (2), 1980-1981, pp. 53-60.
4. Boyer, Peter J. ''Risky Business.'' *American Film* 9(4), January-February 1984, pp. 53-60.
5. Corner, John. '''Mass' in Communication Research.'' *Journal of Communication 29(1), Winter 1979, pp. 26-32.*
6. Custen, George Frederick. *''Film Talk: Viewers Responses to a Film as a Socially Situated Event.''* Unpublished Ph.D. dissertation, University of Pennsylvania, 1980.
7. Ducey, Richard V., Dean M. Krugman, and Donald Eckrich. ''Predicting Market Segments in the Cable Industry: The Basic and Pay Subscribers.'' *Journal of Broadcasting* 27(2), Spring 1983, pp. 155-161.
8. Escarpit, Robert. ''The Concept of 'Mass'.'' *Journal of Communication* 27(2), Spring 1977, pp. 44-48.

9.   Gerbner, George, Larry Gross, Michael Morgan, and Nancy Signorelli. "The 'Mainstreaming' of America: Violence Profile No. 11." *Journal of Communication 30(3), Summer 1980, pp. 10-29.*

10.   Handel, Leo A. *Hollywood Looks at Its Audience: A Report of Film Audience Research.* Urbana: University of Illinois Press, 1950.

11.   Jowett, Garth and James M. Linton. *Movies as Mass Communication.* Beverly Hills: Sage Publications, 1980.

12.   Kerlinger, Fred. *Foundations of Behavioral Research.* New York: Holt, Rhinehart and Winston, 1973.

13.   Levy, Mark R. "Home Video Recorders: A User Survey." *Journal of Communication* 30(4), Fall 1980, pp. 23-27.

14.   Linquist, Rae Andre. "The Evolution of an Image: Marketing Techniques of the American Motion Picture Industry, 1946-1969." Unpublished Master's thesis, University of California, Los Angeles, 1969.

15.   Motion Picture Association of America. *Incidence of Motion Picture Attendance.* New York: MPAA, July 1982.

16.   Olsen, Marvin E. "Motion Picture Attendance and Social Isolation." *Sociologoical Quarterly* 1(2), April 1960, pp. 107-116.

17.   Nie, Norman H., C. Hadlai Hull, Jean G. Jenkins, Karin Steinbrenner, and Dale H. Bent. *Statistititi Package for the Social Sciences,* 2nd ed. New York: McGraw-Hill, 1975.

18.   Sherman, Barry L. "Psychographic Research in Broadcasting." Panel presentation, Broadcast Education Association Fall Seminar, Washington, D.C., October 1982.

19.   Wells, William D. "Psychographics: A Critical Review." *Journal of Marketing Research* 12(2), May 1975, pp. 196-213.

20.   Wimmer, Roger D. and Joseph R. Dominick. *Mass Media Research.* Belmont, California: Wadsworth Publishing, 1983.

4

Teenagers and Teenpics, 1955-1957: A Study of Exploitation Filmmaking

Thomas Doherty

Exploitation filmmaking is a commercial strategy first practiced in earnest by the American motion picture industry during the latter half of the 1950s. Its distinctive product is the "teenpic," a film targeted at teenaged moviegoers to the pointed exclusion of other age groups. The purpose of this study is to trace the economic and demographic realities that encouraged—indeed, forced—the film industry to turn increasingly to teenagers for financial sustenance. *Rock Around the Clock* (1956), the first acknowledged teenpic, will serve as a kind of synecdoche for this investigation. Its history should bring into sharper focus the nature of exploitation filmmaking, one of the ways Hollywood responded to the loss of its mass audience at mid-century.

HOLLYWOOD AND THE TEEN MARKETPLACE

"The Big Bands are breaking up," says an impresario at the beginning of *Rock Around the Clock* (hereinafter *RATC*), "the handwriting's on the wall." The observation could have as well applied to the big Hollywood studios. By the mid-1950s the motion picture industry had lost its preeminent place in American cultural life. Although the promise of spectacle, novelty, or controversy might occasionally lure the mass audience back to theaters, the certainty of a market and the assurance of regular production—the hallmarks of classic Hollywood—had evaporated under the heat of television, divestiture, and shifting demographics (see 7, 17, 27, and 33). In short, filmmaking had become a haphazard business; each picture was a hit-or-miss proposition. If theatrical movies were to have a future as an industry, they would have to find, and discover the means to cultivate, a new, reliable audience with plenty of free time and spending money. Teenagers fitted the bill.

Teenagers had always been around, of course but, prior to the 1950s, neither Hollywood nor anyone else had taken particular notice of them. By 1955, they were impossible to ignore: a statistical anomaly in population distribution had converged with unparalleled economic prosperity to produce the nation's first generation of "true" teenagers. They were distinct from previous generations of American young people in numbers, affluence, and self-consciousness: there were more of them, they had more money, and they were more aware of their unique status. By the late 1930s, the "population trough" of the worst years of the Great Depression had begun to reverse itself. Throughout the war years, there began the marked increase in the birth rate that, after 1946, exploded into the famous postwar "baby boom" (21; 56, p. 32; 57, p. 31). The wartime babies reached adolescence during the mid-'50s, the majority coming of age in homes that, by the standards of their parents and the rest of the world, were luxurious. The increasing uniformity of public school education throughout the states and a national media that doted on their idiosyncracies further standardized their experience. In 1958, when Dwight MacDonald referred to "a new American caste" with "a style of life that was *sui generis,*" he was speaking of this *pre*-baby boom generation (34, p. 57). They, not their celebrated younger siblings of the great baby boom of 1946-'57, were the original teenagers.

Many responded to the sudden prominence of the American teenager with fear and trembling. Throughout the 1950s, cultural guardians likened this "new American caste" to savage hordes descending on a city under seige. But even as editorial writers, law enforcement officials, and parents were shoring up the barricades against them, the business community was welcoming their arrival at the gates. With good reason: there was a fortune to be made selling trinkets to the barbarians.

Newsweek labeled them "the dreamy teenage market" (18, p. 94) and *Sales Management* christened the 13-19 age bracket "the seven golden years" (14, p. 19). In 1959, *Life* reported what was by then old news: "The American teenagers have emerged as a big-time consumer in the U.S. economy . . . Counting only what is spent to satisfy their special teenage demands, the youngsters and their parents will shell out about $10 billion this year, a billion more than the total sales of GM" (40, p. 78). Moreover, as a study for the Bureau of Business Research later documented, those billions were all "largely discretionary" (14, p. 104) which, in entrepreneurial terms, meant that teenage pocket money was basically up for grabs.

Unlike other industries, however, Hollywood was curiously shy in its courtship of the American teenager. Partly the reason for this was that until the mid-1950s Hollywood had only the faintest idea of who its audience was. The only statistical information the industry required was the daily box office report; such data, by themselves, are not amenable to age aggregate partioning. As Martin Quigley, Jr., the influential editor of *Motion Picture Herald* observed in 1957: "In the 'good old days' of dimming memory, no one in the industry—be he producer, distributor, or exhibitor—took any interest in the question *Who Goes to the Movies?* The answer was plain—Everyone . . ." (46, p. 21). Filmmakers were equally confident about predicting what kind of movies "Everyone" wanted. By and large, the forceful personalities who controlled the studio system had depended on little more than hustle and instinct to anticipate and gauge audience tastes. The oft-cited technique of Columbia's Harry Cohn, who claimed he could detect an unprofitable picture if his behind squirmed during the screening, was representative. The prospect of "the whole world wired to Harry Cohn's ass" (as screenwriter Herman J. Mankiewicz retorted) may have been daunting, but his methodology made a certain sense. Moguls like Cohn, Warner, and Mayer had a kinship with their audience that their urbane successors lacked. By the mid-1950s, though, both the audience for motion pictures and the studio executive making them had changed. As the moguls and classic producers who came to power during the go-getting 1920s were replaced by 1950s-style "organization men," the distance between the middle-aged financiers who made the movies and the ever-younger audience who patronized them rendered Cohn's seat-of-the-pants methods hopelessly antiquated. At the same time, the scale of the industry—the complexities and logistics as well as the money at stake—made filmmaking a bigger gamble than ever. Yet compared to their fellows in the automobile or fashion industries, motion picture executives still made production decisions in a stunningly haphazard way (see 3, pp. xx-xxv).

In January 1946, the Motion Picture Association of America (MPAA) first acknowledged modern business and marketing procedures by creating a special department of research. The next year, in a special issue of the *Annals of the American Academy of Political and Social Science,* MPAA department head Robert W. Chambers lamented that so many Hollywood businessmen made decisions in a statistical vacuum. Reiterating the viewpoint of MPAA President Eric Johnston, Chambers noted that "from the standpoint of statistical knowledge . . . the motion picture industry probably knows less about its audience than any other major industry in the United States" (15, p. 169). He commended the industry for taking its first steps towards the emerging science of demographics and spoke of the need for continued movement in that direction (15, pp. 170-171). Elsewhere in the same issue, communications theorist Paul F. Lazarsfeld presented a quantitative analysis of movie audiences. Lazarsfeld reported that "scrutiny of available data" showed "age [as] the most important personal factor by which the movie audience is characterized" and that "the decline of movie attendance with increasing age is very sharp" (32, pp. 162-163). His most significant finding, though, concerned movie "opinion leaders": "In an overwhelming number of cases they are young people, many of them below twenty-five years of age. This is a very remarkable result. Our general notion is that the young learn from the old. In the movie field, advice definitely flows in the opposite direction'' (32, p. 167). In other words, Lazarsfeld was telling the industry that, in 1947, at the height of its prestige as a business and maturity as an art form, its future was with youngsters.

This was not the conventional wisdom. Despite pleas from exhibitors, the MPAA refused to abandon its concept of moviegoing as a family outing. In 1950, Leo Handel's landmark study, *Hollywood Looks at Its Audience,* exhaustively documented the juvenilization of the movie audience (26). Still, statistical reports notwithstanding, moviemakers remained almost willfully blind to the changing nature of their business. ''You can show them (any data) you want,'' said one frustrated exhibitor, ''that's still a long way from getting them to comply'' (37, p. 16). Understandably reluctant to surrender cultural dominance in the entertainment marketplace, they ignored survey after survey which uniformly reported that the nation's typical moviegoer was a teenager. ''Hollywood executives hire you to help them,'' complained market analyst Albert E. Sindlinger, ''But when you don't tell them what they want to hear, sometimes they don't trust your accuracy'' (20). Walter Brooks, writing in his ''Manager's Round Table'' column for *Motion Picture Herald,* voiced a common industry attitude to bearers of unwelcome tidings such as Sindlinger: ''You can prove anything by the statisticians . . . The statisticians assemble all sorts of figures to prove what has happened and to predict what will happen in the future. Personally, we think the statisticians themselves should be laid end to end—to prove that what they find depends on who pays their fees'' (9). Though the great audience for movies no longer existed, the industry did its best to maintain the cherished fiction of service to a grand, broad-based ''public.''

There were two main reasons for Hollywood's astigmatism. First, the ''industry'' didn't operate like other industries in the way it went about selling its products. Moviemakers came out of a show-business, carnival tradition of ''ballyhoo.'' Few had faith or expertise in modern marketing techniques which other industries had used for decades, much less in newfangled forms of consumer seduction such as motivational research and depth psychology. Second, most professionals—producers, directors, and screenwriters—had ''adult'' artistic sensibilities. Whether nurtured in the studio system or recently graduated from television or New York stages, they were serious craftsmen unwilling to let juveniles dictate the exercise of their talents. Thus, many in the film industry worked against their own economic interests by making movies for an audience that no longer attended that often: married adults with children (see also 3, 24).

Though the concept of the movie theater as ''the center of family entertainment'' was encouraged at the industry's highest levels, a growing chorus of voices from the exhibition end of the business and in the trade press called for a recognition of the new demographic realities. A survey for the *Motion Picture Herald* Institute of Industry Opinion reported in 1956: ''The need for pictures appealing to the 15 to 25 age group was listed as most important by all classes of exhibition and by production as well, but distribution placed it fifth. The heavy percentage of opinion for this one factor . . . is an outstanding factor of the survey" (30, p. 12). Quigley used his editorial forum to inform readers that "the most important single area for the present and future well-being of the motion picture industry is the youth of the country . . . the teens up through the mid-twenties" (44). *Variety* agreed, noting at the close of 1956 that "the demand for teenage pictures . . . is coming from all quarters—from small theatres as well as large circuits, from rural towns as well as big cities. The cry to assuage [the] teenage market is so great that some observers are already expressing the fear that the only outlet for mature films will be the art house" (28, p. 86).

Despite the research evidence and urging from certain quarters of the industry, many moviemakers remained recalcitrant. In 1958, producer Sam Goldwyn expressed the anachronistic sentiments of the hold-outs: "I believe in making pictures a man can take his whole family to see" (4). At that late date, of course, most men were not doing any such thing. Quigley warned that "it would be futile to adopt an ostrich-head-in-the-sand attitude and pay no heed to the fact that in relation to their numbers those in the 15 to 25 age-group are the motion pictures' best customers" (45). Even for those who acknowledged the importance of the teenage audience, the time-honored mandate of "entertainment for the entire family" died hard. For example, one exhibitor with a better grasp of statistics than adolescent behavior suggested that "what we need today at the theater is a gimmick to create an incentive to teenagers to come to their neighborhood theaters, enjoy themselves, and bring their families with them" (38).

Such naive remarks highlight the industry's twin dilemma: moviemakers had both to *recognize* that the teen audience was crucial to their economic future and to *court* it successfully. Having identified the problem, they still had to propose a solution. "We know that the juvenile audience is off even though there are more kids around than ever," said one advertising-publicity director, "What we need is a study to indicate to us which way we could get those patrons back again" (37, p. 5). Appropriately, though, a statistical study by a market research firm was not the light which showed the way. Rather, it was the example of Sam Katzman, one of Hollywood's legendary fast-buck boys. The success of Katzman's teenpics led the industry into an earnest and enduring exploitation of the teenage moviegoer.

"JUNGLE SAM" KATZMAN

At the peak of his production schedule in the early 1950s, Sam Katzman churned out an average of seventeen features and three serials a year, none of which lost money or cost over $500,000. One of the industry's most active and successful independents, he specialized in the kind of disposable, low-budget fare whose profit margin was modest but certain. In 1953, for example, cued by the popularity of "sex and sandals" epics such as *Samson and Delilah* (1949), *Quo Vadis* (1950), and *The Robe* (1952), Katzman underwent a prolific Middle Eastern phase, supplying theaters with (successively) *Siren of Bagdad, Flame of Calcutta, Serpent of the Nile,* and *Prisoners of the Casbah.* His production of the lucrative "Jungle Jim" series featuring Johnny Weismuller earned him the moniker "Jungle Sam," but the nickname might just as well have been a tribute to his knack for survival within a treacherous industry and a volatile market. Unfettered by artistic pretensions, Katzman was the definitive exploitation filmmaker. "Lord knows, I'll never make an Academy Award movie," he said, "But then I'm just as happy to get my achievement plaque from the bank every year" (36, p. 82).

Early on, Katzman saw the box office potential of tailoring a motion picture to a matching audience. Following modern business procedures, he always knew his markets, produced pictures with those markets in mind, and merchandized them accordingly. Throughout the 1940s and early 1950s, he catered alternately to preteens (what the trade press called "the cap pistol set") with matinee fare like *Adam Man vs. Superman* (1950) and *Captain Video* (1952) and to a slightly older group composed largely of adolescent boys. In 1946, a series of "quickies" (low-budget, high-speed productions) Katzman made for Monogram and Columbia— *Junior Prom, Freddie Steps Out, High School Hero,* and *Betty Co-ed*—attuned him to an emerging audience for films that were neither "kiddie" nor "Mom and Pop" fare. After television became the nation's most popular babysitter, Katzman increasingly turned his production efforts to films with a decidedly adolescent appeal. "We got a new generation," he told *Time* in 1952, "But they got the same old glands" (31). Katzman stimulated adolescent glands with exotic locales (all filmed in California), freakish creatures (apes, dwarves, and monsters) and disheveled actresses. These items, he felt, had an intrinsic appeal for his target group, an exploitation value that could be grafted onto the flimsiest of storylines.

Given his demanding production schedule, though, not even Katzman could rely on the same half-dozen exploitative elements for every title. For new and exciting ideas he was guided by contemporary journalism: Katzman turned newspaper headlines into film titles. In this the producer was hardly breaking new ground. Since the fast-paced days of silent cinema, "as timely as today's headlines" has been a publicity hook for motion pictures. An economical (in the broadest sense of the word) source of inspiration, the press has long provided the movies with juicy subject matter and, importantly, free publicity. In 1901, Edwin S. Porter did little more than visually render newspaper accounts of contemporary events in *The Execution of Czolgosz, Terrible Teddy and the Grizzly King,* and *The Sampson-Schley Controversy* (39). But in Porter's day filmmakers could crank out dramatizations of current events while the story still dominated the front pages. They could take advantage of transitory public curiosity and reap maximum publicity value from the newspapers' continued coverage of the event that inspired the film in the first place. With the rise of classic Hollywood, such speed was no longer possible nor, so long as the studios had guaranteed exhibition outlets, was it necessary. As the old system faltered and competition for a dwindling audience's attention and time intensified, filmmakers were forced to redefine their industry. Katzman's special contribution was to reintroduce something of the speed of early silent production to the motion picture industry at mid-century.

By minimizing the time lapse between the event and the film that exploited it, Katzman was virtually assured of an intrigued audience and some free publicity. The success of his quickie productions underscored a truism of exploitation filmmaking: be the first, not the best; quickness counts for more than quality. Katzman began work on an atomic thriller the day after he heard the news of the first H-Bomb explosion. A few days after the outbreak of the Korean War, Columbia solicited a suitable war movie. Katzman quickly conjured up a title (*A Yank in Korea*) and delivered the completed product six weeks and two days later (31; 36, p. 82).

Given this modus operandi, Katzman's decision in early 1956 to make a rock 'n' roll exploitation film was predictable. Timely, controversial, and the province of teenagers, rock 'n' roll music was obviously grist for his production mill. Less predictable were the profound, long-range effects this latest assembly-line quickie was to have on the motion picture industry. *RATC* became the first hugely successful teenpic, the picture that announced the coming ascendency of the teenage audience. As such, its production history, exploitation campaign, and ultimate impact bear a closer look.

"ROCK AROUND THE CLOCK"

Exploitation filmmakers are careful businessmen. Generally, they are too careful to attempt a radically new formula. More often than not, they capitalize on successful gambits by the major film companies. In 1955, the profit margins and controversy generated by MGM's *The Blackboard Jungle* and Warner's *Rebel Without a Cause* cued Katzman and several other sharp-eyed independents to the exploitation potential of rebellious youth. Though purportedly "adult" films, *Jungle* and *Rebel* immediately found their own level and were enthusiastically embraced by the nation's young people. A survey for Gilbert Youth Research Organization reported *The Blackboard Jungle* as the favorite film of high school students and *Rebel Without a Cause* star James Dean their favorite actor (2). These two films were usually acknowledged as having spawned the many "youth movies" of the later 1950s, an eclectic assortment of high- and low-budget films dealing with juvenile delinquency, drag racing, high school vice, dating rituals, horror, space aliens, and, of course, rock 'n' roll.

Over the titles to *The Blackboard Jungle*, director Richard Brooks made an audacious choice in background music: "Rock Around the Clock," a minor hit by an up-and-coming band named Bill Haley and the Comets. An amalgam of country and western and rhythm and blues music, the tune marked the first appearance of rock 'n' roll in a major motion picture. Largely on the strength of its use in *The Blackboard Jungle*, "Rock Around the Clock" gained new life on the *Billboard* pop music charts (6). By the end of 1955, the song had sold some two million copies, providing Bill Haley with a lifetime meal ticket (25, see also 16, pp. 17-21).

The scale of Haley's show business success was impressive, but there was nothing, at least in the very early days, to indicate that something more than entertainment-as-usual was going on. After all, shrieking, swooning, and other manifestations of (often well-staged) audience hysteria had been a part of pop music trends since the 1920s: Rudy Vallee, Bing Crosby, Frank Sinatra, and, most recently, the "nabob of sob," Johnny Ray, had each in his turn inspired progressively wilder reactions from claques of devoted fans. Few imagined that "Rock Around the Clock" would become, in the words of rock historian Lillian Roxon, "the Marseillaise of the teenage revolution . . . the first inkling teenagers had that they might be a force to be reckoned with, in numbers alone" (52, p. 216). At the close of 1956, the song, Haley, and the attendant rock 'n' roll hoopla had all the markings of the usual, short-lived musical fad—and, as a fad, it had clear exploitation possibilities for "Jungle Sam" Katzman (see, e.g., 19, pp. 13-20; 35, pp. 40-41; 58).

In Mid-January 1956, Katzman started production on *RATC;* by month's end, shooting was complete. Columbia Pictures, his usual distributor, had placed the first rock 'n' roll musical in selected theaters by March. Directed by Fred Sears and featuring Bill Haley and the Comets, the Platters, and disc jockey Alan Freed, the film was a variation on the venerable Big Band musicals of the 1940s, a form then undergoing something of a resurgence with *The Glenn Miller Story* (1954) and *The Benny Goodman Story* (1955). In terms of production quality and narrative complexity, *RATC* wasn't especially different from the material Katzman had been marketing for years: mildly controversial, timely, teen-oriented, and cheap (under $300,000.) Indeed, with the exception of the rock 'n' roll exploitation angle, *RATC* had a lot in common with an earlier Katzman production, *Teenage Crime Wave* (1955): same director, same teenage topicality, and same filmic antecedent (*The Blackboard Jungle*).

RATC was a model of exploitation filmmaking in two important ways: it was first out of the gate and it had the best title. The rock 'n' roll craze had caught Katzman's nominal competition in quickie production off guard. American International Pictures, Distributors Corporation of America, Allied Artists, and Universal-International all took months to fabricate their own rock 'n' roll teenpics. Foresight was evident in the film's very title: by beating his rivals to the title registration office and filing for the immediately-recognizable catchphrase "Rock Around the Clock," Katzman secured thousands of dollars in free publicity. Articulating another commandment of exploitation filmmaking, the producer defined his narrative guidelines: "We don't get stories. We get titles and then write stories around them or to fit them" (31). Not even a businessman as prescient as he, though, could have realized how big a score he had on his hands or how powerful an influence *RATC* was to have on the motion picture industry.

Although reviewers for mainstream periodicals ignored the film's initial release, the trade press sensed its potential from the beginning. "Nothing massive or pretentious here, but it's as tasty as a charlotte ruse . . . ," commented *Motion Picture Herald* (47). *Variety* enthusiastically predicted that it would "prove a handy entry for exhibitors packaging a show aimed [at] the sweater-levi crowd" (48). Handy it was. In relation to its production costs, the film's financial return was remarkable. With reported world-wide grosses of $2.4 million, or eight times the initial production costs, *RATC* was easily "one of the most spectacularly successful pictures of the year" (49, p. 4). According to *Film Daily Year Book,* 479 features were released in the U.S. market in 1956, of which 272 were American-produced (1, p. 111). *Variety* lists only 109 pictures that grossed $1,000,000 or more in their first full play off (49, p. 1). For Hollywood accountants, however, a picture's total gross receipts are less important than its profit margin, the ratio between box office take and a film's "negative costs." In these terms, *RATC* was as impressive as larger-grossing, but far more expensive, productions such as *Guys and Dolls* or *The King and I,* the box office champions of 1956. In an era in which Hollywood producers were banking more and more on fewer and fewer films, *RATC* showed that with the right project they might gain much while risking little.

"DON'T KNOCK THE ROCK"

There was one significant marketing problem, however: the possibility that the controversy over rock 'n' roll would reach a point of diminishing returns. In late 1955 and early 1956, minor incidents of violence had erupted during live rock 'n' roll shows and in movie theaters during the "Rock Around the Clock" title sequence in *The Blackboard Jungle.* Columbia's release of *RATC* exacerbated an already heated dispute over the music's presumed incitement to violence and juvenile delinquency. Though it is probably true that the average 1950s parent was more worried about fluoridation than rock 'n' roll, the national media found the "rock 'n' roll phenomenon" natural fodder and devoted reams of copy to its colorful stars, fans, and detractors. In retrospect, the intensity of the opposition to the "insidious influences" of rock 'n' roll music is easy to overestimate because historians of the early rock era delight in citing wild pronouncements by contemporary fearmongers (see, e.g., 5, pp. 56-59). Nonetheless, it seems appropriate to quote several statements reflecting something of the level of public discourse on the subject. The nascent racism lurking beneath much of the anti-rock 'n' roll sentiment was brought to the surface by Asa Carter, executive secretary of the North Alabama White Citizens' Council, who condemned the music as an NAACP conspiracy to infect white teenagers via the nation's jukeboxes (54). More in line with the Freudian temper of the times was Dr. Francis Braceland, a noted psychiatrist, who called rock 'n' roll a "cannibalistic and tribalistic form of music," and explained somewhat anachronistically that "it is insecurity and rebellion that impels teenagers to affect 'ducktail' haircuts, wear zoot suits, and carry on boisterously at rock 'n' roll shows'' (50). On balance, the "adult" attitude was perhaps more condescending than alarmist. In 1957, one critic posed what was by then a rhetorical question: "Catering to the teenager's taste has leveled our song standards to the point of vulgarity, banality, and infantilism . . . can this happen to the movies under the prospect of their getting hungry enough to start indulging the banal, untrained, irresponsible tastes of the average teenager" (22)?

RATC was launched directly into the maelstrom. Many exhibitors who played the film encountered resistance from law enforcement authorities, newspaper editorialists, and parents groups concerned that exposure to rock 'n' roll music unleashed the sleeping delinquent in otherwise well-behaved teenagers. Soon after the film's release, a front-page story in *Variety* warned: "Rock 'n' roll—the most explosive show biz phenomenon of the decade—may be getting too hot to handle. While its money-making potential has made it all but irresistable its Svengali grip on the teenagers has produced a staggering wave of juvenile violence and mayhem. Rock 'n' roll is now literally [box office] dynamite—not only a matter of profit, but a matter for the police" (49, p. 1). By the standards of later decades, the juvenile "mayhem" (screaming, foot-stomping, and an occasional scuffle) has an almost benignly nostalgic flavor to it. After a screening of *RATC* in Minneapolis, for example, teenagers snake-danced downtown and broke store windows before "police quelled the youthful rioters" (41). According to *Billboard,* the police at one live rock 'n' roll show were reportedly so jumpy "they even frowned when the kids applauded the acts" (10, p. 22).

Exhibitors were caught between their desire for teenage dollars and their dread of teenage violence. In a delicate balancing act, the publicity department at Columbia exploited the controversy ("Now's the time to book Columbia's *RATC* while it's headline news in the USA!") while at the same time trying to allay the fears and flame the greed of theater owners. "Except for minor incidents, we've had no trouble thus far," said a Columbia spokesman, "It's doing fantastic business" (51). Reflecting the industry's two minds about the teenage audience, the trade press counseled exhibitors to temper the usual ballyhoo with sound judgment. "All these rock 'n' roll stars mean something to rock 'n' roll addicts, and they are very numerous! It's the most . . . They'll be dancing in the streets, in the lobby, and in the aisles," exalted *Motion Picture Herald's* advisor on selling approaches, who was cautious enough to conclude his pitch with the warning: "but don't let them dance all night, the all-night dancethons can get out of control—and do you more harm than good" (55).

Exhibitor misgivings aside, the financial success of *RATC* sent an unmistakable message to the motion picture production companies: there was money to be made from teenagers by capturing the rock 'n' roll craze on film. By the end of 1956, a half-dozen rock 'n' roll pictures had completed production. The recently-organized American International Pictures showed the acumen that was soon to make it the dominant force in teenpics by leading the pack with *Shake, Rattle, and*

Rock (released October 1956); Twentieth Century-Fox had Elvis Presley ready by Thanksgiving vacation in *Love Me Tender* (released November 1956), and for the Christmas holidays the company was busily promoting its second rock 'n' roll offering, *The Girl Can't Help It* (released December 1956); Distributor Corporation of America weighed in with Vanguard Production's *Rock, Rock, Rock* (released December 1956); and Universal-International submitted *Rock, Pretty Baby* (released January 1957). Even the Abbott and Costello comedy series tried to muscle in with the deceptively-titled *Dance With Me Henry* (released December 1956). Katzman, for his part, hoped lightning would strike twice with a sequel, *Don't Knock the Rock* (released January 1957).

Katzman's decision to produce *Don't Knock the Rock* is worth added note as an example of how exploitation filmmaking feeds on itself. *Don't Knock the Rock* exploits not only the rock 'n' roll controversy, but its parent film *RATC* as well. Having scored once, the exploitation filmmaker can usually milk further exploitation value out of the original, successful exploitation. Producer Herman Cohen did much the same thing the next year for American International Pictures, following up the hugely-successful *I Was a Teenage Werewolf* with *I Was a Teenage Frankenstein*. Discussing his exploitation methods with *Variety*, Katzman confided that he never worked too far ahead of a trend and never made more than two or three exploitation pictures on the same subject unless something unusual presented itself (23, p. 5). By Katzman's calculations, the second exploitation picture generally did about 75 percent of the business of the first and the "third begins to level off to the point it's advisable to search for something new" (p. 7).

CALYPSOMANIA

For exploitation filmmakers, the trick is to hit the crest of the wave, ride it, and jump off before wiping out. Attempts by Katzman and several other producers indicate that it is also necessary to catch the *right* wave. Often a good 30 years older than their target audience, moviemakers in the 1950s sometimes found it difficult to anticipate and cultivate teenage tastes. In early 1957, soon after his success with two rock 'n' roll teenpics, Katzman was reported to be biding his time "waiting for something to happen" on which "to base future production" (23). He opted for calypso music, a new and provocative rhythm which, in late 1956 and early 1957, enjoyed a brief vogue on popular music charts (53). The "calypso invasion" was spearheaded by Harry Belafonte's "The Banana Boat Song" and The Easyriders's much-recorded "Marianne." Like all musical crazes, calypso music inspired dances, fashions, and public curiosity. Having always looked upon rock 'n' roll as a temporary affliction anyway, some in the entertainment industry assumed that calypso would displace rock 'n' roll and become the next big teenage music sensation. The Reverend Normon O'Connor, described as a "recognized jazz authority," was quoted in both *Newsweek* and *Variety* predicting that rock 'n' roll was fading fast. "Rock 'n' roll is a stage in popular music similar to the

Charleston, jazz, swing, and the jitterbug of the past two generations and is now on its way out," he claimed. "The present fad is now giving way to calypso music" (60; see also 11).

Low-budget film producers, with the precedent of *RATC* fresh in mind, stampeded to the title registration office. The titles they filed for included *Calypso Rhythm, Calypso Holiday, Calypso Nights, Bop Girl Goes Calypso, Calypso-Gripso, Calypsomania, Calypso Kid, Banana Boat Calypso,* and *Mad Craze from Trinidad* (12). An Allied Artists entry, *Calypso Joe,* and a Sam Katzman film, *Calypso Heat Wave,* were soon neck-and-neck in a race to cash in on the presumed calypso market. In May 1957, Allied Artists won: *Calypso Joe,* promised their ads, was "ready right now for a calypso crazy nation." *Calypso Heat Wave* followed a couple of weeks later.

But there was to be no payoff in the calypso sweepstakes and the "calypso cycle" was short-lived. The "craze" was a show business flash-in-the-pan and an exploitation false alarm. Weighing the prospects of *Calypso Heat Wave,* a trade reviewer noted: "It's none-too-subtly aimed at the teenage market and there will have to find its greatest appeal. Against it is the fact that the calypso song craze is on the wane and some say already dead" (13). By the time *Bop Girl Goes Calypso* appeared several weeks later, it could confidently be pronounced dead on arrival, a "mild musical badly outguessed by events . . . vitiating the potential it might have had earlier as a musical programmer" (8). The remaining calypso titles went unused.

Despite the failure of the calypso cycle, the quick and substantial killings made by the first wave of rock 'n' roll pictures had effectively established the power of the teenage filmgoer. (Many of Harry Belafonte's fans were adults, and the motion picture industry had learned that record sales might not translate into ticket sales unless teenagers were buying the records.) At the close of 1956, *Variety* commented on the importance of the new audience and the kind of pictures it patronized: "The product shortage has brought about a new theory of assembling a show, a practice that has been adopted by several indie producers and distributors. This consists of packaging so-called exploitation pictures. These are low-budget films based on controversial and timely subjects that make newspaper headlines . . . In the main these pictures appeal to 'uncontrolled' juveniles and 'undesirables' . . . Theatermen realize that they are holding a hot potato, but out of desperation are reaching for any straw that spells [box office]. The exploitation pix and rock 'n' rollers, while not drawing the audience 'we want,' are nevertheless bringing crowds to pay-windows" (29, p. 20). Indeed, *Rock, Pretty Baby, Rock, Rock, Rock,* and *Don't Knock the Rock* were each extraordinarily lucrative in relation to their production costs. The success of *Love Me Tender,* the medium-budget Elvis Presley vehicle, was even more impressive. A perfunctory western with no overt rock 'n' roll music, *Love Me Tender* set box office records across the country. Its release was timed to coincide with the school system's Thanksgiving break; at one theater in San Francisco, 200 teenagers lined up for tickets five hours before classes were dismissed, at which time the deluge began (43). Though it had been in release for fewer than six weeks, *Love Me Tender* was twenty-second on *Variety's* year-end list for 1956, grossing $3,750,000 (42, p. 4). The first of a decade-long series of sequels followed with the rock 'n' roll musicals *Loving You* (released August 1957) and *Jailhouse Rock* (released November 1957). With *Love Me Tender* still going strong, Presley finished 1957 with three pictures in *Variety's* top twenty: *Love Me Tender* (number 10, grossing a cumulative $4,500,000), *Jailhouse Rock* (number 15, grossing $4,000,000), and *Loving You* (number 19, grossing $3,700,000). Presley's chief rival for teenage affections, Pat Boone, achieved comparable success in his two 1957 vehicles, *Bernadine* (number 14, grossing $4,000,000) and *April Love* (number 18, grossing $3,700,000). Frank Tashlin's *The Girl Can't Help It* had a heftier budget and loftier ambitions than most of the field (and, of course, Jayne Mansfield's presence up-front gave it broader demographic appeal), but its formidable line-up of rock 'n' roll talent was responsible for much of the $2,800,000 it accrued. At the close of 1957, *Variety's* year-end list of box office hits for the first time included a goodly number of films whose success could *only* be attributed to teenagers (59).

CONCLUSION

Teenagers had made up the most significant part of the moviegoing audience at least since World War II, but it wasn't until 1955-57 that the motion picture industry began to seriously acknowledge them. Though some segments of the business had devoted sporadic attention to the teenage audience with inexpensive serials, "B" westerns, or "weirdie" science fiction quickies, there was no industry-wide consensus of the importance of that market, much less an earnest assault on it, prior to *RATC*. The success of *RATC* and its progeny testified convincingly to the power—and the future ascendency—of the teenage audience. Henceforth, the industry campaign to woo this group would be concerted and conscious: it signaled new production and marketing strategies and gave prominence to a new kind of motion picture, the teenpic. Since the 1950s, this process has only accelerated and teenpics, once the industry's embarrassing underside, have lately become its foundation. Successive generations of teenagers have demanded—and received—the kind of motion pictures that satisfy their special tastes and reflect their distinctive styles: *Easy Rider* (1969) and *Saturday Night Fever* (1977) are two obvious touchstones. More than any other group, teens dictate the terms of commercial American cinema. Exploitation filmmakers for their part, now solidly in the Hollywood mainstream, have become so skilled at taking the pulse of their audience that "calypsomania"-like miscalculations are more and more uncommon. The awesome effectiveness of saturation advertising, simultaneous nationwide exhibition, and a bewildering array of other sophisticated marketing techniques have refined the "pioneering" exploitation methods of entrepreneurs like Sam Katzman to new levels of predictability and profits. The question for the 1950s exploitation filmmaker was which diet would satisfy the teenage taste; the contemporary exploitation filmmaker is more likely to ask: how can I create an appetite? The nature of that new relationship between filmmaker and audience is one focus for future research in mass communication.

REFERENCES

1. Alicoate, Jack (Ed.). *The 1957 Film Daily Year Book of Motion Pictures*. New York: Wid's Film and Film Folk, 1957.
2. "Attendance." *Motion Picture Herald*, March 17, 1956, p. 9.
3. Austin, Bruce A. *The Film Audience: An International Bibliography of Research*. Metuchen, NJ: Scarecrow Press, 1983.
4. "Avoids Gats and Gams." *Variety*, June 4, 1958, p. 1.
5. Belz, Carl. *The Story of Rock* (2d. ed.). New York: Harper and Row, 1972.
6. *Billboard*, May 28, 1955, p. 46.
7. Biskind, Peter. *Seeing Is Believing: How Hollywood Taught Us to Stop Worrying and Love the Fifties*. New York: Pantheon Books, 1983.
8. "Bop Girl Goes Calypso." *Variety*, July 17, 1957, p. 6.
9. Brooks, Walter. "You Can Prove Anything by the Statisticians." *Motion Picture Herald*, January 7, 1956, p. 37.
10. Bundy, June. "Freed Replies to R&R Press Slurs." *Billboard*, April 28, 1956, pp. 19, 22.
11. "The Calypso Craze." *Newsweek*, February 25, 1957, p. 72.
12. "Calypso Films to Flood Market?" *Variety*, March 13, 1957, p. 1.
13. "Calypso Heat Wave." *Variety*, June 5, 1957, p. 6.
14. Cateora, Philip R. *An Analysis of the Teenage Market*. Austin: Bureau of Business Research, University of Texas, 1963.
15. Chambers, Robert W. "Need for Statistical Research." *Annals of the American Academy of Social and Political Science* 254, November 1947, pp. 169-172.
16. Cohn, Nik. *Rock From the Beginning*. New York: Stein and Day, 1969.
17. Dowdy, Andrew. *"Movies Are Better Than Ever": Widescreen Memories of the Fifties*. New York: William Morrow and Company, 1973.
18. "The Dreamy Teen-Age Market: 'It's Neat to Spend.' " *Newsweek*, September 16, 1957, pp. 94, 96-97.
19. Ehrenstein, David and Bill Reed. *Rock on Film*. New York: Delilah Books, 1982.
20. "The Fans: They Like—and Dislike." *Newsweek*, August 4, 1958, p. 69.
21. "Film 'Future': GI Baby Boom." *Variety*, March 5, 1958, pp. 1, 27.
22. Finley, James Fenlon. "TV for Me, If Teens Rule Screens." *Catholic World* 184 (1103), February 1957, pp. 380-381.
23. "$5,600,000 Estimate for Katzman's 12-16 Columbia Pix Up to $6,200,000." *Variety*, March 6, 1957, pp. 5, 7.
24. Garrison, Lee C. Jr. *The Composition, Attendance Behavior and Needs of Motion Picture Audiences: A Review of the Literature*. Los Angeles: Graduate School of Management, UCLA, 1971.
25. "Haley Rocks 4th Disc Into 1,000,000 Circle." *Variety*, April 4, 1956, p. 1.
26. Handel, Leo A. *Hollywood Looks at Its Audience: A Report of Film Audience Research*. Urbana: University of Illinois Press, 1950.
27. Higham, Charles. *Hollywood at Sunset*. New York: Saturday Review Press, 1972.
28. Hollinger, Hy. " 'Lost Audience'; Crass vs. Class." *Variety*, December 5, 1956, pp. 1, 86.
29. Hollinger, Hy. "Teenage Biz vs. Repair Bills." *Variety*, December 19, 1956, pp. 1, 20.

30. Ivers, John D. "Aim at Youth and Reduce Violence, Panelists Insist." *Motion Picture Herald,* September 8, 1956, pp. 12-13.

31. "Jungle Sam." *Time,* December 1, 1952, p. 62.

32. Lazarsfeld, Paul F. "Audience Research in the Movie Field." *Annals of the American Academy of Social and Political Science* 254, November 1947, pp. 160-168.

33. MacCann, Richard Dyer. *Hollywood in Transition.* Boston: Houghton Mifflin, 1962.

34. Macdonald, Dwight. "A Caste, A Culture, A Market—I." *The New Yorker,* November 22, 1958, pp. 57-94.

35. McGee, Mark Thomas and R.J. Robertson. *The J.D. Films: Juvenile Delinquency in the Movies.* Jefferson, NC: McFarland and Company, 1982.

36. "Meet Jungle Sam." *Life,* March 23, 1953, pp. 79-82.

37. "More Data About Audience Tastes? Great! But How Does East Get Studios to Act on Findings?" *Variety,* March 23, 1956, pp. 5, 16.

38. Morrison, James W. "Teenage Incentive." *Motion Picture Herald,* January 5, 1957, p. 7.

39. Musser, Charles. *Before the Nickelodeon: The Early Cinema of Edwin S. Porter* (1983). Documentary Motion Picture.

40. "A New, $10-Billion Power: The U.S. Teen-Age Consumer." *Life,* August 31, 1959, pp. 78-85.

41. "New 'Rock' Explosion of Hot Youth; Branch Mgr. Discounts Morals TNT." *Variety,* May 2, 1956, p. 1.

42. "109 Top Money Making Films of 1956." *Variety,* January 2, 1957, pp. 1, 4.

43. "Presley Sets House Record." *Motion Picture Herald,* December 1, 1956, p. 42.

44. Quigley, Martin Jr. "Youth Must Be Served." *Motion Picture Herald,* June 23, 1956, p. 7.

45. Quigley, Martin Jr. "For the Young Audience." *Motion Picture Herald,* September 15, 1956, p. 7.

46. Quigley, Martin Jr. "Who Goes to the Movies . . . and Who Doesn't." *Motion Picture Herald,* August 10, 1957, pp. 21-22.

47. "Rock Around the Clock." *Motion Picture Herald,* March 17, 1956, p. 818.

48. "Rock Around the Clock." *Variety,* March 21, 1956, p. 6.

49. "Rock 'n' Roll B.O. 'Dynamite.' " *Variety,* April 11, 1956, pp. 1, 60.

50. "Rock-and-Roll Called 'Communicable Disease.' " *New York Times,* March 28, 1956, p. 33.

51. Ronan, Thomas P. "British Rattled by Rock 'n' Roll." *New York Times,* September 12, 1956, p. 40.

52. Roxon, Lillian. *Rock Encyclopedia.* New York: Grosset and Dunlap, 1969.

53. Schoenfeld, Herm. "Hot Trend: Trinidado Tunes." *Variety,* December 26, 1956, pp. 1, 42.

54. "Segregationist Wants Ban on 'Rock and Roll.' " *New York Times,* March 30, 1956, p. 33.

55. "Selling Approach." *Motion Picture Herald,* June 2, 1956, p. 43.

56. *Statistical Abstract of the United States.* Washington, D.C.: Bureau of the Census, 1955.

57. *Statistical Abstract of the United States.* Washington, D.C.: Bureau of the Census, 1982-1983.

58. Thompson, Richard. "Sam Katzman: Jungle Sam, Or, the Return of 'Poetic Justice, I'd Say.' " In Todd McCarthy and Charles Flynn (Eds.), *Kings of the Bs: Working Within the Hollywood System.* New York: E. P. Dutton and Company, 1975.

59. "Top Grossers of 1957." *Variety,* January 8, 1957, p. 30.

60. "Warning: Calypso Next New Beat; R.I. P. for R 'n' R?" *Variety,* December 12, 1956, pp. 1, 79.

5

Subcultural Studies and the Film Audience: Rethinking the Film Viewing Context

Gina Marchetti

"Who is out there?" and "Why are they sitting there paying money to watch this?" are two crucial questions that have puzzled film financiers, producers, distributors, and exhibitors as well as film scholars ever since Lumière put up a bed sheet in a cafe and charged admission. Certainly, the reasons for asking those questions have varied over time, but the nagging issues of audience motivation, participation, and pleasure remain.

Why should the audience continue to be a theoretical thorn after decades of scholarly and entrepreneurial probes? Library shelves are crammed with books and journals, industry tabloids and doctoral dissertations containing graphs, tables, lists, and figures on audience size, composition by race, ethnic group and gender, frequency of attendance, and so on (see 1, 14). Demographers quantify viewers. Behavioral psychologists observe behavior and measure physiological responses. Sociologists count up the hours of leisure time spent in front of the screens and chart film's impact on changing attitudes toward nuclear war or race relations. Industry plots marketing strategy. Although dwarfed by the piles of research devoted to television audiences (who are, after all, "sold" to advertisers based on that sort of data), empirical studies of film audiences have amassed their share of statistical information.

However, beyond quantification lies the *quality* of the viewing experience—its specificity. Why does the viewer find looking at a film pleasurable and exciting or boring and intolerable? Psychoanalysts and various other types of psychologists have stood up to claim this question as their territory. Films have been laid out on the couch, dissected like dreams, and treated like symptoms of a diseased collective mind. With this came an assumption that viewers must be responding to films like social daydreams, group fantasies which key into the structure of the individual's psyche. From this point of view, the audience looks like a collection of identically like-minded individuals who respond to the screen fantasy according to the determinations of the psychological model favored at the moment—Jungian, Freudian, and so on.

With the translation of Christian Metz's work on film semiotics into English in the early 1970s, the determining paradigm for the film viewing experience changed from psychology to linguistics—temporarily. As Metz himself, along with such scholars as Raymond Bellour in Paris and Stephen Heath in London, began to rethink liguistic structures in psychological terms, the image of the film as a dream or symptom reemerged. In the wake of French psychoanalyst Jacques Lacan's work on the way in which language determines ego structure and gender identification and Roland Barthes' application of psychoanalysis, linguistics, and a Marxist critique of ideology to literary theory, film theorists became much more sensitive to the intricacies of the film-viewer relationship. The study of the film-text (fine points of editing, mise-en-scene, sound, and narrative structure) overshadowed historical, cultural, and sociological considerations. Lacan saw language as creating and determining individual psychological make-up and his patient, Marxist theorist Louis Althusser, viewed language, psychology, and ideology as molding and structuring the individual "subject" within the strictures of a class-stratified society. Following their lead, film scholars began to see the film-text as creating its "subject," structuring and determining the viewer's relationship to the screen (see 8 for a relatively uncomplicated summary of this position).

In fact, according to this view, the viewer's position is so textually predetermined that he/she is "sutured" into a place created by the film (see 7, 18). Hence, differences among viewers vanish as they struggle to fit into the mold fashioned by the text. Recently, this view of the spectator as a projection or creation of the film text has been amended somewhat by its early advocates to include the possibility of gender and other differences in viewing practices (see 11). However, the fact that the viewing experience goes beyond an individual viewer's relationship to the screen still seems to elude film theorists. After all, the viewer goes to the cinema as a member of various social institutions—families, schools, governments, churches, businesses—as a creature of a particular historical moment. So the question remains: as film scholars, how do we look at the interaction between the screen and the social and cultural forces which forge the viewer's relationship to that screen fantasy?

By using methods developed by urban anthropologists, film audience researchers can begin to get at the dynamics of the group experience. Coupling these methods with the current work being done on the composition, self-expression, and collective identity of subcultural groups on the edges of the dominant culture, film theory can move even closer to pinpointing how social class, race, gender, or age indentity can shape the viewing experience at a specific moment in history.

SUBCULTURAL STUDIES: A LINK IN A MISSING CHAIN?

With the question of the social position of the viewer, the issue of audience research comes full circle and lands once again in the domain of the sociologist. In a field dominated in the United States for the last several years by statisticians and behaviorists, there seems to be a dearth of methods available to the film audience researcher who does not want to ignore the importance of the film text itself, but who wants to keep close tabs on the viewer's situation as an audience member, as a part of a specific community.

A possible approach to this problem comes from what at first may seem to be a completely unrelated area of sociology—deviance theory. Although the word "deviance" may conjure up images of criminals, jails, and the moral niceties of the science of penology, deviance theory, in certain circles, has also been wedded to the study of social group formations and the development of group and individual identities. Using many of the methodological tools of the anthropologist (particularly the urban anthropologist), sociologists like Howard Becker, for example, look at "deviants" as members of cultural formations with distinctive argot, dress, art forms, institutions, and forms of social interaction. In *Outsiders: Studies in the Sociology of Deviance,* Becker (3, p. 38) looks at deviant groups as "subcultures":

> Members of organized deviant groups have one thing in common: their deviance. It gives them a sense of common fate, of being in the same boat. From a sense of common fate, from having to face the same problems, grows a deviant subculture: a set of perspectives and understandings about what the world is like and how to deal with it, and a set of routine activities based on those perspectives. Membership in such a group solidifies a deviant identity.

Certainly, the concept of "subculture" has been batted around in sociological circles for some time. In *Keywords: A Vocabulary of Culture and Society,* Raymond Williams notes that the term evolved organically out of the way in which the word "culture" has been used in the anthropological sense of human social formations and ways of life (rather than the more arcane, but still common, meaning of the cultivation of the arts and intellectual pursuits). Williams defines "subculture" as "the culture of a distinguishable smaller group" (23, p. 82). Thus, as a category, the concept of "subculture" can cover quite a bit of territory.

However, as a working concept, "subculture" has been increasingly identified with deviance theory of one sort or another. In other words, the subculture is "distinguishable" precisely because it deviates from the norms set by the larger culture. In most current usage, the concept of "subculture" refers to any identifiable and cohesive group which is outside the dominant culture and its ideological norms because of differences of race, age, gender, sexual orientation, lifestyle or outlook. Thus, although subcultures share many common characteristics with the larger cultural formations of which they are a part, they have their own patterns of thought and behavior which are obscure, if not completely incomprehensible, to outsiders.

Like all social formations, subcultures are in a constant state of growth, transformation, and decay. In fact, the term has both structural and historical implications. For example, black subcultures have always existed in American culture; however, dress, argot, language, and so on, associated with various black subcultures have changed over time (from slavery to urban black life today) and are also characterized by geographical, class, age, and other variables within a given historical period (e.g., note the differences between rural and urban black life). Similar observations can be made about youth, gay, and other subcultures.

To assume that every film viewer is a member of an identifiable subculture would be ludicrous. However, the importance of this concept to a study of film audiences cannot be denied. A close examination of one specific type of audience identified with a particular subculture enables the concrete discussion of a viewer who is a member of a specific group with a set of shared economic, social, and cultural circumstances at a specific point in history. This provides an alternative to looking at the audience as merely a dry list of demographic statistics unrelated to the film image. Rather, a study of subculture allows for an examination of the interaction between viewers' cultural circumstances and their perception of, or possible distortion or transformation of, the film's message or presentation of experience. Viewers' relationships with a given film (whether it is a Hollywood feature about a subculture, a feature having nothing to do with the subculture, or a documentary about a certain aspect of the subcultural group) may be completely changed by their identification (or lack of identification) with a subculture.

Perhaps the area of recent subcultural work which will prove to be the most fecund for film audience researchers will be youth subcultural studies. In general, film audiences have become younger. Films that have done well at the box office—from *Star Wars* to *Gremlins*—have been openly directed to this market. Many adolescents become involved in some kind of subcultural activity—ranging from gang deliquency to wearing a spangled glove à la Michael Jackson—in the course of growing up. The interrelationship of youth subcultural activity and film viewership needs to be examined more closely. The ways in which subcultural activities find their way to the cinema screen, as well as the way in which screen fantasies mold and direct subcultural identity and behavior need to be looked at carefully. Specific youth subcultures react to films in very specific, visible ways. For example, youth involved in the punk subculture can enjoy a film which actually condemns their subcultural identity by simply turning up in the theater as a group and vocally cheering on the "villains" while hissing at the "heroes." A film like *Blade Runner* can be enjoyed in this fashion by siding with the punked-out androids against the "straight" humans.

Using youth subcultures as a starting point also makes quite a bit of sense when the existing research on the subject is taken into account. An important body of work already exists in the area of subcultural studies of youth. Since World War II,

a number of sociologists, psychologists, and other cultural analysts have devoted a
great deal of their attention to the study of youth subcultures. Primarily concerned
with working-class youth, these researchers are part of an important tradition within British cultural studies. Like the work of Richard Hoggart, Stuart Hall, Paddy
Whannel, Raymond Williams, and E.P. Thompson, among others, this research
draws a direct link between working-class life and many aspects of popular culture
which could be defined as exclusive to that class.

The focus on youth of this research is not surprising given the visibility of youth
subcultural activity—primarily in Britain, but also in the United States—after the
war. In the early 1950s, youth in Britain and America had more disposable income
available to them to spend on leisure pursuits. These leisure activities developed
into a number of distinctive youth subcultures. Highly visible youth subcultures
have continued to flourish since. In the case of youth subcultures, group identity is
expressed in the form of a distinctive style—in, for example, music, fashion, argot. Although the nature and extent of their critique of the dominant culture and its
norms vary, virtually all youth subcultures have seen themselves, and have been
seen by the dominant culture, as opposed to aesthetic, economic, religious, legal,
sexual, familial, or educational institutions which structure the social system.
Even though subcultural styles are adopted by and adapted to mass commercial
culture, youth subcultures still manage—if only briefly—to convey a sense of opposition and rebellion, though this critique usually remains in the realm of style.

When sociologists first began to consider seriously the phenomenon of youth
and other types of subcultures, the discipline of sociology was dominated by Emile
Durkheim's views on group dynamics and the importance of "outsiders" or "deviants" to the maintenance of the dominant group's own sense of cohesiveness,
common identity, and social order. Most of the earliest research into subcultures,
in fact, fell into this tradition. What became known as the "transactional" approach developed out of this and focused primarily on juvenile delinquents and
petty criminal groups. The social fact of deviancy came to be thought of as a labeling system whereby the dominant culture had the prerogative to set limits and
define itself in opposition to an outside other. In *Subculture: The Meaning of Style*,
Dick Hebdige (12, pp. 178-179) points to Howard Becker's *The Outsiders* as a
classic study of this type:

> One of the best examples of the transactional method in which the construction of de-
> viant groups is interpreted as the result of a dynamic process whereby those in power
> define the limits of acceptable and unaccepatble behavior through *labeling* (e.g. ma-
> rijuana smoker = lazy, long-haired, potentially violent malcontent, etc.)

Becker (3, p.9) summarizes his view as follows:

> Deviance or delinquency are . . . seen, not as arising naturally from the world of the
> "outsider," but as part of an ascribed social identity, arising in the interaction be-
> tween groups which are unequal in the distribution of power. The "deviance" of a
> group is not "natural" but the result of a specific kind of social construction: and one

of the key mechanisms of this process is the power to define situations *for* others, and the power to label others—and make those labels stick. [emphasis in original.]

In "Naturalistic Research into Subcultures and Deviance," Brian Roberts (19, p. 248) explicates this type of analysis further:

> *Social groups create deviance by making the rules whose infraction constitutes deviance,* and by applying those rules to particular people and labeling them as outsiders. From this point of view, deviance is *not* a quality of the act the person commits, but rather a consequence of the application by others of rules and sanctions to an "offender." The deviant is one to whom that label has successfully been applied; deviant behavior is behavior people so label. [emphasis in original.]

Although Becker's work on deviance focuses equally on the way in which the society labels deviant behavior and the way in which the individual subcultural member constructs his/her identity vis-à-vis the dominant culture, other sociologists working within the transactional approach have tended to concentrate on the dominant culture's power to define and label deviations from what it considers the social norm. Erving Goffman, for example, concentrates his attention on how the dominant culture takes some characteristic of an individual outside the norm and elaborates on this in order to create a stereotypic pattern of *stigma* to label that individual as "deviant." Goffman (9, p. 79) states:

> While the stranger is present before us, evidence can arise of his possessing an attribute that makes him different from others in the category of persons available for him to be, and of a less desirable kind—in the extreme, a person who is quite thoroughly bad, or dangerous, or weak. He is thus reduced in our minds from a whole and usual person to a tainted, discounted one. Such an attribute is a stigma, especially when its discrediting effect is very extensive; sometimes it is also called a failing, a shortcoming, a handicap.

For Goffman, deviancy is almost always a fact of outside labeling rather than individual construction of an identity that differs from the norm.

Although this type of research has contributed a number of important concepts to the field of subcultural studies by underscoring the importance of the power struggle existing between subcultures and the dominant culture for control over group identity, this approach also has a number of severe limitations. As Roberts (19, p. 248) points out:

> This now locates deviance *too* much in terms of rule-breaking, too much in terms of the "reaction" of social control agencies, and gives too little to the way the controlled subject or group sees the world from its point of view. [emphasis in original.]

In order to counter this presentation of subcultural identity as something primarily attributed to a group by a more powerful agency of social control, a number of cultural analysts have attempted to place subcultural theory within the broader context of general cultural relationships. To this end, Stuart Hall and his colleagues formed an association at the University of Birmingham in England to

study post-World War II British youth subcultures. First published as a special issue of *Working Papers in Cultural Studies,* a collection of essays summarizing
their research was later brought out under the title *Resistance Through Rituals:
Youth Subcultures in Post-War Britain.* In order to elaborate on the work begun by
the transactionalists in subcultural theory, these researchers draw on Marxist con-
ceptions of class, ideology, hegemony, and cultural struggle in order to situate the
subcultural member in a broader social framework. As stated in the introduction
(10, p.6):

> Our aim . . . remains . . . to explain *both* social action *and* social reaction,
> structurally and historically in a way which attempts to do justice to all the levels of
> analysis: from the dynamism of "face to face" interactions between delinquents and
> control agents to the wider, more mediated, questions—largely ignored by "pure"
> transactionalists—of the relation of these activities to shifts in class and power rela-
> tions, consciousness, ideology and hegemony. [emphasis in original]

By placing subcultural study within a Marxist framework, the members of the
Birmingham School are able to highlight the importance of looking at subcultural
activity within the context of a larger whole. This emphasis on a cultural totality
underscores the interconnectedness of the economic base, class stratifications, social institutions, and the realm of ideas and aesthetics. With economic change
comes changes in the social fabric. This historical dynamic arises out of the contradictions inherent in this cultural whole—between those who control the economic
base and those who do not, between those in political power and those outside the
power structure, hence among members of various class strata. In "Subcultures,
Cultures and Class: a Theoretical Overview," John Clarke, Stuart Hall, Tony
Jefferson and Brian Roberts (5, pp. 10-12) paint a picture of culture as a site of
both structural consistencies and constant struggle and change:

> The "culture" of a group or class is the peculiar and distinctive "way of life" of the
> group or class, the meanings, values and ideas embodied in institutions, in social re-
> lations, in systems of beliefs, in mores and customs, in the uses of objects and materi-
> al life . . . cultures are differently ranked, and stand in opposition to one another, in
> relations of domination and subordination, along the scale of "cultural power" . . .
> it is crucial to replace the notion of "culture" with the more concrete, historical con-
> cept of "cultures"; a redefinition which brings out more clearly the fact that cultures
> always stand in relations of domination—and subordination—to one another, are al-
> ways, in some sense, in struggle with one another.

Various cultures arise out of certain class ties. These relatively large cultural
structures, however, also give rise to a number of smaller cultural units,
"subcultures," which are both like and different from their larger "parent" cultures. Thus, these subcultures bear a certain relationship to both the dominant culture and their parent cultures. Youth, sexual orientation, race, lifestyle, and so on
set the subcultural member apart from both the parent and the dominant culture.

Structurally, the dominant culture, parent culture, and subculture are in conflict. However, the nature of the antagonism among these structures varies. For example, the working class may deny its differences from the dominant culture, because it may be economically advantageous to identify as much as possible with the aims and goals of one's corporation, for example, in order to obtain a promotion or salary increase. Similarly, a subculture may identify very strongly with its parent culture—as in the case of the British Skinheads who vehemently espouse what they perceive to be ''working-class'' values (which often leads them to assault ''decadent'' nonconformists such as hippies or punks). However, for the most part, the parent culture remains quite distinct from the dominant culture, and the relationship between a parent culture and a youth subculture is, more often than not, antagonistic.

Although the apparent difference of age or skin color, for example, is usually perceived by the dominant culture as a negative characteristic, the subcultural member, instead of trying to efface the difference and blend in as well as possible with the dominant ideology's picture of ''normal,'' transforms this difference into a strength, the foundation of individual identity.

All class cultures have, at one point in time or another, been parent cultures for oppositional subcultures. As a parent culture, for example, the bourgeois elite has given rise to the youthful ''jet set'' or ''beautiful people'' subculture, reported in the press as the latest exploits of the ''Kennedy Kids.'' Taking the professional middle classes (petite-bourgeoisie) as the example, the hippies, the beats, the boehmian art circles and much of the illegal drug culture can be pointed out as subcultures arising principally from this class. Mods, skinheads, and rockers (duppers, bikers, and greasers in the United States) are usually cited as examples of youth subcultures principally arising out of the working class.

Thus, affiliation with a particular youth subculture generally does not change an individual's class affiliation. For example, although hippies claim to ''drop out'' of the petite-bourgeois culture of their parents, many still retain that class affiliation by becoming small business entrepreneurs, for example, running health food stores or head shops, becoming skilled artisans or craftspeople. All of these occupations essentially keep them within the same class position as their parents, although they are quite definitely outside the mainstream of occupations generally considered acceptable by other members of their class.

However, although the class affiliations of these subcultures are undeniable, it must be remembered that the subculture is a relatively autonomous structure, with many characteristics which contradict the values and beliefs of the parent culture. Moreover, shared experiences often erode class boundaries. The relationships between a subculture and its parent culture, the subculture and the dominant culture, and between one subculture and another are always in a constant state of change and contradiction.

To cite only one example, Andy Warhol's Factory, a thriving avant-garde institution of the 1960s which still exists today, brought together members of various subcultural groups with diverse class backgrounds to form an important part of the New York Underground—a new bohemianism. In *Stargazer: Andy Warhol's World and His Films,* Stephen Koch (16, p. 5) somewhat histrionically describes this subcultural meeting ground as follows:

> One senses that, in those days, a thrilling complicity united the artistic and sexual and drug subcultures, that some kind of shared refusal threw together mute *seriosos* like the composer LaMonte Young with the hardened, quick-witted, druggy street per- formers with names like Rotter Rita, Narsissy, and Ondine, people living on drugs and their wits, doing their numbers in bars and apartment lofts, of the existence of which the straight world had only the merest dreadful intimations. Men for whom the flamboyant pose and a tongue like lightning were the only life found themselves in a department of limbo adjacent to middle-class artists.

Of course, this is only one very limited historical instance—a time and a place in which various subcultures met and pooled their stylistic resources, magnifying their opposition to the dominant culture. These periods and places of subcultural intermingling are somewhat rare. There are often as many barriers between subcultures as there are points of association. Even among subcultures arising out of the same parent culture, there are antagonisms: Mods despised rockers; skinheads hated punks, gays, and blacks. It is also important to keep in mind that subcultures are fleeting phenomena. Although subcultures are a fact of our social structure, specific subcultural groups form, come to prominence, and suddenly disappear. As Albert K. Cohen (6, pp. 180-181) notes in his study of subcultures and deviancy, *Delinquent Boys:*

> Culture is continually being created, recreated, and modified wherever individuals sense in each other like needs, generated by like circumstances, not shared generally in the larger social system. Once established, such a subcultural system may persist, but not by sheer inertia. It may achieve a life which outlasts that of the individuals who participated in its creation, but only so long as it continues to serve the needs of those who succeed its creators.

Subcultural identification, however, while it does last, serves a very important function for its adherents. As Hall, Clarke, Jefferson, and Roberts (5, p.47) ob- serve, subcultures

> win *space* for the young: cultural space in the neighborhood and institutions, real time for leisure and recreation, actual room on the street or street-corner. They serve to mark out and appropriate "territory" in the localities. They focus around key oc- casions of social interaction: the week-end, the disco . . . They cluster around partic- ular locations. They develop specific rhythms of interchange, structural relations between members: younger to older, experienced to novice, stylish to square. They explore "focal concerns" central to the inner life of the group: things "done" or "never done," a set of social rituals which underpin their collective identity and de- fine them as a "group" instead of a mere collection of individuals. They adopt and adapt material objects—goods and possessions—and reorganize them into distinc-

tive "styles" which express the collectivity of their being-as-a-group. These concerns, activities, relationships, materials become embodied in rituals of relationship and occasion and movement. Sometimes, the world is marked out, linguistically, by names or an *argot* which classifies the social world exterior to them in terms meaningful only within their group perspective, and maintains its boundaries. [emphasis in original.]

One of the more important places in which subcultures have managed to "win space" for themselves is the cinema. Although they often sensationalize and exploit subcultures, films have also helped validate subcultural identity by graphically representing, and often tacitly accepting, subcultural lifestyles and experiences.

SUBCULTURES AND FILM AUDIENCES

Many subcultures have had complex and diverse relationships with the institution of the cinema. At the most basic level, the local cinema has provided a meeting ground for a number of subcultural groups. As a dark, but public, place outside the realm of parental and social authority operating in the home and at the workplace, the cinema is a place to gather and meet like-minded fellows during leisure time. This use of the cinema as a meeting ground can range from the Friday and Saturday night "take-over" of many neighborhood movie theaters by *Rocky Horror Picture Show* fans to the proliferation of all-male pornography cinemas frequented by gay men to find available lovers. In one sense, no matter what may or may not be on the screen, the movie theater has consistently been an important aspect of the lives of many subcultural members.

However, for most subcultures, the cinema remains a comparatively peripheral forum of stylistic expression. *The Rocky Horror Picture Show* phenomenon is the rare exception. Originally produced as a play to exploit the popularity of London's glam subculture (known as "glitter" in the United States) of the early 1970s, the film adaptation surprisingly revived glitter clothing, music, humor, and street theatricality long after the subculture itself had virtually sunk into obscurity. *The Rocky Horror Picture Show* created a subcultural pocket around screenings of this film in major cities. Although this remains a rather unusual offshoot of a once-popular subcultural style, in and of itself, the *Rocky Horror* audience does not constitute a separate subculture. Rather, it is a "sub-" subculture, a variant of the glitter subculture, firmly within the style and issues foregrounded by glitter. (For more information on the *Rocky Horror* phenomenon, see 2, 13, 17.)

The cinema is also an important site for the formation of group identity and feelings of comradeship with subcultural members from other places. In fact, films provide an important channel for the diffusion of subcultural style. For example, the Hollywood film industry will note a new fashion, musical trend, or subcultural style. Small studios like New World Pictures or American International will take a chance on a low budget film exploiting the newly visible subculture; larger studios may also invest money in a feature on the subculture. By making a film about a subcultural group, the studio can profit from two potential audiences. Ostensibly, these "exploitation" films are exposés of juvenile delinquency, the pitfalls of loose sexuality, or the horrors of drug abuse and a life of crime on the fringes of urban society. These activities are condemned as criminal, perverse, or deviant, and the offenders in the films either die, are jailed, or reform. The status quo is affirmed after a journey through this "deviant" underworld, most clearly identified as such by the trappings of a well-publicized subculture, for example, leather jackets and motorcycles in the 1950s, flowered shirts, beads, and long hair in the 1960s, and shaved heads and safety pins in the 1970s.

Of course underneath this apparent condemnation, there is an unmistakable element of titillation for the nonsubcultural audience member. Forbidden desires are indulged by the "naughty" members of the subculture who freely spit on figures of authority, indulge in taboo sexual activities, thumb their noses at conventional morality, and basically have a good time before their inevitable downfall. The viewer's voyeuristic desires are catered to—a well-known subculture provides the perfect vehicle for the expression of socially forbidden wishes. Thus, the general audience indulges in a simultaneous sanctimonious condemnation and vicarious identification with the Hollywood fantasy of the subculture's activities. The forbidden is projected onto the outsiders, the subcultural members.

By comparing themselves with "deviants," members of the dominant culture also solidify their own ranks. Their sense of group cohesiveness is strengthened by opposition to the threat of those who represent alien values. The subculture may represent a fantasy of being free from the constraints of the nuclear family, the work ethic, or the legitimacy of capitalism. This fantasy of freedom, however, coexists with a reaffirmation of the dominant culture's principal values.

On the other hand, the same "exploitation" films can have a radically different significance for another segment of the audience. Although these films ostensibly condemn any type of behavior which goes against the mores of the dominant culture, they can also be looked at and interpreted in radically different ways by members of the subculture represented or by those outside the dominant culture, who may be sympathetic to the position of the characters identified with a subculture in the film. As John Clarke points out, the media's presentation of subcultural activities is subject to "deviant readings" (see 4, p. 186) by those outside the dominant culture. Hence, subcultural members can still enjoy a film in which their activities are condemned by assuming an ironic position vis-à-vis the film's narrative. Removed from a fantasy identification with the negation of the subculture or punishment of its activities by this ironic detachment, the subcultural viewer enjoys variations on style, new music, and interesting "villains" who may fulfill a viewer's secret wishes with impunity. By its very presentation on the screen, the subculture is displayed and tacitly affirmed.

In fact, it is in that way that subcultural styles spread. Although these films ostensibly condemn the subculture and strip it of any real significance other than that necessary to conform to the label of "deviancy" or "villainy" which enables the subculture to fit into the standard exploitation plot, these films also help to popularize the style. Clarke's (4, p. 186) comments on the presentation of subcultures in the news media are equally applicable to the presentation of subcultural activities in Hollywood films:

> Where the news-media strip down and dislocate the indigenous style, in order to make their own symbolic (and derogatory) communication, they may actually widen the "cultural space" which permits the selective re-working and re-appropriation of the style by geographically-dispersed groups. Similarly, the motivations of marketing prompt a generalization and stripping-down of the original sub-cultural style; symbolic elements lose their first, integral relation to a specific life-context, and become thus more open to variation in the precise structuring of their reappropriation by others, whose activities, self-images, and focal concerns are not precisely the same.

Thus, according to Clarke, the subculture is simultaneously "diffused" and "defused" through the media.

The dominant cinema's exploitation of a subculture can extend far beyond these titillating exposes of "deviancy," however. This originally minor, sensationalized "fringe element" may eventually grow into a rather substantial audience in its own right. Eventually, low-budget features made especially for the subcultural market find their way to the local cinema. If popular, a studio may then decide to create bigger budget films about the subculture, hoping for larger profits.

Hollywood films also affect subcultural identity in another important way. Many films, having absolutely nothing to do with subcultures or their activities, find a special place within the subculture's pantheon of valued objects appropriated from the dominant culture. Looked at in a radically different way, these films are transformed by the subcultural viewer's active and deliberate misreading into something of peculiar significance to those involved in the group. Like other objects of mass culture appropriated by the subcultural style makers, these films are not arbitrarily selected but have a particular aspect—or subtext—which allows them to be read in an originally unintended way.

Camp is perhaps the best documented example of this phenomenon. Camp transforms a classic Hollywood film, through a sense of ironic humor, into an object with a totally different significance. In "Rehearsal for a Theory of Subtextual Readings," for example, Chuck Kleinhans (15, n.p.) notes the way in which the Warner Brothers melodrama Now Voyager is transformed by the gay audience into a text with a radically different significance:

> Consider Now Voyager. The plot portrays the gradual emergence of a repressed, mousy spinster (Bette Davis) into a sexually active mature woman under the tutelage of a wise older man (Claude Rains). This emergent butterfly metaphor, while certainly being a universally understood pattern within our culture, has a special resonance for many gay men who themselves have experienced or who are experiencing the conditions of discovering and exploring one's sexuality which has been repressed

within the family and other institutions. In other words, identification with the character and situation is very strong. This is visually enhanced because the changes in the Davis character are signalled in changing dress, hair, style, and physical bearing—precisely those areas which gay men often first publically present their resistance to dominant heterosexual norms.

Thus, a film considered quite straighforward by most members of the audience takes on a special significance for the members of a subcultural group. *Mommie Dearest* provides another example. Marketed as a biographical melodrama which exposes the sadistic underbelly of Joan Crawford's relationship with her adopted daughter, the film was quickly taken up as a camp classic of histrionic dominance fantasies. Mops and wire hangers in hand, the subcultural audience has transformed the film into the "Mommie Horror Show."

Of course, Hollywood features are not the only films to portray or have an impact on subcultures. As an adjunct of the news media, documentaries have also capitalized on and sensationalized subcultural activity. Most often, like their fictional counterparts, these documentaries ostensibly condemn the subculture while titillating the audience with a voyeuristic journey into taboo territory. However, perhaps because of lower costs or a desire to be journalistically "objective" about the phenomenon presented, many of these documentaries have had considerable success with the members of the subcultures presented by the film. Cinéma-vérité documentaries like *Woodstock, Monterey Pop,* and *Gimme Shelter* have been quite successful, providing the subcultural audience with a chance to see their favorite rock group on the big screen.

The large budget commercial documentaries with wide theatrical distribution are, of course, only one end of the spectrum of nonfiction films made about subcultures. With the increased availability of small gauge film and video equipment, many members of subcultural groups are eager to make their own films and videotapes. Occasionally, these "home movies" become parts of feature length documentary films. Others remain private, in-home, personal records. Still others, however, become part of a circuit of avant-garde filmmaking distribution and exhibition.

A cultural space often forms somewhere between the world of the subculture and the institution of independent filmmaking. An audience may be comprised of subcultural members, the local literati, and the curious. Although subcultural members may venture into an avant-garde theater to see a film about a favorite band or even themselves depicted on film, more often new venues are organized to screen these experimental film-subcultural coproductions. Bars, clubs, or local auditoriums may host a band or a dance and show a film as part of the performance. Perhaps the most notorious showcase for this type of activity during the 1960s was Warhol's Exploding Plastic Inevitable. As described by Stephen Koch, it was a bar, a disco, a meeting place, a continuous Op Art light show, a showcase for new talent including the rock group The Velvet Underground, as well as a screening room for Warhol's film productions. Koch (16, pp. 70-71) describes the way in which Warhol exhibited his film *Vinyl* as follows:

> Part of the environment, the film was projected on a screen high above the stage amid five or six other films, light shows, and bursting and sliding abstract images all over the walls. Silently running up there on the wall, *Vinyl* seemed to drown in rampagant [sic] sound and overwhelming blaring fantasy of that first light-blasted multimedia discotheque. And yet, in that ear-splitting, wall-shaking music box, as deafening recorded rock alternated with the utterly deadening music of the Velvet Underground, the Warhol rock group, *Vinyl's* remote, silenced vision of sexual violence assumed a strange admonitory authority over the hall . . . The Plastic Inevitable seemed at first a merely barnlike, faintly tacky discotheque. There were tables placed around the place, and various things were served. There was a dance floor. High on the walls, high above the immense floor-throbbing woofers and merciless tweeters, the films and light shows poured like an endless, drenching visual rain. But as the music alternated between cacophony and the hideous ''acid'' maundering of the Velvet Underground's insufferable navel-gazing guitars, the effort to create an exploding . . . environment capable of shattering any conceivable focus on the senses was all too successful. It became virtually impossible even to dance, or for that matter to do anything else but sit and be bombarded—stoned, as it were—cursing that six-dollar admission fee . . . the environment became a chamber of sensual assault, its aesthetic battery.

The Exploding Plastic Inevitable was really the rough equivalent of DADA's infamous Cabaret Voltaire, a meeting place of popular entertainment, subcultural style, and avant-garde experimentation.

The punk subculture has also given rise to similarly unusual types of film viewing venues. Even before video monitors became standard fixtures in most youth-oriented bars and clubs, punk discos featured televisions or film screens. Many bands included visual materials as part of their performances. Filmmakers found themselves attracted to punk clubs as exhibition outlets with particularly receptive audiences.

Beth B and Scott B's film *The Offenders* offers an interesting case in point. Originally *The Offenders* was shown as a serial at New York's well-known cabaret and showcase for punk artists and musicians, Max's Kansas City. Each episode of the film was, in part, financed from profits of the preceeding week. A great deal of the film was written, performed, and filmed just in time for each week's screening. As a result, *The Offenders* has a rather loose, lumbering, ''home-movie'' structure. Many scenes were improvised, and the film projects this sense of spontaneity and immediacy.

Rather than disguising the passage of time, for example, the Bs self-consciously foreground it. Process becomes part of the film text. Posters for the various episodes of the film appear at some of the locations used to film the following week's episode. The characters act out this week's action in front of the posters advertising the previous week's events.

In addition, the savvy viewer is brought into the filmmaking process in another important respect. The Bs use very familiar local punk haunts as locations in the film. The viewer's own neighborhood is transformed each week into the fantasy of *The Offenders*. In addition, bits of topical material are woven into the film fantasy. The "crime wave" depicted in the film occurred simultaneously with an actual "crime wave" in New York. The Bs exploit this topical goldmine by intercutting sensational headlines from the New York *Post* with the fictional events, for example, bank robberies, murders, and so on, depicted in the film. The gulf between fiction and reality collapses. The viewer recognizes the similarities between current events, actual happenings, and the film's fictional ones. The assumed passivity of the Hollywood spectator is called into question. Viewer participation in the form of retorts to the film, vocal recognition of fellow subcultural members on screen, dancing, drinking, and other active responses to the screen fantasy are expected and encouraged. Cliff-hangers at the end of each week's episode invited the audience to come back next time for the resolution of the crisis. *The Offenders* became a punk version of *The Perils of Pauline*. (For more information on film in the punk subculture, see 17.)

Thus, from the perspective of subcultural studies, specific film audiences become active, creative forces. The subculture opens up the possibility for the viewer to look at a film in a particular way, often actively misreading an apparently straightforward fantasy. Moreover, the subculture may give rise to unique film exhibition environments in which film viewing behavior may differ radically from more common behavior at local suburban multiplexes.

A NOTE ON METHOD

The question of how the film researcher goes about the task of investigating a particular subculture's film-viewing activities remains. An especially fruitful possibility comes from the discipline of urban anthropology. Like an anthropologist, the subcultural analyst not only observes and records the behavior of the group under study, but also participates in the community (see 20, 21). Although the degree of the researcher's participation within the subculture varies (from being openly identified with the group to acting as an outside advocate or simply an interested nonmember), this type of "participant-observer" research avoids many of the pitfalls of statistical studies. For example, the observer's own effects on the phenomenon are taken into account; the researcher becomes, at least to a degree, part of the event analyzed. Also, the analyst develops a sympathy or insider's feeling for the group because of his/her intimate relationships with the subculture. Informal conversations, close observations, and actual participation in group activities reveal a type of information and insight that often substantially differs from findings gleaned from more traditional quantitative methods.

Although the "objectivity" of the results of these urban-anthropological methodologies has been questioned, this issue can also be turned around to expose the falacious "objectivity" of many researchers who ask certain types of questions, in often leading ways, and who are seldom surprised by the results. These methods seldom question the researcher's own prejudices in wording a survey, choosing participants, or analyzing and interpreting data. On the other hand, years of field work and critiques of the anthropologist's methods have brought a certain self-awareness to many working within the discipline and related fields. Personal expectations and prejudices do play their roles, but these biases are offset by self-examination, analysis, and an awareness of the important dialectical relation between sciences and personal commitment. In fact, this self-consciousness has become an indispensable component of the method itself.

"Hanging out" with a particular subculture may strike those who have never attempted this type of work as a rather haphazard method of collecting data. However, close observation of audiences can yield a wealth of information. When do group members attend film performances? How do they dress? What cinemas do they frequent? How do they speak to each other and to outsiders (both verbally and nonverbally)? How do they relate to the screen fantasy—that is, verbal comments, laughter, snickers, quiet talking to one another? With whom do they attend the performance—dates, children, parents, and so on? What kinds of activities go on before, during, and after the screening? What is the physical venue like? How does the viewing environment mold group behavior?

With a solid grounding in participant-observation, most current studies of subcultures (particularly those done under the auspices of Birmingham and Open University in England) have been characterized by a lively eclecticism. Film audience studies inspired by this research likewise tend to draw on several types of information in order to draw as complete a picture as possible of the subculture's peculiar interaction with the screen. This material can range from secondary sociological, anthropological, or historical studies to film reviews or other records about film viewing made by those within the subculture to oral histories and interviews. All of these materials become particularly useful when this information is wedded to a close analysis of a specific film text.

Chris Straayer's "*Personal Best*: Lesbian/Feminist Audience" (22) provides a good example of the fecundity of this openly eclectic type of research method. In this article, Straayer reports the results of a survey conducted with a number of women who identify themselves as either "feminist" or "lesbian" or both. Beyond a simple survey of data, however, Straayer's study places this information within a clear context. Her analysis shows a historical and cultural understanding of the lesbian/feminist community in the United States and a recognition of the importance of a close reading of the text which exposes the ways in which a film can be open to a number of readings.

In fact, a sensitivity to the complexities of the film text itself is crucial to an understanding of audience response. Assuming that a researcher can get at the intricacies of the film-viewer relationship by simply observing the audience or asking questions about a viewer's reaction to a film or viewing habits is naive. A viewer can never be looked at as a completely self-conscious, self-critical, and scrupulously honest source of information. Rather, a film audience researcher must have a good grasp of the workings of ideology within a culture, of the ways fantasies are molded by but also react against the dominant powers, and of the means by which a film text may give pleasure to both those within and those hostile to a subculture.

The potential importance of subcultural film audience studies cannot be overemphasized. Within a culture which is so often perceived as being almost completely homogeneous, subcultures point to important social, economic, political, class, gender, racial, and other differences. Subcultural study takes the diversity of our culture into account. With this diversity comes an implied opposition to—and occasionally a stated criticism of—the status quo. Although primarily through fantasy and the superficial trappings of style, change is still conceived of, and more importantly, acted upon. The dominant culture does not remain an immutable given, but becomes a structure subject to change, an order which can be opposed.

REFERENCES

1. Austin, Bruce A. *The Film Audience: An International Bibliography of Research*. Metuchen, NJ: Scarecrow, 1983.
2. Austin, Bruce A. "Portrait of a Cult Film Audience: *The Rocky Horror Picture Show*." *Journal of Communications* 31, Spring 1981, pp. 43-54.
3. Becker, Howard S. *Outsiders: Study in the Sociology of Deviance*. New York: The Free Press, 1963.
4. Clarke, John, "Style." In Stuart Hall and Tony Jefferson (Eds.), *Resistance Through Rituals: Youth Subcultures in Post-War Britain,* pp. 175-191. London: Hutchinson and Co., 1976.
5. Clarke, John, Stuart Hall, Tony Jefferson, and Brian Roberts. "Subcultures, Cultures, and Class: A Theoretical Overview." In Stuart Hall and Tony Jefferson (Eds.), *Resistance Through Rituals: Youth Subcultures in Post-War Britain,* pp. 9-74. London: Hutchinson and Co., 1976.
6. Cohen, Albert K. "A Theory of Subcultures." In *Delinquent Boys*. New York: The Free Press, 1955. Anthologized in *Social Deviance*, pp. 179-82. Ronald A. Farrell and Victoria Lynn Swigert (Eds.). Philadelphia: J.B. Lippincott, 1975.
7. Dayan, Daniel. "The Tudor Code of Classical Cinema." *Film Quarterly* 28, Fall 1974, pp.23-31.
8. Ellis, John. *Visible Fictions: Cinema: Television: Video*. London: Routledge and Kegan Paul, 1982.
9. Goffman, Erving. "Stigma and Social Identity." In *STIGMA! Notes on the Mangement of Spoiled Identity*. Englewood Cliffs, NJ: Prentice-Hall, 1963. Anthologized in *Social Deviance*, pp. 78-84. Ronald A. Farrell and Victoria Lynn Swigert (Eds.). Philadelphia: J.B. Lippincott, 1975.
10. Hall, Stuart and Tony Jefferson. *Resistance Through Rituals: Youth Subcultures in Post-War Britain*. London: Hutchinson and Co., 1976.
11. Heath, Stephen. "Differences." *Screen* 19, Autumn 1978, pp. 51-112.
12. Hebdige, Dick. *Subcultures: The Meaning of Style*. London: Methuen and Co., Ltd., 1979.
13. Hoberman, J. and Jonathan Rosenbaum. *Midnight Movies*. New York: Harper and Row, 1983.

14. Jowett, Garth. *Film: The Democratic Art*. Boston: Little, Brown and Co., 1976.
15. Kleinhans, Chuck. "Rehearsal for a Theory of Subtextual Readings." Unpublished manuscript. Northwestern University, 1982.
16. Koch, Stephen. *Stargazer: Andy Warhol's World and His Films*. New York: Prager, 1973.
17. Marchetti, Gina. "Film and Subculture: The Relationship of Film to the Punk and Glitter Youth Subcultures." Ph.D. Dissertation, Northwestern University, Evanston, Illinois, 1982.
18. Miller, Jacques-Alain. "Suture (Elements of the Logic of the Signifier)," Oudart, Jean-Pierre, "Cinema and Suture," Heath, Stephen, "Notes on Suture." *Screen* 18, Winter 1977/78, pp. 24-76.
19. Roberts, Brian. "Naturalistic Research into Subcultures and Deviance: An Account of a Sociological Tendency." In Stuart Hall and Tony Jefferson (Eds.), *Resistance through Rituals: Youth Subcultures in Post-War Britain*, pp. 243-252. London: Hutchinson and Co., 1976.
20. Sennett, Richard and Jonathan Cobb. *The Hidden Injuries of Class*. New York: Vintage, 1972.
21. Spradley, James P. and David W. McCurdy. *The Cultural Experience: Ethnography in Complex Society*. Chicago: Science Research Associates, 1972.
22. Straayer, Chris. *"Personal Best:* Lesbian/Feminist Audience." *Jump Cut* 29, February 1984, pp. 40-44.
23. Williams, Raymond. *Keywords: A Vocabulary of Culture and Society*. New York, Oxford University Press, 1976.

6

The Film Industry, Its Audience, and New Communications Technologies

Bruce A. Austin

Painted in broad strokes, the canvas depicting the economic history of the U.S. film industry emerges as a series of peaks and valleys. Intermittently threatened and tumultuous but always, in the final analysis, prolific, prosperous, and profitable, the American film industry has endured as perhaps the preeminent icon (depending upon who is doing the writing) of schlock, pop culture, high art, and so on. For nearly a century the American film industry has confronted and responded to change although rarely does it initiate or welcome such change. Some, in fact, would suggest that Hollywood's typical and most predictable response to any shift in the status quo is to view such movement as revolutionary rather than evolutionary. Jowett and Linton write that "movies have always demonstrated a lack of concern (or very little concern) for anything except the present" (74, pp. 113-114). Thus, the Hollywood-industrial establishment resembles the military-industrial establishment: both are fully prepared to fight and win the previous war. Still, the industry has been resilient so that often—if not usually—by tinkering with the technology it has managed to adapt and adjust to change.

Today the film industry is facing a full frontal assault by myriad new video technologies, each vying for the same slice of leisure time cut for the movies. While earlier changes, such as the introduction of "movies-in-the-home" (TV) conveniently occurred one at a time—and with temporal breathing spells of some duration in between—such is not the case at present. The industry is now confronted with the confluence of multiple technological changes and innovations which may have significant impact on all components of the industry. Observers suggest that we are in the midst of a "communications revolution'' (see 28, 179, 197).[1] And, although some of these new technologies may take considerable time to become formidable competitive forces, they will not simply go away. Nor will dishes, Bingo, double features, stereoscopic and smelly movies, or casual complacency make them go away or diminish their threat. Will merely tinkering with the technology do the trick for Hollywood this time?

This article examines how new communications technologies have—or may have—impacted on the film industry. In particular, the focus is on television-related technologies. Two major aspects of film are discussed: the audience and the business (including production, distribution, and exhibition). This inquiry attempts to sort out what we know to have occurred, that we suspect is occurring, and what we might expect to occur.

TECHNOLOGY AND MOVIES:
A BRIEF HISTORICAL BACKGROUND

At various points in its history, a key threat to the film industry was technological innovation. Radio and later television broadcasting provoked consternation among the Hollywood moguls. Consider the case of radio. Lee de Forest's invention of his audion or triode vacuum tube made possible both radio and sound film (see 171, pp. 29-32). Commercial broadcasting began on August 16, 1922 when WEAF, New York, carried the first paid advertisement (171, pp. 59, 66). Within one year of WEAF's entry to the ether, de Forest had produced and exhibited short, synchronized sound films (106, p. 182)—a parody of a de Forest Phonofilm lecture appears in the 1952 film *Singin' in the Rain*. The development of radio is variously seen as either a modest or a serious threat to the film industry. Taking the latter approach, Wenden writes that radio was "a serious competitor of the cinema in the early 1920s" (194, p. 170). Silent film historian William Everson reports that in 1925 "attendance was way down" and that Hollywood was determined to fight the competition of radio (39, p. 290). Compared to television, which, too,

---

[1] This communications revolution, of course, is of concern to others outside the film industry. Advertisers, for instance, worry about such issues as increasing governmental control over the "new media" as it affects their industry, measurement of audiences, cost-effectivenss of advertising messages, and an inability to penetrate some new media (e.g., video discs) with advertising at all (see 130). Bortnick discusses economic, national sovereignty, and privacy protection concerns faced by U.S. business in the area of information (as opposed to entertainment) data (15). Essentially many of the same arguments, I would suggest, can be raised for both information and entertainment data; although perhaps the latter are more serious than the former. Fombrun and Astley raise the issue of the direction of industrial growth toward centralization or pluralism which

> is largely dependent on social preference and the degree to which government takes on the role
> of network manager, regulating the growth process and restricting the emergence of one kind of
> interfirm structure or another (44, pp. 58-59).

These and other equally important issues are, however, beyond the scope of this article.

was looming on the horizon. Jowett maintained that "the growth and popularity of commercial radio represented a much more immediate threat" and that radio did initially affect movie attendance (73, pp. 191-192, 280). Sklar reports survey data from 1945 in which 84 percent of the sample reported they would relinquish movies in response to the question, "If you had to give up either going to the movies or listening to the radio, which one would you give up?"; only 11 percent said they would give up radio (166, pp. 270-271). Hampton took a more tempered view when writing in 1931 that "for a while radio did affect theater attendance adversely, but not seriously" (58, p. 369). *Variety,* too, was more sanguine, reporting that it was "only in the smaller towns" that radio adversely affected attendance (reported in 186, p. 4). Whichever view is more accurate, an inescapable conclusion is that radio posed a threat of some significance to film.

In conjunction with economic conditions engendered by the Great Depression, network radio became an important part of people's lives as they sought cheaper forms of entertainment (169, p. 86). On November 15, 1926 network radio broadcasting was inaugurated with WEAF's "Big Broadcast" (186, p. 20)—a $50,000, four-hour live program originating in the Grand Ballroom of the Waldorf-Astoria Hotel with remote pickups from Chicago and Kansas City and carried by 25 radio stations (171, p. 107). Walker reports that movie business "was down to twenty to thirty percent" that night. "Just to fight back," he wrote, "the cinema would have to use the human voice as part of their entertainment" (186, p. 20). Moreover, the film industry refused any form of cooperation with radio (180, p. 82)—a not-so-effective strategy also employed when TV was introduced.

Edison, of course, first conceived of movies as merely an extension of his phonograph—a visual aside to complement his more compelling aural invention (for a discussion of the phonograph as a challenge to the movies and how radio affected the phonograph, see 39, p. 118; 180, pp. 46-74). Problems with the technology of synchronized sound films were resolved by 1923 (180, p. 33). Walker recounts that "the talkie revolution in the cinema was preceded, and indeed prepared for, by the talkie revolution at home. Behind both events was—radio" (186, p. 4). Thus, while radio was initially perceived as a new medium menacing the movies, it proved to be the impetus for technological advancement in the film industry (although some critics such as Arnheim remained unconvinced; see 5, pp. 199-230). As Luther pointed out, radio prompted the adoption of sound among film producers and the purchasing of sound equipment and air conditioning among exhibitors (100, pp. 169-170). "By 1938," Jowett writes, "a symbiotic relationship between commercial radio and the movie industry had been established" (73, p. 280)—hardly surprising since the corporations and individuals involved in the development of radio largely overlapped those for sound films (for discussion of the "players" see 51).

In a similar fashion the introduction of television in the 1950s resulted in the adoption (but certainly not the invention) of such technological innovations as various widescreen processes, 3-D, and an industry-wide conversion to—or immersion in—color photography. The impact of television on the film industry has been well-documented (see, e.g., 92, 117, 173). Luther wrote in 1951 "that television is either a colossal hoax or the most dangerous competitive medium ever to face motion picture exhibitors" (100, p. 166). Earlier, in 1946, Harry P. Warner asserted that "it is believed that television constitutes a long-range threat to the motion picture business" (187, p. 16). Anticipating a contemporary issue in 1957, Shaffer wrote: "Should toll [subscription] television meet approval on a national scale and become economically feasible, it might cause an upheaval greater than any experiment to date by movies or television" (162, p. 61).

Imposing as the threat of TV might have been, optimism—however misguided or naive—that movies would meet and beat this challenge remained prevalent. Luther concluded that although exhibitors faced "a serious threat from commercial television," with appropriate "modifications" they would "continue to be a vigorous and profitable medium of mass entertainment" (100, pp. 175, 177). Warner, too, recognized the future symbiosis between TV and movies: "The chief source of motion picture product for the television station will be the short subject and perhaps a greatly modified form of 'B' production" (187, p. 14). Also adding to the clamor of cheerfulness was Samuel Goldwyn who saw TV as similar to radio, "the competition we feared in the past" yet overcame—or at least learned to live with (49). Today, it is clear, the film and television industries are economically interdependent (see 56, p. 511; 114).

LESSONS FROM THE PAST AND HOMEWORK FOR THE FUTURE

One lesson these historical events teach is that, so far, the film industry has had an elastic ability to bounce back from the threat of technology. Indeed it must retain this ability since the introduction and public acceptance of directly competitive media force older media to either satsify new audience needs or wither (see 199, pp. 93-94). McCombs and Eyal's analysis of Americans' spending on the mass media between 1968-1977 concluded that "in terms of mainfest behaviors as well as the underlying motivations and gratifications, [society's use of mass communications] seems remarkably resilient in the face of rapid technological change" (109, p. 158). In particular, movies showed extraordinary economic stability during this period, demonstrating their strong recovery from the introduction of televison (109, p. 157).

History documents Hollywood's skill or luck in adapting to previous technological innovations. But what of today's technological challenges? These, some would say, portend that "the movie business is entering an epochal era" (91, p. 185). The alphabet soup of new technology acronyms which confront the motion picture medium is both numerous and numbing. Unlike radio and television, which both had broad-based audiences as their targets, some of the new technologies appear to be aiming at more narrow-based audiences (albeit *many* narrow-based audiences when all of the new technologies are considered). Unlike radio and TV, the contemporary catchword is technology—or television—of abundance (see, e.g., 196). MDS, LPTV, VCR, HDTV, DBS, STV, SMATV, et al. have also been nearly simultaneous in their development and introduction, quite unlike the quarter-century gap between radio and television. McQuail writes that the new technologies threaten the "established 'media order,' . . . challenge many of the ground rules . . ., take away or redistribute audiences . . . [and] undermine some of the established purposes assigned to media in society" (110, p. 223-224). DeFleur and Ball-Rokeach document the historical trend of a declining movie audience and predict the disappearance of today's movie theater altogether, stating: "Obsolescence is a natural counterpart to innovation" (25, p. 65). Not quite so extreme is Jowett and Linton's argument that pay TV, video cassettes, and discs all "threaten to further fragment and siphon off the potential movie audience" (74, p. 118). And Lees and Berkowitz admonish that "the stubborn tendency of people in Hollywood to lag behind in their understanding of new technology" plainly puts them at a distinct disadvntage (91, p. 186). According to Polon, "film will survive either as the consequence of a reasoned turn in direction of the new technologies or else will be absorbed by an alien force that will reshape film without historic restraint" (137, p. 389).

While certainly there exists no shortage of doomsayers, an opposing view is equally vocal. Perhaps one might dismiss the threat posed by new technologies by referring to the unrealized blue skies forecasts for cable television or, preceding that, the optimism concerning broadcast television's educational and civic potential. Littunen et al. remind us that "every innovation in communications technology has turned out to be less overwhelming in its impact than was initially predicted with the exception of printing" (99, p. 283). Monaco is somewhat more reserved, stating that the challenge of the new media does not approach that of the media revolution when audiovisual media challenged print (114, p. 50). Monaco adds that regardless of the method for delivering or the situation in which audiovisual entertainment is consumed, "the American film industry will most likely be the source of the programming." He concludes, therefore, that "Hollywood is in the best position ever to control audiovisual entertainment" (114, p. 52). Likewise, Syd Silverman, publisher of *Variety,* offered the following in a speech to the Los Angeles World Affairs Council:

> Despite all of the ups and down, feuds and disputes, Hollywood will survive and thrive—because it delivers what people pay for. No one ever bought a ticket to watch technology . . . The people in Hollywood who make the crucial decisions know that *content* will determine the entertainment choices of the public, regardless of the means of distribution (165, p. 13).

Perhaps, though, such comments, coming as they do from an industry insider and an industry notorious for its short-sightedness, can be dismissed as simply ostrich-like behavior. Carey, an academic, offers a middle-ground posture:

Current [technological] changes are rather closer to a civil war than a revolution, are more alterations in surface patterns rather than changes in fundamental structures . . . We are not living through a communications revolution. Rather the traditional patterns of social communication . . . are being intensified, twisted, and extended into international arenas . . . The new wave of innovation in communications is . . . more a reallocation of power than a fundamental alteration of its location, more of an intensification of long-standing patterns of audience distributions than an abrupt change in the nature of the audience (20, pp. 8, 9, 43).

There are thus two competing hypotheses about the impact of new media on existing media: new technologies will diminish the audience for existing media or adopters of technologies are "media addicts" who will integrate them into their existing media use patterns (see 29, p. 5; 112).

NEW COMMUNICATIONS TECHNOLOGIES
AND THE MOVIE AUDIENCE

One approach to examining the impact of new technologies on motion pictures is that of the movie audience. This perspective would suggest that, ultimately, the question of the future of motion pictures as they face new technologies is a question of audience: who will view movies, under what circumstances, and for which reasons. Should new technologies divert audiences to a significant extent, then the medium as we now know it will end. There is, of course, the counterargument that the mass media create an audience—as opposed to audiences which clamor for the development of a mass medium. While recognizing this argument, we nevertheless need to examine what media consumers are doing with new technologies and how this affects their moviegoing. More than a decade ago McCombs wrote that with the development of new technologies, "mass communication will no longer mean the simultaneous diffusion of identical messages to mass audiences." Instead, he predicted we would find "increasing fragmentation and individualization of mass communication" (108, p. 60). The growth—in absolute numbers—of various mass media forms will be governed by the Principle of Relative Constancy:

Only a small and fixed proportion of the economy is available to finance mass communication . . . New media in the marketplace did not produce a bigger pie; instead the old pie was resliced to feed the newcomer . . . For the immediate decades ahead, these two factors—time and money—will jointly constrain the growth of mass media in the marketplace (108, pp. 61, 63).

Maisel echoes this perspective by positing a three-stage theory of social change and media growth. He argues that the post-industrial society fosters specialization of media rather than the rapid growth of mass communications (101).

Time Allocation, Leisure, and Rate of Innovation Adoption

We need to examine the amount of time available to people before analyzing the impact of new technologies on movie audience behavior. Time, of course, is a fixed and finite resource—it is "the ultimate scarcity" (64, p. 395). If the introduction of new technologies results in a reallocation of leisure—or discretionary—time, and if the new technologies are indeed substitutes for motion pictures, then frequency of movie-going will diminish. Such a hypothesis needs clarification. First, as Holbrook and Lehmann note, the allocation of time "becomes particularly salient for activities that are not directly dependent on the consumption of goods and services, but whose primary function is the conscious use of time for pleasure or some other intrinsically worthwhile purpose." Discretionary time refers to "time spent on leisure activities . . . or on other nonroutine pursuits." And, since "an individual's discretionary time budget is essentially fixed in the short-run, the decision to participate in one such activity must necessarily affect the ability to engage in another" (64, p. 395). Second, is the distinction between substitute and complementary activities: two activities (or goods, etc.) "are substitutes if both can satisfy the same need of the consumer; they are complements if they are consumed jointly in order to satisfy some particular need" (60, p. 29). Thus, we need to inquire about people's leisure time availability, their allocation of such time according to various activities, and which of the new technologies function as a substitute for motion pictures.

Leisure activities are very important to Americans. One estimate maintained that the U.S. public would spend some $262 billion on leisure activities in 1982 (183, p. 39). The Census Bureau found that Americans today have greater numbers of leisure time hours availble to them: "Between 1965 and 1975 Americans reported an increase in leisure time of approximately one-half hour a day" (cited in 183, p. 15). Now, with the growth in new communications technologies, one outcome might be that any time devoted to such new technologies will be withdrawn from the expanding leisure account. However, such a banking metaphor may not be applicable.

A recent national study of Americans' leisure time activities found that the general public had 32 hours a week of leisure time available (183, p. 16). Persons 65 years and older had the greatest number of leisure hours (43 hours a week). The elderly population was closely followed by teenagers (41 hours a week), singles (38 hours), and married persons with no children (37 hours). These three groups are also the most frequent moviegoers (see 46, p. 32A; 115, p. 6).

Media use is perhaps the most frequent of all leisure time pursuits. Grunig reported in his study—which did *not* examine movies—that "people who consume the media consume as much as time permits, regardless of whether that content relates to their life situation" (53, p. 255; see also 112). The United Media Enterprises (UME) study concluded that "Clearly, media-related activities play an immensely important role in the way Americans spend their leisure time" (183, p.

29). A corollary to this finding is that most leisure activities are home-centered: "At least eight out of the ten most popular leisure activities are performed in the home . . . We are a nation that values leisure time so that we may relax, enjoy the companionship of our families, and seek information—all in our homes" (183, p. 29). This finding, together with the expanding size of the leisure time pie— suggests that new technologies which are able to be delivered to or consumed in the home will offer the stiffest competition to motion pictures. That the most frequent moviegoers also have the greatest amount of leisure time (except for the elderly) might lead one to conclude that home-based activities may become a substitute for moviegoing. However, the UME study also reported that

> those with relatively few family responsibilities—teenagers, single people, and childless couples—spend a large proportion of their leisure time activities *outside* the home. Only 2% of the teens, 7% of singles, and 11% of childless couples fall into the home-focused range (183, p. 36; emphasis in original).

Thus, despite the home-centeredness of most Americans' leisure time, the key movie audience aggregates do not fit this mold; hence their moviegoing behavior may not be affected—at least not initially. As Monaco notes, movies geared to the 12 to 25 year olds are "the ones who desperately want to leave the house, which is why the theatrical film is really in no danger from the new home-centered media" (114, p. 53). This assertion is underscored by the results of Duncan's study which measured the number of hours people spent engaged in various leisure activities. He indentified an "adolescent social" factor which was defined by dancing, dating, radio/stereo listening, moviegoing, and socializing (33, p. 122). All these activities are exclusively, or largely, out-of-home endeavors.

Two related considerations, however, are the *method* or *form* of theatrical exhibition and the rate of adoption of innovations. The UME's report found that watching television and reading newspapers were by far the two most popular leisure activities (183, p. 29). Similar data were reported earlier by Robinson (147, p. 188) who emphasized the role of television, which, he found, consumed "twice as much primary activity time as all other media combined" (p. 101). The prominance of TV use suggests that technologies such as VCRs, cable TV, premium cable services, and so on are all formidable competition for theaters, especially in light of *how* movies are exhibited. By the early 1970s the trend toward multiplex exhibition had become well-established (see 35). Along with the multiplex came a diminishing screen size which nurtured an audience that may conceive of and be accustomed to the movie experience as virtually identical in form to television— albeit, in most cases, without commercial interruption. When Home Box Office was initiated in 1975, and as it attracted more and more subscribers, movies on the small screen became the movie experience for many. The excitement and the sense of specialness engendered by the large screen format may well become extinct. The new movie audience generation conceptualizes the medium as one run through their home monitor, taped, and played back by their home VCR, rented from the video store, and, on special occasions, reproduced in stereo by their video disc player or (more recently) hi-fi VCR.

The argument for decreased theatrical movie attendance, even among heavy moviegoers, is buttressed by data on the rate of adoption of innovations. Katz, Levin, and Hamilton wrote that "the diffusion of innovation is one of the major mechanisms of social and technological change" (77, p. 237; see also 148 and, for a new technology perspective, 14). Authors such as Rogers and Shoemaker (148) and Toffler (178) have suggested that the rate of adoption of innovations has increased. However, as Olshavsky noted, evidence to support this view was lacking (127, p. 425). He tested and found support for the hypothesis that the rate of adoption of innovations in consumer markets has increased over time by examining the adoption rates for 25 home appliances from 1900, while controlling for purchase price differences. His results may also be interpreted as relevant to, especially, film exhibitors: despite the lengthy time it has taken for the adoption of cable TV, increasing rates of adoption, if applicable to more recent in-home video innovations, emphasizes the urgency of adequate and meaningful preparation and response.

Substitute Technologies for Motion Pictures

Film is predominantly a moving, visual, and entertainment medium. The concept of substitution is related to rate of innovation adoption. Komatsuzaki writes:

> If a new communication medium is promptly accepted, and disseminated widely, the social role of a conventional medium may be substituted by the newcomer. It may fulfill people's needs more efficiently and more conveniently at lower costs (83, p. 271).

Holbrook and Lehmann studied motion picture attendance and other activities in multidimensional scaling space. They found that film could be plotted near the intersection of two axes labeled intellectual demands and degree of physical exertion; movies fell within the low-brow intellectual demand and sedentary quadrant (64, p. 404). In order for new technologies to function as substitutes, they too must share the three attributes of movies noted above and should also fall within the same quadrant. (Holbrook and Lehmann did not examine new technologies.) Thus, such new technologies as videotex, teletext, and other largely linear, verbal, static, and information-oriented innovations will not substitute for movies. Yet numerous substitute technologies exist. The literature on how such substitute technologies affect movie audience attendance is examined below.[2]

---

[2] In the following sections numeric data on a variety of issues and concerns are presented. Although accurate when this article was written, such data change extraordinarily rapidly. As such, they should be viewed as illustrative rather than representative of the contemporary situation.

"Modifications" to Broadcast Television

Since television is the medium which consumes most people's leisure time it remains the most serious competitor for audiences to movies. As a result of new technologies, traditional broadcast TV has expanded by offering viewers increasing numbers of channels from which to select, thus posing an additional threat to the absolute size of the movie audience and their frequency of attendance. This section examines new technologies which modify or supplement existing television broadcast transmission and reception.

Drop-ins are additional—up to 140—VHF TV stations which FCC engineers determined could operate in certain markets without interfering with existing stations (see 52, pp. 81-86). Gross suggests that a combination of the FCC's "benign neglect" toward drop-ins and a lack of interest on the part of potential licensees has, at least for the present, led to few applications for the total available drop-ins. Presently, then, drop-ins threaten neither the movie audience nor traditional TV.

Low Power Television (LPTV) is a "regular" TV outlet operating with only ten watts of power on VHF and up to 1000 watts on UHF. A LPTV signal reaches a 15 to 25 mile radius (52, p. 141). The first LPTV operation initiated service in December, 1981 from Bemidji, Minnesota programming news, sports, and a pay movie service (52, p. 144). Unlike drop-ins, there has been no shortage of license applications. Since 1981, when the FCC invited LPTV applications it has been "deluged" with them and, as of December 1983, had at least 12,000 on file for the approximately 4,000 locations available (36, p. 55). Start-up and operation of LPTV stations is inexpensive, FCC regulation loose, and programming constraints few (52, pp. 141-142). No research has yet been reported on LPTV's popularity among viewers. Compared to drop-ins, though, LPTV may become a serious contender for both movies and traditional TV stations, especially if linked by satellite to form specialty networks.

Multipoint Distribution Service (MDS) is an omnidirectional microwave signal with an effective radius of about 25 miles. Microband Corporation of America was the first MDS operator. In 1975 it began sending pay TV programming to hotels and apartment buildings (158, p. 33). Currently there are more than 300 such operations serving some 750,000 subscribers (70, p. 34; see also 23). Gross indicates that "MDS is used primarily to supply pay movies (52, p. 78). Although hampered by easy signal disturbance from trees, buildings, and such (an unbroken line of sight between sending and receiving units is necessary), start-up costs are signficantly cheaper than for cable systems (158, p. 33). Although nonproprietary audience research is not available, Schwarz asserts that MDS is most likely to find its niche in areas where cable has yet to—or will not—go (see also 52, p. 84). If this is taken to mean rural areas, then the threat to movie attendance may be minimal: there are fewer exhibition sites in such areas and moviegoing is also less frequent as compared to suburban and urban population centers.

Subscription Television (STV) uses the electromagnetic spectrum as do other broadcasters. The difference is that STV, as its name implies, charges a fee for use and scrambles its signal to prevent free viewing. Signal scrambling was first used in 1947 by Zenith with its Phonevision system in Chicago (see 52, p. 70; 136, p. 12). Rather than over-the-air transmission and scrambling, Phonevision used telephone lines. Movie mogul Samuel Goldwyn went so far as to champion the system as having "the greatest" potential for generating revenues for the movie industry (49). The film industry was involved in early STV experiments: Paramount tested a system called Telemeter in Palm Springs in 1953 and again in Etiobicoke, Canada in 1960 (neither was a success); Henry Griffing, an exhibitor, tested a system in Bartlesville, Oklahoma in 1957 which also failed (see 52, p. 70). Perhaps the best-known STV experiment was former NBC president Sylvester L. (Pat) Weaver's 1964 attempt in Los Angeles. It, too, was a failure—in large part due to an emotionally-loaded campaign launched by movie exhibitors (see 52, p. 71; 129). Although "STV is the oldest of the new technologies" (175), its future is grim. Talen reports decreasing numbers of subscribers, STV companies, and revenues (175). *Business Week* reports that "STV owners fear that the window is slamming shut on subscription TV" and that their survival is threatened by multichannel pay TV, rising operating costs, a diminishing subscriber base, and subscriber annoyance over "the number of pay-per-view events that interrupt STV's regular programming" (185; see also 70, p. 34). At present, then, the competitive clout wielded by STV against movie audiences is, at best, weak and, perhaps "the STV business may be terminally ill" (175).

The final new technology which modifies the present mode of television transmission is not a distribution system by rather an image-enhancement system. High Definition (or Density) Television (HDTV) increases the number of TV scanning lines resulting in a higher resolution image—the sharpness, or quality, of the image approximates that of 35 millimeter film. Compatibility between the existing 525-line U.S. system and the 1,125-line HDTV has not been entirely resolved, although CBS, Sony, and the Japanese Broadcasting Corporation (NHK), Panasonic, and Ikegami have each developed proposals (see 52, pp. 148-149; 61; 102; 159). HDTV requires more bandwidth than present TV broadcasting. Its threat to draw away movie audiences currently is nil.

The five modifications to traditional TV discussed here will, at present, do little or nothing to the movie audience configuration. Three are simply not presently or sufficiently available (drop-ins, LPTV, HDTV), one (STV) appears to be disappearing, and the last (MDS) seems unlikely to offer any kind of a reasonable attraction to most moviegoers. Barring unforeseen circumstances, these five technologies do not represent a visible threat to either the size of the movie audience or their frequency of moviegoing.

Satellite Transmission[3]

Since 1962 when the first communications satellite (AT&T's "Telstar") was launched, this mode of transmission has offered a revolutionary method for distributing information (see 181). By themselves satellites do not directly threaten the movie audience structure, but as a means for home television reception of programming, two satellite technologies bear scrutiny; DBS and SMATV.

Making its debut in 1984, Direct Broadcast Satellite (DBS) is described by some as "a heady mixture of aerospace and entertainment in novel partnership" (59, p. 20) and others as "television without the middleman" (138). DBS transmists information directly from its producer, to the transponder of a geosynchronous orbit satellite, and then to the downlink microwave dish placed, for example, on an individual's roof. Two firms, Satellite Television Corp. and United Satellite Communications, largely control the U.S. DBS market. According to Suskin, both are hoping to capture as their customers the 15 million TV homes which "will not have access to cable TV in the foreseeable future" (174, p. 8). Since it is able to address individual homes without the hardware of cable, DBS could be a competitive force for movie audiences (as well as other technologies); its pay-for-view potential is formidable—even in high-density population areas (see 138; 52, pp. 133-135). However, high start-up costs (about $300 million for a nationwide system) and expense to consumers do not bode well for DBS. By July 1984, faced with these financial considerations as well as other, more accessible-to-the-consumer technologies, and concerns over lack of programming, CBS, Western Union, and RCA all bowed out of various DBS exploitation schemes (133). DBS's likely impact on domestic movie audiences will be small; the same may not be true for movie distribution and exhibition.

Satellite Master Antenna TV (SMATV) evolved from MATV systems which were regularly installed in new apartment complexes to ensure clear reception of television signals. SMATV simply couples satellite technology (a receiving dish) with existing technology (see 45; 52, pp. 78-81). Current estimates indicate some 500,000 to one million subscribers with an estimated growth to 3.3 million by 1992 (45). SMATV's threat to movies is similar to that of (especially premium) cable since it is in direct competition with cable. As such, further discussion is reserved for the section below.

Cable Television

Compared to its slow-start beginning in the late 1940s, cable grew at an incredible rate in the 1970s. Today over 40 percent of all U.S. households have cable (124, p. 6; 123)—more than 33 million homes (17)—served by some 6,200 cable systems

---

[3] For information concerning satellite regulation, technological development, costs, control, financing, and so on, see 27, 41, 59, 99, 131, 195.

(21, p. 1).[4] 1983 estimates for the rate of cable adoption ranged from some 250,000 (75, p. 49) to nearly 400,000 (142, p. 3) households a month with a growth rate for basic cable expected to average ten percent a year through the mid-1980s (151, p. 15). The popularity of cable is not restricted to the United States: in the Netherlands 55 percent of the population subscribes to cable, while the percentages for Belgium and Luxembourg are 65 and 90 respectively (136, p. 1). Cable consultant Paul Kagen estimates that by 1993 there will be 104 million pay TV subscriptions and 60 million homes with cable in the United States (90, p. 37) and that overall cable revenues will reach $16.6 billion by 1990 (75, p. 50). The present, as well as the projected, growth rate for basic and premium cable is such that competitors such as STV, MDS, DBS, SMATV, and LPTV may very well be left either in the dust or forced to pick at the scraps ignored by cable operators for one reason or another (see 144).

Premium, or pay, cable's adoption rate rivals that of regular, or basic, cable (of course typically one must first have basic in order to get premium). This is best documented by Time Inc.'s Home Box Office. Beginning in November 1972 with an audience of 365 homes in Wilkes-Barre, Pennsylvania, HBO did not attract much attention until it latched onto a Satcom I transponder and, on September 30, 1975, offered the Ali-Frazier "Thriller in Manila" fight (82, p. 51). Today HBO has some 12.5 million subscribers (see 135 for related data on other pay services) and reported a $100 million profit in 1982 (201). Krugman and Eckrich reported in 1982 that 38 percent of those cable subscribers who have the option of picking up pay cable have done so (86, p. 23). James' 1983 research indicated that 60 percent of all cable subscribers paid extra to receive at least one premium channel (70, p. 33).

Clearly, of all the new technologies examined in the present report, cable and pay cable may represent both the most serious immediate and long-range challenges to the motion picture industry and its audience, although home video appears to have significantly slowed its growth (see 190). O'Connor reports that in 1983 "pay-cable subscribers will shell out about $2.4 billion to watch movies at home compared with the $3.5 billion the entire population will spend to watch movies out" (126, p. 20). Earlier, in 1978, Mayer wrote that cable television "omens for [movie] exhibitors are not favorable" (107, p. 89). To determine the impact of cable and premium cable, the issue will be addressed from three perspectives: demographics, motives for adoption, and effect on movie attendance.

For comparative purposes four groups have been constructed: noncable subscribers, basic cable subscribers, pay (premium) cable subscribers, and frequent moviegoers (attendance of at least one film a month). Frequent moviegoers tend to be under 30 years old (115, p. 6) while cable subscribers are younger than nonsubscribers and pay cable subscribers are younger than cable subscribers (86,

---

[4] By 1979, 36.7 percent of all cable subscribers were served by the ten largest cable organizations. For a discussion of the trend toward multiple-system operator domination, see Howard (65).

p. 29; 136, p. 8; 151, p. 21; 193, p. 121). In short, the pay cable subscriber falls essentially within the same age bracket as the frequent moviegoer. Although one study found that 18 to 24 year olds who had access to pay cable "actually went out to the movie theatre nearly 25 percent more often than the general population" (7, p. 21), this finding is not replicated by other reports. Education level is similar among the four groups and differences are negligible: most fall in the "some college" or "graduated college" categories (86, 103, 115, 151). Also, differences by income are slight when comparing cable and pay cable subscribers to frequent moviegoers (86, 103, 115, 151). Comparisons on three demographic variables, then, suggest considerable overlap among the cable, pay cable, and frequent moviegoers. By itself, this does not bode well for the movie industry, movies are competing for the same demographic aggregate as are cable and pay cable services.

Myriad motives for cable and pay cable subscription have been identified and documented by the research literature. Rothe et al. found that the most important reason for cable subscription was for "more movies" (151, p. 17). Earlier (November 1980), the Roper Organization, too, reported that of six types of programs available on either local or cable channels, movies were ranked as most important (149, p. 7). Metzger's 1983 report, however, found that when asked for reasons individuals *originally* subscribed to cable, movies, sports, and other specific types of programs were ranked third behind variety of programming and better reception (111, pp. 43-44). Still, once "connected," cable subscribers "view movies much more often after they subscribe" than before (151, p. 17). In fact, Rothe et al. found that of 11 program types identified, the only statistically significant change in before-after cable subscription behavior was movie viewing (151, p. 18). Thus Metzger's results may have been due to a novelty effect. Jeffres' research supports this conclusion, stating that while there was "some evidence of increasing selectivity once [cable] viewing has begun, the reverse is found with initiating motives" (72, p. 175). Research on the reasons offered for pay cable subscription are less ambiguous. Without exception, data from four studies indicates that the movies available on pay cable is the chief reason for subscription (see 32, p. 160; 86, p. 26; 111, p. 44; 113, p.64). Moreover, Marcus reports that the greatest amount of his sample's viewing time was spent actually watching movies, followed at a great distance by sports and entertainment specials (103, p. 43). And Nielsen's 1979 study found that premiere and "adult" movies drew consistently large audiences (136, p. 8). Thus, movies are the overwhelmng incentive for cable and pay cable subscription. This suggests that audiences are not so much giving up motion pictures as they are the form of exhibition and viewing context.

Although quite clearly large numbers of individuals are adopting cable, a problem still hounding the cable industry is "churn": subscriber cancellation due to dissatisfaction (172). A 1980 survey conducted by the Opinion Research Corporation for *Panorama* magazine found that 11 percent of the sample reported dissatisfaction with their cable service. However, fewer than ten percent of the disgruntled complained of "not enough movies" (103, pp. 44-45). More recent data, from the Benton and Bowles advertising agency, indicates that churn has increased: "17% of all current or previous subscribers have canceled at least one pay service for reasons other than changing residences" (90). Metzger offers this assessment of the cable industry:

> Overall the reaction is on the plus side, but in relation to comparable questions on many other products, these ratings are low . . . This raises questions about the long-term prospect for growth as well as questions about the ability to maintain the levels that exist now where the systems are fully developed (111, p. 46).

Somewhat surprisingly, research on the impact of cable and pay cable adoption and movie attendance is sparse. Kaplan's early study found that 17 percent of the cable subscribers reported attending movies less often after subscribing (76). By 1980, Marcus reported 46 percent of the cable subscribers sampled said they were going out to see movies and plays less frequently since subscribing (103, p. 43). Rothe et al. found that 1.8 percent of their sample increased movie attendance after cable subscription, while 50.8 percent reported no change and 47.4 percent indicated a decrease in frequency of attendance (151, p. 18). However, only a marginal difference between cable subscribers and nonsubscribers was found for number of movies attended in the previous month (1.0 compared to 1.1 respectively). The results of these three studies, however, are contradicted by another study. Davenport interviewed more than 9,600 people in Albuquerque, Las Vegas, and Tucson and found that "regular viewers of HBO, The Movie Channel, and Showtime attended motion picture theatres some 9.4 percent more frequently than the public at large" (7, pp. 20-21). Moreover, Williams and Shapiro's recent study found that "the most frequent film attenders did not subscribe to cable television" (199); this suggests that there may exist a social group which (thus far) resists the intrusion of cable at the expense of their moviegoing.

Although the results are mixed, the overall conclusion to be drawn from the foregoing is that cable television has had a detrimental effect on frequency of moviegoing. Cable TV and movies share a similar target audience and a key motive for cable subscription is to see movies. Although dissatisfaction over cable has been expressed, at present the number of such individuals is small; thus movie exhibitors in particular can expect no respite as a result. Given the growth projections for cable and premium cable, further nibbling away at the size of the movie audience can be expected. There should be a ceiling to this trend; where that ceiling is, though, is impossible to say given the present data. Further, research (e.g., 7, 199) suggests that a core movie audience will remain despite the pervasiveness of cable.

Video Discs and Video Cassettes

Video disc development began in the late 1960s and, with their potential to store 108,000 frames of information, video discs were heralded as the premiere method for data storage and retrieval. They also offer important educational and training functions (see 52, 104, 155, 160). Initial interest and sales were promising; media consultant David Butterfield estimated that "entertainment video discs [including not just movies but also games] could be a $6.75 billion industry" by 1990 (13). Today the video disc "continues to eke out an unremarkable sales record" (87, p. 43) which may be even less promising since, after taking $580 million loss, RCA announced in April 1984 that it was dropping their disc system (132). Hampered by three incompatible formats (the reflective laser optical disc, capacitance electronic disc, and video high density disc) and the high price for both the player and the software, as well as being commercially restricted to a playback-only format, the video disc does not seem to be a significant competitor for moviegoers' attention. Even though the primary software for video discs is movies, and disc owners purchase up to 30 discs a year (52, pp. 102, 105; 87, p. 43), this technology's drawbacks make it an unlikely alternative for moviegoing. Only about 400,000 players have been sold thus far and 1990 penetration estimates suggest only five to ten percent penetration in the United States (70, pp. 35-36). Far more significant is the video cassette recorder.

Since November 1975, when Sony introduced its Betamax, sales of video cassette recorders (VCRs) for home use have soared. Similar to video discs, VCRs are available in two incompatible formats, Beta and Video Home System (VHS). Sony's monopoly on the market lasted less than one year; by 1976 Matsushita had introduced a VHS machine through Quasar (164, p. 1) and today, the VHS format has captured fully three-quarters of the market (87, p. 42). According to an International Institute of Communications study, "40 million homes in 63 countries will be equipped with videorecorders" by the end of 1983. The IIC study reported that in Kuwait 92 percent of all homes have VCRs; 7,560,000 units have been sold in Japan; 5,750,000 in England; and 3,900,000 in West Germany. 8,750,00 units in use in the United States were expected by the end of 1983 (reported in 57), 13 million by the end of 1984 (88) and 20-25 percent U.S. household penetration by 1990 (189). In Sweden, researchers at Sveriges Radio were predicting a 15-25 percent market penetration by 1985 for home video systems (66, p. 26). An October 1983 Associated Press story reports that Japanese exporting of VCRs was climbing steadily and that the United States was its largest foreign market, accounting for 36.8 percent of all sales; moreover, "exports to the United States rose 77.2 percent from a year earlier" (6). VCR sales should further increase with steadily falling prices and, especially, the introduction of high-fidelity stereo sound and an eight-millimeter format. Projections for VCR penetration in the United States range from a conservative 10-14 percent of all TV households (2, p. 29) to 25 percent of all TV households by 1990 (95, p. 263; see also statements by David Ladd and Jack Valenti in 184, pp. 395, 468).

Margulies reported in November 1982 that moviemakers were rubbing their hands in glee since "the demographics of the theater and home video audiences are thought to be so different as to rule out significant overlap" (105, p. 53). While conjecture may offer consolation, inspection of the available evidence is far less reassuring. In fact, by 1984 a different tune was being sung. Paramount's marketing president, Gordon Weaver, said: "As far as we can tell, the moviegoers and the video cassette buyers are not separate and distinct audiences. They seem to complement each other" (78, p. 62). As was the case for cable, demographic profiles of VCR owners show a clear overlap with the frequent moviegoer. Research by Levy (94, p. 327; 93, p. 23). Dominick (29, p. 4) and Mediastat (in 184, p. 473) indicates that compared to the U.S. population at large, VCR households are better educated, have higher incomes, are more likely to hold professional or managerial jobs, tend to be urban, and are younger. (Similar conclusions were drawn for VCR ownership in Sweden; see 66, 67). Traub reports that in India the wealthy have stopped attending movies in favor of using their VCRs and "in small towns, video parlors constitute an important alternative to movie halls" (182, p. 8). Further, VCR ownership is related to cable subscription and ownership of other home-entertainment technologies, thus lending credence to Levy's comment that "VCR ownership may also affect leisure time budgets and overall media consumption" (96, p. 401). In 1981, Mediastat reported that 35.6 percent of VCR households subscribed to cable and/or pay cable (184, p. 473); Rothe et al. reported in 1983 that cable subscribers were significantly more likely than nonsubscribers to own home computers (8.4 versus 1.9 percent), a VCR (21 versus 10.6 percent), a large screen TV (2.6 versus 2.3 percent), a video disc player (2.3 versus 0.9 percent), and video games (30.4 versus 18.1 percent). Rothe et al. also found similar differences when respondents were asked about their intent to purchase such items in the next year (151, p. 20). Thus, cable TV and VCRs seem to pose a two-pronged threat to moviegoing.

Research on owners' use of their VCRs suggests that recording movies is the most frequent activity. Arbitron found that 36 percent of all recordings were movies while Mediastat reported movies accounted for 27 percent of all recordings (2, p. 34); Levy's research indicated that movies accounted for the largest percentage (24 percent) of videotape recordings and playbacks (96, p. 404; 94, p. 24; 93, p. 329) and that there was some indication that movies and cultural programs may form the core program material for videotape library building (95, p. 265). Early research indicated that VCR owners infrequently used prerecorded rented tapes. Arbitron found that only 22 percent of the VCR owners used such material (2, p. 34) and Levy reported that fewer than one prerecorded cassette a week was viewed (96, p. 402; 94, p. 24). These data, however, were collected in 1980 and most likely are explained by the high cost of prerecorded tapes and the smaller number of tape rental establishments at the time. More recent data indicates that

more than 80 percent of [VCR] owners buy or rent prerecorded programs, mostly movies. An estimated 10 million prerecorded video cassettes will be sold this year [1983] (of which 20 percent will be pornographic). For every video-cassette sale, there are about 10 tape rentals, bringing the total for 1983 to 100 million (87, p. 42).

Jack Wayman, of the Electronic Industries Association, in testimony before the U.S. Senate stated that there were "some 35,000" prerecorded titles currently available. Based upon such data, Kilday concluded that "if videocassettes pose a threat, it seems it's to theatrical exhibition" (184, pp. 49, 62).

Little research has been conducted on the actual effect of VCR ownership on moviegoing and all of the available evidence is dated (especially in view of the rapid adoption rate of VCRs which Lachenbruch (87, p. 42) suggests parallels the growth of color TV "almost unit for unit"). Paramount Pictures reported that the video cassette release of *Flashdance* did "the opposite of what many expected, boosting theatrical receipts instead of annihilating the boxoffice" (161, p. 1). Peter Elson, executive vice president for Guild Entertainment (an exhibition firm), said that for films such as *Raiders of the Lost Ark* and *Flashdance* "the videocassette will probably make people more eager to see the picture in theaters" and he was not disturbed by any negative competitive impact (161, p. 396). Such anecdotal reports are supported by a Mediastat survey conducted in May 1980 for the Motion Picture Association of America. This study found that *new* VCR owners may go out to the movies more often than long-time owners (184, p. 436). However, a UCLA study for Paramount reported that 48 percent of VCR owners went to the movies less often than nonowners, as did pay TV subscribers (184, p. 436). And, in West Germany, the 14 percent decline in 1983 boxoffice was attributed to VCRs (80).

The most optimistic forecast would suggest that VCR ownership will only marginally affect frequency of moviegoing and, in rare instances, may occasionally boost attendance for "blockbuster" films. A 1981 Newspaper Advertising Bureau study found that respondents who preferred to see a movie in a theater were also the most likely to purchase a VCR: "This suggests that many people like movies and like to see them so well that they like to see them in theaters *and* at home" (120, p. 41 emphasis in original). A Swedish study reported that the typical VCR owner's interest in renting prerecorded cassettes declines rapidly. This tended to be true especially among young persons, the group most likely to own VCRs: "Renting films apparently loses its appeal after the first few months" (67, pp. 42, 44). A less favorable forecast is predicted when relying on demographic data as well as recording, playback, and rental behaviors (see also 118).

Summary
The absolute number of technologies which pose a threat to moviegoing is comparable to—in fact fewer than—the number of technologies which do not. To draw reassuring conclusions from such a comparison, however, is to ignore other variables such as rate of adoption and penetration. The extent of penetration, in particular, is important, although reporting data on this factor is virtually pointless since the figures change rapidly. Using Holbrook and Lehmann's study of leisure activities, new technologies which threaten to diminish the size of the film audience apparently fall within the same multidimensional space as did movies: low-brow

intellectually and sedentary. Of course, much of the "software" for these technologies is motion pictures.

A worst-case scenario from the moviegoing perspective would predict greatly diminished frequency of attendance. This is partially true. The greatest impact on moviegoing by these technologies will be among less frequent, or occasional, moviegoers. They will fill their increased number of leisure hours by increasing the already high percentage of time devoted to media use with such technologies. Their already infrequent movie attendance will further diminish as they allocate more time to using the new technologies. With the increasing rate of innovation adoption and the changing (or perhaps more accurately, changed) nature of the movie experience, four technologies are, and will continue to make, a significant impact on moviegoing. To the film industry what this means is an overall decline in the number of ticket sales and fewer blockbuster movies.

Less severely affected by the new technologies—but affected nonetheless— will be the frequent moviegoers. This group has the most leisure time and, like all other social groups, is finding its leisure time expanding. But more than others, this group spends most of its leisure time outside of the home. As such, the impact of such technologies on frequent moviegoers' moviegoing will probably be less dramatic than was the case for occasional moviegoers. What might be expected is that the frequent moviegoers will begin to use proportionately more leisure time in-home but, due to the increase in leisure hours available, only moderately decrease their frequency of movie attendance.

NEW COMMUNICATIONS TECHNOLOGIES AND THE MOVIE INDUSTRY

If the past is even a modestly accurate predictor for the future, the new communication technologies may be seen as harbingers of increased profitability for parts of the film industry. The advent of radio and television did not result in replacing the old medium (motion pictures) with the new media. Instead, new forms served as the impetus for realignment, reassessment, and redistribution of effort and energy for the film industry. In short, although it may not be business as usual for the film industry as it confronts changing technologies there will still be a film business.

Production and Distribution

Since in practice, U.S. film production and distribution are, in the corporate sense, virtually indistinguishable, the benefits—or threats—from new technologies should be shared between these two sectors of the industry. Many of the new technologies discussed in this report are essentially distribution systems. As such, they provide the hardware for information dissemination but are dependent upon others for what they distribute. Home Box Office, the dominant premium cable service, buys some 200 films a year (82, p. 51) and has a policy of "participation" in the production of movies. HBO fronted $3.5 million to the producers of *On Golden Pond* to assure its exclusive pay TV rights for the film. Likewise, Paramount Pictures, at the close of 1983, sold Showtime/The Movie Channel exclusive access to some 75 of its movies over the next five years; a deal worth an estimated $500 million (see 139). And, although some in Hollywood feel as though giants such as HBO unfairly control the industry because of their dominance in the pay TV market (see 122), there is no denying that while control is a point of consternation, cash creates the reality of production.

By 1982 pay cable fees amounted to 17.4 percent of all movie revenues—the second largest source of revenue for the industry. This marked the first time that revenues from this source exceeded foreign sales (47, p. 329). Litman has written that "the steady increase in pay TV penetration in the latter part of the 1970s has meant that new markets and new profit centers are emerging for the theatrical film" (98, p. 34). Likewise, VCRs and video discs are dependent upon the film industry for some, in the first case, and virtually all, in the second case, of their software (see 164).

Such optimistic forecasts are not restricted to the domestic market. Just as the American film industry came to dominate the world's trade in motion pictures (see 54), there is little reason to doubt a recurrence of this pattern for the new technologies. Indeed, the evidence points in precisely this direction. In the United Kingdom pay TV "consists entirely of feature films" and the U.S.-based Motion Picture Export Association is "the most significant supplier" (136, p. 13). An *InterMedia* report suggests that "the growth of pay-TV is likely to be a major force for the further integration of a single national industry; and then of an international industry" due to pay TV's dependence on Hollywood (136, p. 3).

Some would predict that pay TV and related home video technologies "may replace the theatrical market as the primary transmission outlet" due to "superior efficiency in this method of distribution and the rising cost of travel associated with the energy crisis" (98, p. 34). Others suggest a more moderate posture: "For filmmakers the marketing attraction of pay-TV is the new lease of life it might give to films that have had their 'first-run' and reached the 'second-run' generation" (136, p. 13). Regardless of which perspective is more accurate, film producers will undoubtedly see their horizons considerably broadened. Even if half the U.S. movie theaters close as a result of diminished attendance, the in-home entertainment options made possible by the new technologies offer far greater access to audiences than out-of-home entertainment establishments ever did.

In 1981, Krugman and Christians wrote that "if pay cable is to succeed, it must upgrade program quality and expand the range of services" (85, p. 201). Littunen et al., in their discussion of DBS (but equally applicable to other technologies), pointed out

that this technology is only a distribution technology does not necessarily mean that the content structure of mass communications would remain unaffected . . . The multiplication of channel capacity may lead to a lowering in quality of programs as the limited resources must be spread over more programme hours (99, pp. 284, 294).

A counter view to the above is held by the director of such films as *The Dresser, Breaking Away,* and *The Deep.* In a recent interview, Peter Yates noted:

> With the coming of cable and video, the studios are beginning to feel that up to a certain price, they can recoup their money, regardless of a film's theatrical prospects. They're more willing to take a chance if they can count on getting their money back (26, p. 18).

Littunen's assertions address the final product but ignore the production process. By, again, reviewing the history of Hollywood's previous technological competitors—radio and broadcast television—the most reasonable conclusion to be drawn is that external technological threat has resulted in internal technological advances. The impetus for such important innovations as sound, color, and various widescreen (e.g., CinemaScope, Cinerama) processes is largely attributable to broadcasting. These technological advances in the cinema came as a result not of intervention at the time of external threat, but rather exploitation of an existing technology in the face of competition and as a means of either mimicking or outdoing the new technology.[5] Thus, today along with film, we find extended use of videotape in the film industry for instant replay and for editing. Director Francis Ford Coppola rehearsed and pre-shot *One from the Heart* and *Rumble Fish* on videotape and is perhaps best known for adopting similar technical innovations (see 42, 81). Other examples of Hollywood's turn to new technologies include wireless microphones, use of radio to synchronize camera and audio recording, the Steadicam and Skycam, computer-assisted special effects generators, and improved film stocks and lens optics (see 16; 137, pp. 389-390). Moreover, as they learned to do with broadcast TV, moviemakers have begun using the new technologies for cross-media promotion to sell their pictures. A recent development, for instance, is offering music videos derived from a film to MTV, "Night Tracks," and so on (see 38).

Nelson recently wrote:

> Fears that network television, radio, or print will disappear are probably unfounded, since the prophets of doom consistently have failed to foresee how existing technologies can successfully adapt to market changes and weave themselves into a new media mix (119, p. 28).

The same might be said for motion pictures. At least in terms of production, it is unlikely that Hollywood will find itself either out of business or operating under less than full capacity. In fact, with the flourishing myriad of new technological

---

[5] An interesting twist on the typical direction of which medium responds to which other medium's technological advance is stereo television. Motion pictures (as well as radio) have, for years, used stereo sound; although several years off, TV will soon be broadcasting in stereo (see 89). For discussion of color in the cinema, see Andrew (4) and Kindem (79).

delivery systems, the industry may find itself in the comfortable position of being able to pick, and even refuse, projects. Indeed, production projections for 1984 indicate no fewer than 400 pictures in release (22).

As with the production sector, distributors should find themselves with more business than ever. The contemporary market is characterized by many new and different buyers. During the first 45 years or so of their existence, there was but one outlet—or point of distribution—for movies: the theater. Then, with the public's widespread adoption of television, a second major outlet for movies developed. Other nontheatrical, albeit not-so-profitable, ancillary markets for movies emerged in the form of the 16mm. college (among others) circuit, military bases, commercial airlines, penal institutions, and motels/hotels (see 55, pp. 193-201; 107, pp. 81-97). What the new technologies offer is a larger field of potential buyers for that which the film distributors are selling. In addition to demands for current product, pay television, video cassettes, and such have also increased the value of film studios/distributors' libraries (see 156). In 1982 the film studios earned ''between $500 million and $600 million from sales to pay services'' (19, p. 44). So valuable are the new technologies to the earnings of producer-distributors that by 1985 gross revenues from these markets are expected to equal theatrical revenues (19, p.44). Video cassettes, in particular, are an attractive medium for film producer-distributors on both a rental[6] and outright sales basis. According to some observers, the high penetration of VCRs makes this market appear ''more profitable than pay cable is for movie producers'' since 20 percent of the wholesale price returns to the copyright owner—a return greater than that from cable TV (88). Further, as Waterman notes, ''prerecorded home video successfully competes as a delivery system by offering distributors more efficient methods of pricing programs to consumers'' (189).

Current indications suggest an even greater symbiosis among film producer-distributors and the new technologies. Guback reports that in the 1970s the industry majors ''captured between 70% and 89% of the revenue accruing to films earning more than $1 million in rentals'' (55, p. 221). Waterman found that six companies accounted for 89 percent of all 1983 domestic theatrical rentals (189). Gomery reports data similar to Guback and, further, notes that the domination of the medium is a ''bilateral oligopoly'': the few major movie companies control the production sector and sell to an exhibition sector which is largely controlled by even fewer—''five or so''—exhibition chains (50, p. 54). In April 1980 a movies-only pay TV service, named Premiere, designed to compete with HBO was formed by the Getty Oil Company, Columbia Pictures, MCA Inc. (parent to Universal Studios), Paramount Pictures, and Twentieth Century-Fox. Although this venture ultimately failed, it was a clear harbinger of thing to come; following a Justice Department inquiry and allegation of price fixing and conspiracy to create a monopoly, a U.S. District Court found the partnership in violation of the Sherman

---

[6] The copyright issue of first sale, however, remains problematic.

Anti-Trust Act and issued an injunction to halt operation of service on December 31, 1980 (service had been scheduled to begin on January 2, 1981). In January 1983, two premium cable services, Showtime and The Movie Channel, merged; as initially formulated, the deal would have ultimately brought together MCA, Paramount, Warner Brothers, Viacom International (which owned Showtime), and American Express (The Movie Channel was a joint venture of Warner Communications and AE) but ran afoul of the Justice Department (see 150, 153, 200). By mid-1983 Tri-Star Pictures, formed by HBO, Columbia, and CBS, was in operation and had released its first feature, *The Natural*, in early 1984. In late 1983 *Variety* was reporting that Fox, Columbia, and CBS were "in the process of hammering out a major partnership agreement" which would "lock up Direct Broadcast Satellite rights on a global scale" (191, p. 1). While such developments may raise eyebrows among anti-trust scholars and harken back to the pre-1948 consent decree when the film industry was a vertically integrated oligopoly, the trend toward increased concentration and—formal or informal—merger of new and old technologies continues unabated. A relatively recent development suggests the growing interdependence among these industries. On January 17, 1984 TeleFirst, an ABC subsidiary, began broadcasting by a scrambled signal, recent movies to VCR owners in the Chicago market (see 12, 140). TeleFirst represented symbiosis among traditional network television, over-the-air scrambling transmission technology, film producer-distributors, and video cassette recorder owners (since subscribers needed to own a VCR to record the transmissions). Early reports indicated that TeleFirst planned to offer some 33 movies monthly in addition to nonmovie programming (140). Initial indications of the popularity of TeleFirst, however, were not favorable, suggesting no more than 4,000 subscribers after two months of operation and with estimates of 100,000 subscribers needed for the service to reach a profit (141). Indeed, after six months of operation ABC announced that TeleFirst would end operations on June 30, 1984. Losses were estimated a $15 million and ABC Video Enterprises President Herbert Granath cited competing pay TV alternatives and confusion as to how to use the service among TeleFirst subscribers as key reasons for its demise (143).

In short, the distribution sector faces multiple pressures and benefits from the introduction of new technologies. The new forms of communications increase the number of buyers for the distributors' product, thereby increasing competition among buyers for the product. This, of course, places distributors in the comfortable position of dictating financial terms. Writing in 1983, Caranicas stated: "As the studios are learning a bit too late, he who controls the method of distribution controls the industry" (19, p. 43). That it may be too late for Hollywood, though, is doubtful. The intimate corporate relationships between film producers and distributors ensures their continued financial success.

Exhibition

Of the three industry sectors, exhibition appears to have the most to lose as new technologies are introduced. Richard Orear, former president of this branch's lobbying organization, the National Association of Theatre Owners (NATO), stated that "there is no question that near-panic prevails" among exhibitors in response to the "electronic revolution" (157, p. 29). *Variety* reported in late 1983 that exhibitors perceived home video technologies "as a more immediate threat to their business" than cable (18). In particular, home video technology may limit the tiered release of movies by ending the financial feasibility of both re-release and second-run theatrical markets. Although this may be true, it is difficult to pinpoint which of the new technologies poses the most severe threat; it may also be pointless to search for the most menacing medium. For it is the confluence of many new technologies that offers the greatest concern. Exhibitors find themselves having to compete with not just radio, or television, or redistribution of the population from urban to suburban areas. Rather, one-at-a-time competition has given way to all-at-once confrontation.

Hope, however, for the survival of the movie theater is offered by some observers. A panel of industry experts at a 1984 Women in Film symposium held in Los Angeles were unanimous in their optimism on the future of movies and theatrical exhibition (48). On a separate occasion, current NATO president Joel Resnick cited 1983 theatrical grosses, which were up nine percent over 1982, and data showing that moviegoing has increased 20 percent over the past four years as the basis for his positive posture (145). Data collected by the Newspaper Advertising Bureau in 1981 showed that two-thirds of the respondents agreed with the statement that "theaters add something to the movie experience that TV does not"; even greater agreement (74 percent) was found among the key moviegoing group of 18 to 34-year-olds (120, p. 32).

Paramount Picture's Richard Frank states that "the name of the game is sequential distribution [of films] and it starts with the theatrical run" (105, p. 53). Communications consultant Morton D. Wax asserts that "theatrical exhibition anoints, endorses, and awards any picture with commercial value" (192). Litman's research found that "boxoffice performance is strongly correlated to television ratings" (98, p. 50; see also 97, 176). Moreover,

> a feature's value in ancillary markets is increased by even an unsuccessful theatrical release. Exposure of the film in theaters appears to serve as a "quality signal" to later patrons by distinguishing it, for example, from "made-for-TV" movies, which generally cost less and have inferior reputations (189, p. 5).

Michael Nielsen suggests that theatrical release "is increasingly becoming a 'market test'" for ancillary markets (125, p. 39). In short, it is asserted that the theatrical performance of a film is the product value criterion which determines fee schedules for subsequent forms of release. Nevertheless, such common industry wisdom did not deter HBO from producing *The Terry Fox Story* and offering it to subscribers. Thus, on May 22, 1983 this movie became "the first major feature film ever produced for initial release to pay television" (19, p. 43). Ed Bleier, Warner Brothers' East Coast President, warned that, "If HBO's power grows much more, the whole supply of theatrical movies will dry up" (19, p. 44). Although perhaps somewhat hyperbolic, supporting evidence for this may be found in the case of the Oscar-winning *Tender Mercies*. The film was partially financed by HBO with the stipulation that HBO would have exclusive rights to the picture one year after theatrical release. Allegations have been raised, especially after the Academy Awards ceremony, that the film had a slow audience build and had not exhausted its theatrical audience; thus potential admissions were lost to the pay TV service (see 152).

Confidence that theatrical exhibition will remain viable is reflected in the rate at which new screens and/or theaters are being added. According to a May 1984 report in *Newsweek,* "theaters are being built at a record pace" as a result of the increased number of films being released and the consequent need for exhibition sites (134). Estimates of an additional 1,400 screens in 1984 have been offered (116, p. 76). The largest U.S. theater chain, General Cinema Corp., will add 100 screens, AMC Entertainment 132, United Artists Communications, Inc. will add 250 to the more than 1,000 it already has, and Loew's Theatres began a $40 million three-year building program (116, 134).

One clear impact of the introduction of multiple forms of competition is that the window between theatrical and nontheatrical release is closing. The smaller the window, the less the opportunity for some (perhaps most) films to demonstrate their legs, or box office strength. That is, a movie which needs time to generate positive word-of-mouth may suffer by virtue of "small" opening week returns. Anything short of a blockbuster may well be relegated to "marginal" or "failure" status.

In December 1980, 20th Century-Fox decided to release *Nine to Five* on video cassette the same day it opened the picture theatrically. Exhibitors managed to "persuade" Fox to do otherwise by threatening to pull the film from their theaters (see 62, p. 23). Just a couple of years later, however, emboldened by premium TV's increasing audience attraction, Universal became the first studio to release a film theatrically and on pay TV day and date. Although financially disappointing in both venues, the February 18, 1983 release of *The Pirates of Penzance* is an ominous harbinger of what may become at least an optional pattern of film releasing (see 19, 30, 105, 121). Should the strategy prove successful, the product value criterion of theatrical returns will, of course, go by the wayside and exhibitors will be left with fewer and fewer films and patrons.

Still, as was pointed out in the discussion of movie audiences, absolute annihilation of the audience is unlikely. Nevertheless, the new technologies will have clearly dysfunctional consequences to exhibition. The already endangered drive-in theater will likely see its demise hastened in all but the most hospitable climates (see 11). Further ramifications on film exhibition may be gleaned from the history of mass communications; typically, the introduction of new media forms meant that existing media were forced to content-specialize as a result of "demassification" of their audiences. Thus, we might expect film exhibitors, too, to begin focusing their audience appeal. Film exhibition already has outlets for a few distinct genres; perhaps most obvious are theaters which feature sexually explicit movies exclusively. Other types of specialty theaters may evolve including an increase in the number of houses which screen art (see 10), or repertory films, chop-socky movies, and so on (see 168). In a limited number of locations (e.g., Hartford, CT and Burlington, VT), dinner-cinema theaters, much like the stage dinner theaters, have initiated service. And, in addition to such content-related changes, exhibitors may place increased emphasis on concession stands, patron services and conveniences, and use of cinema advertising to bolster their profit margins (see 40).

Advertising of products on movie screens has a long history and can serve as an illustrative example of this last point. In 1931, Chesterfield cigarettes sponsored "Movie Memories" in which the product was advertised in the title credits (128). In 1951 Raines found audience reaction to cinema advertising nearly equally divided between favoring (38 percent) and opposing (35 percent; 27 percent reported no opinion) (146, see also 37). By 1958 *Printers' Ink* was reporting an upsurge of screen ads (1); that television was becoming more widely diffused at this time is not coincidental. By July 1984, Screenvision, a major distributor for movie advertising, claimed it had ads on 3,800 of the U.S. movie screens (34) and projected continued growth (68).

Finally, exhibitors may increasingly turn to new technologies as an aid to their business. Rather than attempting to compete, their strategy may well become cooperation with and cooptation of technology. Not the same technology, of course, but use of selected technologies that will result in brighter, sharper screen images, conversion to projection systems such as Showscan, equipping theaters for satellite reception of high definition images (see 167), and so forth (see 137, pp. 390-402). Already theaters have begun renting and selling in their lobbies video cassettes of the movies they are showing on their screen (see 9); plans for using automatic teller machines to issue and bill for discount movie theater tickets have also been suggested (43).

Historically, exhibitors have, as a group, been skeptical of and slow to adopt new technological innovations, especially those which they perceive as simply adding to their expenses without substantially increasing their revenues. Aldridge has traced this pattern of behavior back to the innovation of sound (3). Contemporary reports suggest the pattern is being broken (see, e.g., 168). Perhaps the most interesting development among exhibitors is what is being labeled "electronic cinema." Broadly defined, electronic cinema includes the production of theatrical films on videotape as well as their distribution (by, e.g., satellite), and exhibition (see 125). Clearly, some of these technological innovations will have to await refinement until they are adopted. Speakers at a 1984 International Tape/Disc Association seminar, including representatives from Sony and General Electric, predicted that satellite-fed video distribution of movies would occur in about five years (154). Likewise, large-screen film is biding its time. Large-screen film differs from wide screen in that it utilizes "nearly the whole field of vision for each audience member" (170, p. 23). Imax, Omnivision, Dynavision, Envirovision, and Showscan are all large-screen processes which are either presently or nearly available (see 24, 31, 63, 168, 170). Showscan, for instance, which is available and has been tested on audiences, is a 70 mm. film projected at 60 frames a second; it more than doubles the standard size of frame and projection speed (84). Showscan's developer, Douglas Trumball, has reported that physiological tests revealed heart rate and galvanic skin response "far exceeding the normal level" among viewers (63). However, he also notes the studios' reluctance to commit the money to produce Showscan movies and exhibitors' reluctance to purchase the new equipment necessary to show the movies (31).

As Polon wrote, with research and development, "the motion picture industry can dominate the very technologies that seem to menace it" (137, p. 402). The production and distribution sectors have taken the lead in this regard; it is likely that the exhibition branch will not be far behind.

Summary

Of the three sectors of the industry, it may be that production and distribution stand to gain the most and exhibition the least as a result of the introduction of new technologies. As Wasko has noted, the continued strength and survival of the production-distribution branches is ensured by at least four factors: Hollywood's large home market guarantees "enough revenue to recoup initial production investments, test risky products or marketing strategies, and develop specialized products for 'minority' audiences"; "de facto protectionism" largely closes the U.S. market to foreigners, thereby lowering the threat of external competition; Hollywood's international distribution system "remains strong, effective, and profitable"; and diversification among the Hollywood majors has prepared them with "new marketing strategies" and "enhanced merchandising schemes" for both software and hardware (188, pp. 102-104). Nielsen has suggested that the new technologies offer, for film producers and distributors, what largely amounts to a trade-off: although the new technologies will cut into box office revenues, such innovations as pay-per-view will replace those lost profits (123). Conglomeration (i.e., the ill-fated Premiere venture and the "up and running" Tri-Star), too, will help reduce the threat of new technologies by spreading risk across several markets. Also, the production sector has embraced technological development as one means for competing: Dolby and stereo sound, Steadicams and Skycams enhance the production values of movies. Thus, although noticeable shifts have taken place in response to the new technologies, the production and distribution branches of the industry are certain to endure, with perhaps minor fluctuations in the precise configuration of filmic content and mode of delivery.

The outlook for exhibitors, while less rosy, is still largely positive. Like the producers, they, too, have embraced technology as a means to compete with technology. Adoption of appropriate high fidelity sound reproduction systems and screen technologies enhance the theatrical experience; even drive-in operators are responsive as increasingly they are implementing high luminance, daylight containment screens such as Protolite (see 11). At the NATO "Supershow '83," industry reporter Art Murphy of *Variety* said that "while some marginal theaters may close, by the end of the century, even if the sky falls in, there will be an irreducible minimum of 10,000 to 12,000 screens" in the United States (quoted in 8, p. 11). (The U.S. Commerce Department estimates that there are some 16,712 theaters and 21,423 screens in the U.S.; see 46, p. 30A.) Supporting data for such optimism includes record-breaking box office for the first nine months of 1983 at $2.937 billion (8, p. 10) and projections for $4 billion in admission in 1984 (177). On the downside, exhibitors are faced with a closing window between theatrical and nontheatrical release, increased ticket prices that may inhibit attendance, and audience research which indicates that, in Sweden at least, although the average amount of time spent at the cinema remained constant between 1977 and 1979, movies accounted for the least amount of total media consumption (see 69, p. 27). Whether "showmanship," by itself, including the glitzy, gauche gimmicks of Hollywood hype so popular in the 1950s and 1960s, can turn the tide against such threats is doubtful.

CONCLUSION

The future of the film audience and of the film industry in light of the new communication technologies are mutually dependent. There is, in short, no strict dividing line between audience and industry on this question; changes in one component necessarily affect the other. As Komatsuzaki has written: "The relationship between technological possibilities and social need is crucial to the acceptance of a new medium in society" (83, p. 273). The evidence does not support extreme predictions which call for the disappearance of the medium or its audience. Instead, what seems most likely to occur is a nearly identical repetition of the kinds of changes which took place when other new media forms entered the marketplace. Although the introduction of television no doubt caused the demise of general circulation magazines, it also caused the development of special interest periodicals.

To paint an overoptimistic picture would, however, be foolish. Exhibitors will be faced with declining admissions; producers and distributors with perhaps a greater number of venues for their product but not necessarily a greater number of independent buyers due to oligopolistic control of the moving image media market; audiences, with perhaps more technological gadgetry but diminished quality of content. Sherman offers an interesting contemporary scenario being played out in Hollywood production offices. Revenues from new technologies are still perceived as a kind of bonus or windfall profit among moviemakers. About one-quarter of the average production cost for a movie may be generated by rentals to HBO-like organizations. Such income provides the illusion of comfort and a financial cushion since the producers have been quite "accustomed to making movies profitably without these extra revenues, [thus] many figure that now almost any film, no matter how awful, is protected to some degree from loss" (163, p. 205). This is plainly deceptive for the financial risks still remain.

Nonetheless, Hollywood learned to live with radio and television; the evidence suggests a similar coming-to-terms with the new communications technologies. Unlike the past, the movie industry seems to be responding reasonably rapidly to technological change, doing more than simply tinkering with the technology, and realizing greater profits in the process.

The changes wrought by the new technologies have clear implications for mass communications theory and research. Just as many of the new technologies are aiming at more narrow or specialized audiences, so too will cinema. This is all part of a trend toward demassification of the media audience. Along with demassification comes fragmentation of the audience and more specialized content. These effects, in turn, result in additional fragmenting of motives for movie viewing ("attendance" may become an anachronism) and increased variety and specialization of gratifications sought and obtained. Reorganization and reconceptualization of the movie uses and gratifications hierarchy, as well as new uses and gratifications, are likely consequences (see 198). Moreover, audiences may be redefining their perceptions of film's value to their lives. Jassem and Desmond point out that the new technologies raise important concerns regarding communications theory and the relevancy of traditional questions employed by media theory (71). The need to consider and revise traditional media theories and assumptions becomes all the more clear and urgent in light of the rapid pace of change. Future research efforts will do well to begin the process of taking into account such issues as we begin to explore the new communications environment.

REFERENCES

1.   "Advertising in the Movies: An Old Medium with New Services, New Strength." *Printer's Ink*, August 1, 1958, pp. 50-51.
2.   Agostino, Donald E., Herbert A. Terry, and Rolland C. Johnson. "Home Video Recorders: Rights and Ratings." *Journal of Communication* 30 (4), Autumn 1980, pp. 28-35.
3.   Aldridge, Henry B. "New York Theatres and Film Exhibition in America." Paper presented at the Society for Cinema Studies conference, New York City, April 1981.
4.   Andrew, Dudley. "The Postwar Struggle for Color." *Cinema Journal* 13 (2), Spring 1979, pp. 41-52.
5.   Arnheim, Rudolf. *Film as Art*. Berkeley: University of California Press, 1957.
6.   Associated Press. "Japan's VTR Exports Hit Record." In *Democrat and Chronicle* (Rochester, NY), October 29, 1983, p. 11C.
7.   Auerbach, Alexander. "Pay Cable Helps Theatre Boxoffice, Market Study Shows." *Boxoffice* 119 (7), July 1983, pp. 20-21.

8. Auerbach, Alexander. "Supershow '83 Bullish on Future of Exhibition." *Boxoffice* 120 (1), January 1984, pp. 10-12.
9. Auerbach, Alexander. "Big Screen + Little Screen = Big Money." *Boxoffice* 120 (5), May 1984, p. 6.
10. Austin, Bruce A. "Portrait of an Art Film Audience." *Journal of Communication* 34 (1), Winter 1984, pp. 74-87.
11. Austin, Bruce A. "The Development and Decline of the Drive-In Movie Theater." In Bruce A. Austin (Ed.), *Current Research in Film: Audiences, Economics and Law*, vol. 1, pp. 59-91. Norwood, NJ: Ablex Publishing Corp., 1985.
12. Bednarski, P.J. "Living with Tele1st." *Channels* 4, May/June 1984, pp. 55-56.
13. Behrens, Steve. "Shortcut to the Home." *Channels* 4 (1), March/April 1984, p. 30.
14. Bolton, Ted. "Videotex and Diffusion Theory." Paper presented at the Eastern Communication Association conference, Ocean City, MD, April 1983.
15. Bortnick, Jane. "Transborder Data Flow Issues." *Electronic Publishing Review* 1 (4), December 1981, pp. 263-266.
16. Brown, Garrett. "It's a Bird . . . It's a Plane . . . It's a . . . Camera!" *American Film* 8 (10), September 1983, pp. 59-61.
17. Brown, Les. "Cable TV: Wiring for Abundance." *Channels* 3 (4), November/December 1983, p. 25.
18. "Cable Execs, Film Exhibitors Pass Small Peace Pipe at NATO." *Variety*, November 9, 1983, p. 27.
19. Caranicas, Peter. "Hollywood Wakes Up and Smells the Coffee." *Channels* 3 (3), July/August 1983, pp. 43-45.
20. Carey, James W. "Changing Communications Technology and the Nature of the Audience." *Journal of Advertising* 9 (2), 1980, pp. 3-9, 43.
21. Clark, Kenneth R. "The Making of a Giant: How Cable Changed America." *Chicago Tribune*, October 30, 1983, sec. 4, pp. 1, 4.
22. Cohn, Lawrence. "400-Plus Pics Skedded for '84 Release." *Variety*, July 4, 1984, pp. 3, 26, 28.
23. Criner, Kathleen. "New Opportunities for MDS Technology." *Presstime* 5 (4), April 1983, pp. 14-15.
24. Crook, David. "Movie House: A Trip to Infinity." *Los Angeles Times*, June 18, 1981, pp. 1, 4.
25. DeFleur, Melvin L. and Sandra Ball-Rokeach. *Theories of Mass Communications*, 4th ed. New York: Longman, 1982.
26. "Dialogue on Film: Peter Yates." *American Film* 9 (6), April 1984, pp. 14-18.
27. Dizard, Wilson P. "The U.S. Position: DBS and Free Flow." *Journal of Communication* 30 (2), Spring 1980, pp. 157-168.
28. Dizard, Wilson P., Jr. *The Coming Information Age*. New York: Longman, 1982.
29. Dominick, Joseph R. "New Technologies: Implications for Research." *Feedback* 22 (3), November 1980, pp. 3-6.
30. "Double-Edged Disappointment." *Time*, March 7, 1983, p. 69.
31. Dowell, Pat and Ray Heinrich. "Bigger than Life." *American Film* 9 (7), May 1984, pp. 49-53.
32. Ducey, Richard V., Dean M. Krugman and Donald Eckrich. "Predicting Market Segments in the Cable Industry: The Basic and Pay Subscribers." *Journal of Broadcasting* 27 (2), Spring 1983, pp. 155-161.
33. Duncan, David J. "Leisure Types: Factor Analysis of Leisure Profiles." *Journal of Leisure Research* 10 (2), 1978, pp. 113-125.
34. "Eastern News—Philadelphia." *Boxoffice* 120 (7), July 1984, p. 29.
35. Edgerton, Gary R. *American Film Exhibition and an Analysis of the Motion Picture Industry's Market Structure, 1963-1980*. New York: Garland Publishing, 1983 (reprint of a Ph.D. dissertation, University of Massachusetts, 1981).

36. Edmundson, Mark. "LPTV: The Sleeping Dwarf." *Channels,* 3 (4), November/December 1983, p. 55.
37. Elliott, Frank R. "Memory for Trade Names Presented in Screen, Radio and Television Advertisements." *Journal of Applied Psychology* 21, 1937, pp. 653-667.
38. Epstein, Becky Sue. "Music Video—The Hot New Way to Sell Hot New Movies." *Boxoffice* 120 (7), July 1984, pp. 12-13, 16-17.
39. Everson, William K. *American Silent Film.* New York: Oxford University Press, 1978.
40. "Extra Income Opportunities in the Theatre, Part II." *Boxoffice* 118 (12), December 1982, pp. 83-85.
41. Fagan, Keith N. "Direct Broadcast Satellites and the FCC: A Case Study in the Regulation of New Technology." *Federal Bar News & Journal* 29 (1), November 1982, pp. 378-384.
42. Fielding, Raymond. "Recent Electronic Innovations in Professional Motion Picture Production." *Journal of Film and Video* 36 (2), Spring 1984, pp. 43-49, 72.
43. Fisher, Gary. "Computers in the Theatre." *Boxoffice* 120 (3), March 1984, pp. 44-46.
44. Fombrun, Charles and W. Graham Astley. "The Telecommunications Community: An Institutional Overview." *Journal of Communication* 32 (4), Autumn 1982, pp. 56-68.
45. Friedman, Mel. "SMATV: Stealing Cable's Thunder." *Channels* 3 (4), November/December 1983, p. 28.
46. Gertner, Richard (Ed.). *Motion Picture Almanac 1983.* New York: Quigley Publishing Co., 1983.
47. Gitlin, Todd. *Inside Prime Time.* New York: Pantheon Books, 1983.
48. Glasser, Kit. "Experts Upbeat on Film Future." *Boxoffice* 120 (4), April 1984, pp. 50-51.
49. Goldwyn, Samuel. "Hollywood in the Television Age." *New York Times Magazine,* February 13, 1949, pp. 15, 44, 47.
50. Gomery, Douglas. "The American Film Industry of the 1970's: Stasis in the 'New Hollywood.'" *Wide Angle* 5 (4), 1983, pp. 52-59.
51. Gomery, J. Douglas. "The 'Warner-Vitaphone Peril': The American Film Industry Reacts to the Innovation of Sound." *Journal of the University Film Association* 28 (1), Winter 1976, pp. 11-19.
52. Gross, Lynne Schafer. *The New Television Technologies.* Dubuque, IA: Wm. C. Brown, 1983.
53. Grunig, James E. "Time Budgets, Level of Involvement and Use of the Mass Media." *Journalism Quarterly* 56 (2), Summer 1979, pp. 248-261.
54. Guback, Thomas. *The International Film Industry: Western Europe and America Since 1945.* Bloomington: Indiana University Press, 1969.
55. Guback, Thomas. "Theatrical Film." In Benjamin M. Compaine (Ed.), *Who Owns the Media,* pp. 179-241. White Plains, NY: Knowledge Industry Publications, 1979.
56. Guback, Thomas H. and Dennis J. Dombkowski. "Television and Hollywood: Economic Relations in the 1970s." *Journal of Broadcasting* 20 (4), Fall 1976, pp. 511-527.
57. Guild, Hazel. "As Vid Recorders Gain Ground, Worries Over Porno Grow, Too." *Variety,* October 19, 1983, p. 34.
58. Hampton, Benjamin B. *A History of the Movies.* New York: Covici, Friede, 1931 (republished as *History of the American Film Industry.* New York: Dover Publications, 1970).
59. Hawkins, John. "Satellites: The Next Wave of Television." *InterMedia* 9 (4), July 1981, pp. 14-25.
60. Henderson, James M. and Richard E. Quandt. *Microeconomic Theory: A Mathematical Approach.* New York: McGraw-Hill, 1958.
61. "High Definition Television." In Richard Patterson and Dana White (Eds.), *Electronic Production Techniques,* pp. 21-25. An *American Cinematographer* reprint, 1984.
62. Hill, Doug. "It's Not All Popcorn and Profits Now." *TV Guide,* March 20, 1982, pp. 20-23.
63. Hoban, Phoebe. "Fast Films." *American Film* 6 (5), February 1984, p. 100.

64. Holbrook, Morris B. and Donald R. Lehmann. "Allocating Discretionary Time: Complementarity Among Activities." *Journal of Consumer Research* 7, March 1981, pp. 395-406.

65. Howard, Herbert H. "Ownership Trends in Cable Televevision: 1972-1979." *Journalism Quarterly* 58 (2), Summer 1981, pp. 288-291.

66. Hulten, Oluf. "Home Video—A Threat to Public-Service Television?" *EBU Review* 31 (2), March 1980, pp. 24-26.

67. Hulten, Oluf. "Using Video in Sweden." *InterMedia* 11 (1), January 1983, pp. 42-44.

68. "In-Theatre Commercials on Upswing in 1984." *Boxoffice* 120 (4), April 1984, pp. 65-67.

69. Ivre, Ivar. "Mass Media: Costs, Choices and Freedom." *InterMedia* 9 (5), September 1981, pp. 26-31.

70. James, Watson S. "Jay." "The New Electronic Media: An Overview." *Journal of Advertising Research* 23 (4), August/September 1983, pp. 33-37.

71. Jassem, Harvey C. and Roger Jon Desmond. "Theory Construction and Research in Mass Communication: The Implications of New Technologies." Paper presented at the Eastern Communication Association conference, Philadelphia, PA, March 1984.

72. Jeffres, Leo W. "Cable TV and Viewer Selectivity." *Journal of Broadcasting* 22 (2), Spring 1978, pp. 167-177.

73. Jowett, Garth. *Film: The Democratic Art.* Boston: Little, Brown and Co., 1976.

74. Jowett, Garth and James M. Linton. *Movies as Mass Communication.* Beverly Hills: Sage Publications, 1980.

75. Kahn, Robert D. "More Messages from the Medium." *Technology Review* 86 (1), January 1983, pp. 49-51.

76. Kaplan, Stuart J. "The Impact of Cable Television Services on the Use of Competing Media." *Journal of Broadcasting* 22 (2), Spring 1978, pp. 155-165.

77. Katz, Elihu, Martin L. Levin and Herbert Hamilton. "Traditions of Research on the Diffusion of Innovation." *American Sociological Review* 28 (2), April 1963, pp. 237-252.

78. Kilday, Gregg. "Ninth Annual Grosses Gloss." *Film Comment* 20 (2), March-April 1984, pp. 62-66.

79. Kindem, Gorham. "The Demise of Kinemacolor: Technological, Legal, Economic, and Aesthetic Problems in Early Color Cinema History." *Cinema Journal* 20 (2), Spring 1981, pp. 3-14.

80. Kindred, Jack. "West German Exhibs Hit by Homevid." *Variety,* January 25, 1984, pp. 5, 34.

81. Klein, Judy E. "Coppola Makes 'Rumble Fish'—The Coppola Way." *Boxoffice* 119 (11), November 1983, pp. 10-11.

82. Kleinfield, Sonny. "Time Inc. is Everything." *Rolling Stone,* Issue #407, October 27, 1983, pp. 48-56.

83. Komatsuzaki, Seisuke. "Social Impacts of New Communications Media: The Japanese Experience." *Telecommunications Policy* 6 (4), December 1982, pp. 269-275.

84. Krohn, Bill and Harley Lond. "Showscan: A New Type of Exhibition for a Revolutionary Film Process." *Boxoffice* 120 (2), February 1984, pp. 10-11.

85. Krugman, Dean M. and Clifford Christians. "Cable Television: Promise versus Performance." *Gazette* 27 (3), 1981, pp. 193-209.

86. Krugman, Dean M. and Donald Eckrich. "Differences in Cable and Pay-Cable Audiences." *Journal of Advertising Research* 22 (4), August/September 1982, pp. 23-29.

87. Lachenbruch, David. "Home Video: Home is Where the Action Is." *Channels* 3 (4), November/December 1983, pp. 42-43.

88. Lachenbruch, David. "The VCR is Changing the Whole TV Picture." *Channels* 4 (1), March/April 1984, p. 16.

89. Lachenbruch, David. "Hear Ye! Hear Ye! Stereo Comes to TV." *TV Guide,* June 9, 1984, pp. 41-44.

90. Landro, Laura. "Pay-TV Industry Facing Problems After Misjudging Market Demand." *Wall Street Journal*, June 29, 1983, p. 37.

91. Lees, David and Stan Berkowitz. *The Movie Business*. New York: Vintage Books, 1981.

92. Levin, Harvey J. "Competition Among Mass Media and the Public Interest." *Public Opinion Quarterly* 18 (1), Spring 1954, pp. 62-79.

93. Levy, Mark R. "Program Playback Preferences in VCR Households." *Journal of Broadcasting* 24 (3), Summer 1980, pp. 327-336.

94. Levy, Mark R. "Home Video Recorders: A User Survey." *Journal of Communication* 30 (4), Autumn 1980, pp. 23-27.

95. Levy, Mark R. "The Time-Shifting Use of Home Video Recorders." *Journal of Broadcasting* 27 (3), Summer 1983, pp. 263-268.

96. Levy, Mark R. "Home Video Recorders and Time Shifting." *Journalism Quarterly* 58 (3), Fall 1981, pp. 401-405.

97. Litman, Barry R. "Predicting TV Ratings for Theatrical Movies." *Journalism Quarterly* 56 (3), Autumn 1979, pp. 590-594, 694.

98. Litman, Barry R. "Decision-Making in the Film Industry: The Influence of the TV Market." *Journal of Communication* 32 (3), Summer 1982, pp. 33-52.

99. Littunen, Yrjo with Pertti Hemanus, Kaarle Nordenstreng, and Tapio Varis. "Cultural Problems of Direct Satellite Broadcasting." *International Social Science Journal* 32 (2), 1980, pp. 283-303.

100. Luther, Rodney. "Television and the Future of Motion Picture Exhibition." *Hollywood Quarterly* 5, 1951, pp. 164-177.

101. Maisel, Richard. "The Decline of Mass Media." *Public Opinion Quarterly* 37 (2), Summer 1973, pp. 159-170.

102. Marbach, William D. with Jennet Conant and Nancy Ukai. "TV's High-Tech Future." *Newsweek*, January 2, 1984, p. 70.

103. Marcus, Stanley. "The Viewer's Verdict So Far—On Cable TV." *Panorama* 1, October 1980, pp. 42-45.

104. Mareth, Paul. "The Video Disc: Shining a New Light." *Channels* 4 (1), March/April 1984, pp. 24-30.

105. Margulies, Lee. "Will Movie Theaters Survive Video?" *Home Video* 3, November 1982, pp. 50-53.

106. Mast, Gerald. *A Short History of the Movies* (3rd ed.). Indianapolis: Bobbs-Merrill, 1981.

107. Mayer, Michael F. *The Film Industries* (2nd ed.). New York: Hastings House, 1978.

108. McCombs, Maxwell E. "The End of Mass Communication." *Journalism Monographs* 24, August 1971, pp. 60-63.

109. McCombs, Maxwell E. and Chaim H. Eyal. "Spending on Mass Media." *Journal of Communication* 30 (1), Winter 1980, pp. 153-158.

110. McQuail, Denis, *Mass Communication Theory*. Beverly Hills: Sage Publications, 1983.

111. Metzger, Gale D. "Cable Television Audiences." *Journal of Advertising Research* 23 (4), August/September 1983, pp. 41-47.

112. Meyersohn, Rolf. "Television and the Rest of Leisure." *Public Opinion Quarterly* 32 (1), Spring 1968, pp. 102-112.

113. Mink, Edward. "Why the Networks will Survive Cable." *Atlantic Monthly*, December 1983, pp. 63-68.

114. Monaco, James. "The Silver Screen Under Glass." *Channels* 1 (3), August/September 1981, pp. 50-53.

115. "Movie Audience Marquee Values Traced Since 40s." *Gallup Report* #195, December 1981, pp. 3-26.

116. "Movie Screens are Popping Up All Over." *Business Week*, May 14, 1984, pp. 76, 81.

117. Murray, Lawerence L. "Complacency, Competition and Cooperation: The Film Industry Responds to the Challenge of Television." *Journal of Popular Film* 6 (1), 1977, pp. 47-70.
118. Nadel, Mark and Eli Noam (Eds.). "The Economics of Physical Distribution: Video Cassettes/ Discs & Movie Theater (*sic*) an Anthology." New York: Columbia University, Research Program in Telecommunications and Information Policy, 1983.
119. Nelson, Richard Alan. "Entering a Brave New World: The Impact of the New Information and Telecommunications Technologies." *Journal of the University Film and Video Association* 35 (4), Fall 1983, pp. 23-34.
120. Newspaper Advertising Bureau. *Movie-Going in the United States and Canada.* New York: Newspaper Advertising Bureau, October, 1981.
121. Nicholson, Tom with David T. Friendly and Peter McAlevey. "Hollywood's Play for the Pay-TV Crowd." *Newsweek,* February 21, 1983, p. 66.
122. Nicholson, Tom with Janet Huck and Peter McAlevey. "HBO Versus the Studios." *Newsweek,* November 15, 1982, p. 83.
123. Nielsen, Arthur C., Jr. "The Outlook for Electronic Media." *Journal of Advertising Research* 22 (6), December 1982/January 1983, pp. 9-16.
124. A.C. Nielsen Company. *1983 Annual Report.*
125. Nielsen, Michael. "Hollywood's High Frontier: The Emergence of Electronic Cinema." *Journal of Film and Video* 36 (2), Spring 1984, pp. 31-42, 72.
126. O'Connor, J. Patrick. "Cable Viewers: How to Pick the Right Channel for You." *TV Guide,* October 29, 1983, pp. 20-22.
127. Olshavsky, Richard W. "Time and the Rate of Adoption of Innovations." *Journal of Consumer Research* 6, March 1980, pp. 425-428.
128. "An Opinion on Screen Advertising." *Educational Screen* 10, April 1931, p. 112.
129. Ostroff, David H. "A History of STV, Inc. and the 1964 California Vote Against Pay Television." *Journal of Broadcasting* 27, (4), Fall 1983, pp. 371-386.
130. Ostrow, Joe. "Media Perspectives for the 80s: Nine Key Media Problems." *Media Asia* 7 (4), 1980, pp. 202-204, 214.
131. Paterson, Owen. "The British Renaissance: An Assessment of Satellite Development in the U.K." *Satellite Communications* 7 (1), January 1983, pp. 28-34.
132. Pauley, David and Connie Leslie. "The Videodisc Strikes Out." *Newsweek,* April 16, 1984, p. 69.
133. Pauley, David with Christopher Ma and Madlyn Resener. "Cracked Dishes: DBS's Doom" *Newsweek,* July 23, 1984, pp. 58-59.
134. Pauley, David with David T. Friendly and Michael Reese. "Big Bucks for the Big Screens." *Newsweek,* May 28, 1984, p. 63.
135. "The Pay Services: A Guide." *Channels* 3 (4), November/December 1983, p. 39.
136. "Pay-TV: An InterMedia Survey." *InterMedia* 10 (1), January 1982, pp. 1-16.
137. Polon, Martin. "Future Technologies in Motion Pictures." In Jason E. Squire (Ed.)., *The Movie Business Book,* pp. 388-403. Englewood Cliffs, NJ: Prentice-Hall, 1983.
138. Pollon, Michael. "DBS: The Space Race is On." *Channels* 3 (4), November/December 1983, p. 12.
139. Polskin, Howard. "Paramount Deal with Showtime Shakes Pay-TV." *TV Guide,* December 31, 1983, p. A-1.
140. Polskin, Howard. "ABC to Telecast Recent Movies to VCR Owners." *TV Guide,* January 14, 1984, p. A-1.
141. Polskin, Howard. "Few Subscribers to Wee-Hour Pay-TV Service." *TV Guide,* April 14, 1984, p. A-1.
142. Polskin, Howard. "What You Can Expect from Cable Now." *TV Guide,* June 2, 1984, pp. 2-8.
143. Polskin, Howard. "ABC Folds TeleFirst." *TV Guide,* June 23, 1984, p. A-1.

144. Pottle, Jack T. "Pay Television: A Primer on Competition." *Satellite Communications* 6, November 1982, pp. 26-30.

145. Quinn, John. "Resnick Offers Show-A-Rama Up Note on Future of Exhibition." *Variety,* March 21, 1984, pp. 4, 34.

146. Raines, I.I. "Preferences of a Small Town Motion Picture Audience." *Current Economic Comment,* May 1951, pp. 51-59.

147. Robinson, John P. *How Americans Use Time.* New York: Praeger Publishers, 1977.

148. Rogers, Everett M. and F. Floyd Shoemaker. *Communication of Innovations: A Cross-Cultural Approach* (2nd Ed.). New York: The Free Press, 1971.

149. Roper Organization, Inc. *Evolving Public Attitudes Toward Television and Other Mass Media.* New York: Television Information Office, 1981.

150. Rosenthal, Sharon. "Snapping Back at the Crockodile that Ate Hollywood." *TV Guide,* March 3, 1984, pp. 4-8.

151. Rothe, James T., Michael G. Harvey, and George C. Michael. "The Impact of Cable Television on Subscriber and Non-subscriber Behavior." *Journal of Advertising Research* 23 (4), August/September 1983, pp. 15-23.

152. Sanello, Frank. " 'Tender Mercies' Kept Out of Theaters Because of HBO." UPI report *Democrat and Chronicle* (Rochester, NY), April 12, 1984, p. 5C.

153. Sansweet, Stephen J. "Pay TV's Showtime and Movie Channel Agree to Merge in Five-Company Venture." *Wall Street Journal,* January 10, 1983, p. 4.

154. "Say Vid Exhibition 5 Years in Future." *Variety,* April 14, 1984, p. 7.

155. Schneider, Edward W. and Junius L. Bennion. *Videodiscs.* Englewood Cliffs, NJ: Prentice-Hall, 1981.

156. Schwarz, Michael. "A New World: Hollywood." *Channels* 1, February/March 1982, pp. 26-28.

157. Schwarz, Michael. "Turning Movie Houses Into Video Houses." *Channels* 2, April/May 1982, pp. 29-30.

158. Schwarz, Michael. "MDS: The Newest Channels in Town." *Channels* 3 (4), November/December 1983, pp. 33, 36.

159. Schwarz, Michael. "HDTV: High Resolution for the '90s." *Channels* 3 (4), November/December 1983, p. 56.

160. Sebestyen, Istvan. "The Videodisc Revolution." *Electronic Publishing Review* 2 (1), March 1982, pp. 41-89.

161. Seidman, Tony. "Homevid Aids Cinema B.O. for Two Pics." *Variety,* October 26, 1983, pp. 1, 396.

162. Shaffer, Helen B. "Movie-TV Competition." *Editorial Reports,* January 18, 1957, pp. 45-61.

163. Sherman, Stratford P. "Coming Soon: Hollywood's Epic Shakeout." *Fortune,* April 30, 1984, pp. 204-216.

164. Shyles, Leonard. "The Video Tape Recorder: Crown Prince of Home Video." *Feedback* 22 (4), Winter 1981, pp. 1-5.

165. Silverman, Syd. "Entertainment in the Satellite Era." *Variety,* October 26, 1983, pp. 13, 99.

166. Sklar, Robert. *Movie-Made America: A Cultural History of American Movies.* New York: Vintage Books, 1975.

167. Smith, F. Leslie. "Technology and Introduction to Broadcasting." *Feedback* 23 (4), Winter 1982, pp. 1-4.

168. Stabiner, Karen. "The Shape of Theaters to Come." *American Film* 7 (10), September 1982, pp. 51-56.

169. Stanley, Robert. *The Celluloid Empire.* New York: Hastings House, 1978.

170. Stegman, Allan. "The Large-Screen Film: A Viable Entertainment Alternative to High Definition Television." *Journal of Film and Video* 36 (2), Spring 1982, pp. 21-30, 72.

171. Sterling, Christiopher H. and John M. Kittross. *Stay Tuned: A Concise History of American Broadcasting*. Belmont, CA: Wadsworth Publishing Co., 1978.

172. Stoller, David. "Cable Industry: End of the Gold Rush." *Channels,* 3 (4), November/December 1983, p. 26.

173. Stuart, Frederic. *The Effects of Television on the Motion Picture and Radio Industries*. NY: Arno Press, 1976 (reprint of a Ph.D. dissertation, Columbia University, 1960).

174. Suskin, Philip A. "Satellite to Viewer: Will the Direct Connection Work?" *TV Guide*, March 24, 1984, pp. 8-9.

175. Talen, Julie. "STV: Going, Going . . ." *Channels* 3 (4), November/December 1983, p. 33.

176. Taylor, Ryland A. "Television Movie Audiences and Movie Awards: A Statistical Study." *Journal of Broadcasting* 18 (2), Spring 1974, pp. 181-186.

177. "TEA Meeting Looks to Bright Future." *Boxoffice* 120 (7), July 1984, p. 18.

178. Toffler, Alvin. *Future Shock*. New York: Bantam Book, 1970.

179. Toffler, Alvin. *The Third Wave*. New York: Bantam Books, 1980.

180. Toll, Robert C. *The Entertainment Machine*. New York: Oxford University Press, 1982.

181. Traub, James. "Satellites: The Birds that Make it All Fly." *Channels* 3 (4), November/December 1983, pp. 8-9.

182. Traub, James. "The Big Turn-On in India." *Channels* 4 (1), March/April 1984, pp. 7-8.

183. United Media Enterprises. *Where Does the Time Go? The United Media Enterprises Report on Leisure in America*. New York: Newspaper Enterprise Association, 1983.

184. United States. Senate Committee on the Judiciary, 97th Congress, 1st and 2nd Sessions. *Copyright Infringements (Audio and Video Recorders)*. Serial No. J-97-84. Washington, D.C.: U.S. Government Printing Office, 1982.

185. "Viewers Turn Off Subscription TV." *Business Week*, May 16, 1983, pp. 28-29.

186. Walker, Alexander. *The Shattered Silents: How the Talkies Came to Stay*. New York: William Morrow and Co., 1978.

187. Warner, Harry P. "Television and the Motion Picture Industry." *Hollywood Quarterly* 2, 1946, pp. 11-18.

188. Wasko, Janet. "Hollywood, New Technology and Interntional Banking: A Formula for Success." In Bruce A. Austin (Ed.), *Current Research in Film: Audiences, Economics, and Law,* vol. 1, pp. 101-110. Norwood, NJ: Ablex Publishing Corp., 1985.

189. Waterman, David. "Videocassettes, Videodiscs, and the Role of Theatrical Distribution." Paper presented at the Columbia University Research Program in Telecommunications and Information Policy conference, New York City, March 1984.

190. Waters, Harry F. with Mark D. Uehling. "Cable's Lost Promise." *Newsweek*, October 5, 1984, pp. 103-105.

191. Watkins, Roger. "Show Biz in Int'l TV Power Play: Giant Companies Form Satellite Consortium." *Variety*, November 9, 1983, pp. 1, 68.

192. Wax, Morton D. "When Do the Exhibitors Get a Piece of the Royal Pie?" *Boxoffice* 120 (3), March 1984, p. 54.

193. Webster, James G. "The Impact of Cable and Pay Cable Television on Local Audiences." *Journal of Broadcasting* 27 (2), Spring 1983, pp. 119-126.

194. Wenden, D.J. *The Birth of the Movies*. New York: E.P. Dutton, 1974.

195. Wigand, Rolf T. "The Direct Satellite Connection: Definitions and Prospects." *Journal of Communication* 30 (2), Spring 1980, pp. 140-146.

196. Williams, Donald O. "Television of Abundance—The Challenge." *Feedback* 22 (3), November 1980, pp. 9-10.

197. Williams, Frederick. *The Communications Revolution*. Beverly Hills: Sage Publications, 1982.

198. Williams, Frederick, Amy Friedman Phillips, and Patrical Lum. "Gratifications Associated with Communications Technologies." Paper presented at the Speech Communication Association conference, Chicago, IL, November 1984.

199. Williams, Wenmouth, Jr. and Mitchell E. Shapiro. "A Study of the Effects In-Home Entertainment Alternatives Have on Film Attendance." In Bruce A. Austin (Ed.), *Current Research in Film: Audiences, Economics, and Law,* vol. 1, pp. 93-100. Norwood, NJ: Ablex Publishing Corp., 1985.
200. Ziegler, Peggy and Joe Boyle. "Three Studios Buy into Movie Channel." *Multichannel News,* November 17, 1982, pp. 1, 139.
201. Zuckerman, Laurence. "Pay TV: HBO & The Also-Rans." *Channels* 3 (4), November/ December 1983, p. 32.

7

Industrialization of Entertainment in the United States*

Calvin Pryluck

By the time movies were first introduced at the end of the nineteenth century, entertainment was already a semi-industrialized enterprise; some branches of show business operated under patterns of industrial organization that emphasized standardized product, division of labor, and centralized control. At the same time, other entertainments continued under earlier, more amorphous, and less industrialized patterns of organization. In the current era of hundred million dollar deals and complex organization in the film industry, it is easy to forget that the mass production characteristics of the industry are not twentieth century aberrations; these are practices that stem from historical developments that stretch back at least 150 years.

Understanding the various levels of industrialization and their development can be useful since they established the matrix of choices that were available to entrepreneurs presenting new forms of entertainment at the end of the nineteenth century. The point is a simple one: the history of film did not start just on April 23, 1896, with the first commercial showing at Koster and Bial's Music Hall in New York City. An indication of the state of writing in film history is that considerable effort has been expended arguing priorities of invention and presentation; yet it does not matter which dates are chosen as the "first," because the results have been the same. Much that has been written treats "pre-cinema" as a technological story, isolated from a larger context, although we are dealing with a single phenomenon—entertainment—of which movies are only a part.

* A version of this article was presented at the Eastern Communication Association Convention in Philadelphia, March 1984.

Except for occasional efforts (e.g., 11, 34, 35), the history of entertainment in the United States as it has been written has been a history of particular types. Legitimate theater, circuses, minstrel shows, vaudeville, motion pictures, phonograph recording, and broadcasting have been studied in isolation from each other and only incidentally cross-referenced. Some doctoral dissertations in the past several years have tried to broaden the context, but typically this work consisted of connecting film to a single branch of the entertainment industry, such as vaudeville, television, or theater (2, 9, 20).

Scattered through all of these accounts are common threads that can be integrated in an attempt to deal seriously with the complex relationships between older entertainment forms and the newer mass entertainment forms. This chapter draws upon various of these secondary accounts in an attempt to elaborate the historical context for the current structure of the film industry, examining particularly the development in entertainment of the industrial patterns of organization that stressed standardization, specialization, and centralization.

IN THE BEGINNING . . .

In contrast to the highly organized industry of the late twentieth century, entertainment in much of the nineteenth century was a diffuse, undifferentiated, itinerant trade that slowly evolved industrial characteristics. This was a trade practiced by largely anonymous strollers whose names are known only by the accident of surviving issues of newspapers, or incidental mention in the memoirs of others.

A few examples may give some sense of entertainment in this period. At one tavern, whose owner kept a diary, guests were entertained by a Mr. Neventon, his wife (name unknown to us), and a Mr. Todd in a performance that included a live wolf, a wildcat, a magic lantern, plus acrobatics on the slack wire and slack rope. Later, the same tavern had the opportunity of displaying a puppet show if the tavern owner were willing to offer the single puppeteer free room and board and a percentage of the ticket sales (27, pp. 115–116).

A man whose name may have been Jacob or David Crowinshield or, perhaps, John C. Crownshield apparently traveled alone with the first elephant in the United States, charging "twelve and a half cents a look" (6, p. 2; 11, p. 40; 22, p. 125). An early display was in York, Pennsylvania in 1796; a year later the elephant and its owner were in Massachusetts, and Charleston, South Carolina. In 1806, they were in Philadelphia, and five years later in Gettysburg, Pennsylvania (22, p. 125).

Many other troupes were family groups such as the Brittinghams—father, mother, and more than one daughter apparently—who travelled through the upper reaches of the Missouri River "at the border of civilization," in a pair of lashed-together canoes. Itinerant artist Alfred Waugh, who left a long-unpublished memoir, witnessed performances by the family at Lexington, Missouri in the winter of 1846 and again 12 miles west in Independence, early in May of the same year. One program consisted of songs, dances, and a parody of David Garrick's play *High Life Below Stairs*, entitled in this version *Low Life Above Stairs*. Mr. Brittingham was apparently also a dancing master, offering lessons at the various stops in their travels (36, pp. 78, 105–106). The scattered dates that are known for people like Crowinshield and the Brittinghams are evocative for their suggestion of continuity; one can wonder what the performers were doing between the documented dates.

Other family groups are better known. There was William and Sarah Chapman, their four children, a daughter-in-law, and a grandson who traveled and performed in a "Floating Theater." In the period between 1831 and 1847, the Chapman family performed in most towns accessible to rivers, including, at one point, New York City (12).

About the same time, a young man in his twenties, Fayette Lodawick Robinson—who adopted the name Yankee Robinson—started on his career as an entertainer "with a second hand curtain depicting a Grecian urn, and two paintings of the life of Christ . . . . During the next few years, Robinson tried everything from blackface to high tragedy, went out with two different circuses, leased a musuem . . . toured with his own *Uncle Tom's Cabin* show under canvas" (22, p. 196).

The most elaborate form of organization early in the nineteenth century was an entertainment troupe, managed by one of the performers, that traveled on unplanned tours, presenting something for everyone in a single performance. Shows would be a mixture of divertissements that might include a performance of *Hamlet* and a farce comedy with a title such as *The Day After the Wedding* or *The Pet of the Petticoats*. Interspersed in this double feature would be variety acts such as popular songs, dancing, juggling, and bird imitations. In other shows, the farce and variety would be accompanied by circus elements; horses were prominently featured in some of the dramas.

The principal economic characteristic of these and the thousands of similar undertakings is that they were simple proprietorships that intermixed business and personal fortunes or partnerships where income was distributed in equal shares for each performer with an additional share for the performer who served as manager and a few shares "for the show" to cover the costs of costumes, scenery, and props. The minimum investment required by these enterprises was gathered from personal resources—savings, personal loans, and the like—a process similar to childhood newspaper routes or lemonade stands. Bookings were equally casual. Such groups would "barnstorm" or "wildcat"; they would arrive at a locale and try to arrange a performance, staying as long as it seemed profitable. The venue for the performance would be any available space—sometimes literally a barn, often a tavern, occasionally a school; when all else failed, the company could "busk," entertaining on the streets for whatever change passers-by would be willing to contribute. This form of organization continued into the twentieth century for some shows. In an odd throwback, busking has become the venue of choice for contemporary street performers in some urban centers such as New York and San Francisco.

In the 1830s, other shows became more formal in their organization; performers were now salaried employees; a bonus at the end of the season might be used to reduce employee turnover; outside investors began to supply the necessary financing. Entertainment was becoming a business, not a calling.

Accompanying these changes was increasing differentiation of shows. Blackface acts that had been part of many shows from the beginning of the century became minstrel shows for a whole evening of blackface entertainment. Dramatic troupes increasingly emphasized the play; the entr'acte began to disappear in some companies. In the 1830s, other shows began to elaborate in the direction of modern circuses, distinct from theatrical performances. Exhibits of a single exotic animal expanded into menagerie shows; these shows added human performers: equestrians, acrobats, clowns and human freaks. Circuses were becoming the spectacles they are today.

These developments had consequences for the pattern of organization. Circuses and menageries were in their nature touring attractions; in any one season they had fundamentally one show to present; they quickly exhausted their audience potential. Rather than extended stays in one place, circuses returned annually for one-day stands that were the occasion for a festival day (11, pp. 284–286).

The repertoire of early theatrical troupes, by contrast, ranged from a half dozen or so plays to perhaps several dozen. These troupes stayed in one place as long as they were able to attract audiences with their repertoire. As these localities became larger and more established they were able to support semi-permanent stock companies capable of presenting a season of plays ranging from Shakespeare to the latest farce comedy. Instead of touring at random, theatrical companies built theaters—often aided by local investment—and tried to establish circuits of towns where they could present annual seasons.

As a consequence of the fundamental differences between outdoor entertainments and theatrical entertainments these two major branches of show business evolved different patterns of organization and control. While these developments were still in primitive stages, in the 1830s and 1840s, there were examples of attempts at monopoly control. These stories are worth recounting for what they suggest about the development of effective monopolies.

Early in the nineteenth century, Hachaliah Bailey (not the Bailey of Barnum and . . .) toured the Northeast profitably displaying his single elephant, Old Bet. Soon many of his friends and neighbors in Westchester County just north of New York City were in the business of exhibiting menageries of exotic animals, or supplying goods and services to touring menageries, or simply investing in such shows. In 1835, these people formed the Zoological Institute, a joint venture that merged at least nine major menagerie shows with a capitalization of $329, 325 and 128 signatories to the Articles of Association. Their goal was centralized control of the import and exhibition of exotic animals. It worked for a while in the limited area of the Northeast; before long, however, the Zoological Institute was out of business (6, pp. 29–33).

At about the same time, theatrical entrepreneurs were waging a battle for control of the business in the Mississippi Valley between New Orleans and St. Louis. While James H. Caldwell led the preeminent English language theater company in New Orleans, Noah Ludlow and Sol Smith headed the dominant theatrical company in St. Louis that also played a winter season downriver at Mobile (about 150 miles from New Orleans).

Ludlow and Smith used both of these towns as bases for tours in the surrounding territory which impinged on part of what Caldwell could have seen as his domain. Caldwell tried to drive Ludlow and Smith out of Mobile by building a showcase theater; the partners responded by moving into a theater in New Orleans in direct opposition to Caldwell. Much was at stake in this encounter; domination of these three towns could have meant control over theatrical activity in the almost 700 mile Mississippi Valley between St. Louis and New Orleans.

Through move and counter-move, each company tried to control particular venues through control of theaters and presentation of attractions. The episode ended after four years when Caldwell ran out of money and energy in the 1840s and the partners ran out of patience with each other a few years later.[1]

The key point to these tales is that while the intent at monopoly was present 150 years ago, the conditions for success were not. Neither in theater nor in circus was it possible to preclude the entrance of other entrpreneurs into the business. There was no way to preempt the opportunities to offer entertainment in particular venues. At that time entertainment companies and circuses were easily formed and places to present shows were easily arranged. By the 1840s, as potential audiences grew larger with expanding population and increased settlement, numerous entrepreneurs formed various entertainment troupes, minstrel shows, dramatic companies, and circuses.

These shows were constantly in competition with each other and competition increased during theatrical hard times—such as the 1840s. As employment in theatrical centers declined, troupes would be formed to go on tour for subsistence. Most of these shows were ephemeral, as easily disbanded as formed. The most stable element in this story were the resident stock companies which were part of their communities.

The tenuous stability of resident stock companies was initially buttressed by the appearance of individual stars in guest performances with local stock companies. Yet, as it turned out, the popularity of guest stars led to increased specialization, division of labor, and standardization—crucial elements in the development of industrialization (3).

---

[1] For a summary of this affair, see (10). Ludlow and Smith each wrote memoirs in their retirement years (18, 29). See also (14) for more on Caldwell.

Stock companies typically operated with a form of typecasting where players were designated as playing certain classes of roles; in the phrase of the time, players had certain "lines of business." The idea remains with us in such terms as leading man, character woman, ingenue; in the nineteenth century there were dozens of distinctions: leading tragedian, first old man, second tragedy, soubrette, eccentric woman, and so on.[2]

When stars toured, they specialized even further by playing a limited number of their favorite roles. Many stars specialized in Shakespearean tragedy (they had such meaty roles), particularly *Macbeth* and *Richard III,* ignoring the rest of the tragic repertoire. The stars gave the same few performances in each town—a crude, but clear, beginning to standardization of product for diverse audiences.

With the increasing power of the stars, in the 1820s and 1830s, management was becoming separated from performance. Actor-managers became managers. They spent less time with the show and more time arranging for a season of star players. The star system created inflationary pressures on established stock companies, increasing the budget beyond the capacity of smaller venues. Since theater is labor-intensive, the salaries of local players suffered; better, more aggressive performers left resident companies and tried for bookings as guest "stars" or toured in small companies of their own.

As the local stock companies became weaker in their ability to supply adequate support for the star, visiting stars began to travel with key supporting players further separating local managers from the performance. By the time of the Civil War, the railway system had developed sufficiently to make it possible to travel with a complete show, including the full cast, costumes, and sets in what were called combination companies.

Theaters that had featured resident stock companies shifted to a policy of booking combination companies. Between 1871 and 1878, the number of resident stock companies had declined from 50 to "seven or eight." One of the last of these companies, Mrs. Drew's Arch Street Theater in Philadelphia, lost $9,000 in its last year as a resident stock theater. The following year it had a net profit of $12,000 showing the productions of touring companies (19, p. 7).

The move to combination companies was perhaps the key event in the industrialization of entertainment. The production of plays for tours was centralized in specialized production organizations in the major theatrical centers: New York, Chicago, San Francisco; the organizational pattern of these production groups increased the division of labor and standardization. Players and other personnel were hired for the specific purpose of the particular play and particular role; several identical versions of a popular play might be sent on tour. Some kind of record must have been set in 1896 when the play *Trilby* had 24 companies touring the country simultaneously (25, p. 69).

---

[2] An extensive list of these lines of business can be found in (19, p. 13).

By the end of the nineteenth century, much of the business had become specialized. Most participants in the theatrical enterprise were hired hands; many worked for producers who organized shows to be presented at various theaters across the country. Local theater managers were no longer impresarios; now they kept the theater clean, promoted coming attractions, and booked a season of shows. As arrangements became increasingly complicated, agents emerged to represent theaters and productions.

The more successful agents booked shows for a number of theaters in a geographical region that included major cities where profitable showings were possible, with one-night stands along the railroad route between these cities to help pay the overhead. Agents with the best routes had the first choice of the better productions. Some agents produced shows to fill out the season in theaters they represented. Soon they were producing shows for their own account, backed by the guaranteed routes they controlled. In other words, agents were becoming the fulcrum in economic integration between production and theaters. In about 25 years following the Civil War, businessmen had replaced showmen.

MEANWHILE, OUT IN THE COUNTRY . . .

These developments directly affected the structure of the industry in the leading theaters of the major cities and the satellite one-night stand theaters. In less expensive theaters in big cities and in smaller towns throughout the country, the industry remained amorphous and less industrialized. Casually organized small troupes—again, often families—continued to barnstorm for bookings from one appearance to the next, as had earlier itinerant players.

In cities with more than one theater, there were "popular-priced" (that is, cheap) theaters that depended on available talent or operated as part of a system that imitated the dominant one. In towns and villages there were single all-purpose spaces called the Town Hall, the Opera House, or some such generic term with the town name appended; often the owner's name was used to designate the space. Musser's Hall for instance—H.A. Musser, manager and bill-poster—had an announced capacity of 800 in Orangeville, Illinois, a town that claimed 700 population in 1896 (4, p. 261)[3]. There were probably few towns so remote as to be out of reach of a circus or other entertainment.

One of the consequences of industrialization was the growth of repertory entertainment companies that played one-week stands—often in tents—with a different show each night, before moving on to the next small town (28). These touring companies, called 10-20-30 shows in recognition of their admission scale, filled a specialized niche providing entertainment in territories that the industrialized entertainment companies had abandoned.

---

[3] See (15) for a description of the operation at the end of the nineteenth century of the Concert Hall in Beaver Dam, Wisconsin, then a town of about 4200 population, 25 miles north of Madison.

An ironic, and perhaps important, point about the 10-20-30 shows is that the number of companies grew at exactly the same time that movies were increasing in popularity in the years between 1897 and 1910. Precise figures are difficult to obtain but one estimate based on various published sources claimed that the number of 10-20-30 shows increased fourfold (from around 20 to around 80) between 1897 and 1910 (19, p. 8), a period when the United States population increased by 46 percent and the rural population increased by 22 percent.

These forms of entertainment are not directly involved in the story being told here, yet they should be kept in mind; the distinction between big-time and small-time is apparent only at the extremes. These small theaters and performers who appeared there are supporting players who add richness to the more obvious drama. For some of the performers these companies were their training ground; others spent their lives touring and never played towns larger than 10,000 population. It can be argued that the existence of these widely scattered venues and companies were important to the development of the film industry (24). But even if the argument—or the fact that the argument is possible—were not true, accurate history is more than the story of grandiose events.

OLD MONOPOLIES

In the summer of 1896, just over four months after the commercial introduction of motion pictures in the United States, three separate firms joined to form the Theatrical Syndicate in an attempt at monopoly control of theatrical production and presentation.

One of the firms, Hayman and Frohman, had a factory system for combination company productions. They controlled booking in 300 theaters; they had on their payroll stars, directors, technicians, and the members of the Empire Theatre Stock Company in New York, one of the few remaining resident stock companies, where players could gain experience and be available for combination company tours. Another firm, Klaw and Erlanger, was a prominent New York booking agency. The third firm, Nixon and Zimmerman, owned theaters in Philadelphia and booked shows for other theaters in Pennsylvania and Ohio.

Between them, the Syndicate firms controlled booking in approximately 500 theaters. Hayman and Frohmam controlled routes between New York and the Pacific Coast, while Klaw and Erlanger controlled all of the important routes in the South, including numerous one-night stand theaters. Shows desiring any kind of decent route had to deal with the Syndicate. Theaters desiring any kind of decent season had to deal with the Syndicate. To further enforce Syndicate control, theaters and producers had to sign exclusive contracts, that limited them to dealing only with other Syndicate participants (17).

This arrangement worked for a while, until the Syndicate was challenged by the Shubert brothers, who introduced a new element into the process. The Syndicate was a closely-held monopoly with financing based on internally-generated capital at a time when theaters began to be an attractive investment possibility for outsiders. In contrast, the whole Shubert undertaking was based on outside investment; the Shuberts and their associates owned many of their own theaters which gave them absolute control over booking instead of the weaker form of integration represented by the booking contracts that formed the basis of the Syndicate strength.

The Shuberts established a prominent presence in most of the major markets, yet they remained weak in one-night stands which were still controlled by the Syndicate and were necessary to break up lengthy, unprofitable jumps between major cities. However, a nonexclusive open-booking policy brought the Shuberts enough major stars and shows to force many one-night stand theaters to abandon their exclusive contract with the Syndicate. The Shuberts were teaching the industry a lesson that would be relearned 15 years later by the film industry: control of talent can lead to control of other elements in the theatrical enterprise. In the case of the Shuberts this meant complete vertical integration from commissioning specially written shows, supplying scenery and costumes through booking routes.

As it turned out, the Shuberts survived the Syndicate. With the incorporation of Sam S. and Lee Shubert, Inc. in 1905 with a capitalization of $1.4 million, they established an institutional continuity that would outlive any of the individual participants. Shubert interests continue to be a dominant, though not overriding force in theater (3, 31).

The Syndicate-Shubert confrontation added a twist to the experience of the Zoological Institute and Caldwell, Ludlow and Smith fifty years earlier; total control was still not possible but it took a sufficiently well-financed competitor to push its way into a share of a highly industrialized market.

The weak could compete with the apparently strong, however, in the early stages of industrialization, as in 1908 when Edison, Biograph, and other film and projector manufacturers formed the Motion Picture Patents Company, in an attempt to monopolize the burgeoning movie industry. There had been talk of potential monopoly as early as 1901[4]. But it took a series of court cases to sort out the various claims to patent rights. Finally, Edison, Biograph, Vitagraph, and Armat were each found to hold some valid patents. Between them they held all of the effective patents to motion picture technology; these patents were pooled in the Patents Company (or Trust, as it came to be called).

The company licensed firms at every level in the process from projector manufacture to exhibition, collecting license fees and royalties at every point. Again, as in the Syndicate, the Trust imposed an exclusive clause in all of its licenses (5).

---

[4] H.N. Marvin of Biograph and Thomas Armat made separate attempts as early as 1901 to enlist Edison in plans for "the formation of a trust . . . a real monopoly." Edison's response in a handwritten note to Gilmore, his general manager, was: "I fail to see it." Letter, Armat to Edison, November 15, 1901. File D1901, Motion Pictures, Edison National Historical Site Archives. The Archives contain other similar letters from Armat. See also file Motion Pictures 1903 for other monopoly proposals advanced by Marvin in letters to Edison.

This was effectively economic integration, albeit a weak form since contracts can be broken.

Although the Trust seemed sturdy enough at the time, from a historical vantage point the effort was doomed almost from the start: There was no way to preempt the production and exhibition of motion pictures. Once the technological problems were solved, entrance into the market was easy; movie projectors and movie cameras were mechanically simple devices that could be readily copied.[5] Elements of the opposition—the Independents—could and did successfully compete with the Trust companies, as is well-known. Antitrust suits were filed by some of the Independents but the Trust had failed through structural weakness before the cases were adjudicated. Moreover, the firms in the Trust themselves were bound only by contract and some of the patent companies cooperated with the Independents when it was mutually advantageous (1, pp. 130–134).

All of these attempts to gain monopoly control of an aspect of show business, from the Zoological Institute in 1835 to the Patents Company 75 years later, were constructed as closed systems—attempts to gain total control of key elements in the system, whether it was the importation of elephants or the technology of motion pictures. With one exception, all of these attempts failed through their inability to preclude outsiders from entering the field.

Only in vaudeville was this pattern of control successful. Control of the major vaudeville theaters owned by the several circuits that constituted the United Booking Office effectively led to the control of vaudeville at the beginning of the twentieth century. Monopoly control of big-time vaudeville was possible because of the character of the vaudeville show which typically included eight or more unrelated acts.

Between performers and theaters it was a buyer's market. Performers were independent contractors in competition with each other for places on the bills of theaters while to the theaters individual acts were interchangeable parts (30). Recalcitrant performers could be deprived of bookings at no cost to the theater; replacements were always available. However, theaters did need a new program every week. Under these conditions the booking office can exercise effective control by being at the center of a complicated process of allocating thousands of performers among hundreds of theaters.

During a lull in their own battles, the Shuberts and the Syndicate formed the United States Amusement Company with the intent of using vaudeville to fill the playing time in their own theaters. Given the structure of vaudeville, the Shubert tactic of using headline performers to break the opposition would not work. The Amusement Company started with 19 theaters while the United Booking Office booked for hundreds of theaters and could—if it wished—grant a full season of 40 weeks to an act. Despite having signed some big names, the United States Amuse-

---

[5] A list of a number of bootleg projectors that had been advertised as early as 1897 can be found in (24).

ment Company went out of business in January 1908, after eight months existence (3, pp. 68–69). It was a matter, perhaps, of insuffient strength to make an effective challenge.

At the end of the nineteenth century, size became an element also in the pattern of dominance emerging in circuses and outdoor entertainments. Theater-based expansion depended on control of a large number of theaters over a wide geographic area. In vaudeville, for instance, Keith controlled the major venues east of the Mississippi and Orpheum controlled the major venues west to the Pacific Coast. No such control was possible in circuses and outdoor entertainment since the "venue" for them is an open field where tents can be raised for a day.

Over the years following the Civil War, size of a circus became a key competitive strategy. The circus itself was the star; bigger is better, larger is more spectacular. Circuses expanded the size of their shows. One-ring shows became two-ring shows, then three rings were used. Standardization of railroad gauges made it possible for circuses to travel on specially designed railroad cars; the size of the train became a measure of the appeal of the show. At the end of the century, major shows were traveling in trains that had more than 80 cars, playing only the major markets where the large audiences and the large profits were.

Barnum and Bailey and the Ringling Brothers were the principal competitors in the battle of the giants. In 1896, James A. Bailey planned routes to puts his shows in day-and-date competition with the Ringling show no less than 45 times. The encounter was a stand-off; a few years later, the Ringling Brothers bought Bailey's shows from his estate, giving them integrated ownership of the largest shows: Ringling Brothers World's Greatest Shows, Barnum and Bailey Greatest Show on Earth, and Buffalo Bill Wild West and Congress of Rough Riders of the World (6). Ringling Brothers dominated their market by size; no other shows were large enough to compete seriously with the Ringling-owned shows. The numerous smaller independent shows avoided competition with these shows by playing in places that Ringling ignored (see e.g., 16). A similar pattern of dominance and competition would emerge in motion pictures and broadcasting as they developed into mature industries later in the twentiety century.

There was one more attempt at closed system control in show business, undertaken in the late 'teens of the twentieth century when Adolph Zukor and the groups associated with Paramount Pictures used control of popular movie stars as the key to their policy of block-booking; exhibitors who wanted pictures with popular stars also had to take other pictures whose main value was that they filled out the program and were inexpensive to produce. Although block-booking would continue as a policy in the whole film industry for 30 years, it failed in its original intent to support a monopoly by the Zukor interests. Major theater chains organized a counter-offensive under the name First National Exhibitors' Circuit. First National entered production; Zukor began to buy theaters.

NEW PATTERNS OF CONTROL

This was the last overt effort to completely preempt production and exhibition. But in the process a more powerful structure of control was created. Production, distribution, and exhibition became integrated under unified corporate control at Paramount, while First National had a weaker form of integration based on contracts with producers and agreement for exhibition with "five or six thousand theaters" (13, p. 177). Other leading motion picture firms were also partially integrated at that time.

What evolved under the aegis of a newly formed film industry trade association, the Motion Picture Producers and Distributors of America, was an arrangement whereby the integrated studios cooperated in a system of industry-wide control.

The association may have been innocent enough, it may have been formed to deflect demands for censorship—the best known function of the Hays office, as it came to be called—but it seems less than coincidental that the membership roster was—and remained for many years—a list of the major integrated corporations and their affiliated companies, yet did not include producers operating independently of the major studios.[6]

The difference between this plan and earlier ones, such as the Syndicate and the Patent Companies, is that this system was open to any competitor potentially strong enough to challenge the control.

In the course of the 1920s, the line-up of major motion picture powers changed; Loew's Corporation became fully integrated with the formation of Metro-Goldwyn-Mayer Studios; First National collapsed and was absorbed by Warner Bros.; and Fox went bankrupt. The new participants—Warner Bros. and the corporate predecessors of RKO—had been minor competitors at the beginning of the decade, and not members of the MPPDA. But both firms had become fully integrated by the end of the decade and were participants in the system of control.

While some of the participants had changed, the game continued under the old rules—the pattern of control remained the same. Under this system, the integrated companies had guaranteed markets for their films in their own theaters, and traded bookings of profitable films in the theaters of their presumed competitors.

In the early 1930s, two more participants joined the game. Columbia Pictures, a former poverty row production company, was not a fully integrated company; they did not own theaters. But Columbia had something of value to offer the system. Their generally standard quality budget pictures were used to balance top-of-the-bill pictures in double feature programs that were becoming popular in the Depression years. More: Columbia also produced the popular films directed by Frank Capra that might have drawn business from the studio-owned theaters if

---

[6] See photograph of original membership in (13), plate 75, between pp. 238-239; 1940 membership roster in (33, p. 68). For a discussion of organizations of various types of producers, see (8, p. 230).

they had been booked into independent theaters. By including Columbia in the system of control, the majors profited from the pictures of potential opposition, while continuing to subordinate independent theaters and preempt screen time from independent producers.

In 1933, a small company, Twentieth Century, was formed by two leading industry executives, Darryl Zanuck and Josph Schenck, under the patronage of Louis B. Mayer, head of Metro-Goldwyn-Mayer. Through a merger, two years later, this company relieved Chase National Bank of the responsibility for the old Fox studios, becoming a fully integrated corporation and a full member of the system of control.

In contrast to the older patterns of control that tried to exclude new entrants or deprive competitors of resources, the pattern of control developed in the 1920s allowed players to enter the game so long as they had something to contribute as in the case of Columbia Pictures, or had a large enough stake as did RKO and Twentieth Century-Fox.

Gone were the bitter circus booking wars when bill-posters would tear down or cover over announcements from the opposition, battling physically when caught at it; gone too were the scurrilous denunciations of the Syndicate-Shubert era. The film industry had become more sophisticated than the days of physical violence between Trust and Independents. Rather than try to eliminate competition directly, the new rules allowed the old hands to co-opt potential serious competitors to their mutual benefit. The only losers were those outside of the system of control.

By the 1930s, entertainment was dominated by industrialized motion picture companies and broadcasting networks. By their nature, broadcasting networks are capital intensive industrialized entities with standardization of product, division of labor, and centralized control. Three major networks had evolved in the early days of radio, before 1930; they dominated by size. Until recently, subsequent efforts at building a major fourth network have failed. It takes an HBO to compete with an NBC, or to collaborate with a CBS for mutual benefit. In the 1930s, broadcasting and motion picture companies did collaborate for mutual benefit; Publicity for the studios and programming for the networks.

Independent entrepreneurs existed only at the margins in such things as touring carnivals, the remnants of tent repertory, poverty row film production, operation of local radio stations. The largest of these enterprises were independent motion picture theater chains.

On the initiative of some of these chains, the United States government filed a series of antitrust actions, known collectively as *United States v. Paramount Pictures et al*, that stretched from 1938 to 1949. The effort was to breakup the integrated system of control of the film industry (7). By then it was too late; the major studios were too well-entrenched.

The *Paramount* defendants—Paramount, MGM, Warner Bros., RKO, Twentieth Century-Fox, Universal, Columbia, and United Artists—signed consent decrees subsequent to the adverse decision of the Supreme Court in 1949 that, among other things, forced divorcement between production and exhibition.

The old monopoly was broken up. The theaters were sold off. Without guaranteed markets, the moviemaking factories of the old days began to be shutdown. Contracts with stars, directors, writers, producers, and the rest were allowed to lapse. Everybody, it seemed, would be "independent." Well, not really. The major studios still had the only effective national film distribution systems; they still had the principal resources for the financing of films.

POST-INDUSTRIAL PATTERNS

It is now just over 30 years since the old system was broken up. All the old-timers such as Louis B. Mayer and Adolph Zukor are dead. But it does not matter. During the 25 or 30 years that the system introduced during the Hays office years operated, participating corporations had developed institutional continuity which transcends the importance of particular individuals. The corporation has a life of its own.

The *Paramount* defendants still dominate production; despite initial timidity, they quickly became a principal source of product for television and now cable and all of the new methods of exhibition. They are in the same position as the broadcasting networks and Ringling Brothers were—they dominate by size.

In 1983, Columbia, MGM/UA, Paramount, Twentieth Century-Fox, Universal, and Warners released 147 pictures that accounted for 89 percent of the $3.7 billion box office income in the domestic market. An additional 7 percent of the market was accounted for by the 15 pictures released by mini-majors—Buena Vista and Orion. These market shares left 4 percent of the market for the 202 pictures intended for general release by independent distributors.[7]

The majors had bought land and built studios when both were very cheap; during the period of unchallenged dominance of the movie industry they had built up libraries of product whose value is probably incalculable. One financial analyst made what he said was a conservative estimate of over two billion dollars as the current value of the approximately 11,000 films in the libraries of the major studios—the former *Paramount* defendents (21).

These kinds of assets—typically undervalued on balance sheets—made the studios attractive targets for corporate takeover. The studios became bargaining chips in high stakes corporate gambling. Following the period of divorcement each of the major studios passed into the hands of financiers and conglomerates. As a re-

---

[7] Compiled from *Variety:* Major and mini-major releases, October 5, 1983, pp. 3, 35; market shares, January 18, 1984, pp. 5, 40; independent releases, March 7, 1984, p. 414. Box office income is only a rough guide to film rental, the figures that really matter. In practice, the higher grossing pictures are able to get higher proporations of the box office income as film rental. For the curious, the figures above yield per picture averages of $22.4 million for major releases, $17.3 million for mini-major releases, and $733 thousand for independent releases.

sult of corporate reorganization and the reorganization of the production process, the structure of decision making around the production of films became more complicated.

From the beginning, each stage in industrialization of entertainment was accompanied by a lengthening of the chain of command between the show and the management decisions that made the show possible. In simple stock companies the manager was also one of the performers. The managerial function became separated from performance with the increased use of guest stars; the introduction of booking agents between combination companies and theaters further lengthened the management chain. Even before movies became part of the story, bureaucracy increased with each step toward mass production of entertainment.

The development of organizational machinery to produce and sell films repeated the earlier experience. At first, film production was organized along the lines of any cottage industry; one or two people did everything. Increased demand for product on a regular basis brought with it all of the organizational paraphernalia of mass production (32). By the time of the movie factories, executives in New York set policy, including the annual production schedule and overall budget; the head of production in Hollywood carried out this schedule through staff producers.

Under the system that followed the breakup of the movie factories, the film corporations (still called studios) depended on outsiders—so-called independents—for increasing proportions of their product. Although producers are not on the corporate payroll, the term "independent" is misleading in this context since studios still exert substantial control and influence on the activities of the people directly responsible for making the films.

About a third of the films released by the majors in 1983 were "in-house" productions, made by producers and others hired for specific properties developed under studio control. Some affiliated production units have contracts with the studios for a certain number of pictures to be produced for the studio over a period of two or three years. Other films come to the studio more-or-less complete and are purchased as negative pick-ups or released as part of a distribution deal.

These various arrangements between the studio and outsiders brought about an interposed layer of bureaucracy; someone has to deal with the outsiders on behalf of the corporation. Producers continue to be directly responsible for the production, but in development they work with production executives during writing and rewriting scripts, casting of stars and director, and establishing production budgets. Production executives negotiate for changes in negative pick-ups and deal with affiliated producers. Production executives have power that is unstated but well-understood—they can say "no" or influence the decision. However, only at the highest corporate levels can the decision be made to "go to picture," that is, invest several million dollars.

Each further conglomeration brings with it further bureaucracy. Broadcasting networks and cable services, such as HBO, have program executives to represent their corporation in similar fashion when negotiating for product. It is a system where responsibility without authority is spread through a lengthy chain of command; it is a system that encourages the manufacture of safe, highly saleable pictures. It is not a system that encourages risk or diversity.

Personalities sometimes do make a difference; "bankable" people such as Clint Eastwood, Woody Allen, and Steven Spielberg can do pretty much whatever they want to do, so long as they want to do "commercial" pictures. Other presumably bankable stars—Barbara Streisand and *Yentl* is the most recent example—have difficulty obtaining support within the mainstream for offbeat pictures.[8] More: The executive cadre that had successfully run United Artists until the early 1980s is responsible for the current success of Orion. At the same time, past success is no guarantee of future success. The Ladd Co., formed by Alan Ladd, Jr., and 12 executives from his successful tenure as production head of Twentieth-Century-Fox, suffered declining good fortune following the less-than-successful release of *The Right Stuff* and *Star 80*. Despite his mixed record of success, Ladd was subsequently appointed President of MGM/UA, responsible for the separate production schedules of the merged companies.

The allure of the new markets of cable pay television, home video, and the like, in addition to the old markets of theaters and over-the-air television continues to draw new aspirants into the marketplace. Yet, the failed attempts by Melvin Simon and Lorimar to establish a presence in motion picture production during the late 1970s and early 1980s, at reported costs of approximately $40–$50 million each, demonstrates that the ante has been raised considerably. The fate of Coppola's Zoetrope Studio in Hollywood makes the same point, as does the appearance and disappearance over the last decade or so from the list of successful competitors of names such as National General Pictures, American-International, and Embassy.

The major studios do not constitute a monopoly such as the Theatrical Syndicate; a better model for today is the way circuses operated around 1900, when the market for smaller competitors was whatever was left over by the Ringling Brothers. The majors have the most extensive structures for financing and distributing product; they can spread their risk over a large release schedule; they can absorb larger losses then their smaller competitors; their size increases their negotiating power for talent, product acquisition, and screen time.

At the far edges of this story are the genuine independent entrepreneurs who try to produce films outside of the mainstream; these are unstable undertakings without an adequate machinery for financing, distributing, or exhibiting their product. They are as ephemeral as the nineteenth century strollers, forced by structural considerations to move into the mainstream (if they can) or leave the field altogether.

---

[8] There is speculation that among the sources of disinterest in *Yentl* were the peculiarly ethnic and feminist themes and Streisand's multiple production roles as producer, writer, director, and star.

CONCLUSIONS

There is no large moral, ethical, or political point to be made by these observations. This has been more a cautionary tale about the writing of film history. As the picture business emerged from show business, it repeated in condensed form some of the earlier experiences. Tracing the development of film as part of a larger story can help us understand what was unique and what was commonplace.

A broader context also encompasses failed attempts which are as important as the successes. One example that leads in unexpected directions deals with the role of established theatrical producers in the emerging film industry. We know that Klaw and Erlanger, among others, tried to establish themselves in the film industry around 1915; they failed in the attempt. Was their failure simply bad judgment on properties and stars, as the older film histories would have us believe? The answer seems too simple. A knowledge of the fiscal and managerial policies of the Syndicate and the failure of the United States Amusement Company suggests the possibility of inappropriate financial and organizational structures.

In contrast to Klaw and Erlanger's lack of success, the Shubert brothers' biography (31) contains numerous clues about the participation of Lee Shubert in the formation and financing of the Loew's empire. A tantalizing part of the story is the claim (23) that Robert Rubin, attorney and confidante to Marcus Loew, had previously been legal counsel to the Shuberts and, yet earlier, been a classmate of Sam Shubert, back in Syracuse, preparing together for bar mitzvah.

This long-time relationship, and other similar ones, raises again questions that have been previously muted about the role of cultural nepotism and competition. At least one partner of each of the firms in the Syndicate was from an earlier generation of German-Jewish descent, while the Shuberts, Loew, Zukor, Goldwyn, and others were of a younger generation of Eastern European Jewish immigrants, that often found itself in conflict with the established German-Jews. At the same time, there were numerous gentiles prominent in the early film industry and show business generally. Surely it was not that Eastern European Jews were smarter and wilier. We know better than that, even if Ramsaye (26) did not. More likely there are structural explanations for the way things worked out.

If history is not exactly a seamless web, there are continuities among the disjunctures. Tracing some of these threads leads us backward and forward, not in the mechanistic sense of "the lessons of history" but in providing the basis for imaginative leaps among the clues that can aid in knowing what to look for. It seems relevant, for instance, that movies and phonograph recordings came to the fore as technological entertainments at about the same time and under similar circumstances; at first both were used as vaudeville acts, as entr'actes in various other shows, and as the featured attraction in itinerant shows. How one became mass entertainment and the other home entertainment is worth looking at more closely than we have.

In short, the writing of film history will be much richer when we begin to look beyond the narrow confines imposed by a single-minded interest in movies.

REFERENCES

1. Allen, Jeanne Thomas. "The Decay of the Motion Picture Patents Company." In Tino Balio (Ed.), *The American Film Industry*, pp. 119–134. Madison, WI: University of Wisconsin Press, 1976.
2. Allen, Robert C. "Vaudeville and Film: 1895–1915: A Study in Media Interaction." Ph. D. Dissertation, University of Iowa, 1977.
3. Bernheim, Alfred L., assisted by Sara Harding. *The Business of the Theatre: An Economic History of the American Theatre: 1750–1932*. New York: Actors' Equity, 1932 (Reprinted, New York: Benjamin Blom, 1964.)
4. Cahn, Julius. *Julius Cahn's Official Theatrical Guide, 1896*. New York: Author, 1896.
5. Cassady, Ralph, Jr. "Monopoly in Motion Picture Production and Distribution: 1908–1915." *Southern California Law Review* 32(4), Summer 1959, pp. 325–390.
6. Chindahl, George L. *A History of the Circus in America*. Caldwell, ID; Caxton Printers, 1959.
7. Conant, Michael. *Antitrust in the Motion Picture Industry*. Berkeley and Los Angeles: University of California Press, 1960.
8. Dawson, Anthony H. "Motion Picture Economics." *Hollywood Quarterly* 3(3), Spring 1948, pp. 217–239.
9. Dombkowski, Dennis J. "Film and Television: An Analytical History of Economic and Creative Integration." Ph. D. Dissertation, University of Illinois at Urbana-Champaign, 1982.
10. Dorman, James H., Jr. *Theater in the Ante Bellum South: 1815–1861*. Chapel Hill: University of North Carolina Press, 1967.
11. Dulles, Foster Rhea. *A History of Recreation: America Learns to Play*, (2nd ed.). Englewood Cliffs, NJ: Prentice-Hall, 1965.
12. Ford, George D. *These Were Actors: The Story of the Chapmans and the Drakes*. New York: Library Publishers, 1955.
13. Hampton, Benjamin B. *A History of the Movies*. New York: Covici, Friede, 1931. (Reprinted as *History of the American Film Industry*. New York: Dover Publications, 1970.)
14. Hostetler, Paul Smith. "James H. Caldwell: Theatre Manager." Ph. D. Dissertation, Louisiana State University, 1964.
15. Hoyt, Harlowe R. *Town Hall Tonight*. Englewood Cliffs, NJ: Prentice-Hall, 1955.
16. Hunt, Charles T., Sr. as told to John C. Cloutman. *The Story of Mr. Circus*. Rochester, New Hampshire: The Record Press, 1954.
17. Lippman, Monroe. "The History of the Theatrical Syndicate." Ph. D. Dissertation, University of Michigan, 1937.
18. Ludlow, Noah M. *Dramatic Life as I Found It*. St. Louis: G. I. Jones, 1880. (Reprinted, New York: Bejamin Blom, 1966).
19. McArthur, Benjamin. *Actors and the American Culture*. Philadelphia: Temple University Press, 1984.
20. McLaughlin, Robert. "Broadway and Hollywood: A History of Economic Interaction." Ph. D. Dissertation, University of Wisconsin, 1970. (Reprinted, New York: Arno Press, 1974.)
21. McMeekin, Thomas. "Filmed Entertainment Industry." *Institutional Research*. Philadelphia: W. H. Newbold's Sons and Company, December 9, 1983.
22. Murray, Marian. *Circus: From Rome to Ringling*. New York: Appleton-Century-Crofts, 1956.
23. Provol, W. Lee. *The Pack Peddler*. Philadelphia: The John C. Winston Co., 1933.
24. Pryluck, Calvin. "The Itinerant Movie Show and the Development of the Film Industry." *Journal of the University Film and Video Association* 35(4), Fall 1983, pp. 11–22.

25. Purcell, L. Edward. "Trilby and Trilby-Mania." *Journal of Popular Culture* 11(1), Summer 1977, pp. 62–76.
26. Ramsaye, Terry. *A Million and One Nights,* 2 vols. New York: Simon and Schuster, 1926.
27. Rice, Kym. *Early American Taverns: For the Entertainment of Friends and Strangers.* Chicago: Regnery Gateway, 1983.
28. Slout, William Lawrence. *Theatre in a Tent.* Bowling Green, OH: Bowling Green University Popular Press, 1972.
29. Smith, Solomon Franklin. *Theatrical Management in the West and South.* New York: Harpers, 1868. (Reprinted, New York: Benjamin Blom, 1968.)
30. Snyder, Frederick E. "American Vaudeville—Theater in a Package—Origins of Mass Entertainment." Ph. D. Dissertation, Yale University, 1970.
31. Stagg, Jerry. *The Brothers Shubert.* New York: Random House, 1968.
32. Staiger, Janet Kay. "The Hollywood Mode of Production: The Construction of Divided Labor in the Film Industry." Ph. D. Dissertation, University of Wisconsin-Madison, 1981.
33. Temporary National Economic Committee. The Motion Picture Industry—A Pattern of Control. Monograph No. 43. 76th Congress, 3d Session, Senate Committee Print. Washington, DC: Government Printing Office, 1941.
34. Toll, Robert C. *On With the Show.* New York: Oxford University Press, 1976.
35. Toll, Robert C. *The Entertainment Machine.* New York: Oxford University Press, 1982.
36. Waugh, Alfred S., John Francis McDermott (Ed. and Comp.). *Travels in Search of the Elephant: The Wanderings of Alfred S. Waugh in Louisiana, Missouri and Santa Fe in 1845–1846.* St. Louis: Missouri Historical Society, 1951.

8

Before Laurel: Oliver Hardy and the Vim Comedy Company, a Studio Biography

Richard Alan Nelson

INTRODUCTION

The rapid transition of moving pictures from a peep-show amusement into a multimillion dollar enterprise by the end of the 1920s was without direct precedent in the entertainment field. A historical comparison of the various traditional components of "show business" (including legitimate stage, vaudeville, carnivals, circuses, Wild West Shows, motion pictures, radio, and television) demonstrates that the cinema was the first to develop into an industrial mass medium.

The other major national media of today, ranging from broadcasting to syndicated publishing, have subsequently followed patterns of industrial development remarkably similar to those experienced by the movie business (10). To some extent these capitalistic media enterprises, like traditional forms of commercial marketing, have the same underlying financial bases and thus adopted similar organizational methods (34). Yet in several key respects, the motion picture business departed from earlier organizational models by pioneering concepts and strategies now common to other information- and entertainment-based industries. "Its product—mere shadows on a curtain—suggests the art of the magician rather than the prosiac, everyday labors of men," notes a Harvard Business School publication of 1927.

> Its mushroom growth, the reports of fabulous salaries earned and the huge fortunes acquired, make it seem fantastic and legendary rather than real. In its adventurous and speculative features it has been compared to gold mining. Its potential social influence cannot be doubted. Its esthetic standards, wavering between intrinsic quality

and commercial value, have revived ancient and seemingly interminable controversies. Yet the film industry is not less an industry because it provides entertainment or . . . because the commodity in which it deals is human emotions (38, p. ix).

Surprisingly, there are few major analyses of filmmaking as a commercial enterprise (a recent exception, 94)—even though by the 1920s the production, distribution, and exhibition of photoplays had become an American trade medium whose cultural and financial impact was felt world-wide. The majority of studies detailing the development of the motion picture industry concentrate on film's growth as an art form, emphasizing the beginning of structural narrative, following with the visual and editing contributions of D. W. Griffith, and then culminating with a discussion of particularly noteworthy productions, genres, stars, directors, producers, and perhaps studio "styles." And yet the origins of the industry and subsequent cinematic history can be analyzed not only for what can be said about artistic contributions, but also in terms of the broader economic forces and social patterns shaping this art form. At the same time an overemphasis on the creative aspects of cinema neglects the more mundane, but crucial, interplay of the capitalistic realities which impelled the organizational development of the producing firms and the industry institutions directly responsible for employing the filmmaking talent.

The early organizational years and the epoch of silent filmmaking extending until about 1930 is a particularly fertile period for renewed investigation by researchers. Financially, this phase in the industry's history marked the entry of Wall Street into the motion picture world. From an organizational standpoint this was also an era which witnessed the gradual consolidation, after bitterly incessant rivalry as well as many business failures, of the major companies which dominated "filmdom" for decades. And from a historical perspective, a renewed look at specific elements of the early industry can help us discover new linkages to more accurately reconstruct the past.

METHODOLOGICAL APPROACH

A growing number of revisionist scholars have in recent years begun to challenge the often parochial and distorted emphasis on "Hollywood" in film studies by utilizing local and trade materials overlooked by more conventional authors (for example, 4, 21, 22, 26, 27, 29, 35, 36, 46, 47, 50, 61, 62, 83). Their approach to historical research involves a reversal of looking at filmmaking from a monolithic Hollywood perspective through concentration on the industry as a collective expression of local and regional developments. While some fine traditional analyses continue to make their way into print, the localists are a necessary antidote for the all-too-often shoddy and ill-researched work which unfortunately passes itself off as film scholarship today. Historical studies of early studios and trends, particularly, can help illustrate the weaknesses of mainstream cinema scholarship when it fails to delve deeply beyond publicist mythology into the mercantile structure of the film trade (65). Even in extended works on California's film heritage rarely does one find citations made to business sources, let alone to local newspapers, periodicals, and other materials. Not all the blame for this, of course, can be attributed to poor methodology or ahistorical bias. One reason for this neglect is simply the tedious search time which must be invested in scanning literally years of issues. Until recently, too, the lack of microform materials meant that runs of newspapers and periodicals were widely scattered and haphazardly collected. A third limiting factor may stem from a failure to realize the wealth and extent of coverage local news sources give early media such as the motion picture industry where reportage proves unusually detailed and can clarify numerous omissions in national trade and popular sources.

Several assumptions underlie use of local materials. One is that such resources are closer to the events they report. Particularly where more than one newspaper or magazine journalist covers the activities of motion picture companies, the different interests and emphases of the reporters provides for fuller coverage than one finds by simply relying on a reading of the trade press and secondary materials. By the very nature of trade and popular journalism, articles published in national magazines long have been for the most part dependent on the publicity efforts of the various film manufacturers. This has a legitimate and useful role. But by also referencing local publications, one at least maximizes data gathering from independent information sources, even though there is no certainty that reliability and validity factors are enhanced. At the same time, because of the increased body of available literature from which to draw, various local developments and controversies which may have lacked national interest at the time can now be illuminated and integrated within a historical framework.

This article emphasizes use of local and trade materials to take an authoritative case study look at one typical expansionist venture representative of the early industry—the Vim Comedy Company. Adopting a Shakespearean jester as its widely promoted advertising logo, Vim controlled studio facilities in both New Jersey and Florida in addition to sales offices in New York. Comedies were the "spice of the programme" during the silent era, turned out with amazing rapidity by dozens of largely forgotten filmmakers. Despite their neglect by scholars, these weekly one- and two-reel releases proved important both to audiences and exhibitors who relied on them to complete an attractive supplement to the playbill of feature, newsreel, comedy, and scenic or cartoon films (52). Vim, by the sheer number of films released (156 one-reelers) as well as the personalities making them, historically is one of the more interesting of the early companies producing comedy shorts. An appended filmography demonstrates that such studio firms should not be neglected in reconstructing American production trends and statistics.

HISTORICAL DEVELOPMENTS

Early Industry Conditions

The incredible growth of the motion picture business during the mid-teen years encouraged investors on Wall Street and boosters in local communities to speculate in underwriting a number of new film companies (91). By 1915, an estimated $500 million were already invested in the American industry (24). Audience demand for even more varied product, rising production costs necessitating increased capitalization, and the potential for fabulous profits led additional "picture gamblers" to invade a field already overrun with promotional businessmen whose methods were questionable at best (23).

At the same time, other conditions also helped fuel the speculative "get rich quick" studio stock boom (12, 64, 71). The panic abandonment of comedy short production by many major studios and stars seeking bigger hits and greater artistic control through features, plus stringent World War I production and import/export restrictions on European film producers created shortages of available photoplays for both domestic and international markets (3, 8, 73, 92). Decentralization of production at a number of movie centers outside New York and Southern California, and the open market aided by the breakup of the Motion Picture Patents Company monopoly also emboldened American film veterans to form new studio ventures.

The resulting short-term production glut (4,850 reels were released in the U.S. market in 1916, declining to 4,056 in 1917, and 3,171 in 1918) temporarily crippled the orderly development of the industry, but ultimately encouraged mergers into stronger vertically-integrated film combines controlling studios and theaters so that revenues could be leveraged to cover future production costs. The consolidation of the film business during the 1916–1920 period into a "Hollywood" dominated by a handful of major studios directly resulted from the competitive failures and successes of companies such as Vim during these preliminary years.

Executives Controlling Vim

Vim was founded by two of the more flamboyant figures of the early industry, Louis Burstein and Mark Dintenfass, who went into partnership late in 1915 to make their fortune in mirth on the cutting edge of the boom then engulfing the movie business (66, 89). As *Variety* observed during this period: "Talk of new studios fills the air in every section of the country" (86). Both men had colorful histories typical of the promotional and legal nature of the industry. Dintenfass was a pioneer motion picture executive who entered the industry as one of the first independents when he founded the Champion Film Company in 1909. When Champion merged to become part of the Universal Film Manufacturing Corporation in 1912, his block of stock proved crucial in deciding control of the company. Dintenfass eventually left Universal in a bitter power struggle, after helping bring former diamond salesman Lewis J. Selznick (father of David O. Selznick) into the picture business. He then headed several other independents before linking himself with Burstein and Vim as the studio's New York-based treasurer (16; 53; 83, p. 128).

Burstein, Vim's director-general stationed in Jacksonville, became involved in the movie business through his training in law. With Adam Kessel, Jr., Charles O. Bauman, and Fred Balshofer, in 1909 he helped found the New York Motion Picture Company (and was rewarded with a one-fourth interest for his legal advice). Catching the movie bug, Burstein then moved on to assist Kessel and Bauman organize the Reliance Film Company in 1910 and was responsible for studio construction with that concern in New York. That same year, he was instrumental in putting together the Motion Picture Distributors and Sales Company as a national outlet for independent product. Subsequently, Burstein continued his work with Kessel and Bauman when in 1912 they, too, joined in forming Universal to combat the Motion Picture Patents Company trust and expanded to create the Keystone Film Company (later famous for Keystone comedies) as a New York Motion Picture Company subsidiary (48, 49). Kessel and Bauman backed out of the Universal combine in the same power dispute which ultimately led both Burstein and Dintenfass to depart the organization. Burstein briefly left the industry entirely in 1914, but returned the following year as the key figure in the Wizard Film Company. The potential upsurge in demand for comedy films in 1915–1916 and the availability of inexpensive talent and studio space in Jacksonville, Florida (then a burgeoning rival to Hollywood), prompted Burstein to contract with former Lubin and Sterling stars Bob Burns (''Pokes'') and Walter Stull (''Jabbs'') to create an updated series of their pratfall comedies for Wizard (78). When Wizard was merged in late 1915 with Equitable, Burns' and Stull's contracts stayed with Burstein and they remained in Florida to become headliners with Vim.

Comedy Films Popular

One reason for Vim's optimism was that comedy teams were a proven component of the genre (43). In the teen years, among the most popular besides Pokes and Jabbs were Ham and Bud, Oscar and Conrad, Kolb and Dill, and Heinie and Louis. To increase its teamed offerings Vim also quickly obtained the services of Oliver ''Babe'' Hardy, another Lubin comedy veteran, who was engaged to perform opposite diminutive Billy Ruge in a second unit of 35 hobo slapstick ''Plump and Runt'' one-reelers released through General Film Company in 1916 (2, 72, 84, 95).

General Film originally started in 1910 as the releasing arm for the Motion Picture Patents Company alliance's attempt to curb independent competition. However, in response to government orders finding it part of an unlawful conspiracy to restrain trade, as well as the precipitous decline by the Patents Company member firms, in 1915 General opened up its program to a variety of producing companies. Prior to its demise in 1919 as part of the shakeout of the industry occurring during the World War I period, General desperately tried to maintain a presence by turning increasingly to smaller independents as its main suppliers (30, 74, 76). Vim's "Pokes and Jabbs" comedies entered the market in November 1915 to replace MinA ("Made in America") films on the General program (43, pp. 40–41; 55), when a dispute between General and MinA head David Horsley led him to disband the company, form other brands, and move his releasing program to Mutual.[1]

The prescription for succes by the new company, noted Burstein, was:

First of all, every one of our comedies must have a plot. Although slapstick in nature, we must not insult the intelligence of our audience by making the film a hodgepodge. We are going to demonstrate that slapstick comedies can have plot. Secondly, our comedies must be clean. We will not tolerate vulgarity. There will be nothing in the picture that one need be ashamed to laugh at. We will hire only the best of talent and will spare no expense in the making of the film. We consider that stinting in the production of a picture is acting on the principle of penny wise and pound foolish. In short, our comedies will be high class and clean and (most importantly of all) really funny (90, 95).

Hardy's Early Career

The opportunity to work regularly at Vim in a starring role proved singularly helpful to Hardy's career, which had already begun to show promise. "Babe," as he was known to all his friends, entered show business as a tenor singer, and established his long association with the film industry in 1910 initially as a theater manager and projectionist in Milledgeville, Georgia. According to his widow, Lucille Hardy Price:

In 1913 he decided to leave the movie theatre business having heard that openings for actors existed in Jacksonville. He got a job singing in a cabaret and during the day haunted the film studios watching how they worked . . . One day while watching the Lubin Company work it turned out they needed a "fat boy" for a comedy sequence . . . and he was afterwards hired by Lubin at five dollars a day, with a contract for three days work each week (80).

Hardy steadily progressed at Lubin in a range of comedy and heavy roles for three years until the firm stopped production and sold its assets. He also appeared in releases by Pathé, Gaumont, Edison, Star Light, and then contracted with Wharton Bros. Inc. where Babe was featured in "The Get-Rich-Quick Wallingford" series before joining Vim in November 1915 (54, 85). That month, Vim had taken over the former Lubin studio lease at the Jacksonville Yacht Club building in the fashionable Riverside district (earlier described by *Moving Picture*

---

[1] For a time in 1916–1917 Benjamin B. Hampton, later to author the standard work *A History of the Movies* (1931), served as president of General. MinA was a continuation of the Méliès Company's U.S. arm. Following Horsley's unsuccessful dispute with General, eventually the Méliès name was resurrected as the releasing agency on the General program for Vim's series of Myers-Theby pictures.

World as ''the best outdoor studio this side of Los Angeles'') (32). An interior stage was artificially lighted, but as was common for the period most of the films were shot outdoors to take advantage of the free sunlight. The exterior stage measured 52 x 125 feet and was fitted with a muslin sun screen rigging that could be moved over the bare board platform as needed either for effect or changes in weather.[2] In this grind-'em-out training ground, long before his teaming with Stan Laurel, Hardy developed the talent and mannerisms that would later influence his screen persona as the lovable bumbler ''Ollie.'' As Jordan R. Young notes, the ''Plump and Runt'' pictures ''are of particular interest, as an examination of their content reveals what are possibly the first-sown seeds of the Laurel and Hardy concept. Besides many of the comedies sounding like typical L & H situations, the character relationships and plot developments coincide frequently, sometimes to an incredible degree'' (95, p. 3). After the ''Plump and Runt'' films started to show a deterioration in quality noticeable enough to be reported in the trade press, Hardy was teamed with the popular comedienne Kate Price who had signed with Vim following her stint at Vitagraph. They appeared in up to 14 films together before Vim ceased releasing in 1917 (37).

Myers and Theby Films

Along with a third Vim unit featuring the talents of Harry Myers and Rosemary Theby in weekly domestic comedy releases, the box office of these films ''added spice to the floundering program of General Film'' (43, p. 41). Myers and Theby joined Vim under personal contract to Mark Dintenfass in April 1916, following experience at a number of studios. They had been teamed together earlier with Lubin and then Universal, where Myers and Theby had first worked under Dintenfass' management. They usually played a young couple and did a refined style of polite low-key domestic comedy popularized earlier by Mr. and Mrs. Sidney Drew (6, 57). The Vim series is today considered well-produced, and the pictures, while they ''offered little in the way of marked story originality, pleased audiences'' (28).

Key supporting roles at Vim were played by Ethel Burton, ''a vivacious and pretty ingenue''; ''Spook'' Hansen, a former Hippodrome clown; and Edna Reynolds, ''a popular stock favorite'' among others. Including casts, directors, cameramen, crew, and administrative personnel, the Vim studio in Jacksonville employed nearly 50 people plus extras, with a regular weekly payroll of approximately $3,800 (82).

---

[2] The studio address in Jacksonville was 740-750 Riverside Drive. Lubin had stopped comedy production in 1915 following the failure of English vaudevillian Billy Reeves to appeal to the American market. Instead the company concentrated on features in the ill-fated merger with Vitagraph, Selig, and Essanay in V-L-S-E. In 1916 Lubin completely sold out its interests to Vitagraph. But since the studio in Jacksonville was only leased, it was not involved in the transfer and was only briefly used in the interim before Vim assumed control.

Attractiveness of South

That Vim's executives chose to work in the South is not unusual given its scenic attractions and the longstanding interest in the region's film potential by motion picture producers (9). Selig, for example, early had been active in New Orleans and other sunbelt cities (44). Although most cinema historians are unaware that Florida was a major studio center during the silent film era, the state (particularly the greater Jacksonville/St. Augustine area) served as the location for many early productions and engaged in a serious effort to establish a permanent presence as "the Klondike of the growing motion picture industry" (11, 56, 58, 63). Many film executives visited the state, and new contracts for studio facilities were being announced in the press at increasingly regular intervals.

Dintenfass himself in 1916 declared he was "converted to Florida" after personally touring Jacksonville with members of the city's motion picture committee and predicted it would be the "future Los Angeles" soon to have well over 100 active film companies. Local officials were so pleased by these remarks that they actually gave Dintenfass a silver loving cup in tribute (18, 20, 71).

Failure of Vim

Market uncertainties, poor quality, and lack of distribution led to the failure of a number of expansion studios during the late teen years, but Vim might have continued indefinitely had in not been for a financial scandal involving the two owners.

According to Billy Bletcher (who with his wife Arline Roberts also played lead and supporting roles at Vim)[3], the partners were "cheating each other":

> Vim wasn't exactly destroyed by business reverses. Dintenfass was the man in New York—really the head man. Burstein was down in Florida. I'll tell you the truth about it. There was a little crooked business going on between Dintenfass and the man that ran the Florida office. A little hanky-panky was going on as to payroll. "Babe" Hardy was the one who discovered it. The New York partner and the Florida partner were cheating each other and the actors were suffering for it to a certain extent. Our salaries were pretty secret and so you just didn't ask the other guy "What are you getting?" The money was in cash in an envelope every Saturday and actors were told "That's for you." Well, Babe discovered the salary list which showed how much we were all being credited with. But the amount the New York office was sending down was more than the actors were really getting. Babe was furious and said, "Hey, you dirty bastards—you're only paying me so much, but you're charging the guy in New York to pay a lot more." When that got out, boom, it wrecked the company (5).

Dintenfass and Burstein were soon engaged in legal battles with one another, forming an unfortunate but not atypical epitaph for such a promising company.

---

[3] In later years Bletcher worked as a character actor in many films, including a number of Roach comedies with Laurel and Hardy and others in the 1930s. Interestingly, he was the voice of the Big Bad Wolf in Walt Disney's classic *Three Little Pigs* cartoon.

EPILOGUE

While Vim had succumbed, that was not the end of the story. In a complicated series of legal maneuvers connected to its release agreements with General Film Company, Vim's interests were taken over by the Amber Star Film Corporation, a subsidiary of Eastern Film Corporation of Providence, Rhode Island (35; 59, p. 36). The key figure in these arrangements was Frank Tichenor who managed to stave off General Film's complete bankruptcy for several years while important backers (including Frederick S. Peck, a Republican national committeeman) salvaged their investments. Peck owned the General Film Company studios in Providence and earlier joined with Tichenor to form Eastern in 1915 (42). Now with two studio facilities, Tichenor traveled down to Florida to reorganize the business. None of the intricacies of the failure of Vim reached the trade press, but a local Jacksonville news item does confirm Bletcher's statements. In reporting the "Old Vim Concern Bawled Up in Finances," the *Florida Times-Union* notes:

> According to Mr. Tichenor, who came here from the home offices of the Amber Star Film Corporation . . . the financial affairs of the local branch are in a muddled condition, and steps are being taken to straighten them out. He declared that there is a large shortage of company money, which is being traced by expert auditors now working on the books . . . (Although) Mr. Tichenor did not go into details as to the company's affairs, he declared that the shortages were thought to have been caused by padding the payrolls and redating of old accounts held against the Vim Company by local concerns (70).

Tichenor promptly took charge and renamed future release product, as of March 1917, under a new "Jaxon" promotional logo (33). Jaxon used the local facility to produce several series of new "Pokes and Jabs" (the latter name was shortened) and "Sparkle" comedies (featuring Kate Price and Billy Ruge). When Bobby Burns left "Pokes and Jabs" later that year, Hardy's former Runt partner Billy Ruge then teamed with Walter Stull to become "Finn and Hattie" first for Jaxon and then other independent comedy producers into the 1920s (14, 67, 77, 81). Ruge later disappeared from leading roles and faded into obscurity, another casualty of the early screen. After a few months, Tichenor allowed the Florida lease to lapse to concentrate studio work in Rhode Island and further experiment with features. A disastrous fire there late in 1917 destroyed much of the remaining complex (estimated losses $75,000–$100,000) and led to a scaled-down shifting away from commercial into nontheatrical educational and business productions. In mid-1918 the Jaxon name was abandoned except for rare features, and the company no longer proved an important factor in the commercial industry (43, p. 41).

After the failure of Vim and another Florida producing firm, the Eagle Film Manufacturing and Producing Company, several of the leading players from those organizations joined together in January 1917 to form Encore Pictures Corporation (apparently figuring their careers were worth another try). Beginning with $30,000 of paid in stock (and a capitalization of $50,000), Encore's two principal founders were Harry Myers (who continued to star with Rosemary Theby in their series of comedies) and Fernandez "Tweedledum" Perez (who earlier had left Vim for Eagle after completing four pictures). The Myers-Theby Comedies were two-reelers; Tweedledum's were one-reelers (60). Unfortunately for Encore, they had trouble getting additional financing and distribution. By March, Myers and Theby renegotiated their contract with Mark Dintenfass who in turn arranged for Myers-Theby Comedy Corporation films to be released through Pathé (15, 17, 75). Dintenfass then had some success investing in features, most notably *My Four Years in Germany* (1918) where he met an astonished Jack Warner on the film's set in New Jersey escorting a beautiful woman with one arm and carrying $28,000 out of a promised $50,000 ("all he could spare") inside a shoe box under the other[4] (93, pp. 91–92). But by January 1920, Dintenfass was back in Florida making Cuckoo Comedies with Jobyna Ralston and Bobby Burns (19). These, along with a line of "race comedies" with black casts, had little impact at the box office. As Cripps (13, p. 85) observes: "There were also white failures such as Mark Dintenfass, who, having failed in the larger white markets, opened a small studio in Jacksonville in order to make Negro movies in a marketplace already beset by tiny margins, cutthroat competition, limited outlets, and empty pockets." Dintenfass' subsequent attempt to promote a pro-Ku Klux Klan film in 1921 failed badly and he seems to have dropped out of the industry after that disappointment (69).

King Bee and Billy West

Burstein rather surprisingly also remained in Jacksonville for a time to make Billy West comedies under his new King Beę Film Company brand, proof to the resiliency of many of the originators of the industry (25, 39). Burstein had obtained

---

[4] Jack Warner, in his autobiography, graphically describes how his brother Harry took advantage of the unusual business methods of Dintenfass to help underwrite production on *My Four Years in Germany:* "None of us had a dime to finance the picture, but Harry went into a basement somewhere in New York and found a gnomish character with the improbable name of Mark M. Dintenfass. We used to call him inkwell, not only because the word *Tintenfass* is German for inkwell, but because he boasted that he was always in the black. By a strange coincidence he could have passed for Kaiser Wilhelm's twin brother. The long points of his mustache were so heavily waxed that they stuck up like tines on a pitchfork, and he pretended to have a withered arm like the Kaiser. Inkwell promised to put up $50,000 and pay production costs as they arose. The first and only time he showed up we were doing exteriors on Arthur Brisbane's New Jersey farm . . . . We had just finished shooting a scene showing American doughboys chasing the Huns down the street when Inkwell turned up with a shoe box, an apple, and a beautiful young girl who was introduced as his secretary. The shoe box was filled with paper money, the apple was his lunch, and the girl, I think, was really there to take care of the fountain pen. When he had finished counting the cash in our presence, he had only $28,000, and he said that was all he could spare. We had to scurry around New York and dig up the other $22,000 ourselves, but it was worth the trouble. *My Four Years in Germany,* distributed by First National, grossed $1,500,000, and after paying off all expenses and loans we had a net profit of $130,000. I don't recall how much Inkwell got, but hiring beautiful girls to carry shoe boxes was a luxury. When he died he had run out of ink, and my brother Harry paid the funeral and burial costs."

control of the contract for Billy West (Roy B. Weissberg), the foremost imitator of
Charlie Chaplin and a talented comic performer in his own right (31, p. 64; 43, pp.
42 and 102–108; 45, pp. 398–405; 51; 79). Beginning in March 1917, King Bee
began production of a series of two-reel comedies which at first proved quite
popular in filling the program vacancy left by Chaplin who had greatly slowed his
output by going into features (41, 88).

Several of the former lead and supporting players at Vim (including Babe Hardy, Frances McLoughlin, and Ethel Burton) made their peace with Burstein and
were selected to join West in making the new pictures. Before joining King Bee,
Hardy (as "The Ton of Jollity") managed and was featured singer at the cabaret of
the Hotel Burbridge in Jacksonville which catered to the theatrical and movie
crowd. Hardy's first wife also worked at the Hotel where she directed the ragtime
orchestra (1). King Bee additionally controlled the former Vim studios in
Bayonne, New Jersey, and production was moved there late in the summer of 1917
(87). Rather than returning to Florida, however, the following winter the King Bee
players made the jump to California with much of the rest of the industry (40).

King Bee chose not to release through General, Universal, or Mutual and instead became a leading independent, but went out of business when Burstein became financially overextended—forcing him to temporarily give up production.
Billy West left for other studios, including a brief return to Florida in 1920 in an attempt to rebuild his languishing career (68). Burstein, undaunted by his earlier re-
verses, reached new heights of success as a feature film producer following a name
change to "Burston" before experiencing tragic death in a 1923 Los Angeles auto
accident which brought his colorful career to a sad close (7).

CONCLUSION

In reviewing the tubulent genealogy of Vim and its successor studios, one can observe a microcosm of the film world for that day. The search for stability and desire to coordinate the industry on a sound economic basis led to major and lasting
changes in the post-World War I movie business. Cost efficiencies through land
acquisition in California and the creation of industry finance, talent, and equipment pools encouraged New York-based film accountants and executives to drastically cutback East Coast work—marking the clear rise of Hollywood to its
preeminence as the American and world motion picture production center. These
capitalistic imperatives further aided the large studios in acquiring assured screen
outlets to dominate the industry, while the importance of the smaller independents
declined proportionately. Film entrepreneurs and actors such as Burstein and
Hardy who could adjust to the new oligopoly continued to enjoy success, while
others such as Dintenfass simply faded into obscurity.

REFERENCES

1. Advertisements, Hotel Burbridge cabaret. *Florida Times-Union* (Jacksonville), February 22 and 26, 1917.
2. "Babe Hardy, the Fat Boy with Vim." *Florida Metropolis* (Jacksonville), February 20, 1916, p. 5–C.
3. "Bankruptcy in Pictures Laid to War Conditions." *Variety* 52 (9), October 25, 1918, p. 32.
4. Beutel, Paul. "Development of the Feature Film Industry in Texas, 1955–1965." Unpublished master's thesis, University of Texas at Austin, 1979.
5. Bletcher, Billy and Arline Bletcher. Personal interview, Hollywood, California, September 1978.
6. Brodnax, Eleanor. "Harry Myers, of the Vim Company." *Florida Metropolis,* April 30, 1916, p. D–5.
7. "Burston Killed in Accident; W.E. Lusk Dies; Both Popular." *Moving Picture World* 61 (6), April 7, 1923, p. 618.
8. Bush, W. Stephen. "Are Short Subjects Coming Back?" *Moving Picture World* 29 (13), September 23, 1916, p. 1947.
9. Campbell, Edward D.C., Jr. *The Celluloid South: Hollywood and the Southern Myth.* Knoxville: University of Tennessee Press, 1981.
10. Cochran, Thomas C. "Media as Business: A Brief History." *Journal of Communication* 25 (4), Autumn 1975, pp. 155–165.
11. Craig, James C. "Jacksonville—World Film Capital." *Papers—The Jacksonville Historical Society* 3, 1954, pp. 117–127.
12. Crain, G. D., Jr. "Mushroom Film Concerns." *Moving Picture World* 25 (7), August 14, 1915, p. 1187.
13. Cripps, Thomas. *Slow Fade to Black: The Negro in American Film, 1900–1942.* New York: Oxford University Press, 1977.
14. "Debut of 'Sparkle Comedies.' " *Motography* 18 (1), July 7, 1917, p. 23.
15. "The Delicatessen Mystery." *Moving Picture World* 32 (8), May 26, 1917, p. 1307.
16. Dintenfass, Mark M. "Tenth Anniversary Recollections." *Moving Picture World* 31 (13), March 31, 1917, p. 2113.
17. "Dintenfass Company at Jacksonville." *Moving Picture World* 32 (4), April 28, 1917, p. 627.
18. "Dintenfass Gets Loving Cup." *Moving Picture World* 27 (12), March 18, 1916, p. 1836.
19. "Dintenfass to Visit Florida." *Moving Picture World* 43 (5), January 31, 1920, p. 738.
20. "Dintenfass Would see this City a Future 'Los Angeles' of Motion Picture Industry." *Florida Times-Union*, February 9, 1916, section 2, p. 13.
21. Edgerton, Gary R. *American Film Exhibition and an Analysis of the Motion Picture Industry's Market Structure, 1963–1980.* New York and London: Garland Publishing, 1983.
22. Edgerton, Gary R. "The Film Bureau Phenomenon in America: State and Municipal Advocacy of Contemporary Motion Picture and Television Production." This volume.
23. Fink, Harold S. "The Good and the Bad in Motion Picture Securities." *The Magazine of Wall Street* 16 (6), July 10, 1915, pp. 406–407.
24. "$500,000,000 Invested in Motion Picture Industry." *Variety* 38 (3), March 19, 1915, p. 19.
25. "Form King Bee Corporation." *Variety* 46 (4), March 23, 1917, p. 17.
26. French, Warren (Ed.). *The South and Film.* Jackson: University Press of Mississippi, 1981.
27. Grisham, William Franklin. "Modes, Movies, and Magnates: Early Filmmaking in Chicago." Unpublished doctoral dissertation, Northwestern University, 1982.
28. "Harry Myers in New 'Vim' Series." *Moving Picture World* 28 (6), May 6, 1916, p. 949.
29. Henritze, Ksue. "Motion Picture and Television Advisory Commissions: The Colorado Experience." Unpublished master's thesis, University of Denver, 1975.
30. "How the Film Trust Lost its Hold." *Variety* 61 (6), December 31, 1920, pp. 4 + .

31. Huff, Theodore. *Charlie Chaplin*. New York: Henry Schuman, 1951.
32. "In the Field with Hotaling." *Moving Picture World* 15 (2), January 11, 1913, pp. 139–140.
33. "Jaxon Film Corporation Enters Field." *Moving Picture World* 31 (12), March 24, 1917, p. 1934.
34. Johnston, William A. "The Motion Picture Industry." *Annals of the American Academy of Political and Social Sciences* 127, September 1926, pp. 94–101.
35. Karr, Kathleen. "Films Made in Rhode Island During the Silent Period." Unpublished report and register, Rhode Island Historical Society, Providence, n.d.
36. Karr, Kathleen. "Hooray for Providence, Wilkes-Barre, Saranac Lake—and Hollywood." In Tom Shales and Kevin Brownlow and others, *The American Film Heritage: Impressions from the American Film Institute Archives*, pp. 104–109. Washington, DC: Acropolis Books, 1972.
37. "Kate Price Now a Vim Star." *Moving Picture World* 30 (2), October 14, 1916, p. 245.
38. Kennedy, Joseph P. (Ed.) *The Story of Films, As Told by Leaders of the Industry to the Students of the Graduate School of Business Administration George F. Baker Foundation Harvard University*. Chicago: A. W. Shaw Company, 1927.
39. "King Bee Comedies." *Variety* 46 (13), May 25, 1917, p. 23.
40. "King-Bee to Coast." *Moving Picture World* 33 (13), September 29, 1917, p. 2013.
41. "King Bee's Young Director." *Motography* 18 (2), July 14, 1917, p. 84.
42. Krows, Arthur Edward. "Motion Pictures—Not for Theatres, Part 11: Frank A. Tichenor and his Eastern Film Corporation." *Educational Screen* 18 (7), September 1939, pp. 242–245.
43. Lahue, Kalton C. *World of Laughter: The Motion Picture Comedy Short, 1910–1930*. Norman: University of Oklahoma Press, 1966.
44. Lahue, Kalton C. (Ed.). *Motion Picture Pioneer: The Selig Polyscope Company*. New York: A. S. Barnes, 1973.
45. Lahue, Kalton C. and Samuel Gill. *Clown Princes and Court Jesters*. New York: A. S. Barnes, 1970.
46. Lamb, Blaine P. "Pioneer Film Making in the West." Unpublished master's thesis, University of San Diego, 1972.
47. Lamb, Blaine P. "Silent Film Making in San Diego, 1898–1912." *Journal of San Diego History*, Fall 1976, pp. 38–47.
48. "Louis Burstein." *Moving Picture World* 32 (11), June 16, 1917, p. 1769.
49. "Louis Burstein is a Pioneer in the Movie Field." *Florida Metropolis*, February 13, 1916, p. B–5.
50. Lyons, Timothy J. *The Silent Partner: The History of the American Film Manufacturing Company, 1910–1921*. New York: Arno Press, 1974.
51. MacKnight, F. C. "Collecting Chaplin, Part 8: The Imitators, Billy West and Others." *Classic Film Collector* no. 51, Summer 1976, pp. 29–30+.
52. Maltin, Leonard. "The Spice of the Programme." *The Silent Picture* no. 15, Summer 1972, pp. 19–24.
53. "Mark M. Dintenfass." *Moving Picture World* 20 (16), May 9, 1914, p. 800.
54. McCabe, John. *Mr. Laurel and Mr. Hardy*. New York: Signet/New American Library, 1968.
55. "Melies Offers New Comedies." *Moving Picture World* 28 (12), June 17, 1916, p. 2039.
56. "Metro Motion Picture Head Boosts Jacksonville as a Film Producing Community." *Florida Times-Union*, May 2, 1916, section 1, p. 6; reprinted from *Motion Picture News*.
57. "Miss Rosemary Theby in Light Comedy." *Florida Metropolis*, April 23, 1916.
58. "Motion Picture Men Hail Jacksonville as Klondike of this Growing Industry." *Florida Times-Union*, March 15, 1916, section 2, p. 17.
59. *Motion Picture Studio Directory and Trade Annual 1917*. New York: Motion Picture News, 1917.
60. "Myers Forms Encore Pictures Corporation." *Motion Picture News*, January 22, 1917, p. 587.

61. Nelson, Richard Alan. *Florida and the American Motion Picture Industry, 1898–1980.* Two volumes. New York and London: Garland Publishing, 1983.

62. Nelson, Richard Alan. "Utah Filmmakers of the Silent Screen." *Utah Historical Quarterly* 43 (1), Winter 1975, pp. 4–25.

63. Nelson, Richard Alan. "Movie Mecca of the South: Jacksonville, Florida, as an Early Rival to Hollywood." *Journal of Popular Film and Television* 8 (3), Fall 1980, pp. 38–51.

64. Nelson, Richard Alan. "Stock Failures and Con Men: A Neglected Economic Aspect of America's Early Motion Picture Industry." *Journal of Popular Film and Television* 11 (1), Spring 1983, pp. 12–23.

65. Nelson, Richard Alan. " 'High Flyer' Finance and the Silver Screen: The Rise and Fall of the National Film Corporation of America." *Film & History* 13 (4), December 1983, pp. 73–83, 93.

66. "New Brand of Films for General Program." *Motography* 14 (19), November 6, 1915, pp. 963–964.

67. "New Jaxon Product Announced." *Motography* 18 (5), August 4, 1917, p. 244.

68. "New York Movie Co. Buys Klutho Filming Studio." *Florida Times-Union,* July 28, 1920, p. 11.

69. "No Great Demand for 'Ku Klux' Film." *Variety* 64 (8), October 14, 1921, p. 47.

70. "Old Vim Film Concern Bawled Up in Finances." *Florida Times-Union,* November 7, 1916, p. 14.

71. "100 Companies of Movie Actors for this City is Dintenfass Prediction." *Florida Times-Union,* February 12, 1916, section 2, p. 15.

72. "One of the New Plump and Runt Comedies Produced by the Vim Company." *Florida Metropolis,* March 19, 1916.

73. "One-Reelers Going." *Variety* 38 (12), May 21, 1915, p. 15.

74. "Passing of General Film Marks End of Old Regime." *Variety* 54 (7), April 11, 1917, p. 61.

75. "Pathe Gets Dintenfass Comedies." *Moving Picture World* 31 (13), March 31, 1917, p. 2126.

76. "Picture Independence Won." *Motography* 17 (17), April 28, 1917, p. 675.

77. " 'Pokes and Jabs' Popular." *Motography* 17 (17), April 28, 1917, p. 896.

78. "Pokes and Jabbs." *Moving Picture World* 25 (11), September 11, 1915, p. 1811.

79. "Popular Picture Personalities." *Moving Picture World* 32 (7), May 19, 1917, p. 1453.

80. Price, Lucille Hardy. Personal interview, Studio City, California, November 1978.

81. "Prompt Rebuilding of Eastern Studio." *Moving Picture World* 33 (11), September 15, 1917, p. 1675.

82. "Scenes at the Vim Studio." *Florida Times-Union,* January 16, 1916, section 3, p. 5.

83. Spehr, Paul C. *The Movies Begin: Making Movies in New Jersey, 1887–1920.* Newark: The Newark Museum, 1977.

84. "Story of a Fat Boy." *Motography* 16 (22), November 25, 1916, p. 1211.

85. "Studio Directory." Oliver Hardy biography in *Motion Picture News* 14 (16), October 21, 1916, section 2, p. 26.

86. "Studios Must Quit the City Declare New York Officials." *Variety* 40 (3), September 7, 1915, p. 22.

87. "Summer Activities of King Bee." *Moving Picture World* 33 (7), August 18, 1917, p. 1089.

88. "Three King-Bees." *Moving Picture World* 32 (9), June 2, 1917, p. 1461.

89. "Vim Comedy Players Lease Lubin Studios." *Florida Times-Union,* November 4, 1915, p. 3.

90. " 'Vim' on the General Program." *Moving Picture World* 26, October 30a, 1915, pp. 946–947.

91. "Wall Street Promoters Invade Feature Film Field." *Variety* 37 (8), January 23, 1915, p. 23.

92. "War Curtails Picture Production." *Motography* 19 (5), February 2, 1918, p. 213.

93. Warner, Jack L. with Dean Jennings. *My First Hundred Years in Hollywood: An Autobiography.* New York: Random House, 1964.

94. Wasko, Janet. *Movies and Money: Financing the American Film Industry.* Norwood, NJ: Ablex Publishing Co., 1982.

95.   Young, Jordan R. "Early Ollie: The Plump and Runt Films." *Pratfall* 1 (12), 1975, pp. 3–7.

VIM STUDIO FILMOGRAPHY

Company personnel, as of January 1916, at the Jacksonville studio:

Treasurer (in New York): Mark M. Dintenfass.
General manager: Louis Burstein.
Secretary: Mildred Burstein.
Directors: Walter H. Stull, Robert Burns, Edward McQuade, and Will Louis.
Assistant directors: Harry Narthton, Bert Tracy, Roy Gahres, and Ernest Boehm.
Male stars: Bobby Burns, Babe Hardy, Billy Ruge, Fernandez/Fernando Perez ("Tweedledum"), Robin Williamson, Billy Bletcher, Spook Hansen, James B. Schroed, and Joe Cohan.
Female stars: Elsie MacLeod, Ethel Burton, Edna Reynolds, Frances McLoughlin, and Helen Gilmore.
Male supporting actors: Harry Byrnes, Walter Baker, George Marks, and Bert Tracy.
Female supporting actresses: Anna Mingus, Arline Roberts, and Violet Burnes.
Cameramen: James L. Carlton, Al Ausbacher, H. E. Partridge, and Howard Green.
Carpenters: W. O. Jelf, P. M. Jones, and A. L. Stokes.
Stage men: C. V. Sherwood, Vernon Eldert, Clarence Fisk, F. J. Wagner, and Emory Buzhardt.
Property and technical men: Daniel Stull in charge; Emory Hampton and John Gray, assistants.
Scenic artist: Bruno Ulm.
Chauffeur: Henry Bard.

Later additions:

Actor/Director: Harry Myers.
Female Leads: Rosemary Theby, Kate Price.
Director: Al Ray.
Female support: Ray Godfrey, Mudge Cohen, Melba Andrews.
Male support: Dad Bates.

Abbreviations:

B = Bungles (starring Tweedledum)
HP = Hardy/Price
MT = Myers/Theby

P&J = Pokes and Jabbs
P&R = Plump and Runt
VFC = Vim Feature Company

Note: Dates are release dates as reported in the trade press. Typical for smaller studios in the teen years, Vim Comedies were not copyrighted.

Midnight Prowlers (11-12-1915)—P&J
A Pair of Birds (11-19-1915)—P&J
Pressing Business (11-26-1915)—P&J
Love, Pepper and Sweets (12-3-1915)—P&J
Strangled Harmony (12-10-1915)—P&J
Speed Kings (12-17-1915)—P&J
Mixed and Fixed (12-24-1915)—P&J
Ups and Downs (12-31-1915)—P&J
This Way Out (1-7-1916)—P&J
Chickens (1-14-1916)—P&J
Frenzied Finance (1-21-1916)—P&J
A Special Delivery (1-27-1916)—P&R
Busted Hearts (also referred to as ''Busted Hats'') (1-28-1916)—P&J
A Sticky Affair (2-3-1916)—P&R
The Getaway (2-4-1916)—P&J
Bungle's Rainy Day (2-10-1916)—B
The High Sign (2-11-1916)—P&J
One Too Many (2-17-1916)—P&R
Pluck and Luck (2-18-1916)—P&J
Bungles Enforces the Law (also referred to as ''Bungle's Inforces the
    Law'') (2-24-1916)—B
Love and Lather (2-25-1916)—P&J
The Serenade (3-2-1916)—P&R
The Artist's Model (3-3-1916)—P&J
Bungles' Elopement (3-9-1916)—B
Their Wedding Day (3-10-1916)—P&J
Nerve and Gasoline (3-16-1916)—P&R
A Pair of Skins (3-17-1916)—P&J
Bungles Lands a Job (3-23-1916)—B
Behind the Footlights (3-24-1916)—P&J
Their Vacation (3-30-1916)—P&R
Anvils and Actors (3-31-1916)—P&J
Mamma's Boys (also referred to as ''Mamma's Boy'')
    (4-6-1916)—P&R
In the Ring (4-7-1916)—P&J
The Battle Royal (4-13-1916)—P&R
The Sleuths (4-14-1916)—P&J

All for a Girl (4-20-1916)—P&R
Hired and Fired (4-21-1916)—P&J
What's Sauce for the Goose (4-27-1916)—P&R
The Rivals (4-28-1916)—P&J
The Brave Ones (5-4-1916)—P&R
Home-Made Pies (5-5-1916)—P&J
The Water Cure (5-11-1916)—P&R
The Pretenders (5-12-1916)—P&J
Thirty Days (5-18-1916)—P&R
A Fair Exchange (5-19-1916)—P&J
Baby Doll (5-25-1916)—P&R
Villains and Violins (5-26-1916)—P&J
The Schemers (6-1-1916)—P&R
The Land Lubbers (6-2-1916)—P&J
The Sea Dogs (6-8-1916)—P&R
A Dollar Down (6-9-1916)—P&J
Hungry Hearts (6-15-1916)—P&R
The Raid (6-16-1916)—P&J
Never Again (6-22-1916)—P&R
For Better or Worse (6-23-1916)—P&J
Better Halves (6-29-1916)—P&R
For Value Received (6-30-1916)—P&J
Housekeeping (7-5-1916)—VFC/MT
A Day at School (also referred to as "A Day in School")
    (7-6-1916)—P&R
Furnished Rooms (7-7-1916)—P&J
Spring Cleaning (7-12-1916)—VFC/MT
Spaghetti (7-13-1916)—P&R
The Great Safe Tangle (7-14-1916)—P&J
The Connecting Bath (7-19-1916)—VFC/MT
Aunt Bill (7-20-1916)—P&R
Help! Help! (7-21-1916)—P&J
Will a Woman Tell? (7-26-1916)—VFC/MT
The Heroes (7-27-1916)—P&R
What'll You Have? (7-28-1916)—P&J
Hubby's Relatives (8-2-1916)—VFC/MT
Human Hounds (8-3-1916)—P&R
Wait a Minute (8-4-1916)—P&J
That Tired Business Man (also referred to as "The Tired Business Man")
    (8-9-1916)—VFC/MT
Dreamy Knights (8-10-1916)—P&R
Rushing Business (8-11-1916)—P&J
Their Dream House (8-16-1916)—VFC/MT

Life Savers (8-17-1916)—P&R
Comrades (8-18-1916)—P&J
The Lemon in their Garden of Love (8-23-1916)—VFC/MT
Their Honeymoon (8-24-1916)—P&R
The Tryout (also referred to as "The Try-Out") (8-25-1916)—P&J
The Tormented Husband (8-30-1916)—VFC/MT
An Aerial Joyride (8-31-1916)—P&R
The Reward (9-1-1916)—P&J
The Chalk Line (9-6-1916)—VFC/MT
Side-Tracked (9-7-1916)—P&R
A Bag of Trouble (9-8-1916)—P&J
His Strenuous Visit (9-13-1916)—VFC/MT
Stranded (9-14-1916)—P&R
Payment in Full (9-15-1916)—P&J
Honeymoon Car (9-20-1916)—VFC/MT
Love and Duty (9-21-1916)—P&R
The Man Hunters (9-22-1916)—P&J
Artistic Atmosphere (9-27-1916)—VFC/MT
The Reformers (also referred to as "The Reformer") (9-28-1916)—P&R
Tangled Ties (9-29-1916)—P&J
A Grain of Suspicion (10-4-1916)—VFC/MT
Royal Blood (10-5-1916)—P&R
Strictly Business (10-6-1916)—P&J
Their Installment Furniture (10-11-1916)—VFC/MT
The Candy Trail (also referred to as "The Candy Trial")
    (10-12-1916)—P&R
Watch Your Watch (10-13-1916)—P&J
A Persistent Wooing (10-18-1916)—VFC/MT
The Precious Parcel (10-19-1916)—P&R
Here and There (10-20-1916)—P&J
Green-Eyes (also referred to as "Home Made Horrors")
    (10-25-1916)—VFC/MT
A Maid to Order (10-26-1916)—HP
The Frame-Up (10-27-1916)—P&J
Gertie's Garters (11-1-1916)—VFC/MT
Twin Flats (11-2-1916)—HP
In the Ranks (11-3-1916)—P&J
Marked 'No Funds' (11-8-1916)—VFC/MT
A Warm Reception (11-9-1916)—HP
Hot Dogs (11-10-1916)—P&J
His Wedding Promise (11-15-1916)—VFC/MT
Pipe Dreams (11-16-1916)—HP
Good and Proper (11-17-1916)—P&J

The Good Stenographer (11-22-1916)—VFC/MT
Mother's Child (11-23-1916)—HP
Money Maid Men (11-24-1916)—P&J
Hubby's Chicken (11-29-1916)—VFC/MT
The Prize Winners (11-30-1916)—HP
Ambitious Ethel (12-1-1916)—P&J
The Guilty Ones (also referred to as "The Guilty One")
    (12-7-1916)—HP
A Rare Boarder (12-8-1916)—P&J
Charity Begins at Home (12-13-1916)—VFC/MT
What's the Use? (12-15-1916)—P&J
They Practice Economy (12-20-1916)—VFC/MT
He Winked and Won (also referred to as "He Went and Won" with a 20
    December release date) (12-21-1916)—HP
Reckless Romeos (12-22-1916)—P&J (Note: release date postponed to
    1-12-1917)
A Financial Frenzy (also referred to as "Her Financial Frenzy")
    (12-27-1916)—VFC/MT
Fat and Fickle (12-28-1916)—HP
Before the Show (12-29-1916)—P&J (Note: release date postponed to
    1-12-1917 with the new title "The Property Man")

Note: All 1917 releases are by Vim Feature Company

The Boycotted Baby (1-4-1917)—HP
His Movie Mustache (1-11-1917)—HP?
Terrible Kate (1-18-1917)—Kate Price (without Hardy?)
War Correspondents (1-19-1917)—P&J
The Love Bugs (February 1917, #21667)—HP
It's All Wrong (February 1917, #21670)—MT
The Other Girl (February 1917, #21689)—HP
A Job For Life (February 1917, #21694)—Charles Dudley
Nora Declare's War (February 1917, #21711)—Cast?
Happy Nat's Dilemma (February 1917, #21713)—Cast?
Seeing Double (February 1917)—Charles Dudley
Harry's Pig (February 1917)—Cast?
The Newlyweds' Mistake (March 1917)—MT
Art and Paint (March 1917)—Cast?
Seeing Double (March 1917)—Cast?
This is Not My Room (March 1917)—Cast?
A Deal in Furniture (March 1917)—Cast?
Deep Stuff (March 1917)—Cast?
Willie Walrus Pays Alimony (March 1917)—Cast?
In Stump Land (March 1917)—Cast?

Wanted a Bad Man (March 1917)—Cast?
Somewhere in Mexico (March 1917)—Cast?
Nellie's Nifty Necklace (March 1917)—Cast?

Vim Feature Company's March release list repeats in April 1917 issues of *Moving Picture World*, then disappears in May as Vim ends releasing. NOTE: "Caught With The Goods" (6 January 1916) is implied to be a Vim release in some of the company's early advertising, but actually was a MinA production.

Total releases equal 156 one-reel films:

61 Pokes and Jabbs	(39.1%)
35 Plump and Runt	(22.4%)
14 Hardy/Price	(9.0%)
27 Myers/Theby	(17.3%)
4 Bungles	(2.6%)
2 Charles Dudley	(1.3%)
13 Miscellaneous/unidentified cast	(8.3%)

9

The New Wave and the Post-War Film Economy

Steve Lipkin

Film history has firmly associated the "politique des auteurs" and the late 1950s *La Nouvelle Vague* with the intellectual and aesthetic currents that stirred the depths of postwar French culture. As a film movement, however, the New Wave also had its roots in the structure of France's postwar film economy. An examination of the first clarion call for the *politique,* François Truffaut's "Une Certaine Tendance du Cinéma Francais" (which appeared in *Cahiers du Cinéma* no. 31, January 1954) shows that even the aesthetic "tendencies" denouned by the *Cahiers* staff sprung from economic determinants as well as aesthetic sources. In order to situate both the postwar French film establishment and the New Wave in a proper economic context, it is necessary to examine what the "tendency" attacked by Truffaut was, who represented it, and to confirm what kinds of films were the result. Only then is it possible to understand how the pattern attacked by "A Certain Tendency of the French Cinema" became established. If there was a tendency to repeat a particular approach to making films, then a logical source of such repetition was economic reinforcement of the aesthetic product. This article examines the economic system which sustained what Truffaut called in "A Certain Tendency" the "tradition of quality."

THE TRADITION OF QUALITY AND THE FILM ESTABLISHMENT

For Truffaut, the "tradition of quality" was the "acclaimed" critical status of about a dozen films made by the French industry. Truffaut coined the phrase from the 1952 law awarding governmental financial aid to the "films of quality," that is, films which had well-known, reputable writers and technicians enlisted in their production. For Truffaut, the "tradition of quality" had several defining characteristics:

1. Psychological realism, which evolved out of a "poetic" realism, attributable chiefly in France to Marcel Carné and was itself in imitation of American films of the 1930s.
2. Adaptation of well-known literary works: most of Truffaut's attack was leveled at the claimed "faith to the spirit" of the original works which became nonsensical in the face of the extreme diversity and complexity of the original sources and the essential similarity and simplicity of the range of completed adaptation.
3. "Refinement" of technique, due to the use of "scholarly framing" and dialogue to overcome shortcomings in the adapted works.
4. Use of "accepted" screenwriters.

Above all, for Truffaut the dependence on an "establishment" of scenarists created the mediocrity of the French commercial cinema. Jean Aurench and Pierre Bost received the brunt of Truffaut's attack; however, the cavalier attitude of Aurench and Bost was infectious to the extent that newcomers such as Jean Ferry, Jacques Sigurd, Roland Laudenbach, Robert Scipion, and even the established playwright Jean Anouilh would "make sacrifices for fashion." Truffaut argued that, ultimately, the eight or nine working scenarists in the French cinema created only "one story" for all the hundred or so French films: a victim, usually a cuckold, was led to his doom by the hatred and evil of his family, and the "injustice of life" (27, p.35). On a polemical level, Truffaut was concerned with exposing the truly bourgeois nature of the facile, antibourgeois gestures in the quality films. The attitude toward the "victim" favored social statement by inoculation, made palatable and commercially salable through thoroughly incorporating traditional theatrical and literary conventions. Truffaut was also concerned with advocating a cinema of the *auteur* ("author') in a more honest sense of the term. The formulaic nature of the French film of this period which he points out *en route*, however, is of foremost concern here.

Besides reducing a variety of novels and plays to this "one story," access to studio technology and striving for a studio "look" was also responsible for the repetitious nature of these films. The "scholarly framing" and "sound track resolutions" that quality films used to circumvent aesthetic difficulties signaled an artistically questionable effort to create a polished and refined studio product just like cherished American models. The scramble to make wide screen processes and color the norms of French production over to the following two years (1954–56) confirmed Truffaut's implication that the "quality" adaptation depended on studio technology for its cinematic elements. The *metteur-en-scéne* simply set up and photographed the scenes as written. Technology served the script, creating a primacy of literary values. Thus all French films made under the establishment of scenarists became essentially the same story told the same way. Beneath the formula, Truffaut further asserted there are not ''men of the cinema'' but men of literature who, in their contempt for both the medium and its audience, leveled out the aesthetic of the film in order to repeat their same hypocritically antibourgeois statements'' (27, p. 33).

Before turning to the economic structures of the 1950s film establishment, it is helpful to confirm and then to supplement Truffaut's remarks by briefly noting other observations about the personnel and genres of films which composed the commercial French cinema of the 1950s.

The Film Establishment

Truffaut included Claude Autant-Lara, Jean Delannoy, Rene Clement, Yves Allegret, and Marcel Pagliero within the tradition of quality. To these, he opposed Jean Renoir, Robert Bresson, Jean Cocteau, Jacques Becker, Abel Gance, Max Ophuls, Jacques Tati, and Roger Leenhardt as directors who also wrote their own dialogue and invented their own stories. The only study in English devoted to the broad range of postwar commercial filmmaking in France is Armes's *The French Cinema Since 1946* (3), which makes a division between ''old'' and ''new'' as the two fundamental kinds of directors, those of ''The Great Tradition'' and those who represent ''The Personal Style.''

If one considers only the directors who launched their careers before the late 1950s (excluding directors of short films), the defining characteristics of the commercial French cinema identified by Armes confirm those attacked by Truffaut. First, Armes found that the commercial French film was essentially that of ''Méliès rather than that of Lumière, being concerned not with the recording of reality but with the creation of an illusion of reality and having its home therefore in the film studio'' (3, vol. 1, p. 7). The earlier directors (those who began their careers before World War II) were Méliès-like too in their interest in illusions, dreams, myth, and fairy tales, rather than ''realism.'' They brought to the cinema formative influences from other arts, particularly literature and theater (3, vol. 1, pp. 17–18). Armes was not arguing, as did Truffaut, that these directors would sacrifice the cinema to any other art; rather he wished to indicate their aesthetic sources. Thus the group included René Clair and Marcel Carné, as well as Renoir, Ophüls and Cocteau.

Armes attributed the characteristics Truffaut considered aesthetic shortcomings to the group of directors who began to make films immediately after the war. Here Armes grouped Henri-Georges Clouzot with Clément, Jean Delannoy, Yves Allegret, and Autant-Lara. Armes agreed with Truffaut that ''with all of these directors the script-writer is the key collaborator on whom the success or failure of a film largely depends, for great reliance is placed on dramatic construction and dialogue. The limitations of the great majority of this generation can be ascribed to this dependence on script-writers'' (3, p. 20). These directors, too, rely wholly on the studio; Armes further characterized them as ''craftsmen . . . exploiting to the fullest the great wealth of experienced acting talent available in France'' (3, p.20).

The Cinema of the Art and Essay

The other major "kind" of film besides the commercial feature consituted more of a style than a genre. The short film, or "films of art and essay," were characterized primarily by "their spirit of artisic exploration" (23, p. 125). Since double features had been prohibited before the war, the short film was traditionally a valuable addition to distribution catalogues.

The most important function the short film served was to allow films to be made each year by younger members of the industry who were neither allowed access to studio facilities for their own projects, nor given conventional production financing. Roles in the production situation were hierarchical. Only after years of "apprenticeship" as an assistant could one hope to have a chance to direct. From 1950 to 1960 over 300 short films were made, costing anywhere from 15,000 to 500,000 francs (10, p. 15).

Before new means of financing feature films opened up, several important New Wave-era directors were able to get their starts by making short films: among them were Alain Resnais, Jean Rouch, Chris Marker, Jacques Baratier, and Truffaut. Short films provided a valuable starting ground for these filmmakers because they allowed the most control over the production situation, resulting in a tremendous variety of subject matter. Jeanne and Ford list the following genres of short films: films of exploration and voyages, science films, histories and biographies, short fictional works, films about art, "fantasies" and film poems, animations, and documentary films over a range of subjects as equally varied (20, vol. 5, p. 98)

Key Production Roles

The inability for newcomers to commercial films to work as directors became one of the main industrial constraints Truffaut condemned as a critic. The hiercarchy of responsibilities in the studio system was established both internally and externally; internally, by the unions of creative and technical industry workers, and externally, by the larger economic and legal structure which tried to maintain the production of films as a profit-making business.

Legal definitions existed delimiting the responsibilities and rights of all personnel associated with the conventional production of a film. Probably the most important and interrelated were the definitions of the *"auteurs"* and the "producer" of the work. These definitions by law placed creative workers, and film *auteurs*, under the control of the administrative powers of the producers.

While the producer was "the person . . . who took the initiative and responsibility for the *réalisation* of the work," the *auteur* (as legally defined) was the person and/or persons responsible for the creation of the work (10, p. 93). Individual *auteurs* were rare; group *auteurs* were termed as either collective or collaborative, and in either case the rights varied accordingly. In the instance of a "collective" *auteur* there was no mention of the various individual authors, hence there was complete, common fusion of the contracts (and rights) of all involved. *Auteurs* in collaboration were the most common—here the author of the scenario, the author

of the adaptation, the author of the dialogue, the author of music especially composed for the film, and the director were accorded status as collaborative *auteurs*.
Until 1964, collaborative *auteurs* shared proportionally in monetary remuneration
as determined by the producer. In all contracts the various *auteurs* would under-
take with a producer, the producer had total, exclusive rights to benefits from the
exhibition and distribution of a film. The *auteurs* received their payment directly
from the producer (28, pp. 240–241).

Some protection of rights came from the unions in the French film industry
which maintained an equilibrium in the division of profits. Unions intervened in
effecting a major policy change in 1964 which resulted in the distributor, rather
than the producer, computing remuneration for contributors based on returns from
theaters. Prior to that, the basis for computing the percentage for remuneration was
problematic. Further, even if the producer held all collaborator's rights it did not
necessarily follow that the producer should be the sole party to determine the com-
pensation of contributors. By computing the contributor's percentages on the basis
of the money due to the distributor after exhibitors had received their share, all parties might then benefit from the relative success or failure of a film, depending on
its public reception (28, pp. 242–243).

The definitions of roles in the production situation, like the characteristics of
the films themselves, reflected only the visible surface of the industry. It is necessary to examine the economic structure of the film establishment to understand
more fully why French film production in the 1950s ran the course outlined by
Armes and Truffaut.

ECONOMIC STRUCTURE OF THE FILM ESTABLISHMENT

The end of World War II found the French film industry in a shambles. Any film
production or renovation of existing production and exhibition facilities after the
German occupation was slowed not only by the effects of war destruction, but also
by excessive postwar taxation (18, 1945, p. 963). Economic ill health had begun
to plague the film industry even in the decade before the war, however, due to the
generally depressed economic conditions in Europe and the rest of the world.

> The fringe industries of vulnerable countries,and of France in particular, based their
> production and commercialization strategies on those of the dominating industries,
> but the fringe industries maintained an artisan-like character and found themselves at
> the mercy of the least shock. Thus between wars the French cinema knew a succes-
> sion of highs and lows. (7, p. 58).

By 1936, both Gaumont-Franco Films Aubert and Pathé Cinéma were for sale.
These were the only two large consolidated production, distribution, and exhibition complexes in France.

As early as 1931 the Conseil National Economique had initiated reports on all
major areas of the French economy. Guy de Carmoy, the Minister of France, de-

livered a timely report of the state of the French cinema in July 1936. de Carmoy cited two major areas as the source of the crisis in the French film industry. Film production expenses were the primary cause of unprofitability due to the costs of updating film technology. There was also, however, a crippling imbalance of foreign and national films: five out of 13 distributors in France were actually American companies resulting in the distribution of 186 American films in 1935 as opposed to only 47 French productions (21, pp. 121–124). In order to "put an end to the anarchic regime" of the film industry ". . . the Conseil National Economique had recommended exceptional corrective measures allowing the marked intervention of the State in the event that the profession did not prove itself capable of accomplishing the necessary reforms." (21, p. 129). Specific proposals for immediate action included a delay on the projections of imported films (as well as a reduction of import licenses), a temporary reduction of national production, and most significantly, the formation of a central organization which would govern the functions of the film industry in France. This would be ". . . a fiduciary body termed as financial center for the film industry, which would exercise control over the diverse branches of the industry from the beginning of work in the studio to the counting of receipts in the theaters, in order to facilitate the granting of banking credit" (28, p. 50). Legislation was ready by 1939 which specified in detail the functions of the state-sanctioned, central organization mandated with the control of the French film industry. The organization would begin as a committee which would be replaced by a permanent, professionally-run agency. The committee would regulate distribution throughout the country, limit the opening of new theaters, and have complete control over all theatrical receipts. The committee would also initiate the legislative determination of terms such as "auteur," "producer," "French film," and "foreign film," and would develop a means of extending the Labor Code to the cinema industry. The French government passed legislation on March 17, 1939, containing 59 articles administering the original recommendations of the Conseil National Economique (27, pp. 50–51).

While aimed at creating financial stability, the 1939 legislation marked the beginning of government influence, and the weakening of private control over the administration of the film industry. The 1939 articles began a chain of legislation which continued through the German occupation and the Vichy regime, culminating in 1946 with the formation of the Centre National de la Cinématographie (CNC). Gérard Valter, in a massive study of the legal status of the CNC, showed how the government intervention brought on by the crisis of the industry in 1936 resulted in the gradual but complete takeover of the control of the industry by the government (28, p. 23). Increased judicial, rather than administrative, safeguards and the direct appropriation by the State Treasury of the program of aid to the industry annexed responsibilities initially allocated to the director of the CNC. Committees, rather than individuals, determined CNC policy by 1952, contributing to an ossification of industry practices.

The legislative strategy of the late 1930s and 1940s, including the formation of the CNC, however, aimed at government regulation of measures the industry would take to help maintain itself. "It was a perpetual question of not only substituting for the normal mechanisms of common law—civil or commercial— mechanisms of constraint which would determine the processes of authorization, control, and disciplinary codes; but also of entrusting the establishment and administration of those codes either wholly or partly, directly or indirectly, to the professions themselves" (28, p. 61). Formed at the end of 1946, the CNC was a body between public and private realms. Representing the intersection of state interests and private business, the CNC consolidated in one body all the exigencies of administering what was essentially a five-headed financial animal, including all production, distribution, exhibition, importation, and exportation concerns. In order to fully understand the scope of the CNC's responsibilities it is helpful to look first at the problems and possibilities of autonomous, private financing in the French film industry.

Traditional Means of Film Financing

Until the creation of the CNC and governmental aid to the cinema, there were two basic sources for production funding loosely termed "internal" or autonomous financing, and "external" or "loan" financing (10, pp. 79–80). A film would be produced internally if the producer individually provided the necessary financing, usually from revenue generated by prior films, or prior wealth. Distributors would also provide their own funds directly to producers.

More frequently, a film would be funded through loans of varying sorts to the producer. In the decade prior to the war distributors customarily signed for a loan, since they could easily secure bank financing against existent film holdings (7, p. 59). The distributor could also guarantee another kind of collateral in foreign sales; accepted financing practice would allow up to 15 percent of the total budget against projected export sales. Another kind of loan called a "professional credit," could come directly from within the profession itself. Studios and laboratories would simply extend an account to a producer, effecting a loan, or, the technicians and actors working on a particular film would forego direct salary in return for a percentage of the film's profits.

The various means of film financing entailed not only risk for the guarantor of a loan or the provider of direct sources of cash, but also allowed varying degrees of control over the production of a film. A privately financed film carried total risk for whoever financed it, but since this was usually the producer, it would also allow complete control over the creation of the film product. A producer would inevitably lose some control in relying on professional credit. Actors and technicians would require some influence on the choice of subject or method of presentation, since the risk would be distributed among creative personnel. Bank loans, although the most secure method of financing, would also be the most conservatively controlled, since only low risk projects could qualify.

The early years of governmental aid prior to and concurrent with the formation of the CNC allowed advances on production by means of the Crédit National. A producer would submit the budget for a film, and if the Crédit National approved aid funding, it would forward 25 percent of the estimated budget (7, p. 27). Films received a total of 50 million francs in funding from the Crédit National in 1941; 500 million francs in 1947; and one billion francs in 1949 (7, p. 144).

Creation of the Centre National de la Cinématographie

Although the immediate cause of creating a central governmental agency to administer the French film industry was simply the inability of private capital to balance profits against losses, Guback noted that the causes are deep within the structure of European culture:

> In Europe . . . there has been the belief which holds the state responsible for the maintenance and perpetuation of national heritage and culture. The authority of the state gives it the mission to preserve and encourage art and culture, for it is the only institution representative of its people and their traditions. In execution of this obligation, the state is empowered to assist morally and financially all types of art for their qualities of national expression and creativity (17, p. 144).

The program initiated by the Conseil National Economique in 1936 recognized that the film industry, as an integral element of both the French economy and the French culture, required the means to both promote and sustain film production. After the war (and even to present day), the government recognized an additional responsibility in renovating theaters destroyed by the war. Government regulation of the industry centered on five main areas: (1) the control of box office receipts; (2) aid to national (and eventually international) film production; (3) regulation of imports by establishing and enforcing screen quotas; (4) determining salaries and remuneration within the industry proportional to a contributor's status as a ''creator''; and (5) balanced distribution of films among theaters throughout the country (28, p. 24).

The Centre National de la Cinématographie was founded on October 25, 1946, to replace the Office Professional du Cinéma and the Direction Général de la Cinématographie. The CNC ''. . . was charged with administering the regulations . . . which concerned the production, the exhibition, the distribution, and the exportation of films earmarked to be shown in public'' (13, p. 62). As the culmination of a succession of temporary governmental agencies, the CNC maintained the contractual relations between the various branches of the industry while providing a controlling structure. The CNC combined professional self-direction with external regulation which would hopefully ''normalize'' the economics of the film industry within a few years. The CNC was legislated originally as a public establishment with financial autonomy, under the auspices of the Minister of Information. The director of the CNC wielded the authority of the organization and was its chief representative in all acts of civil life. As part of its legislative mandate, certain regulatory powers were delegated to the CNC. No branch of the film industry could operate without its official authorization. Principal creative collaborators on a production were required to hold a professional identity card, which was not only revocable by the director of the CNC as a disciplinary measure, but also protected and validated the qualifications of skilled technicians (28, pp. 59–63). In general, the powers of regulation charged to the CNC were ''to ensure the coordination of work programs in order to utilize more rationally manpower, the modernization of enterprises, the coordination of the diverse branches of the film industry, the statistical observation of professional activity, and generally, to develop the French film industry; and (further) to arbitrate eventually the conflicts resulting from such regulations . . .'' (28, p. 63).

The responsibility for regulating the film industry was divided into three basic mandates, including *''attributions d'animation,''* *''attributions de contrôle,''* and *''attributions de coordination.''* *Attributions d'animation* included, besides the specified powers of regulation, studying all proposes laws, decrees, and cases pending related to the film industry. *Attributions de contrôle* (of finances) allowed the CNC to administer all theatrical receipts, then to funnel revenue into the financing of film production, and also entailed the thorough keeping of admissions statistics and ticket sales records. The CNC was charged with having immediate accountability for the financial state of the film industry on any given week. As information center for the industry, the CNC was communicate ''to distributors, producers, and those holding rights to a percentage of a film's receipts any information relative to those receipts and products of any kind relevant to the exploitation of the films in which they (held) an interest'' (28, p. 69). Among the *attributions de coordination* of the CNC were the responsibilities for developing the noncommercial sector of the cinema, the ''cinema of the art and essay''; organizing France's contributions to national and international exhibits, such as the Cannes Film Festival; and overseeing the development of the professional and technical character of the industry. Besides issuing industry identity cards, the CNC was responsible for maintaining the Institute d'Hautes Etudes Cinématographique (IDEHC) (28, pp. 65–73).

As a national center, the CNC was the funnel through which literally all industry revenues would pass. The gross receipts taken in by all theaters in France were sent directly to the CNC for accounting, where the income would be split among the exhibitors, the distributors, and the contributing creators in predetermined percentages. The CNC also received a percentage of theater revenue for providing its accounting and statistical services.[1]

The director of the CNC at its inception and until 1952 was Michel Fourre-Cormeray; Fourre-Cormeray was succeeded by Jacques Flaud through the end of

---

[1] The CNC also had income from dues paid by professional organizations, taxes on licenses issued, fines levied by the director of the CNC, and a percentage of the fees charged to all producers for registering their films at the Registre Public (see 28, pp. 77–78).

the decade. Besides ensuring the professional character of the industry by controlling possession of identity cards, or, in extreme cases, banning personnel from working at all (the director of the CNC was also empowered to close companies for up to a year), the director also determined the rules which located films in theaters on the bases of both earned and potential receipts. The director was not, however, allowed to shoulder the total responsibility for the Center. Administrative and disciplinary tasks were divided among several commissions and committees consisting of representatives of the industry, government ministries, and the CNC director. A "Conseil Paritaire," which considered the CNC budget and heard all cases bearing on CNC regulations, was composed of 16 members, including eight representatives of industry employers and eight representatives of salaried workers. A larger Central Commission on the Control of Receipts took responsibility for the overall administration of the Center, functioning like a board of trustees. Members included the director, government ministry representatives, and representatives from each major branch of the industry. Gérard Valter's claim is that in 1959 a subtle shift in the structure of the CNC virtually converted the organization from a meeting of government and commercial industrial interests into a simple tool of the government. A 1953 revision of law moved the source of authorization of funds for aid to film production from the director of the CNC to a representative of the state treasury who was also on the Central Commission. The director then was left in a position only to administer the ministerial decision (20, p. 228).

Aid to the Cinema

Although the formation of a national center for the film industry allowed more centralized economic control, the purpose of such control was to facilitate and stimulate the production of films. The main change in traditional financing caused by state centralization was the creation of a new source of production funding through direct financial assistance by the government. In 1948, the "Fonds de Développement de l'Industrie Cinématographique" were only a temporary measure; however, in 1953, legislation renewed this revenue as "Soutien Fiancier a l'Industrie Cinématographique" on a permanent basis (28, p. 121). Aid money went directly to producers from the budget of the CNC and was furnished by a tax passed at each stage of renewal of the aid fund. The temporary aid began in the form of "advances on receipts," but over 15 years evolved to become available in different forms subject to varying criteria.

The source of aid funds was a tax imposed on virtually every ticket sold in commercial cinemas. Aid was thus, in a sense, the French government forcing the film industry to help itself. The tax on theater tickets was nothing new; a three-level tax had been levied on cinema ticket purchases in France since 1920.[2] After Septem-

---

[2] The "three-level" tax included the "droit des pauvres," an entertainment tax originally declared by Charles VI for the benefit of the Hospital of Saint-Julien; a state tax which was imposed on cinema

ber 16, 1948, tickets in the 45- to 95-franc range increased five francs, while there was a 10-franc tax levied on tickets costing 100 francs or more (1, 1957, p. 802). The admissions tax was supplemented by another tax on the length of the film to be distributed, paid by the producer. French feature films were taxed 400 francs per meter, while undubbed foreign features incurred a tax of 25 francs per meter. Short films (films less than 1,300 meters long) were taxed 50 francs per meter. These taxes generated an average of 125 million francs per year in the first years of the temporary aid fund (28, p. 196).

The 1948 aid consisted of an automatic advance on the receipts of a film in circulation, either for paying off production debts, or for financing a new film. Eligible French films had to be made by French producers in the French language using all French creative personnel (including authors, technicians, and actors). The subsidy advanced 13 percent of a film's earnings, and seven percent after receipts reached 7.5 million francs (17, p. 156; and 7, p. 80). The automatic subsidy was "calculated proportionately on the receipts from release in the City of Paris and in the overseas departments and territories . . . and in the French provinces and in foreign countries" (11, p. 37). Although the advance on receipts had a major problem in that, by definition, it could aid no new projects, it did encourage economically successful productions. In 1956, Jacques Plaquin traced the "lives" of the 123 French films made in 1952, and found that government aid had funded only 36 percent of the financially unsuccessful films made that year, while 65 percent of the profitable films had been financed with state aid (10, pp. 76–77).

In 1953, the renewal of the aid laws brough a shift in criteria which allowed aid to be granted based on the "probable quality" of a film. here, "probable quality" is based on the reputation of the production team, and is equivalent to box office potential.

The law of 6 August 1953 made its contributions to the problems of quality . . . Advances on receipts could be decided before production . . . based on . . . characteristics and qualities of the cinematographic work and from the conditions of its production (28, p. 207)

Criteria for aid in 1954 continued in the same spirit: the *International Motion Picture Almanac* reported that advances would "be given sparingly," even to the extent that 50 million francs would be given to one film, rather than 25 million to two. "Under the new decrees enacted by the Government, a minimum sum of 15 million francs may be used to subsidize films other than those financed with foreign capital. The decree lay down [sic] that such films must serve the cause of the

receipts in 1916; and a local municipal tax which legislation enabled in 1920. The local tax (which was dropped from the General Code of Taxes in 1968) could range up to 8.5 percent of the price of sale. Tax "breaks" were granted to small exhibitors (those with fewer than 1200 weekly admission totaling no more than 2400 francs); the receipts of "Youth and Family Nights" (which received exemptions totalling 800 to 1000 francs); and exhibitions of "Art and Essay" films which were subject to graduate scales of taxes (10, pp. 60–61 and 21, pp. 51–52).

French cinema'' (15, 1956, p. 782). There were also two significant changes in aid by 1954; exhibitors became eligible to receive up to 70 percent of the cost of redecorating old theaters, and short films became eligible for subsidy (10, p. 63). Short films received their aid in the form of jury prizes. Criteria for "artistic quality" would depend on the particular jury; however, the prize was considered an incentive to production since it was a direct grant, as opposed to an advance on receipts for a film already in circulation. Prizes to short films averaged 10,000 francs each. Other bonuses were possible for outstanding use of color, or for a short film of "quality" released with a feature. This award could amount up to one percent of the total aid granted the feature itself (10, p. 78; and 17, p. 145).

The fundamental structure and intentions of governmental aid to the cinema remained stable until 1959, with the exception of an abortive attempt by the government to eliminate the tax on tickets priced under 165 francs in 1956. Such a move would have eliminated much of the aid fund. In 1959, subsidies were extended for seven years with provisions included for gradually diminishing aid payments. In place of aid, loans would become available at low interest (five percent). The hope was that an era of transition would allow the industry to return to a state where it could become self-supporting. By 1967, aid did become basically limited to bonuses on foreign and domestic receipts. The most important change in aid (especially to the group of new directors who would constitute the New Wave) was that, in 1959, "quality" feature films became eligible to receive both bonuses granted by jury selection, as well as advances on receipts (5, p. 770). The basis for a jury prize was to be the scenario of a film, submitted in advance of production; unlike the 1953 aid, which was awarded primarily on the basis of reputation, the 1959 aid was conceived as an award for aesthetic quality. From 1948 to 1953 over 13 billion francs in aid revenue were disbursed to producers, distributors, and technicians; from 1954 to 1959 the "Fonds de développement de l'Industrie Cinématographique" totaled 46 billion francs (17, pp. 29–30). Through the 1950s, aid ultimately accounted for an average of 20 to 25 percent of the total investment needed each year for film production.

Governmental aid gave the industry the support and sustenance it needed to gain financial health after the war. The cost of financial recovery came in the form of sacrifice of control to government influence. The extent of the CNC (and thus governmental) control over the functions of the film industry is evident in a survey of industry activities in the 1950s.

ELEMENTS OF INDUSTRY ACTIVITY IN THE 1950S
PRODUCTION, DISTRIBUTION, IMPORTATION,
EXPORTATION, AND COPRODUCTION

Production

The average cost of a French feature film almost doubled from 47 billion francs in 1952 to 81 billion francs in 1956. In 1956 producers provided an average of 38.5 percent of the total budget for their films, either through their own funds or through financing they received from the CNC (24, pp. 80-81).

The producer was the vital link between the financial and creative energies necessary to complete a film. One of the constraints in the film production system which both Truffaut and Astruc condemned was that only rarely (as in the instances of Jean Cocteau, Jean Renoir, and Jacques Tati) would creators also produce their own films. By controlling budgets, producers would delegate creative authority in a production any way they wished. The producer of a film was by legal definition the agent wholly responsible for its completion. As a consequence, all creative collaborators signed a contract granting the producer sole control over rights to the distribution of a film (28, p. 37). The producer was also responsible for registering the film with the Registre Public by filing the title of the film and copies of all contracts along with a synopsis, a budget, and a short statement explaining the original sources of the film and justifying why this film was being made from the original work. If a producer failed to register the project with the Registre Public, all contracts signed with collaborators became null and void, and the film could not become eligible for governmental aid.[3] The Registre Public also mediated guarantees between producers and technical services. If a lab or studio offered its services in return for a percentage of the earnings, utilizing the Registre Public guaranteed that the level of payment would be determined by the official accounting services at the CNC.

The quantity of French production increased steadily throughout the 1950s, reaching a peak in 1961. The production increase at the end of the decade was due in large part to the changes in the aid criteria in 1959 which allowed aid to be granted to new feature films of "quality," effectively laying the economic groundwork for the New Wave. Production became more expensive due not only to the inflated costs of materials, which increased from ten to 100 times in the 15 years after the war, but also because of the increased use of color and wide screen processes (10, p.148). As early as 1951, *Film Daily Yearbook* reported that "quality is now the foremost care of the producers, inasmuch as like everywhere else the B pictures are more and more unprofitable to turn out and audiences are getting increasingly choosey" (p. 754). The hope in the use of wide screen and color was

---

[3] A production project was also required to receive a second authorization on the basis of the editing script, the definitive budget a complete crew list, and submission of copies of all documents related to the financing of the film (28, pp. 41 and 86).

that audiences could be drawn away from the television and other consumer distractions and back into the theaters, a problem discussed in more detail below. Thomas Guback offers the following analysis of the increase in production costs through the 1950s:

> While costs [rose] for both types [national and coproductions] the cost of making a French national film increased the most sharply, presumably because there was more room for expansion into higher budgets from the relatively small ones in the early 1950s. In addition, it could very likely be that cheap productions had been forced out by competition and that there is a smaller market for them today'' (17, p. 186).

Distribution

From 1951 to 1956, only 1.5 percent of all films produced failed to reach distribution (10, p. 148). Contractual relations between producers and distributors depended on the relative indebtedness of the producer. By law the producer owned (and therefore controlled) all negatives and prints of a film, and was entitled to a defined percentage of a film's distribution returns. A distributor who had financed the film originally, however, could claim a share of the ownership either by holding rights to the title of the film or the rights to the adaptation, or by claiming a share of any aid funds advanced to the producer.

Although distributors were directly responsible for the number of films they held in their catalogues and the number (and nationality) of films acutally in distribution at any given time, the specific regional locations of films in distribution in France and the amount of time a film could spend in any one location was regulated by the CNC. The actual number of films in distribution remained stable from the middle until the end of the decade (1, 1956, p. 617; 1, 1961, p. 786). The stability of the distribution system was due in part to the rigid accountability of theater managers. Theaters were required to use an official ticket system allowing for a close accounting for receipts from ticket sales. Theater managers were then responsible for declarations of their receipts not only to the CNC, but also to film distributors and the Society of Authors, Composers, and Editors of Music (SACEM). Theater accounts were subject to weekly inspection by itinerant represenatives of the CNC and managers could incur stiff fines for infractions. In return for close regulation, most theater managers benefitted from a set of distributor/exhibitor understandings which were recognized by the CNC. The ''Conditions générales de location de films'' represented an agreement between the Fédération Nationale des Cinémas Francais and the Fédération Nationale des Distributors des Films which determined the privileges accorded to types of theaters in the order and clearances of films within distribution zones throughout France. The Conditions générales also defined a protective period during which before and after a film had run a particular theater, the film could not be shown again in the same zone (27, pp. 265-266).

Importation

In the years immediately following World War II, American aid and American films flowed into a temporarily crippled Europe. Since production was well below capacity, foreign exhibitors were dependent on a large influx of American films to keep their screens filled. The glut of American films on the French market was officially sanctioned by both governments in May, 1946 when Léon Blum, French minister of commerce, and James Byrnes, the American Secretary of State, signed what became known as the infamous ''Blum-Byrnes Agreement.'' This agreement annulled the quota set on American films before the war, which had limited imported American films to 120 a year (17, p. 21). Subsequently, in 1946, there were 182 American films exported to France, which jumped to 336 American films in 1947, a figure nearly triple the national French film production (1, p.804). The Blum-Byrnes agreement also reserved the first four weeks out of the thirteen-week ''quarter'' of the fiscal year in French theaters for French films. Although French exhibitors could reap immediate benefits from the dumping of the popular American films on the French market, that market was ''scarcely large enough for the cheaper French film to recover its cost'' (14, p. 49). A 1950 UNESCO report stated that

> The large number of cheap American films available . . . apart from adding to the dollar deficit, is only one of the factors prejudicing the development of national film industries. These industries, unable to recover their outlay on the films which they produce, are stunted in growth and become unable to meet the demands of the national market. The exhibitors, therefore, are driven to depend for their existence upon foreign, largely American, films (17, p. 16).

The causes of American dumping ran far deeper than mere economic opportunism allowed by hungry French theater circuits. Guback viewed the influx of American films as part of a larger attempt to ''Americanize'' Europe immediately after the war through the aid made possible by the Marshall Plan:

> While the [Marshall] aid was supposed to strengthen faltering economies against risings from the left, American films were seen as propaganda vehicles for strengthening western European minds against pleas from the left. The argument to foreign governments was: If you take our dollars, you can take our films. Considered in these terms, it is not surprising that American films received advantageous terms in many western European markets at the expense of competitors (17, p. 73).

The traffic of American films through France was so great as to not only threaten film production, but also to create a dangerous imbalance of cash flow from France to the United States. As a consequence, in 1946 French banks simply ''froze'' the revenue generated by American films in France, and the release of frozen American dollars became a key lever in subsequent renegotiations of the import and screen quotas. The strategy was not only to protect home industry, but also to channel this ''borrowed'' currency toward solving domestic economic problems while it was still accessible within national borders. A new Franco-

American agreement, signed in September 1948, broached both problems; it reinstated the prewar import quota at 111 American films and raised the screen quota for French films in any theater to five weeks out of thirteen for each theater. France also agreed to release $9 million in blocked funds over a four-year period (18, 1948-1949, p. 694). "The pact listed several ways in which these frozen funds could be spent: joint production of films with French companies, construction of new studios, acquisition of distribution rights to French films, acquisition of story rights in France, etc. (17, p. 19).

The restrictions on transferring American earnings out of France began to be lifted with some qualifications by revisions of American-French agreements in 1951. For example, two years later a provision was added to existing agreements that $430,000 in francs were "to be reserved from U.S. film earnings to assist in the promotion and publicity of French film in the U.S." (1, 1954, p. 877). The basic policy of granting about 110 export licenses a year to American companies persisted throughout the decade, while France continued to attempt to manipulate U.S. revenue until 1960, when restrictions on American earnings were lifted completely.[4]

Exportation

Although France found itself on the receiving end of most international film traffic in the early part of the decade, by the mid- to late-1950s film exportation had become a flourishing part of the industry. France's efforts to crack American distribution circuits began as early as July 1951, when the CNC attempted, as a condition of returning "frozen" dollars, to require the American Motion Picture Export Association to donate $250,000 to finance a French film office in the United States. In a compromise, French export licenses were given a discount which amounted to a negligible level of American support for French exportation. France did manage to export 33 films to America in 1950 (almost one-third of its total production) and 28 in 1951; exportation prospered as the earnings of French films in all countries doubled between 1953 and 1954 (18, 1953-1957, and 1, 1952-1956).

The overall number of French films distributed in America doubled again between 1958 and 1960. The coincidence of the jump in French exports with the New Wave years in France was not accidental. The phenomenal success of Roger

---

[4] The following data illustrate the stable progression of licenses and remission of blocked U.S. dollars (see 1, 1953–1961, and 18, 1954–1962.)

Year	Licenses	Remitted
1952	121 licenses	$120,000 remitted
1953	121	200,000
1954	90	200,000
1955	90	235,000
1956	110	235,000
1960	446 (over three years)	

Vadim's *Et Dieu Créa la Femme* (1956) caused a huge demand for French films
for several reasons, Brigitte Bardot not the least among them. *Et Dieu Créa la
Femme* alone earned $4 million in 1957, a year in which the total French film earn-
ings in America were only a little over $8 million. "The prospects were so good at
the end of [1957] that the French were busily plotting the invasion of the greater
American hinterland, with a plan for buying up showcase houses in various key
cities" (1, 1958, p. 878). American distributors came to hope that the spicier
French films would, like wide-screen processes, serve as a lure to draw audiences
away from television and back into the cinema:

> With competitive free entertainment being offered (in the form of TV) exhibitors rea-
> soned that perhaps the public was tiring of paying for Hollywood's traditional con-
> tent, so well spelled out in the old Production Code. Acquisition of foreign films
> offered the chance to experiment in luring the missing millions of viewers back to
> theaters. Foreign films with fresh (and flesh) appeal were called upon to revitalize
> theater programs. This experiment produced mixed results, for some foreign films
> brought in attractive revenues while many others failed to display any box office
> value (17, p. 71).

Jacques Flaud, the director of the CNC, pointed out in an interview with *Cahiers du Cinéma* (no. 71, May, 1957) that French exportation was succeeding not
only because of the content of the films, but also because of the methods of exportation the CNC was attempting to develop. Flaud referred specifically to Unifrance
Film, an autonomous organization which promoted groups of French films abroad
by organizing French film weeks and publishing a journal containing interviews
with the actors and directors, critical reviews, script extracts and stills.

Coproduction

Coproduction, like exportation, gained economic importance as the decade progressed. Coproduction began in 1948 in part as a means of loosening blocked American funds, and developed within a few years into a definite style of filmmaking. In
the loosest sense, coproduction is the sharing of financial and creative responsibilities for the production of a film. The implications of a coproduced film were complex, since most European countries granted governmental aid to film production
projects. A means for international definition of the nationality of a production in
order to divide both expenses and profits became essential. Coproductions had
three major advantages: a broader (and potentially more secure) investment base; a
doubled marketability; and access to a larger group of creative personnel.

The criteria for determining the nationality of a film were established by the
Conseil de la Communauté Economique Européene (CCEE) in 1953. These criteria considered the original language in which the film was shot; the nationality of
the authors, technical collaborators, and actors; and the locations in which at least
30 percent of the shooting of the film had taken place (28, pp. 184-185). Interna-

tional coproductions, however, were established through individual treaties between various producing partners.

> Coproduction takes place within the framework of bilateral treaties among partner countries. The treaty's value is that it established the context for such activity while formalizing the responsibilities of the commercial partners, minimum financial participation of partners, minimum budgets, the employment of artistic and technical personnel, and the permissable places of shooting and laboratory work (17, pp. 192-193).

Coproductions became more frequent through the 1950s because they provided a means to cope with the rapidly rising costs of film production, in particular allowing the use of expensive technologies such as color and wide-screen processes. As more expensive films, coproductions could compete with the American presence in Europe. Guback notes that:

> By pooling resources, a more elaborate picture with bigger stars can be made than if only one country were financing it . . . While lavish production techniques, color, scope, processes, and big stars are not necessarily prerequesites [sic] for good films, they do perform the vital functions of attracting audiences in several nations and competing on more or less even terms with the costly productions from other countries, notably the United States. Thus, bipart and tripart films may be considered as bargains in cost terms in that producers in two or three countries receive revenue (and subsidies) from a bigger film than any could afford to produce separately (17, pp. 192-193).

French coproduction developed slowly until 1953, when there were 45 coproductions as opposed to only four the year before. The number of coproductions dipped below 40 once between 1953 and 1960 (see 18, 1946-1965). Among all of France's coproduction partners Italy was the most popular; France and Italy shared approximately 70 of each other's coproductions from their first corproduction agreement signed October 1949, until 1966. From 1950 to 1965, the average cost of Italian/French coproductions was $465,000 with Italy supplying 52 percent of the total investment. These coproductions were at least one-and-a-half, and often up to three times as expensive as normal national productions (17, pp. 185-193).

A 1966 treaty between Italy and France recognized three classes of coproductions: "normal coproductions," coproductions of artistic value," and "coproductions of exceptional entertainment value." Normal coproductions cost at least $285,000 with the minority partner's financial contribution amounting to at least 30 percent of the total cost. Films of artistic value cost somewhat less, and lowered the minority partner's contribution to no less than 20 percent of the production cost. Coproductions of exceptional entertainment value, however, had a minimum budget of about $509,000, with similarly lowered requirements for the minority partner's contributions, including funding and commitment of creative personnel (17, p. 193).

The aims of Italian and French coproduction were defined as the improvement of the production values of films through creating the opportunities allowed by an increased budget. The ultimate goal was to improve the reputation of Italian and French film in general: "The agreement was. . . to facilitate the production of Films of Quality; moreover, the essential idea was to make films of such value *that they could serve the expansion of French and Italian film world-wide"* (italics in original, 10, p. 31).

Whether or not coproductions actually attained this goal is far less tangible than the investment coproduction came to represent in France between 1952 and the mid-1960s; as of 1959, investment in French coproduction doubled and climbed steadily, so that by 1966 the amount of money invested in coproduction had increased twelve-fold since 1952, while the investment in national production in the same period had only doubled (17, p. 188).

In 1957, Jacques Flaud hoped that French/Italian coproduction had surpassed the stage where expense of production would superficially be equated with quality, and that a new epoch of coproduction was under way.

> Coproduction . . . has known two periods; in the first it was praised. It brought teams with industrial, technical, and artistic skill, but they would often produce films without authentic inspiration which finally were harmful to the art [of the cinema] of the two or three countries engaged in these coproductions. Presently coproduction has entered a second period . . . notably in French and Italian coproduction . . . What [now] matters is that France help Italy make films in the Italian tradition, and vice-versa. This system, which is essentially financial, seems to be bearing happy fruit (5, p. 14).

As the costliest of the costly European film, coproduction represented a logical conclusion to the production tendencies of the "tradition of quality." With famous international technicians and multinational markets, coproductions, like films shot in wide-screen formats, gave hope to an industry confronted with sagging sales. Attendance trends show that even with government control and reinforcement, inclinations toward increased financial investment could not surmount the larger causes of a late 1950s crisis in attendance. Toward the end of the decade, it became clear that "quality" production in France could not pay for itself.

ATTENDANCE

In the 15-year period from 1950 to 1965, the French cinema lost a total of 130 million viewers, while the overall population in France increased by one percent (12, p. 24). The causes of the deterioration in film viewing and its relationship to a similar crisis in cinema attendance in other countries must be considered within the larger context of film exhibition, particularly the number and distribution of theaters and the levels of admissions revenues generated in this period.

The number of 35-millimeter format theaters in France steadily increased from 1945 to 1960, due to the effort to rebuild theaters destroyed during the war and the need to either renovate old theaters or build new ones to accommodate the wide-screen processes which became integral to the industry in the mid-1950s (18, 1946–1963). There have traditionally been four kinds of theaters in France: "Salles d'exclusivité," the larger, more plush theaters in main cities; "salles de quartier," or "local" urban theaters; smaller, "theaters of the film of art and essay" or art houses; and the theaters located in rural areas. In the mid-1950s, "salles de quartier" and local rural theaters generated over half of all exhibition receipts, making them the most financially significant theaters (24, p. 78).

With some increases, the gross receipts of French theaters remained very steady from the late 1940s to the late 1950s, rising from 14 billion francs in 1947 to 30 billion francs in 1951, and reaching 49 billion francs in 1955 (1, 1948, p. 804; 1, 1952, p. 734; and 1, 1956, p. 617). Receipts rose a further eight percent in the New Wave years from 1959 to 1962. The main reason for the steady climb in receipts was not a proportionate increase in attendance, but instead from steady increases in both the price of admissions and the tax levied on admissions tickets. Viewed in proportions to account for the change from old to new francs a ticket which cost .33 francs in 1947 cost 1.86 francs in 1960, and had skyrocketed to 5.26 francs in 1971, an overall increase of 1600 percent (7, p. 73). *Film Daily Yearbook* reported that a ticket in 1952 in any theater cost 15 times its price in 1938. The tax on the purchase price of the ticket rose from 20 percent in 1946, to 35 to 50 percent in 1950. After 1954 the increase in the tax percentage was limited to the more expensive seats costing over 120 or 130 francs. Even at that time there was speculation that the tax might backfire by keeping spectators away from the cinema, and decreasing the amount of revenue it would bring to the aid fund.

The actual drop in spectators in the 10 years from 1947 to 1957 was slight (12 million)—the crucial attendance factor centered on the number of times an individual would go to the cinema. Filmgoing depended on access to theaters and other leisure time distractions. Although there were 424 million admissions in 1946 and 412 million ten years later, the average individual frequency of paid film admissions through this period dropped from 10 a year in the early 1950s to eight in 1960, and to six in 1962 (25, p. 65). By 1961, attendance had fallen off 20 percent overall from 1957 (1, pp. 804–805). Although different sources indicate a variety of possible reasons for the drop in viewer attendance[5], the two major causes were an increase in leisure-time options (particularly in the quality of television broadcasts and the availability of television receivers) and a general trend toward

[5] For example, the 1953 *Film Daily Yearbook* attributed major responsibility for the drop in commercial film attendance to noncommercial screenings by private clubs, public education offices, and cultural and religious groups and institutions. Distribution contributed indirectly to the decrease: smaller houses had less likelihood of getting good films, causing a tendency for the local theaters to close.

suburbanization in France, which took potential customers away from larger theaters in the cities.[6]

Sadoul attributes the drop in individual viewer frequency directly to television;
however, he also points out that Italy, with comparable access to television programming in 1960, had twice as many theater admissions per capita (25, p. 140).
The effects of television were delayed from 1952 to 1957. In 1952, there were only
100,000 TV receivers in all of France, with only government-sponsored programs
on the air 30 hours a week. By 1957, there were approximately 750,000 television
sets, providing five percent of French households with television (1, 1953, p. 892;
1958, p. 878). Decreases in attendance began to correlate directly with television
ownership:

> A study of the effects of TV inroads on film attendance in the mining regions of the
> Northern France, where set sales had shown a considerable increase, showed a pro-
> portionately heavy decline in movie attendance. The noncommercial French televi-
> sion continues to operate on a few hours a day schedule, and the artistic level of the
> programs is hopelessly low, but the Lille region study seemed to demonstrate that
> even with these handicaps, TV could play hell with the movies (1, 1955, p. 878).

Television was only one of several possible forms of leisure which became
available to the French population during the 1950s. Jacques Cleynen estimates
that leisure expenses constituted 8 to 8.5 percent of the average French household's budget, and that prior to the war, one-fifth of the leisure budget was devoted
to the cinema. During the war, the cinema gained in importance as a leisure activity as it was highly available. By the late 1950s, cinema expenditures accounted for
only three percent of the money an individual might spend on leisure activities,
compared with 20 percent in 1946 (7, pp. 87–88). As the French economy improved through the 1950s, so did individual purchasing power through increased
income and increased credit. The increased purchasing power of French consumers led them to funnel money into hobbies, records, photographic equipment,
vacations, the obligatory television set, and camping gear (17, p. 181). These habits persisted through the 1960s: according to the Centre de Recherches et de Documentation sur la Consommation, in 1965 French consumers put 36.1 percent of
their investments into "devices" (photography apparatus, musical instruments,
and TV and radio sets); 25.5 percent into spectacles (11.6 percent of this to the cinema, as opposed to only 2.9 percent for theater and concerts) and 38.6 percent for
"art works" including photos, records, books, and journals (17, p. 182).

The late 1950s and early 1960s saw a trend toward large shifts in population
away from urban centers and rural areas and toward rapidly developing suburbs.
By the late 1950s, about one-third of the French population had moved, with the

---

[6] A demographic factor also predetermined a partial drop in attendance; since the beginning of
1950s, the largest single population sector supporting the cinema has been the 15 to 24 year age group,
averaging 22 admissions yearly per individual. From 1945 to 1962, however, the segment of the French
population in this range decreased by about 10 percent from 6.5 to 5.9 (7, pp. 65 and 23).

result that 44 percent of those who had moved went to the cinema less frequently than they had before and 17 percent no longer went at all (12, p. 25). The tendency to move to another city or within one city was accompanied by a trend for attendance to drop by 25 percent in smaller towns and as much as 50 percent in larger cities. Theaters responded by either moving out to the growing suburbs or remodeling (usually by decreasing the number of seats, following the lead of the smaller, newer suburban theaters). Smaller theaters attempted to offer more varied programs to attract viewers. Viewer preference in city centers, however, was for larger, more comfortable theaters, so that the local, neighborhood cinemas which throughout the decade had provided a majority of exhibition revenues were forced to close in spite of their efforts to remodel and renovate (7, pp. 66, 77–79).

One consequence of suburbanization was a general decrease in the amount of time devoted to traditional media. During the 30 years from the period before the war to the late 1960s, French newspapers lost three million readers, and 30 daily newspapers closed shop. The theater suffered a similar decline (17, pp. 156–157). French consumers had more money to spend on more things but less time for each: "There are a lot of ways to kill time, but there is no more time to kill" (7, p. 721).

CONSTRAINTS OF THE AID SYSTEM

The crisis in theater attendance and efforts to ease the crisis by enlarging, moving, or renovating theaters, or turning more and more to lavish international coproductions illustrates a defining characteristic of the direction of the French film industry: a formulaic response to change. The essence of the formula equates quality with monetary investment, and simultaneously assumes that quality of the product will suffice to draw an audience with evolving interests. Two factors invited such a film industry formula: the dependence of the film industry in general on technology, which Minister de Carmoy labeled as early as 1936 as the expensive fertilizer prerequisite to industry existence and growth; and in France, the addition of government to the balance of art, industry, and business that produces cinema in any country.

Jacques Cleynen suggested that in the early years of its life, the film industry grew out of elements in its environment highly favorable to its development, that the newborn industry gropingly found the most effective ways to become profitable (7, p. 72). Cleynen's argument runs as follows: an industry develops through the evolution of certain technologies. Yet the wants and needs of a receiving public must also determine the structure and functions of an industry. Industries must develop *with* the technologies they employ as well as with public interests. The failure of an industry is then a failure to adapt to changes in the environment which nourishes it; here, the failure of the cinema to draw audiences suggests that it has become an outmoded leisure activity:

The established organization is relatively rigid, and adapted to its environment; in the event that this environment changes, necessitating adaptation, structural rigidity hinders development. The industry becomes outmoded from the moment the organization no longer has the flexibility necessary to adapt . . . Thus changes in life-style and possible diversions, television in particular, gives cinema the final blow (7, p. 72).

In short, the cheaper, more accessible technology of television made it a more attractive medium.

The participation of the government in the film industry in France, with the purpose of reinforcing the basic structures and functions of the pre-existing industry, only led to rigidity, or as Cleynen argues, to further rigidity. Cleynen points out that the very necessity to turn to a system of governmental aid was a characteristic sign of an industry that has lost its liveliness. An examination of the effects of aid on the creation of films shows in what sense the processes of administering and receiving aid may have been responsible for contributing to rigidity and aesthetic stagnation in film production.

Because aid guaranteed advances on receipts, films were produced which would have the most potential to generate those receipts. Aid encouraged ''safe,'' commercially reinforceable films, that is, films which tended away from creative experimentation and relied on financially satisfying formulas (see 2, p. 19; and 4, p. 375). Aid emphasized a production as a business product in the mind of its creator(s), so that, in the terms of Jacques Flaud, director of the CNC through the 1950s, creators ''acquire a producer's mentality, shying away from taking risks'' (5, p. 6). Aid had brought prosperity to the French cinema, but also ''routine, and a lack of imagination and heart.'' With the possibility of aid, artists became conservative, unwilling to take risks, resulting in a general stagnation of the creative work. Flaud extended the analogy, stating that a logical consequence of the producer mentality was an ''exporter'' mentality, further fueled by the then recent successes of French exports:

In 1956, almost 40 percent of the receipts of the French cinema came from abroad. The creative mentality becomes changed, and [creators] come to estimate that the better films are those that guarantee a 40 percent return from abroad, that is, films shot from known authors [films tirés d'auteurs connus] about proven subjects (thus they tend to be remakes or adaptations) and which re-feature proven talents and confirmed actors with international reputations.

These producers seek less to take risks on the level of the subject or the film's distribution, than to insure themselves against the risks of production by choosing infallible subjects and actors and crew which are sure to make money (5, p. 6).

Claude Degand, the director of the CNC in the mid-1960s, also argued that aid too easily led to too many films made too fast. ''The obligation put upon producers to reinvest their subsidies in a new film carrie[d] with it the risk of overproduction—the producer must make a film willy-nilly to obtain the subsidy'' (11, pp. 39–40).

Aid also tended to encourage more expensive productions, simply because, by definition, the advance on receipts necessarily had to be invested in new production. The larger the advance the larger the investment, and thus the emergence of the equation of expense of production yielding higher financial return (in the form of aid) constituting ''quality'' production. The system did not favor the smaller producer:

It restricts itself to assuring the industry a certain level of rentability, in favoring, *a priori* by advances on receipts films with big budgets and recognized stars, and *a posteriori,* through subventions successes consecrated by the public; it ''aids'' above all the large, internationally competitive production companies, scarcely preoccupying itself with the ''cultural contributions'' of independents and marginal producers that the present system tends to eliminate (7, p. 82).

The original phenomenon of government reinforcing existent industry structures was only further aggravated by increasing government encroachment on the actual administrative functions of the industry. The film industry was transformed into a government bureaucracy in several distinct stages, rather than maintaining its status as a government- ''advised'' but otherwise autonomous entity. Any rigidity inherent within the industry structure could only become worse as the aims and directions of the industry became determined by committees of government ministries, rather than individuals within the industry itself.

The balance shifted toward government as early as 1953, when the director of the CNC became determined by a decree of the council of government ministers, on recommendation from the minister charged with the film industry, rather than directly selected from within industry ranks (28, p. 118). Also in 1953, the means of forming and initiating industry regulations was transferred from a ''conseil paritaire'' to a ''conseil supérieure'' on which representatives of the film industry had only minority membership, 12 members out of 30. The profession therefore lost its direct administrative reins, and saw its consulting influence diluted.

The direct participation of the French government in the film industry also made it easier to cast the more ominous shadow of censorship over the production of films. Through the 1950s censorship was the responsibility of the Film Control Board, a group composed of representatives of the government, the industry, and members of the Family Association (18, 1950, p. 870). The Control Board and the CNC were separate by definition. With the turn to aid granted on the basis of ''quality'' in 1953 and 1959, however, the possibility arose of refusing aid on the grounds that a proposed project would be unsatisfactory to the censor. Although Flaud argued in 1957 that the number of ''refused scripts'' was actually very small, in 1960 the government announced that it would refuse aid to anyone who had signed the petition upholding the right of French youths not to fight in Algeria

(5, p. 8). This announcement immediately followed the suppression of Jean-Luc Godard's *Le Petit Soldat*.

If, at bottom, the essential problems of the film industry were manifested in a stagnant output of films, the solution to the problem was the need to grant aid on the basis of potential quality outside of commercial success, rather than advancing funding on earned receipts; such a measure would potentially reinforce different, more creative films. As early as his 1957 interview swith *Cahiers du Cinéma*, Flaud called for criteria for granting aid which would be more flexible and more appropriate to the current needs of both industry and audience. Flaud pointed out that the 1953 aid law had provided a precedent in granting aid based on the criterion of "probable quality" (reputation of the production team) and the same approach could be taken to funding features of "aesthetic quality" (5, p. 10). "Aesthetic quality" would be determined by an examination of the scenario for the film.

Flaud also wanted any new measures to overcome a problem of ignorance of the aid system which plagued the earlier aid options. If only a limited number of producers know about the award, only a limited number would receive it.

> The mechanism of this procedure is very badly known. Producers themselves are badly informed. They know that there exists a prize for quality, but its functions escape them somewhat. Therefore, the first reform . . . consists of informing and producers that if they take the risk of making a film with any audacity, that they can be underwritten, thanks to the jury prize (5, p. 10).

Through legislative approval of aid to features based on quality, Flaud was confident in the resurgence of the health of the industry. In fact, the system he forecast in 1956 was precisely the set of economic conditions which produced the New Wave three years later—the predictive detail of his description of the aid system and the results which would ensue is uncanny:

> This system would consist of creating a sort of prize to the first film of a new director, as there exists a prize for a first play. Thus, not on the basis of the completed film, but on the basis of a film project, after examining the scenario and the production team, [there would be] aid given before the production began . . . This would give to a producer the possibility of making a film without a star, with an original scenario, or even with a qualified director as yet untried in feature films. With this system of a "prize to the first film" the producer would have some advantage in taking a risk, an advantage evident the moment he undertook the production of the film (5, p. 12).

THE NEW WAVE AS AN ECONOMIC REACTION

It is a point of general agreement among those who write of and about this period that the New Wave was largely an aesthetic reaction against the typical French film of the 1950s. Claire Clouzot, for example, writes:

The French cinema . . . in 1958 was in a state of sclerosis, stuck between a drama-
turgy inherited from the theatre . . . an aesthetic based on a "success formula"
(well-crafted scenarios, sure-fire stars and dialogue writers) and a closed system of
product based on the antiquity of the makers, large budgets, the lack of imagination
of the promoters and the routine intelligence of the public (8, p. 3).

It was the very changes in the aid laws in 1959, predicted by Jacques Flaud in
1956, which allowed the New Wave to work in "total liberty" from the industry
and its established preconceptions about production (6, p. 415).

Truffaut's 1954 attack against the film establishment specifically condemned
the system of production being utilized and a creative mode which entailed dependence on "successful" directors and "sure-fire" scenarists. In the early and
mid-1950s potential directors needed a long career as an assistant, a scenarist, a dialogue writer, or technician to have a chance to make a feature. The number of
new directors was actually numerically reduced each year, so that in 1955, there
were only four "beginners," and three in 1956 (discounting Vadim and Marcel
Camus who were assistant directors previously) (8, p. 1).

The 1959 changes in the aid laws, which allowed aid to a first film on the basis
of a submitted script produced an explosion in the output of films by new directors
which was one source of the label "La Nouvelle Vague." There were over 100 out
of a total of 133 feature films made in France by new directors with proportions remaining the same over the next few years (26, pp. 116–118).

Fueling the New Wave explosion was the success of the first New Wave features in not only international festivals, but also in general international distribution. Truffaut's *Les Quatre Cents Coups,* winner of the award for "Best
Direction" at Cannes in 1959, brought $500,000 for American distribution rights
alone. Marcel Camus's *Orpheu Negro,* which won the "Best Film" award at
Cannes the same year, had been made in Brazil and had an "international flavor"
which piqued possibilities for international exportation much like Vadim's first
film had a few years earlier. The first New Wave films virtually reversed the usual
distribution patterns:

> Prior to the New Wave, a French film would circulate exclusively in French metro-
> politan areas. This would take a long time, especially if the film was exceptionally
> popular . . . With the New Wave, low-budget films circulated abroad before do-
> mestic runs were exhausted (8, p. 18).

Not wanting to miss the chance to ride the crest of the distribution "wave,"
producers became extremely willing to put money into low-budget, "fast" productions by unknowns, adding a new source of financing to the government aid already available. Truffaut wrote:

> We were in a state of euphoria. In '59 the situation was abnormally good. It naturally
> encouraged many, sometimes rather wild dreams. This was also true of some produc-
> ers who believed that the secret lay in youth, in innovation, and who hastened to pros-
> pect for new talent (16, p. 13).

While on the one hand, the plethora of willing producers (one article mentions a possible 600 available) depended on the few successful films to carry financially the many failures, on the other hand, the sheer quantity fostered competition between producers and allowed filmmakers a new arena of creative freedom (19, p. 8; 22, p. 7). While there were more opportunities and more channels for productions, the inevitable glut of financially unsuccessful "New Wave" productions (in 1962, there were 30 "mostly bad" New Wave productions circulating within France) ultimately led to producers and distributors who were shy of the "New Wave" label, making it extremely difficult after 1962 or 1963 for a new director to get a first film into production (15, p. 25).

In the first few years after the 1959 aid law, however, the possibilities for a newcomer were tremendous. For the first time, any new filmmaker could, in effect, act as producer, either through receiving aid advanced on a script, or by working with a producer who would allow the freedom desired for a particular project. Two productions which were close predecessors of the New Wave, Claude Chabrol's *Le Beau Serge* and Louis Malle's *Les Amants* had both been financed completely by their directors' own private funds.[7] In order to work within the economic limits inscribed by such sources of funding, the New Wave productions were necessarily low-key, rejecting big name stars and scenarists, studio shooting, and complex production technology in general. With a lower budget, directors gained control they would not have had through established production channels: "For the young cinéaste, it is the seal of liberty, the possibility of being himself without being obsessed with losing money for the financier who has given you his confidence; for the producer, it is a reduction of risk and a better guarantee of profit, especially from sales abroad" (8, pp. 16–17). Much of the early New Wave production was a result of group in-breeding; for example, Chabrol financed Jacques Rivette's first short film, which was shot in Chabrol's apartment and featured Jacques Doniol-Valcroze. Rivette began his first feature film, *Paris Nous Appartient,* in the summer of 1958 through a loan from *Cahiers du Cinéma,* the camera and lab fees borrowed on credit, actors and technicians who took a percentage in lieu of salary, and out-takes which Chabrol had left over from *Les Cousins.* Chabrol also produced Eric Rohmer's first 35-millimeter short film, *Véronique et Son Cancre* (9, p. 20).[8]

---

[7] Malle had utilized his own fortune, and Chabrol, his wife's inheritance. (Chabol subsequently got 45 million francs in aid to produce *Les Cousins,* which cost only 58 million francs total (see 8, p. 15).

[8] Crisp reports the following:

Chabrol, Truffaut, Godard, Rohmer, and Rivette had a scheme for ...several of them to make their first films: since the average cost of a film was little under 100 million francs, and they were convinced they could produce them for as little as 20 million, they would offer a producer five films for the price of one. And so that the producer would not take fright at the thought of so many untried directors, they would get the help of Astruc and Resnais. Thus, Resnais, for instance, would shoot the first one with Rivette as assistant. Astruc the second with Truffaut as assistant, Rivette the third and Truffaut the fourth, with other members of the group as assistants,

The notion that financial control and autonomy would allow for a cinema of personal expression had begun as a seed planted by Alexandre Astruc's landmark "Le Caméra Stylo" in *L'Ecran Française* (no. 144, March 1948) and was fertilized not only by Truffaut's polemics in "A Certain Tendency of the French Cinema" and other reviews and articles, but also by independent, inexpensive productions throughout the 1950s, such as Jean-Pierre Melville's *Le Silence de la Mer* (1947) and Agnes Varda's *Le Point Courte* (1956). The New Wave was thus not only a new style of making films, it was also specifically (in its most lasting representations) a personal expression, a way of producing a "personally" created work—in direct opposition to the more formulaic establishment output of the preceding years—which was enabled by sources of funding more accessible to the less-essential, individual filmmaker:

> The desire to work in a cinema of the auteur had led to a modification of the ordinary system of production. In its turn, this modification has resulted in changes in shooting methods. Finally, these renovations have had aesthetic repercussions in the choice and treatment of subjects (8, p. 18).

CONCLUSION

Truffaut's reaction to the established French commercial cinema of the 1950s foresaw the aesthetic necessity of the cinema of the *auteur*. By viewing the historical depth of the economic roots of the commercial cinema, one source of the tradition of quality clearly becomes the economic structure of the industry. Production of financially successful films was reinforced through a system of financial aid designed to ensure that a high level of investment would perpetuate a studio style of filmmaking. There were then two main kinds of constraints in the French film industry in the 1950s: first, the industry favored long, expensive productions utilizing only established workers, especially in film direction. The second kind of constraint was the general governmental control, influence, and preservation of industry tendencies. "Quality" was as much an economic category as an aesthetic designation; by legally redefining "quality" in 1959, production more closely resembling the cinema of the *auteur* flourished in the New Wave years. The older films of "quality" became stale and repetitious because economic determinants equated creativity with financial reinforcement.

In Truffaut's view the nontraditional cinema of the *auteur* placed the control of the original conception of the work in the same hands which controlled the actual production of the film. Within the context of making films, such "personal control" was available initially in the short film, and then later allowed in the production of features by new government financing.

---

and so on. The system never came to anything, largely because producers were simply not interested in making cheap films (9, p. 20).

The New Wave "happened," then, economically, for several key reasons: films like Malle's *Les Amants* and Vadim's *Et Dieu Créa la Femme* widened public support for the subject matter which was to become indigenous to New Wave films, the preconceptions which forced producers to finance only certain kinds of productions began to dissipate; filmmakers themselves realized the feasibility of shooting films with unknown actors and on locations, rather than in the studio; and government subsidies became more generally available.

REFERENCES

1. Alicoate, Jack (Ed.), *The Film Daily Yearbook.* Fort Lee: J.E. Brulatour, 1947–1961.
2. Allen, Irving. "Subsidy Creates Mediocrity.," *Journal of the Screen Producers Guild* 9, June 1967, p. 19.
3. Armes, Roy. *The French Cinema Since 1946.* 2 vols. New York: Tantivy Press, 1970.
4. Baumol, William J. and William G. Bowen. *Performing Arts: The Economic Condition.* New York: The Twentieth Century Fund, 1966.
5. Bazin, André and Jacques Doniol-Valcroze, "Entretien Avec Jacques Flaud." *Cahiers du Cinéma* no. 71, May 1957, p. 14.
6. Butcher, Maryvonne. "France's Film Renaissance." *Commonweal* 71, January 8, 1960, p. 415.
7. Cleynen, Jacques. "Histoire Economique du Cinéma." L'Ecole Practique des Hautes Etudes (typewritten). n.d.
8. Clouzot, Claire. *Le Cinéma Français Depuis La Nouvelle Vague.* Paris: Fernand Nathan, 1972.
9. Crisp, C.G. *Francois Truffaut.* New York: Praeger, 1982.
10. Degand, Claude. *Le Cinéma . . . Cette Industrie.* Saint Etienne: Editions Techniques et Economiques, 1972.
11. Degrand, Claude [*sic*]. "Film Subsidy in France." *Journal of the Screen Producers Guild* 9, June 1967, p. 37.
12. Derogy, Jacques. "La Crise du Cinéma?" *L'Express*, December 28, 1964, pp. 24–25.
13. Doniol-Valcroze, Jacques and Claude De Givray. "Tentative d'Analyse Spectrale du C.N.C." *Cahiers du Cinéma*, no. 161–162, January 1965, p. 62.
14. Durgnat, Raymond. "A Mirror for Marianne," *Films and Filming* 9, November 1962, p. 49.
15. Gary, Romain. "The Foamy Edge of the Wave." *Show* 4, April 1964; p. 75
16. Graham, Peter. "The Face of 1963." *Films and Filming* 9, May 1963, p. 13.
17. Guback, Thomas H. *The International Film Industry.* Bloomington: Indiana University Press, 1969.
18. *International Motion Picture Almanac.* New York: Quigley Publications, 1946–1963.
19. Jacob, Gilles. "Nouvelle Vague or Jeune Cinéma? *Sight and Sound* no. 34, Winter 1964–1965, p. 8
20. Jeanne, René and Charles Ford. *L'Histoire Encyclopedique du Cinéma.* 5 vols. Paris: S.E.D.E., 1962.
21. Léglise, Paul. *Histoire de la Politique du Cinéma Français.* Paris: Librairie Générale de Droit et de Jurisprudence, 1970.
22. "Meeting La Nouvelle Vague," *Films and Filming* 6, October 1959, p. 7.
23. Mitchell, B.R. *European Historical Statistics.* New York: Columbia University Press, 1975.
24. "Quelques Statistiques." *Cahiers du Cinéma* no. 71, May 1957, pp. 78 and 81.
25. Sadoul, Georges. *Le Cinéma Français 1890–1962.* Paris: Flammarion, 1962.
26. Sicilier, Jacques. "New Wave and the French Cinema." *Sight and Sound* no. 30, Summer 1961, pp. 116–118.

27. Truffaut, François. "A Certain Tendency of the French Cinema." *Cahiers du Cinéma* (in English) no. 1, January 1966, pp. 31–41.

28. Valter, Gérard. *Le Régime de l'Organisation Professionelle de la Cinématographie. Due Corporatisme au Régime Administratif.* Paris: Librarie Générale de Droit et de Jurisprudence, 1969.

Canadian Feature Films in the Chicago Theatrical Market, 1978-1981: Economic Relations and Some Public Policy Questions*

Manjunath Pendakur

INTRODUCTION

Canada embarked on a program of producing feature films with the intention of cracking the most lucrative theatrical market in the world, the United States, when in 1975, it extended the 100 percent tax write-off policy to private investors in feature films. Faced with market domination by U.S. distributors and lack of opportunity for Canadian talent and capital in the domestic market, the Canadian federal government appears to have opted for this policy of subsidizing film production through a taxation mechanism but seeking profits in the United States and other foreign markets while creating jobs at home in the short run.[1] An estimated $170,000,000 were spent on film production in 1980, and an average of 50 feature films were being produced in Canada between 1978 and 1980 (1). Some Canadian-produced feature films have played on American theater screens, as well as network and pay-TV screens. Many of these films featured American stars

* An earlier version of this article was presented at the Western Social Sciences Association Annual Conference, Albuquerque, New Mexico, April 27-30, 1983. This inquiry would have been impossible without the cooperation of many persons in the Chicago film industry. We are deeply indebted to them for sharing their knowledge with us. Robert Winning, who was the graduate research assistant, contributed well with energy and interest.

Thanks are also due to the National Film Board of Canada for supporting this study with a grant.

[1] The Canadian Film Development Corporation, a government financing agency, invested $26 million in the production of films between 1968 and 1978 and recovered only $5 million. See, Canada, *Report of the Federal Cultural Policy Review Committee*, Ottawa: Information Services, Department of Communications, 1982, p. 254. For an analysis of how Canadian films are systematically excluded from the domestic market by U.S. distributors and major theatrical chains, see (4). For a historical analysis of government policy contributing to the underdevelopment of Canada's film industry, see (5).

such as George C. Scott, Burt Lancaster, Jack Lemmon, and Bill Murray in leading roles as a marketing strategy to make these films attractive to the American and other markets. However, no systematic analysis of the Canadian-produced films' penetration into the U.S. markets has been undertaken so far.

Additionally, no systematic analysis of the performance of those films that have entered the U.S. markets exists, which can be immensely helpful for Canadian filmmakers and government officials. This study, a pilot effort in that direction, examines the performance of selected Canadian feature films that found entry into one important market, Chicago, and provides a partial picture of the marketing strategy used by the dominant distributors (Majors) and the dominant theater chains in the Chicago area. This article is also a micro-look at the existing economic relations among the major film producer-distributor combines in the United States and the major theatrical chains.[2]

Although nation-wide generalizations are difficult to make from such a small study, the sample examined and the method utilized point out viable opportunities for conducting an expanded study of Canadian films' market performance in the American theatrical and ancillary markets. This case study has also been useful for generating some research questions for further work in this area of inquiry.

In the last two decades, many scholars around the world have been concerned with the study of cultural domination and resistance. One-way flow of cultural goods from the United States into Canada has been examined as a process of asymmetric power relations between two countries (5). Current Canadian film policy rests on the ground that a capitalist cinema could be created at home if market entry into the United States is assured and if Canadian films are treated in a nondiscriminatory manner by the American Majors. This study attempts to lay the groundwork to evaluate such policy by examining the patterns of distribution and exhibition of a selected number of Canadian feature films produced since 1978, which have gained access to the Chicago film market.

METHOD

The Sample of Films
Ten Canadian feature films were selected for the purposes of the study for three major reasons. First, all 10 received play dates on Chicago area screens both in urban and suburban locations. Second, with the exception of *Atlantic City*, they

---

[2] The eight leading firms with integrated production-distribution operations were: Universal Pictures, Paramount Pictures, Twentieth Century-Fox, MGM/United Artists, Warner Bros., Columbia Pictures, Orion Pictures, and Buena Vista (Disney). Orion is a newcomer to this powerful group of corporations. It was created by some of the executives of United Artists when that company was absorbed by MGM in the recent years. They are called the Majors because of their historic control of the U.S. motion picture industry which, measured in terms of annual film rentals received by them, is usually greater than 90 percent. The steady decline in the number of films they produce, however, has no bearing on their high market share. For an analysis of these factors see (3).

were all given play dates in a single theatrical chain, the Plitt Theaters, which dominates the Chicago markets. Third, it is believed that these 10 films represent fairly the types of films that Canada is producing with the American market in mind under the 100 percent Capital Cost Allowance Program.

The titles and their completion dates are: *Atlantic City* (December 1979), *Meatballs* (September 1978), *Scanners* (December 1979), *Terror Train* (December 1979), *Heavy Metal* (November 1980), *The Changeling* (February 1979), *Tribute* (May 1980), *Prom Night* (September 1979), *Happy Birthday to Me* (September 1978), and *My Bloody Valentine* (October 1980).

Variables and Definitions

1. *Distribution Company:* Perhaps the most important part of the film business is carried on by a distribution company, the function of which is to arrange for the marketing of films. Acting as the middle agent between the producer and exhibitor (retailer), the distributor often finances production, as well as shares the costs of advertising and promotion. The distributor works out specific contracts with the exhibitor in terms of sharing the costs and revenues from exhibiting a film and, in turn, does the same with the film's producer.

2. *Nature of the Contract:* As the study focused on relations between the distributors and exhibitors in the Chicago market, the following aspects of the contract were researched for each of the ten films: Was the picture put up for a bid to obtain the best terms from the exhibitors? If yes, what was the advance paid by the exhibitor to the distributor? If no, was it negotiated? What were the terms of sharing the revenues under both conditions? What was the committed playing time for each picture? If the picture was not put up for a bid, why not? The assumption here was that a bid brings in more revenues to the distributor and, in turn, may be shared by Canadian producers. We were also interested in determining the conditions under which pictures were put up for bids and the conditions under which they were negotiated with the theatrical chains.

Since the ten films considered in this study had been awaiting release for a year or two before entering exhibition, they may not have been blind bid. Consequently, a relevant question was: did the exhibitors trade-screen these films before booking them, or did the bookers go only on reviews and word of mouth information?

3. *Guarantee:* It is an assured sum of money that an exhibitor promises to pay a distributor to secure a film for release in its theater(s). This amount represents a nonrefundable dollar commitment to the film. Often it may have to be paid before a film's opening.

4. *Advance:* This is the amount paid by the exhibitor to the distributor in advance of a film's release to secure that picture for its theater(s), usually within seven or 14 days. It is paid against anticipated rentals and may or may not be part of the exhibition contract. Unearned portions of this amount are refundable.

5. *Box Office Gross:* These are revenues collected from ticket sales and do not include candy sales, and so on. What did each of the ten films gross in the Chicago theatrical markets?

6. *Rental Revenues:* This is the most important parameter of how a film performed at the box office. These are gross box office revenues minus exhibitor's fees and costs (the "house nut") agreed to by the distributor. It is from the rental revenues that the distributor takes its share (commission, advertising costs, etc.) and pays the producer its share.

We did not attempt to determine how the individual distributors of these 10 Canadian films shared their rental revenue with the respective Canadian film producers. Important though that might be, this study was limited to the relations between distributors of these films and exhibitors in the Chicago area due to time and funding limitations.

7. *Advertising Budgets:* This variable is the most revealing indicator of an exhibitor's and a distributor's confidence in the film's grossing potential and their commitment to a picture. Basically it indicates whether or not they believed that the picture had the potential to return a profit.

Advertising expenses are often shared between distributors and exhibitors, and the distributor may pass on part or all advertising costs to the film's producer. This study examined advertising practices for the 10 Canadian films in the Chicago theatrical market and thereby suggested patterns of practices among the distributors and exhibitors. It could not be determined how these costs were shared between distributors of these 10 films and their respective Canadian producers as that was not part of the study.

8. *Indirect Advertising:* We explored such factors as local film critics' reviews in the various media, television coverage of film-related events, if any, and talk show appearances by film personalities. Data were gathered from interviews with local film critics, television industry personnel, and published newspaper reports.

Interviews With Key Industry Personnel

Initially, a general survey of the trade press—*Variety, Cinemag/Cinema Canada*—was undertaken, which was useful in providing the background information for the study.

We identified several persons in the Chicago theatrical market from whom we could generate the data for the study. Generally, they fall into the category of accountants in the theatrical chains, bookers at various chains as well as independent theaters, and three distributors. In all, we interviewed five bookers, three of whom were most helpful. Three theater managers were interviewed, two of whom worked for Plitt Theaters, and the other, worked for M & R Theatres, another chain. Three distributors—one representing Avco-Embassy, Orion, and Columbia Pictures—were interviewed for the study. We approached the distributors only to corroborate the data and to ask general questions about industry policies and practices. Local representatives did not seem knowledgeable about such data as national box office grosses, specific information regarding producer-distributor contracts, and nationwide advertising costs, and so on. They advised us to contact their head offices in New York for such information.

With the background information gathered, we approached the industry persons for specific data that were needed for the study. The data found were further corroborated from more than one booker to make sure that they were authentic. We were specifically requested *not to reveal* their names by most of the interviewees, consequently individual pieces of information gathered for the study are not credited to any particular person(s). Names appear in the article only when that person has permitted us to do so.

ANALYSIS AND FINDINGS

Market Size and Importance

Chicago is recognized industry-wide as one of the three most important markets in the United States. Chicago is second only to Los Angeles and New York City in the attention given it by the film industry. According to one investigator at the Chicago Bureau of *Variety,* the Chicago market can be counted on to produce in excess of one-quarter of a million dollars a week in gross box office revenues. Those revenues represented $150,000-200,000 in rental revenue to the film distributors.

Almost everyone interviewed agreed that the Chicago market possessed certain unique qualities that distinguished it from other major markets. According to a public relations manager for Columbia Pictures:

> L.A. and New York are 'scale-markets' where we can weigh a picture's chutzpah. Chicago is a revenue market. We can put a picture in somewhere in Chicago and make money on it.

Researching the performance of certain films in this market confirmed that observation. For example in June-July of 1981, the French production *Lou-Lou* was nationally grossing $603,000. In a six-week run in Chicago, *Lou-Lou* was grossing $84,000. This is nearly one-sixth of the national figure. A representative of Orion Pictures, a major production-distribution company, stated that on the average, the Chicago area would generate about four to five percent of the box office revenue of the U.S. market (7). He explained the reasons for it in the following way:

> On a theater-by-theater basis you will find that the average theater's gross on a given picture here will be higher than you will find elsewhere. But it's due to the fact that Chicago is a good movie-going town to begin with, but the higher seating capacities of the auditoriums are the basic reason for the higher average gross per auditorium that you will find here.

Another important reason for Chicago's ability to produce higher grosses per theater is its size and range. In what is called "the Chicagoland," there are seven counties: Cook (which contains the City of Chicago), DuPage, North and South Lake Counties, and the outlying counties of Kane, McHenry, and Will. The Chicagoland area has an estimated population of eight million potential moviegoers. It includes 327 theater screens, housed in 200 theaters, of which 165 screens are controlled by five major theater chains. Table 1 presents a breakdown of screens controlled by the major chains on the basis of their location in Chicagoland in 1983.

The remaining screens can be divided into two categories. First, there are many independent chains, which are operated by a single entrepreneur who controls three or more screens. They are not affiliated with any nation-wide theater chain. These independent chains control about 40 to 45 screens in the Chicagoland area. Second, there are the neighborhood screens, numbering approximately 116. They are independently owned and operated and cater to the largely neighborhood, often ethnic, clientele.

The independent chains generally have very little impact on the bookings of the major chains' screens though, in certain isolated instances, they must compete directly with them for pictures. These houses are a combination of first-run, discount, and first-run "art-speciality" houses, such as Chicago's well-known northside Biograph theater. The neighborhood theaters, on the other hand, are generally reduced-admission houses and offer a wide variety of second-runs and reissues.

The focus of this study is on the 165 screens controlled by the five major chains, which we call here the Chicago market. Of these 165 screens, only four are not first-run. The rest, while sometimes conceding to play reissues and second-runs during periods of industry "droughts," do figure significantly in the competition for the booking of feature films. It is this specific group of screens that forms a block over most of the north and south Chicago suburban areas, where brisk competition is enhanced by the building of new screens by various exhibitors. This be-

Table 1.   Screens Controlled by Major Chains in the City and Suburb of Chicagoland, 1983

Chain	City screens (theaters)	Suburb screens (theaters)	Total screens (theaters)
Plitt Theaters	14(10)	46(12)	60(22)
General Cinema Theaters		34(10)	34(10)
Essaness Theaters	1(1)	29(9)	30(10)
M&R Theaters	2(1)	27(7)	29(8)
American Multi-Cinema		12(2)	12(2)
TOTAL	17(12)	148(40)	165(52)

Source: Respective Theater Chains

comes apparent when one considers that in the city of Chicago, there are 21 screens, whereas the suburbs have approximately 259 screens—over two-thirds of the total screens in the Chicagoland.

General Cinema, a solely suburban operator, controls 34 screens in the Chicago market. Essaness, another company of similar size, operates 30 screens in both city and suburban area, but is predominantly a suburban chain in the Chicago market. M & R Theaters operates 29 screens in this market. As can be seen in Table 1, it has 27 screens in the suburbs. M & R's downtown location, the Fine Arts I & II, is quickly becoming Chicago's most important and perhaps most lucrative full-time "art-speciality" complex. M & R has enjoyed previous success in this area at their now-closed Sandburg Theater, where *Atlantic City* became one of Chicago's all-time top specialty films at the box office.

It is interesting to note that General Cinema, Plitt, and American Multi-Cinema ranked among the ten largest theater circuits in the United States-Canada market (8). While all of the major chains in the Chicago market are privately-held corporations, Essaness and M & R are "home-grown" theater chains.

The most significant and complex chain operator is Plitt Theaters, which controls 60 screens in the Chicago marketplace. While it is only about one-ninth of Plitt's screens nationwide,[3] Plitt may have a competitive edge over the other four major chains because of its concentrated buying power. A chief executive for Plitt declared that Chicago was their most lucrative market situation. A substantial part of this is due to their domination of the Chicago downtown theaters. In the area designated as "downtown," there are 14 screens; seven of these are on the lucrative, prestigious "Near-North Gold-Coast" area. Plitt operates ten of the downtown theaters; six of these are in the "near-north" area.

According to representatives of Plitt's competitors, this entitles them to certain "considerations" from the distributors of feature films. The most significant among them is a "first-deal" option on films not being offered for competitive bidding. This is the most important consideration for the purposes of this study. In the case of some specific groups of formula films, such as horror-films (e.g., *Scanners, Prom Night, Terror Train, Happy Birthday to Me,* etc.), they are seldom bid for competitively. Instead, a single exhibitor is approached and offered an opportunity to give said films screen-time. According to one major distributor, competitive bidding was abandoned in the Chicagoland in the late 1970s, because of increased availability of films, compared to the number of theater screens in the market. It is to the advantage of the major chains not to bid for pictures, but to negotiate the terms as they would be more favorable to the chains. The effect of this policy may be devaluation of the film's potential to produce revenues for the distributor, because competitive bidding would force up the terms.

---

[3] Plitt Theatres controls approximately 550 screens in the United States, according to Jerry Winsburg, a retired vice-president of that company in Chicago. He asserted that Plitt was the fourth largest theater chain in the country. Jerry Winsburg, *Interview with the author,* Chicago, July 6, 1983. Also see (8).

Plitt theaters are also in the desirable position of operating the three largest and most productive houses in the Chicago-Loop area: the 2,400 seat State-Lake Theater, the 1,126 seat United Artists Theater, and the 2,800 seat Chicago Theater. All three of these houses maintain an average ticket price of $4.00. In addition, all three houses have a solid industry reputation for their success in playing the so-called "exploitation films." *Scanners, Prom Night, Terror Train, My Bloody Valentine,* and *Happy Birthday to Me* have all played one or a combination of these houses. According to one Plitt competitor, "if a distributor wanted a wide play on a questionable title, he wouldn't look at anyone but Plitt."

In contrast to these big houses in the downtown area, Plitt also controls the Water Tower Theaters, which are a quadraplex located on the main level of the high-rise shopping facility called The Water Tower Place. While the largest of these houses seats just in excess of 400, their desirable location and box office consistency make them a lucrative booking for a wide range of films. Water Tower Theaters were the first-run bookings for *Heavy Metal* and *Tribute.* These screens meet a variety of market needs and are considered to be desirable locations by distributors. In the case of the two Canadian films in question, *Heavy Metal* was a moderate success, while *Tribute* completed only one-half of its committed run.

Plitt Theaters, then, almost wholly dominate the Chicago market. The combination of the number of screens in the urban center and their strategic suburban locations make Plitt an important booking for any distributor. As this analysis progresses, it will become apparent that this entitles Plitt to a great deal of booking leverage. With no critical competition downtown, many market practices used by distributors to enhance the value of a film, such as blind bidding and securing premium play dates, are not necessary. As will be shown in subsequent pages, this has serious implications for the grossing potential of the 10 Canadian films in the study.

Table 2 presents a marketing summary of the 10 Canadian films that have been distributed in the Chicago area and shows the structure of exhibition deals.

Patterns of Booking

There are several ways in which a film can enter the Chicago marketplace. One means of entry is "competitive bidding." Bidding is the highest valuation of a film and enhances its potential in the marketplace. Competitive bidding, by its nature, forces up the amount of guarantee exhibitors will pay to secure a booking. Also, the bidding situation forces exhibitors to commit themselves to longer guaranteed runs. Finally, having made a lengthy and expensive commitment to a booking, the exhibitor is then in a position of having to make a similar commitment to advertising and promotion.

This was the case in the Chicago market with the Kemeny-Heroux, Canadian production *Quest for Fire.* Based on the earlier success of their production, *Atlantic City*—which was *not* a bid picture—*Quest For Fire* was put up for competitive bidding. It appears to have benefitted by this type of booking. Pre-opening adver-

Table 2. Structure of Exhibition Deals for Ten Canadian Films in the Chicago Market

Title	Distributor	Theater (seats)	Opened	Length of run	run	Deal guarantee	rental terms
Atlantic City	Paramount	Sandburg (600)	May 5, 81	12	6	$25,000	weeks 1 & 2 at 70% of receipts / weeks 3 & 4 @ 60% / weeks 5 & 6 @ 50%
Scanners	Avco-Embassy	United Artists (1126)	Jan. 30, 81	5	4	$10,000	week 1 at 70% / weeks 2 & 3 @ 60% / week 4 @ 50%
Terror Train	Twentieth Century-Fox	State-Lake (2400)	Oct. 2, 80	3	3	$ 5,000	week 1 @ 70%
		Ford City 2 (900)				$ 5,000	week 2 @ 60%
		Norridge (700)				$ 5,000	week 3 @ 50%
Prom Night	Avco-Embassy	Woods (1200) / Woodfield Mall (602)	Aug. 6, 81	2	open based on box office	none	@ 50% of receipts
Happy Birthday to Me	Columbia	United Artists (1126)	May 20, 81	2	open	none	@ 50% of receipts
My Bloody Valentine	Paramount	State-Lake (2400)	Feb. 13, 81	2	open	none	@ 50% of receipts
Heavy Metal	Columbia	Water Tower 2 (302)	Aug. 7, 81	4	4	$15,000	week 1 @ 70% of receipts / weeks 2 & 3 @ 60% / week 4 @ 50%
Meatballs	Paramount	Water Tower 2	Aug. 11, 81	4	4	$10,000	Terms Unknown
The Changeling	A.F.D.		Mar. 27, 80	2	2	none	flat rental of $4,500 for two weeks
Tribute*	Twentieth Century-Fox	Water Tower 2 / Woodfield Mall	Sept. 81	4	4	$10,000	week 1 @ 70% / weeks 2 & 3 @ 60% / week 4 at 50%

*This picture was bid competitively. Plitt Theaters withdrew the picture from the two screens after two weeks due to poor performance of the film and ran it as a double-bill with *Nine to Five* at another screen for two weeks to meet the commitment to the distributor.

tising for the film was done over two weeks at a cost to the distributor of $3,500. In its sixth week of run, the exhibitor, Plitt Theaters, was spending $800-$1,000 a week in advertising. Among the films in this study, only *Tribute* was a bid picture. According to one booker in the Chicago area, the deal that Twentieth Century-Fox was asking for was so light in the sense that it stipulated a short length of run which thereby demonstrated a lack of commitment to the film by that distributor. The rest of the films in the study entered the marketplace through negotiation, which will be discussed later.

According to one informed theater manager, in the downtown Chicago market "bidding can be a deception." With Plitt's almost total control of this exhibition area bidding becomes a formal ploy. Distributors are always aware of the availability of screen time. With Plitt having only three screens to compete in the downtown area, it is possible that a picture may be offered for bid with the distributor (and perhaps the exhibitor as well) knowing full well that only a single exhibitor is available to bid on it. The distributor then appears to have met their commitment to the producers of the film, while actually having only dealt the film to a favored exhibitor. A booker-competitor of Plitt Theaters suggested that *Scanners* was dealt to Plitt in just that way. He further stated that *Scanners* was opened for bids, but only Plitt had open dates so a booking was then negotiated.

The avenue through which the films in this study reached the marketplace was negotiation. A negotiated booking generally involves either the exhibitor or distributor approaching the other about booking a specific picture or type of picture. More often than not in Chicago, according to those interviewed, it is the distributor approaching an exhibitor with whom they would like to get a play date. Among the films in the study, only *Atlantic City* seems to be an exception to that pattern of booking. The booker for M & R Theaters revealed that he had seen *Atlantic City* at the Venice International Film Festival 1980-81. Initially, he attempted to contact the Canadian representatives of the film, but was told that Paramount Pictures was making a deal to secure its distribution. The booker then contacted local representatives of Paramount who displayed no knowledge of the availability of the film. A booking was finally negotiated by M & R directly with Paramount in New York.

When *Atlantic City* opened in Chicago on May 5, 1981, it still had not had a significant market test. M & R booked *Atlantic City* to an "exclusive" six-week run, with the run to be augmented at the end of six weeks in the event of a holdover. The film was booked into M & R's exclusive, downtown-near-north, speciality theater, the Sandburg. While the distributor was now assured of a preferred booking, the exclusivity of the booking, however, restricted the film's full grossing potential as the market later proved. While the Sandburg run was highly successful, the market demand suggested that the film had the potential for wider success. The recent reissue success and the previous second-run success of *Atlantic City* supports this proposition.

To secure a booking of *Atlantic City*, M & R put up a $25,000 guarantee. This assured M & R's commitment to the film and to its run. While the pre-opening advertising was handled by Paramount—at a total commitment of about $500—only a portion of advertising was paid by the distributor during the run. This support by the distributor lasted only six weeks, the length of the guaranteed run. Subsequently, the cost of advertising by M & R reached about $10,000 throughout the run. The positive impact of this commitment on the success of the film was considerable. *Atlantic City* became the Sandburg's longest running and highest grossing film in its history.

The opening week box office gross on *Atlantic City* was $20,000 plus. The second week's gross on the film was $23,272. These first two weeks were sufficient to pay the $25,000 guarantee, while nearly a $2,500 profit was realized. In the course of the six weeks of guaranteed-run, *Atlantic City* grossed $104,685 while paying $64,666 in rental. This success warranted a six week holdover at greatly reduced rental percentages. In the final six weeks, the film grossed $59,450 versus $15,044 in rentals.

When we asked the booker for M & R about various factors that may have influenced the booking of *Atlantic City,* he suggested that in terms of "bookability," Louis Malle and Susan Sarandon had been a successful box office mating in *Pretty Baby*. This, coupled with the "speciality-nature" of the film, made it potentially attractive for the audience at the Sandburg. Its box office potential was further enhanced by the fact that a major local and national critic, Roger Ebert, saw the film at Venice and spoke highly of it. The booker felt the extra press gave the film an added boost. In addition, Ebert gave the film time on his nationally syndicated television program, *Sneak Previews,* which aired the week of May 14, as well as a special spot on his Oscar previews program.

The pattern of how a film with a certain box office appeal as *Atlantic City* entered the Chicago market suggests that the major distributors often do not give the product acquired abroad as big a push as it might deserve. There may be a number of reasons as to why that happens which is not a part of this inquiry. However, it is worthwhile to ponder the possibility that if Paramount had realized the grossing potential of this film, it could have demanded a bid, and released it in more theaters, thereby increasing the potential revenues by several times. Its advertising budget could have been larger and consequently a better exposure to such a film might have been gained.

Table 3 indicates how each of the 10 selected Canadian feature films performed at the box office in the Chicago area, the type of deal between each film's distributor and exhibitor, and the total rental figure for each film. It is to be noted that, except *Atlantic City,* all others played a double-bill at one time or another. Consequently, gross box office data do not represent revenues generated by that film alone.

Two most notable findings indicated in Table 3 are the waiting periods for these Canadian films and the double billing policy's impact on their revenue generating capacity in the Chicago theatrical market. The 10 films chosen for the study had to wait from one to three years to enter the Chicago market. As reported, Chicago is

Table 3.   Market Performance of Selected Canadian Films in the Chicago Area

	Release Date	Chicago Playdate	Negotiated Deal	No. of Screens	Advance/ Guarantee	Gross Box Office	Rental
Atlantic City	Dec. 1979	May 1981	6 weeks	1	$25,000	$166,186	$ 79,713
Scanners	Dec. 1979	Feb. 1981	4 weeks	1	$10,000	$244,113	$128,096
Terror Train	Dec. 1979	Oct. 1980	3 weeks	3	$ 5,000 $ 5,000 $ 5,000	$ 31,454 $ 47,742 $ 59,125	$ 19,756 $ 29,226 $ 34,132
Prom Night	Sept. 1979	Aug. 1981	2 weeks	1	* * *	$ 91,949	$ 55,169
Happy Birthday to Me	Sept. 1978	May 1981		1	* * *	$ 33,314	$ 16,657
My Bloody Valentine	Oct.	Feb.	2 weeks	1	* * *	$ 33,661	$ 16,830
Heavy Metal	Nov.	Aug.	4 weeks	1	$15,000	$ 54,126	$ 33,788
Meatballs	Sept.	Aug.	4 weeks	1	$10,000	$ 51,753	$ 34,596
The Changeling	Feb.	March	* * *	1	* * *	$ 19,444	$ 4,500
Tribute	May 1980	Sept. 1981	Bid 4 weeks	1	$10,000	$ 19,444	$ 13,609
	(Tribute closed after 2 weeks.)						

the second largest market in the United States and a film's favorable market performance here can be used by its distributor to boost audiences elsewhere. Consequently, early entry into this market will be beneficial to the producers. The longer a film waits to reach the market, the higher the interest and other costs that a producer may have to bear. Furthermore, investors' confidence in film business rests on the possibility of immediate market entry after a film's completion and quick returns from the box office. As Canada's current national film policy is aimed at strengthening entrepreneurial capitalists who could bring a heavy dose of private venture capital into film, as opposed to complete state subsidies, long waiting periods for films produced in Canada may have an adverse impact on their profitability.

The booking policies for films such as Scanners, Terror Train, Prom Night, Happy Birthday to Me, and My Bloody Valentine—all horror films—are significantly different from that of Atlantic City. To understand these films in the marketplace, it is necessary to understand them categorically. Unlike Atlantic City, which was booked on the basis of certain unique qualities, the horror films rely on their similarity to one another to enhance their bookability. It is precisely this criterion which is important to Plitt Theaters, Chicago's major booker of "exploitation" films. The term exploitation in the industry refers to taking advantage of a specific market's expectations. This expectation is in part reinforced by the image of the film, and in turn, influenced by the image of a theater in which a film plays. Both exhibitors and distributors are keenly aware of those marketing factors which have a direct impact on the manner a film is handled.

Seldom do films of this kind play a run alone. They are often double-billed, even if for only a portion of a run. There are several ways and reasons a second picture can and will be inserted into a run. In some instances, if a film is producing poorly at the box office, a second picture will be added to boost its grosses. Still another reason for inserting a second picture might be to allow a strong running picture to revive a film which has done poorly at the box office in its own runs. A case in point discussed below is Columbia's *Hardcore*. The policy of double-billing of exploitation films is preferred by exhibitors for two additional reasons: it keeps their screens playing new titles all the time, which is hoped to bring a steady flow of audiences into their theaters; and, it would also reduce the number of films which are waiting in line to enter the market. This is particularly the case and policy of Plitt Theaters at their Chicago-Loop locations.

Double-billing is an important marketing tool to the distributor in particular. The distributor can represent the box office figures from other major markets as those of either film when presenting a picture to exhibitors. Among the films studied here, *The Changeling* was caught in this situation in the Chicago market. That film never received a first-run date in Chicago. Essaness Theaters first tested the market for *The Changeline* on a double-bill in their large Chicago-Loop location, The Woods Theater. It was then booked for a flat rental of $4,500 for two weeks. *The Changeling* opened with a first billing picture that turned in a weak run, thereby gaining a negative box office reputation for both films in this market. As a result, *The Changeling* was not given a significant first-run in Chicago which ruined its box office potential.

All of the horror films in the study played for at least portions of their runs on double-bills. *Happy Birthday to Me,* for instance, played a two-week run for Plitt Theaters accompanied by a Columbia reissue of *Hardcore*. This pairing of films was actually a package that was used nation-wide. One representative of Columbia suggested that this was an attempt to earn revenues on a film which played ''miserably'' earlier that year. He further stated that this reissue anticipated the first run release of *Hardcore 2* as well. *Terror Train,* on the other hand, booked into three separate engagements, ran alone for the entire run at Ford City Theaters. In the other two situations, it ran only the first week alone. At Plitt's State-Lake, located downtown, it ran the final two weeks with a Twentieth Century reissue of the highly successful *Suspiria*. At the Norridge Theaters, *Terror Train* ran the second week with *The Day After Graduation Day*—a Group-One International release—and the final week with Avco-Embassy's *The Exterminator*. Even the extremely successful *Scanners* ran on a double-bill in its final week. Also, *Scanners* was later reissued to boost another Avco-Embassy release, *Graduation Day,* in September 1981.

This booking practice has several implications on a film's evolution in the marketplace. One implication briefly discussed above is the dependency of films running together. The films must either share success or failure as if they were a single picture. Double-billing is a useful tool for the distributor, who can utilize pictures together to either salvage a run or a single picture's future. However, the distributor also faces the risk of losing the picture's potential earning power. A picture's future bookings and the deals for these bookings are often directly tied to grossing productivity of a double-bill. Distributors just as often use double-bills only to satisfy their commitments to the producers of films.

In addition, doubling cuts the revenues effectively earned by a picture. Generally in a doubling situation the pictures on the double-bill will be products of the same distributor. In this event, the revenues from the run are returned to a single source. However, the distributor then holds the option of reporting them as the grosses of one film or the other. In the case of doubling films of two different producers, it is impossible to conclusively determine to which film the revenues are to be attributed.

A more complex booking practice can be observed in the case of *Terror Train* which was distributed by Twentieth Century-Fox. The film opened alone at one theater (Norridge) and grossed a rental of $19,756 in its first week. In the second week, it was coupled with *Day After Halloween,* another horror film distributed by Group-One International, when the two films together grossed a rental of $29,226. In the third week, *Day After Halloween* was dropped and *The Exterminator,* an Avco-Embassy picture, was added. That week's gross rental for the double bill was $34,132.

In the case of both films doubled with *Terror Train,* the exhibitor paid flat rentals to their respective distributor out of the revenues generated by both pictures in the package thus perhaps cutting into those revenues earned by the strong running film. This policy of beginning one run before another has been completed, referred to as "cheating-a-run," results from the theaters' need to secure bookings on films as they become available and to keep new products appearing. While all the bookers interviewed agreed that this practice did not cut into their revenues, and perhaps affected the strong running films' box office share more adversely, they believed it was necessary to keep screens "playing fresh."

The policy of double-billing is beneficial from the viewpoint of distributors, as their products keep moving into the market. Marginal films that may never get screen time do get exposure. If by piggy-backing on a stronger film, a marginal film can earn some revenues it is even better for all concerned with that film. The producers of the films in the package, however, have no way of knowing their films' box office performance.

Chicago is a very important market for "exploitation" films, according to a representative of Plitt Theaters. This was corroborated by the distributors and available data seem to support that view. According to *Variety* (October 28, 1980), *Terror Train* grossed $929,603 nationally in four weeks of running. The

Chicago run of *Terror Train* (three screens for three weeks each) resulted in a total box office gross of $138,321. This represents nearly one-sixth of the national figure over the film's opening in 11 cities. While the figures suggest an inevitable success for films of this kind in the Chicago market, the fact that Chicago is also the initial market for these films results in substantially less-profitable deals for their screentime. The commitments also tend to be substantially lower by both the exhibitor and the distributor.

Distributors do not stand strongly behind films of this kind unless they develop an extraordinary pattern of success. In part, this falls into the nature of the business of "exploitation" films. The industry policy about these films is "Short-runs—Quick-revenues" and keep the screens "playing fresh." The result of this policy, for our purposes, is that films of this kind are booked with only a commitment to earning revenues and making way for the product that may be waiting in line to reach the market. For instance, each film in this study was pre-opened by a single advertisement in each of the local newspapers paid for by the distributor. The distributor also provided the run with a large opening-day advertisement. From that point on, the exhibitor paid the costs of advertising. From the exhibitor's standpoint, if a film is booked for only two weeks of screen-time, costly advertising is not feasible. The total cost of advertising in the case of each of the horror films in this study was about $500. The only exception was *Scanners.* In addition to the print advertising for *Scanners,* Avco-Embassy purchased 21 television spots over five weeks. That difference in the advertising strategy may have directly contributed to the film's box office gross of nearly one-quarter of a million dollars in Chicago.

Once a picture proves itself at the box office, the attention it receives from the industry is somewhat different. For instance, in *Variety,* June 10, 1980, a double-page advertisement appeared stating that *"Happy Birthday to Me* grossed $10,609,514 in its first three weeks." Columbia Pictures purchased this advertisement to boost the bookings for the film. What appears to be an overwhelming success for that film was in fact a composite box office figure for a double-bill package which, in many cases, consisted of *Happy Birthday to Me* and *Hardcore.* In the Chicago market, *Happy Birthday to Me* was booked into a negotiated two weeks run by Plitt Theaters and grossed only $33,314. When representatives of Columbia were questioned about the advertisement in *Variety,* they offered no explanation of how *Happy Birthday to Me* could have grossed such high revenues in three weeks having been opened in only 21 cities.

Patterns of Advertising and Promotion
A final concern with regard to "exploitation" films are other marketing variables affecting their box office performance. According to one booker, films meant to exploit this kind of market rely very little on variables such as support from critics and other forms of promotion. The audience for these films is generally not concerned with popular criticism or television talk shows. Generally, the economic

factors of production are not conclusive to hiring bankable star commodities to appear in the films. Therefore, actors' personal appearance are not useful. Of the films studied, only *Scanners* was treated to a formal review (Roger Ebert, *Chicago Sun Times,* February 7, 1981). It did not prove to be favorable to the film in any case. So, for the most part, such promotional variables do not apply to this category of a film's success or failure at the box office.

There is only a little to be said about the remaining films, *Heavy Metal* and *Meatballs.* Both films were booked into Plitt's most prestigious complex downtown, The Water Tower Theaters. This four-screen complex is a conscientious attempt on the part of Plitt to supply a variety of market needs under a single roof. The gamut of markets range from "dramatic-art" films (*Tribute* perhaps) to "exploitation" films like *Halloween.* For this reason, the booker at Plitt assured the author that both were "sound bookings."

Heavy Metal was booked into a four-week run at Water Tower 2. This smaller of the two "main-aisle" screens seats 302 persons. Plitt advanced Columbia $15,000 for this booking. In addition to purchasing pre-opening advertising at a cost of nearly $1,000, Columbia also shared a portion of the advertising cost for the entire four weeks of run. This gave Plitt, and subsequently *Heavy Metal,* a significant boost. As a result of $1,500 worth of advertising, *Heavy Metal* grossed $19,724 in the first week, and paid rentals of $13,806. By the end of the four-week engagement, *Heavy Metal* had grossed $54,126 while paying $33,788 in rentals.

The pattern of booking and advertising was similar for *Meatballs.* This film was booked for a four-week run with an advance of $10,000 into one of Water Tower's "rear-aisle" screens, Water Tower 3, which seats only 280 persons. The pattern of advertising and cost sharing in the case of *Meatballs* indicated the distributor's confidence in the film. Paramount not only purchased pre-opening advertising but paid a portion of the advertising costs as well throughout the run. Generally, in such instances where the distributor pays a portion of the advertising costs during the run, it is done so on a percentage basis, which is commensurate with the percentage of rental being paid. In the case of *Meatballs* and *Heavy Metal,* the exhibitor was paying 70 percent of the gross box office to rental while the distributors were assuming 70 percent of the advertising cost in their first week of run. This figure then diminished accordingly. This is a standard entry in most exhibition contracts these days. It makes advertising of a larger scale feasible for the exhibitor and is certainly in the best interests of the film.

Both *Heavy Metal* and *Meatballs* represent fairly standard examples of industry booking for multiple-screen situations. Both films produced modest revenues, but neither of them beyond expectations,according to their bookers. This, in part, is due to the nature of booking in multi-screened situations with the given limitations of space, resulting in smaller seating capacities, diffused displays, and promotions. Although national box office data were unavailable, one major distributor suggested that both films did better in their suburban runs. This would seem accurate at least in the case of *Meatballs* with its $55,000,000 nationwide box office gross.

CONCLUSIONS

The analysis presented in this paper was based upon the marketing relations between major distributors and major theatrical chains in the Chicago markets. It suggested patterns of how the Canadian films in the study sample came to enter the Chicago market, the nature of the deals that distributors and exhibitors entered into, and the box office performance of these films. As the study did not include examining the relationships between producers of these films and the major distributors, we cannot argue whether or not marketing of these films in the Chicago area is in fact beneficial to Canadian producers. An expanded study which examines the relationships between Canadian producers and U.S. distributors, and relationships between distributors and exhibitors in the United States needs to be undertaken to tackle such a question.

To increase the generalizability of this study, it is necessary to obtain data for a bigger sample of Canadian films marketed in the United States. Additionally, comparisons between Canadian-made and American-made films along the dimensions used in this study may offer new insights into the process of distribution and exhibition of feature films in the United States.

Although eight out of 10 films in the study sample were "exploitation" pictures, we do not believe that it imposes any limitation on the conclusions drawn. Canada has carved itself a niche in the global film market in making such films and has built an international reputation as can be observed by their film sales around the world. It is believed that the study sample represented the typical "Canadian" film made in the 1978–81 period with the goal of entering the U.S. market. Exceptions to the typical low-budget "exploitation" film are represented by the two films—*Atlantic City* and *Tribute*—which had bigger budgets and other box office ingredients and also acquired a certain degree of critical acclaim. By including them in the study, it is believed that the economic relations between the major American distributors and major theatrical chains in Chicago are explored reasonably well.

What is, however, lacking in this study is comparative data for similar pictures produced by the American majors themselves or in partnersip with others to analyze any discriminatory treatment given to films produced in Canada. That analysis would be useful to Canada's policy makers, as it would bear on the profitability of films produced in Canada significantly and the viability of Canada's feature film industry. It was not done, however, due to funding and time limitations. Although it is easy to speculate on the possbility of discrimination by the American majors against the films they acquire abroad, one would have to carefully examine the specific deals in as much detail as done in this study to arrive at such a conclusion.

From within the scope of the present study, the following conclusions can be drawn:

1. The play dates obtained for the selected Canadian films in the Chicago markets are generally good for the Chicago area. This finding is consistent with some

studies (6) done on the American film industry that as the principle suppliers of blockbuster films, the U.S. majors command the good play dates available on major theatrical chains, despite the divorcement of theaters due to the Paramount Consent decree in 1948.

2. The deals we examined for the 10 selected films in the study suggest a general pattern of lack of interest or commitment on the part of the Majors to push these films in the market to the extent that they could generate higher revenues. Except for *Tribute* all other pictures were negotiated deals. Consequently, Canadian producers *may* have lost sizeable revenues potentially accruing to them. Since we did not inquire into the deals between the producers and distributors, this observation cannot be more conclusively stated.

3. The practice of double-billing used for nine out of the 10 films in the study makes it difficult to determine which of the two films in the package contributed to the box office gross. Double-billing provides an opportunity for the distributor to juggle the figures especially when the package consists of one of their own productions. This raises some interesting questions for further investigation. How were the rental revenues divided between two films that formed the double-bill package? As five of the nine films were combined with the Majors' own product, how were rentals divided up in such cases?

4. The waiting period involved for the Canadian films in the study to enter the U.S. markets was between one to three years. This may have serious implications for economic viability of Canadian film production companies since investors' confidence in the industry rests on a certain degree of assured returns in the shortest time possible after a film is completed. If profitability for the Canadian film industry, and hence its long term growth is based upon U.S. market entry, then the long waiting periods pose difficult obstacles to the success of current national film policy in Canada.

REFERENCES

1. Adilman, Sid. "B.O. Climbs But Tix Sales Even." *Variety,* November 25, 1981, p. 39.
2. Guback, Thomas H. "Theatrical Film." In Benjamin M. Compaine (Ed.). *Who Owns the Media?* White Plains, NJ: Knowledge Industry Publications, 1979.
3. Larmett, John, Elias Salvada, and Frederick Schwarts, Jr. *Analysis and Conclusions of the Washington Task Force on the Motion Picture Industry.* Unpublished report, June 8, 1978.
4. Pendakur, Manjunath. "Cultural Dependency in Canada's Feature Film Industry." *Journal of Communication* 31 (1), Winter 1981, pp. 48–57.
5. Pendakur, Manjunath. "Film Policies in Canada: In Whose Interest?" *Media, Culture and Society* 3 (2), April 1981, pp. 155–166.
6. Phillips, Joseph D. "Film Conglomerate Blockbusters: International Appeal and Product Homogenization." In Gorham Kindem (Ed.). *The American Movie Industry: The Business of Motion Pictures.* Carbondale, IL: Southern Illinois University Press, 1982.
7. Silk, Paul. Branch Manager, Orion Pictures, *Interviews With the Author,* Chicago, July 15, 1983.
8. "U.S. & Canada Theater Circuits Ranked By Size," *Variety,* January 16, 1985, p. 38.

11

The Film Bureau Phenomenon in America: State and Municipal Advocacy of Contemporary Motion Picture and Television Production

Gary Edgerton

Economic development is today a pursuit for the government of each and every state and major municipality in the United States. The promotion of tourism and local industries form the backbone of this endeavor as politicians and businessmen work hand-and-hand to further the commercial and job prospects of their respective regions. For the most part, though, America's motion picture business has annually been a billion dollar proposition that has held little relevancy beyond the states of New York and, especially, California. Certainly film theaters have always been dispersed nationwide; still, the industry's more lucrative production and distribution arms have, for the most part, been centered in either Hollywood or New York City for more than three generations. Since the 1950s, however, this condition has been gradually changing; Hollwood has outgrown its geographic boundaries and now goes on location more and more across the United States. All of America's 50 states and major metropolitan centers have set up local governmental agencies in order to attract the business of movie and video production to their area. This is a brand new and exciting development for the domestic mass media that translates into millions of dollars and thousands of jobs throughout every U.S. region. This essay identifies and explains the film bureau phenomenon from both a historical and a definitional point of view. A number of questions are addressed: What is the history of America's movie and TV commissions over the last two decades and how does the appearance of these offices fit into the overall context of an evolving U.S. motion picture industry? What is a film bureau and what does it do? How does it operate and function as an organizational midpoint between the aesthetics, the politics, and the business of Hollwood moviemaking? Lastly, what is the purpose of a local commission and its corresponding importance for regional America in particular, as well as the contemporary movie and video industries in general? These are no doubt challenging queries; nevertheless, this paper begins to address their significance and at the end offers suggestions for future and related research.

HISTORY AND DEVELOPMENT

Hollywood itself is not an exact geographical area, although there is such a postal district. It has commonly been described as a state of mind, and its exists wherever people connected with the movies live and work.
—Hortense Powdermaker, 1950 (37, p. 18)

Hollywood, Ohio can be any Ohio town when the Ohio Film Bureau is successful in convincing filmmakers to shoot on location in Ohio. —Eve Lapolla, assistant manager, Ohio Film Bureau, 1983 (21)

During the past 15 years, a significant transformation has been slowly taking place within the production tier of the American movie business. No longer operating exclusively in either Southern California or New York, America's major film and television producion companies are now beginning to seriously consider domestic locations that had hitherto been ignored by Hollywood for the better part of four decades. At first, U.S. moviemakers went overseas during the 1950s as a means of escaping the ever-increasing costs of film production in Los Angeles, while correspondingly exploiting various government subsidy programs in England, France, and Italy. By the mid-1960s, these major companies would also be experimenting with a number of alternative locales within the United States. New York, New Jersey, Illinois, Florida, and Texas along with those states in close proximity to California (namely New Mexico, Colorado, and Arizona), all experienced intermittent production activity from major U.S. moviemakers prior to 1970. It wasn't long, however, before these initial encounters with Hollywood encouraged a number of state and municipal governments to take further action in order to attract additional productions to their home terrain.

In 1966, Major John Lindsay established a New York City office which would serve as the prototype for today's film bureaus. His intention was to create a center under municipal jurisdiction which would monitor and encourage film and video production, while minimizing government red tape and trouble with the private sector. By and large, though, this film commission suffered through a decade of inattention and uneven support. As a result, the operation lay virtually dormant until Ed Koch became mayor in 1977. However, a number of other cities and states in the Southwest, the Midwest, and the deep South successfully explored the enormous potential of attaching local fortunes to the money, industry, and glamour of a major Hollywood production.

Today, 91 municipal and state film bureaus exist in the United States and its surrounding territories, although more than 70 percent of these agencies have appeared since 1976. This extensive proliferation, slow moving at first, was ultimately contingent upon a number of interrelated factors including geographical location, weather patterns, scenic variety, availability of professional and technical expertise, and most importantly, citizen and governmental support. As the last vestiges of the old Hollywood production system were being liquidated with the auction and sale of studio real estate and property during the late 1960s, major American filmmakers were increasingly inclined towards scouting outside Southern California for novel, unused, and authentic domestic locations, as well as finding the means of escaping the rising cost of taxes and union crews at home. Not surprisingly, the first localities that major California film and television producers explored in earnest were their sunny, neighbor states directly to the east.

Probably more a matter of proximity than anything else, the Southwest offered Hollywood an immediate and easily accessible alternative. In response, official action was quickly mobilized as a way of more effectively attracting studio filmmakers to this region. New Mexico was the first state in the nation to form a film commission on an ad hoc basis. Located in Santa Fe, the New Mexico commission was formed in 1968 (50). Actually, New Mexico had a long tradition of moviemaking, being the first state west of the Mississippi to have a film shot on-location: Thomas Edison's *Indian Day School* (1898). Since then, parts of more than 400 movies and a multitude of commercials have been shot in New Mexico (49).

A similar account of production activity is also evident in Colorado, Arizona, and, to a lesser degree, Utah. In fact, the Colorado Motion Picture and Television Advisory Commission was the first legislated film bureau in the United States. It was created July 1, 1969, and budgeted with an appropriation of $5,000 a year for the first two years. During these subsequent 24 months, major movie and television companies spent $3.25 million in Colorado as astronomical profits were returned on the state's initial investment (40). Other states were quick to notice the benefits being experienced by Colorado, New Mexico, and Arizona for bringing the substantial and windfall economics of major motion picture production into their own environs. More and more, Hollywood was going on-location across America, and a handful of state officials had the presence of mind to recognize that public and private prosperity could be critically interfused at this industrial juncture for the betterment of all involved.

Overtures from Louisiana, Georgia, and Mississippi next attracted the purview of studio filmmakers into the deep South. Somewhat unexpectedly, Florida at first failed to fulfill its considerable potential by not becoming the dominant center of film and video work in this region. Gubernatorial priorities were disinclined towards taking the lead in media production, despite Florida's long tradition of moviemaking in Jacksonville, Tampa/St. Petersburg, and Miami prior to the 1927 coming of sound. The benefits afforded by this state's climate and scenic beauty did ensure a certain amount of sporadic activity in both feature films and prime-time television programming throughout the 1960s. Nevertheless, until 1976 Florida suffered from the lukewarm attention that was paid to this whole matter by its state and municipal offices of economic development. In contrast, there has been a complete turnabout over the last seven years with the formation of the Florida Office of Film and Television Coordination. It now operates on a $400,000 annual budget, and generates approximately $250 million a year in production revenues (20).

On the other hand, Georgia's promotional ploy to become "the best back lot you've ever had," enabled this state to get a much needed headstart on a then disinterested Florida. The Georgia Film Office was officially established in 1973 by Governor Jimmy Carter, and has subsequently attracted over $535 million to the state in production monies across the last ten years (14). During this same period, Louisiana and Mississippi also had a considerable share of success with Hollywood by serving as the setting for literally dozens of feature films. In fact, moviemaking in the whole region during the 1970s spawned a new genre of Southern, action-oriented, "country" films, such as *Deliverance* (1972), *Macon County Line* (1973), *Buster and Billy* (1974), *Walking Tall* (1974) and *Smokey and the Bandit* (1976). Finally, Alabama likewise became involved in the world of big-time moviemaking when Steve Spielberg arrived to shoot *Close Encounters of the Third Kind* in 1976. In response to this experience, the Alabama Film Commission was created by an executive order during the next year. As this commission's director, Phil Cole explains: "The film woke everybody up. People [in the state] began to see that tremendous benefits could be realized from on-location shooting" (17, p. S1).

Texas, of course, has had a long and illustrious history of feature film production. Such classics as *The Big Parade* (1925) and the first Academy Award-winning best picture *Wings* (1927) were shot in large part in the San Antonio area. Although Hollywood only used Texas as a location for 10 of its feature films through 1949, in the 1950s production activity began to slowly escalate with eight movies (including *The Sundowners* [1950], *Viva, Zapata* [1952] and *Giant* [1956]. During the 1960s, this number mushroomed to 10, as the evocation of the Texan landscape and culture added immeasurably to such offerings as *The Alamo* (1960) *Hud* (1963), *Baby, the Rain Must Fall* (1964) and *Bonnie and Clyde* (1967).

In 1970, the Office of the Governor began taking an active part in promoting the potential of this rapidly growing industry in the "lone star" state. The Texas Film Commission, mandated in 1971, resulted in the on-location producion of 114 theatrical and made-for-TV movies over the next decade. Today, Governor Mark White oversees the coordinated success of one state and five separate municipal film bureaus whose combined performance allows him to unabashedly boast that

"Texas stands as a genuine 'Third Coast' alternative to the traditional production centers" (10, p. iii). An outside consultant estimated that film and tape production injected approximately $500 million into the economy of Texas in 1980 (42).

America's next region to "go Hollywood" was the Midwest. Unlike the Sunbelt or the South, the heartland had neither proximity, an overabundance of sunshine, nor an exotic terrain to offer on-location moviemakers; what it did provide, though, was a degree of stark and commonplace authenticity. In 1976, a handful of major feature films paved the way toward establishing the business of motion picture production in this region: *F.I.S.T.* (Dubuque, Iowa), *The Betsy* (Detroit), and *The Deer Hunter* (Cleveland and Struthers, Ohio). For each of these pictures, the gritty, industrial ambiance that is evident in the Midwest was essential. In turn, the major movie companies began exploring the pros and cons of filming in one Midwestern state over another. As is presently the case in all parts of the United States, competition to attract major productions is especially intense between neighboring cities and states. By 1977, as *Time* was heralding the fact that movie crews were pouring millions of dollars into the Midwest, Illinois and Ohio were emerging with the first film bureaus and the most business in the area (43). Toward the end of the 1970s, Kentucky and Michigan would also begin to actively promote themselves as well.

The influx of motion picture and television production was not without its growing pains in the Midwest however. Detroit's major automakers were upset about the apparent social and political viewpoint of Paul Schrader's *Blue Collar* (1978), while Chicago was essentially off-limits to Hollywood until the death of Mayor Richard J. Daley in 1976. Nevertheless, reluctance would change to responsiveness and enthusiasm in the "windy city" between 1977 and 1981. During this same time period, major film projects ended up creating an economic impact of $57 million in Illinois and $35 million in Kentucky (32, p. 1; 44). With comparable success, Ohio and Michigan pursued the route of all productive film commissions by branching out beyond only theatrical and TV movies to the related promotion of documentaries, network and public television series, music videos, commercials, and industrial films as well.

Happening simultaneously with this growth of on-location work in the Midwest, was the reemergence of both New York and New Jersey as major production centers. Today both states, along with Massachusetts and Pennsylvania, dominate motion picture and television activity in the Northeastern United States. Actually, it's been nearly a half-century since the movie production business prospered in this region after the 30-year heyday that ranged from the earliest shorts that were manufactured by the Edison Company in West Orange, New Jersey in the late 1890s to the 1930s when Adolph Zukor and Jesse Lasky ran the old Astoria Studio for Paramount in New York. Television production also flourished in New York City during the early 1950s, but a similar exodus west eventually curtailed the amount of east coast work done in that medium as well. Clearly, New York and New Jersey suffered from an image problem in Hollywood, and only a concerted effort between a group of aggressive municipal and state film commissions, an attentive private sector, more flexible unions, and the considerable effort of certain elected officials were able to turn this negative impression around since 1977.

Again, community adjustment in New York was a significant adjunction to this growth pattern in on-location shooting. With *Cruising* (1980), *Nighthawks* (1981), and *Fort Apache, the Bronx* (1981), Manhattan alone had had three of the more celebrated examples of the public protesting either the nature of the filmed content or the inconvenience caused by a major motion picture crew.[1] Still, $750 million was spent in New York City in 1981 as a direct result of motion picture and television costs, while the number of feature films shot in the greater metropolitan area tripled in the five years between 1977 and 1981 (1). Moreover, New York City production revenues skyrocked even further to $2 billion in 1982, with additional published estimates that local film and video output will grow into a $6 billion industry by 1990 (35).

New Jersey is also an essential part of the Northeast megalopolis; it too is enjoying a production renaissance of sorts. Since the 1977 creation of the New Jersey Motion Pictures and TV Commission, a reported $100 million of media location work has been infused into the New Jersey economy (55, p. 180). In New England, Massachusetts is far and away the leader in theatrical film and television activity. In 1982 alone, $54 million was spent on production, yielding "an economic impact upwards of $135 million in ultimate benefits" to the state (23, p. 3.). This added increase is possible because of a consideration that economists call the multiplier: when an extra dollar is put into a market it regenerates itself many times over with each subsequent use.

The most underdeveped part of America, as far as films and television production is concerned, is the Northwest territory from the Dakotas to the Pacific. So far, the high-power Washington motion picture bureau has enabled that state to attract 27 theatrical and TV movies during the 1970s, and an additional 19 more from 1980 through 1983 (31). Until 1981, however, most film offices in this region languished under the burden of having to prove their income-generating capabilities with no staff or budget to speak of. Slowly but surely, this condition is changing as all Northwestern states now have either a legislated or an ad hoc motion picture and TV commission; Idaho has even opened a Hollywood office in order to attract major moviemakers to their state (6). All the same, Thomas M. Forsythe, the film coordinator for North Dakota, points to the attitude that still pervades much of this region in respect to movie and TV promotion: "North Dakota is a very conservative state. Our legislators are mostly farmers and business people.

---

[1] In 1979, the shooting of William Friedkin's *Cruising* sparked a wave of demonstrations from the gay community in Greenwich Village. Residents of Roosevelt Island, in the East River, subsequently protested the use of their tramway to Manhattan for a hijacking scene in the Sylvester Stallone film *Nighthawks* in 1980. That same year, blacks and Latinos vigorously complained about the making of *Fort Apache, the Bronx* in their South Bronx neighborhood.

They work hard to keep government lean and small. Requests to create new state agencies are generally unpopular ideas'' (13).

Presently, Hawaii, Alaska, Puerto Rico, and the Virgin Islands also have small but vital film and television bureaus well underway. In fact, commission budgets in the 49 states (excluding California) now average $163,000 a year. The annual outlay for project development is considerably higher for that handful of high-profile states now boasting their own production centers. For example, New York, New Jersey, Texas, Florida, Georgia, and Illinois, all operate on allocations ranging from $250,000 to $500,000 (45, p.1). Clearly, the amount of reward that is possible in attracting a major motion picture or television production on-location has encouraged each and every state to institutionalize an extreme form of civic boosterism in the hope of a richly rewarding potential return.

The self-promotion and economic aggrandizement is paying off. In 1983, more movies were being made domestically outside of California than in the state for the first time in over 50 years (7). Most importantly, this trend signals a major procedural transformation in U.S. motion picture and television production that ultimately has both economic and aesthetic ramifications. California's present $1 billion annual loss in revenue from ''runaway productions'' has subsequently created a financial boon in the media prospects of many cities and states nationwide. In turn, these indigenous parts of the United States also provide America's art directors and production designers with a countless number of previously unused, authentic, and richly varied locales that regionally distinguish themselves in the resultant mise-en-scene.

HOLLYWOOD'S RUNAWAY PRODUCTIONS

Hollywood doesn't know anything about the United States. From the old cathedral towns in the top end of Illinois, to the Basque colonies in Washington and Oregon, to the Italians in the low, scrubby hills of West Virginia, to the French Canadians in Maine, you could route a factual crew of moving men for years recording the looks and the customs indigenous to this country and not be tiresome or repetitious. —Pare Lorentz, August 1939 (24, p. 171)

In his 15 years as a film critic, one of Pare Lorentz's most prominent themes was his persistent lament that Hollywood rarely shot on-location. In fact, during this 1927-1941 period, the dominance of the ''classical Hollywood style'' corresponded with the emergence and entrenchment of Los Angeles as the film production capital of the world. The major American companies were by this time vertically integrated, while the majority of product they manufactured is usually characterized as exhibiting well-known stars and a strong identifiable plot line, the idiom of melodrama, as well as in-studio mise-en-scene and an emphasis on ''invisible'' techniques. Certainly, when considering the quantity of Hollywood's output during these years, there were many minor variations in this classical style.

Still, Hollywood's propensity to stay indoors, or at least inside the friendly confines of Southern California for the most part, uniquely affected the look and content of the American mainstream cinema from the coming of sound through World War II. Any inclination towards regional expression in U.S. feature filmmaking was involuntarily submerged by the dictates of the Hollywood studio system. Furthermore, the desire to appeal to a broad-based, mass audience also contributed to this tendency towards product homogeneity.

The first of Hollywood's contingencies to change was its industrial structure. The 1948 Paramount Decision irrevocably altered the neatness and parochialism of vertical integration forever, while nearly simultaneously, the growth of television had its own impact. The history of the Paramount litigation has been thoroughly documented elsewhere, and all the particulars need not be resurrected here (4). Nevertheless, one important theme should be emphasized: the divestiture order not only fragmented exhibition, but ultimtely led to decentralization in the production tier as well.

Increasingly during the 1950s, successful above-the-line personnel formed their own production companies, as many entrepreneurs from both within and outside the film industry experimented with being dependent producers. Ever so slowly and cautiously, the major producer-distributors also shifted more of their emphasis in the production process to financing and providing facilities and services for various independent companies, while making a fewer number of movies themselves. In this way, these studios remained in the crucial position of delivering the eventual product for nearly every proven production source in America to exhibitors nationwide. The studios' immediate reaction to the ever worsening market conditions of the 1950s was to cut their feature film output in half from 448 to 223 during the first 15 years following the Paramount case (11, p. 28). In turn, this product shortage created a void which was somewhat filled by a supply of movies manufactured by companies other than the major studios, though many times these pictures were underwritten by them. Specifically, the number of independently produced motion pictures rose from 49 percent of all features in 1949 to 71.3 percent in 1964 (19, p. 20). The role and function of each tier-production, distribution, and even exhibition—was rapidly evolving into a new, modern context, while the verities of the old studio system were clearly elapsing forever.

By the early 1960s, production was restructuring itself differently than either distribution or exhibition. The overriding arrangements in this tier reformalized more according to the dictates of craft than the usual bureaucratic demands. In other words, an above- or below-the-line worker in Hollywood became part of a network determined more by his or her union and skill than by any relationship to one specific company. In retrospect, the ramifications of this new condition were twofold. First, the required cost of motion picture production escalated as unions became strengthened by the increased attention and alignment of their respective memberships. Second, this shift in worker allegiance also freed personnel from holding an exclusive obligation with any one company and its accompanying studio grounds. Consequently, as the price of feature filmmaking skyrocketed throughout the 1950s, the reasons to stay in Hollywood concurrently evaporated. In fact, both major and independent film production companies began to seriously test the potential of controlling expenditures further by shooting outside of Southern California by the end of the decade.

Initially, Hollywood's runaway productions went primarily overseas. In this respect, the use of cheap, foreign labor by the U.S. movie business was not unlike the expansionist tendency demonstrated by each and every leading American industry after World War II. Moreover, a number of attractive film subsidy programs in Western Europe made the internationalization of Hollywood's production tier a high priority. ''It is not surprising then that through the 1960s, American-financed films abroad rose from about 35 percent to 60 percent of the total output of American producers,'' although this figure has decreased to an average of 46 percent during the intervening 14 years.[2] In its place, the decline in overseas filming has been more than offset by location shooting at home. By 1983, an additional 30 percent of the total domestic output was being lensed on American soil outside of California. Obviously, the dictates of the old-time studio system have now changed dramatically, as three out of every four U.S. movies can today be called runaway productions. This cost-effective decision by Hollywood to venture beyond its own immediate environs and employ the other 49 states as an extended backlot is a tendency that is increasing annually.

Today, there is also a greater emphasis on pictorial verisimilitude than there was in the 1950s, and this evolving aesthetic consideration had its influence on the increase in locationing as well. An identifiable turning point was the gritty and realistic mise-en-scene of *On the Waterfrront*. With that feature, Richard Day became the first art director ever to win an Academy Award (1954) for work done primarily on-location. The reaction in Hollywood was telling; there was a strong undercurrent in the Academy that complained that Day was being recognized for a mood and ambiance that the New Jersey shore provided on its own. Evidently, after spending nearly 30 years within the studio system, even a significant contingent of Hollywood professionals were naive to the intricate difficulties of designing a set for a real location. Day had, in fact, done his job so effectively that his direction was undetectable to an eye conditioned to the exclusivity of Hollywood's classical style. In a much broader sense, this particular example points to the fact that on-location moviemaking in America was from the very outset irreversibly undermining the former aesthetic and technical imperatives that had been previously codified over many years within the controlled environment of Hollywood's shooting stages and studio back lots.

Television, of course, added to this change in the pictorial expectations of the American viewing public. Domestic audiences quickly became accustomed to the

---

[2] The first two percentages are found in Guback (15, p. 348); the most recent statistic was computed from figures that are available in McCarthy (26, p. 52 and 27, p. 26).

appearance and texture of this medium's location work which perceptively increased during the 1960s with the advent of smaller and more mobile film and video equipment. Not only was 35 mm. motion picture equipment becoming more portable, but also the 16 mm. format was being used by movie and TV professionals as well. Moreover, the Cinemobile Mark IV was employed by Hollywood's major companies for the first time in 1967. Essentially, this enormous trailer truck functioned as an elaborate motion picture studio on wheels: and within five short years, cinemobiles were being used in the making of nearly 50 percent of the feature films done by Hollywood's major production companies (3, pp. 373-374). In turn, subsequent, updated versions of this compact and movable unit were further perfected for both film and video during the 1970s. Thus, the consistent evolution of media technology over the last three decades was another important factor that contributed heavily to the number of productions that "ran away" from Southern California.

Finally, this increase in location activity from America's production tier simultaneously encouraged an ever-widening responsiveness from both the private and public sectors across the United States. Beginning in 1970, a larger number of regional entrepreneurs were then entering the media ranks because of the relative inexpensiveness of this smaller equipment. Local support systems, a feature that will be discussed at length later, were clearly mobilizing in most major urban centers nationwide, providing a certain degree of specialized service and expertise for incoming production companies from Hollywood. Furthermore, municipal and state boosterism was rapidly rising. In 1976, 26 film and television commissioners convened their first national cineposium in Denver, Colorado as an initial step towards defining and better understanding the evolving functions, operations, and objectives of their unique occupation. By 1981, a national organization, the Association of Film Commissioners, was next created in order to centralize membership and representation, as well as set the agenda for what has since become an annual convention. These signs of growing maturity and formal sophistication merely reflect the level of development and success that is presently enjoyed by motion picture and television bureaus in each and every section of America. In response to this pattern of progress and proliferation outside its boundaries, two new bills are presently before the California legislature which are designed to ease the tax, permit, and fee burdens which are today driving more and more major productions away from that state (47, p. 1). In other words, California is apparently in a position where it must now adjust its own business environment, if it is to cultivate the billion dollar industry which it took for granted for more than 50 years. Curiously, one of these antirunaway measures would legislate a new gubernatorial appointment for the very first time in California—a film commissioner with statewide jurisdiction! (48, p. 3).

CIVIC BOOSTERISM

The film commission, wherever it is located, is the point where the art, the industry and the politics of filmmaking converge.—Nancy Littlefield, former president, Association of Film Commissioners, 1982, (22, p. 12).

If I'm a better salesman than John Earle in Utah or Joel Smith in Texas, or any other film commission, and it's more economic to come to Arizona, than that's where it will come.—Bill MacCallum, President, AFC and Arizona motion picture development Coordinator, 1984 (8)

The big difference is what we get for nothing from a community that really wants you.—Martin Jorow, independent producer, 1981 (28, p. 141)

Boosterism itself is nothing new to the American character; it is the drive and hustle of businessmen and public officials as they collectively foster and engineer trade and commerce within their immediate environment. Unquestionably, the vim and vigor of the booster spirit built America, promoting everything from ice, to fish, to cotton, to lumber, to wheat, to minerals, and livestock. From the mid-nineteenth through most of the twentieth century, the abundance of these resources and the occasional demonstrations of both the ingenuity and the luck of local rooters ushered in an age of heavy manufacturing and U.S. urbanism. Today, the domestic landscape is changing again, and so are the raw materials that concern the successful promoter. Boosterism assiduously cultivates progress and gambles on the future; it also naively basks in that "honeymoon period" when a new discovery appears to have no limitations. In this way, the overstatement and hyperbole of the Hollywood institution has for decades symbolized an extreme form of this attitude, while at the same time seeming to be inaccessible, unattainable, and isolated from the rest of the country. In the 1980s, however, both the economic prospects and the corresponding myth of the U.S. movie business presses outside its usual confines in Southern California, as state and municipal governments compete among themselves to lure the glamour and windfall potential of the mass media, and ultimately the information age, into their own backyards.

By the end of 1984, nearly 95 film and TV commissions will be operating domestically. First and foremost, these offices are all publically affiliated, and they function primarily as intermediaries between various production companies, the civil bureaucracy, the private sector, and the local community. Most bureaus are created for reasons of economic development, and therefore are encouraged to go out and aggressively recruit business for their respective states and municipalities. In contrast, a few offices still suffer from severe staff and budgetary limitations, and merely react to sporadic, incoming inquiries. To put this into perspective, the typical commission averaged just over three employees in 1982, most of whom were political appointees with little or no media background, and were learning the particulars of their assignment as they went along.[3] Additionally, job turnover tends to be high, as is the case with most civil service positions. In fact, only 11 representatives attending the 1983 annual cineposium in San Jose, California had ever been to any of the previous seven conventions before (12, p. 8).[4]

Consequently, the glamour and excitement of movie and TV production is sometimes counteracted by problems of worker continuity and expertise. Bureau employees are essentially public relations people who must establish connections and maintain open lines of communication with the motion picture and television industries. They characteristically publicize themselves and their surroundings in three ways: (1) by producing and distributing a location manual which emphasizes the uniqueness and variability of the home terrain and the accessibility of support services; (2) by advertising in the trade papers; and (3) by hosting courtesy parties for studios executives in Hollywood and New York City if, of course, their budget permits. Clearly, the more prosperous commissions hold a definite financial advantage over their smaller counterparts when it comes to high profile boosterism.

Actually, the kind of self-promotion that emanates from each and every motion picture and television office resembles the language and slick exaggeration that is characteristic of the techniques of U.S. advertising in general. Even medium- and small-sized operations boast that "we are willing to do *anything* and *everything* to assure that your shooting experience [in Idaho] is both enjoyable and profitable" (56, p. 3.). The customary hard-sell also includes claims that border on the extravagant; for instance: "we feel that Montana has what you need for virtually every shooting situation" (58). In fact, prior to 1981 the Ohio Film Bureau employed a promotional strategy which spotlighted the state as having four distinctly different looks: the cosmopolitan Northeast, the Mississippi River Valley, Kentucky bluegrass country, and the industrial Midwest. Later, this commission narrowed its focus to merely stressing the last image since experience made it apparent that production companies scouting for the first three regional areas were consistently going elsewhere to shoot their pictures. Overall, this example suggests that bureau officers are progressively becoming more astute at the booster aspects of their jobs, learning and improving how and what to best present to prospective clients about themselves, their cities, and their state.

Next, film and TV offices assist incoming companies in the surveying and selection of locations. Presently, 85 percent of the bureaus nation-wide provide helicopter transportation, while 20 percent have installed toll-free phone numbers in order to better facilitate this service (45, p. 1). Usually, any individual commission is contending with a number of other states and cities in their region at this

---

[3] This average is computed from figures available in Littlefield (22, pp. 14–15).

[4] This attendance pattern is revealing since member turnout for the annual AFC cineposium is always very high. For instance, only four commissioners did not come to the 1984 meeting in Mobile, Alabama. The convention is consistently attractive because it offers an essential and alternative learning experience to merely relying on the "trial and error" lessons that are absorbed on the job. In this way, the cineposium creates a situation where film bureau employees can share information as well as receive advice and training about the particulars of this new profession from both industry insiders and fellow commissioners.

stage of preparation. Any combination of production representatives, including the producer, director, assistant director, writer, set director and/or the production and location managers will scout a variety of possible shooting sites. Typically, the motion picture or television company will solicit competitive bids from each prospective film and TV office concerning the cost and availability of lodging, meals, transportation, equipment, sets, props, storage, local labor, studio facilities, as well as police, fire, sanitation, and medical services. More often than not, the film bureau and locale that has been the most responsive in finding ways to off-set production expenses is the one ultimately chosen. In this respect, the skill and public relations capabilities of any commission is a crucial determinant in attracting business according to its degree of influence in centralizing and simplifying the process of acquiring permits and paying fees; in negotiating lower prices with local merchants, businessmen, and unions; and by monitoring any rent-gouging or shysterism directed towards this new influx of media capital.[5]

The boosterism of most successful film bureaus also extends to taking an active role in the development of a skilled infrastructure for production purposes in their immediate environs. Today, these duties include the fostering of a local talent pool, participating in minor casting and locating extras; assisting with wardrobes and props, as well as cataloguing the statewide availability of production service personnel and technology. On one hand, the "right-to-work" laws in many states make it possible for movie and TV companies to save a great deal of money by hiring nonunion professionals on-location. Still, a major motion picture or television production demands a high degree of technical and creative expertise. Therefore, an amalgam of skilled workers in each and every region of the country is nowadays an alternative that has previously been unavailable ever since the rise of the studio system. As an example, "producers from Hollywood can come [to Illinois] with a skeletal staff, and the Chicago production community will supply the rest" (39, p. 5).

Indeed, this sophisticated level of community support now extends to the growth of satellite studios in New York, New Jersey, North and South Carolina, Georgia, Florida, Texas, along with Chicago, Illinois (2, 16, 29, 46, 51). Since May 1982, for instance, the newly constructed $12 million Dallas Communication Complex at Los Colinas has made it possible for incoming companies to develop a motion picture or a television program from preparation through the final stages of post-production without ever leaving Texas. Consequently, the open-door policies of many film and TV commissions are today seizing the opportunity offered them by the commercial fallout surrounding the rapid decentalization of media production in America. Moreover, the better bureaus are also becoming an integral part of the industry in their own right, building a solid reputation based on per-

---

[5] Teamsters locals in Kentucky, Illinois, and Texas have even been convinced to write letters of welcome and introduction which are, in turn, included in the production packets that are currently being distributed by the respective film bureaus in these three states.

sonality, ability to juggle logistics, and dependability. These offices provide an invaluable and unique service as they work with major productions from start to finish, minimizing every possible local problem from handling traffic, security, and safety to arranging and controlling publicity and press interviews. In turn, Hollywood subsequently bolsters these respective state and municipal economies with ample returns on their booster efforts by providing a substantial potential for additional industrial growth and an inestimable amount of public relations benefits besides.

LOCAL BENEFITS

My job is economic development. My job is to get that picture to shoot here and spend its $3 million here rather than have it shoot in Michigan. My job is to bring dollars in and create jobs.—Lucy Salenger, managing director, Illinois Film Office and TV Services, 1983 (9, p. 7)

It's an argument you can't resist. Any way you choose to measure it, the state comes out on the winning side.—Mary Lou Crane, director, Massachusetts Film Bureau, 1980 (30, p. 40)

In 1980, the Massachusetts Film Bureau commissioned a study that measured the financial impact of film and video production on the state's economy. A survey conducted by the Regional Services Research Institute at the University of Massachusetts demonstrated a steady growth pattern in media revenues over the previous five years. This study also accurately predicted an even brighter future for motion picture and television work in the commonwealth during the next half decade (53). Similar research in one form or another has been conducted under the auspices of nearly every film and TV commission nation-wide. Since all of these offices are funded by government monies, supporting data are generally required as the means for either establishing a brand new bureau, or justifying substantive budgetary increases after several years of operation. As a result, self-study or outside documentation are the ways by which a commission can establish its reasons to be. In addition, these research projects time and again outdistance even the more optimistic predictions concerning economic and job development for what these public officials and/or outside researchers expect to discover.[6]

Texas, for example, hired professor Don Umphrey from Texas Tech University to conduct a survey of state-wide film, television, and video production work and its subsequent effect on the domestic business climate for the year 1980. His findings were an encouraging surprise for the Texas Film Commission: somewhere between $500 and $900 million was infused into the state's economy that year,

---

[6] Film bureau self-studies are initiated and conducted in a number of different ways. On one hand, a governor, a state official, or a mayor may mandate the research in order to better determine their respective agency's needs and/or usefulness. In contrast, the film commissioner may conduct or commission a survey himself as a means of proving a point or arguing a case to a higher-up.

depending on whether a conservative or liberal multiplier was used (51). Either way, however, the fiscal rewards accorded to Texas by this growing media enterprise makes mass communications one of the leading industries in the state. Similar results were reported in contracted studies performed for Louisiana, Arizona, California, and New York (51, pp. 5-7).

Two of the primary benefits from this ongoing increase in runaway productions are the substantial financial gains in these respective states and municipalities, along with the creation of new jobs, albeit temporary in nature. Illinois is a case in point. Whenever a feature film is produced, anywhere from 25 to 33 percent of the total budget is consistently left in the surrounding environs. *The Blues Brothers* (1980), for instance, "spent $6 million to $7 million in Chicago" (38, p. 4). To gauge the liquid effect of this money on the local economy, the exact dollar figure is then subject to the aforementioned multiplier to compute the regenerative power of this capital. The Federal Reserve turnover formula is 3.57 which, in turn, is multiplied to that part of any feature film's budget that is expended on-location. In this way, *The Blues Brothers* alone was responsible for a gross worth of between $21.42 and $24.99 million in Chicago during 1979. Futhermore, the potential for jobs is equally as startling.

Between 1965 and 1975, only five major productions for movie theaters and television combined were filmed in Illinois. Over the next seven years, this number mushroomed to 95 movies, creating approximately 48,000 temporary jobs in the state (36, p. 6). In this same time frame, total expenditures for motion picture and television production in Hawaii amounted to $155.35 million, which concurrently generated 11,756 new jobs (57). To illustrate this same pattern on a much smaller scale, the Institute for Economic and Business Research at the University of Kansas studied the influence of producing the made-for-television movie, *The Day After* (1983), on the economy of Lawrence, Kansas and the neighboring region. The resulting report, "An Analysis of the Economic Impact of a Motion Picture Production in Lawrence, Kansas, 1982," stated that the $1.1 million spent in Lawrence subsequently produced an estimated total income of $2.147 million in Lawrence itself and an additional $.55 million for the rest of Kansas (5). This influx of outside money also created 169 jobs in the interim. Across the board, therefore, the business of media production translates into measues of growth and fiscal accord; this unique industry is at the same time nonpolluting and only provisionally disruptive for wherever the location shooting happens to be.

Another significant attraction that follows any major production into an area is a noted increase in publicity and public relations value. Through years of myth-building and tradition, Hollywood actors and actresses offer a certain degree of glamour and prominence by their very presence. This fact certainly does not go unrecognized by either local politicians or businessmen who are eager to court the increased prestige and potential image improvement that is available in being pictured with visiting celebrities in the local and sometimes national media. A city or a state can enjoy an invaluable amount of civic promotion merely by serving as the setting for a successful movie or a television series. San Francisco is characteristically cited as the first locale to realize such benefits, although most film and TV commissions now take it for granted that a residual reward offered to them by attracting a local shoot is the probability of a subsequent boost in the regional tourism industry.

SUMMARY AND DIRECTIONS FOR FUTURE RESEARCH

The past decade has seen an enormous growth in regional theater. Why not a similar growth in regional films? . . . A story indigenous to Texas, made by Texans, can be shown and understood in northern Michigan. A story rooted in northern Michigan, such as *Anatomy of a Murder* (1959), might possibly be made better by indigenous Michiganders than by a team from Hollywood that moved into the area with its preformed script and its preconceptions. What I'm arguing is a film that recognizes the multiplicity of this vast country, a film that places differences above similarities.— Arthur Knight, 1978 (18, p. 340)

With the results of the 1948 Paramount Decision and the ultimate demise of the studio system, the production tier of the American movie business has become slowly and progressively more decentralized. A similar trend is evident in the U.S. television industry because of separate consent decrees signed by NBC, CBS, and ABC during the past decade which limit network involvement in the production of prime time programming and its subsequent syndication.[7] The dominant pattern for both movies and TV today provides that individual above and the below-the-line talent come together for each "package," and then this crew will fragment again when the project is completed. In turn, the major Hollywood studios and the networks function primarily as distributors, although, importantly, they also provide the stability and capital needed for most of America's mass-consumed films and prime time diet which after all guarantees their control over what gets made and seen nation-wide. Therefore, the production arms of the contemporary motion picture and television industries are no longer geographically bound to Southern California as they previously were when most shooting was done in-house. Instead, the 1950s and 1960s marked the beginning of an unhurried, though deliberate, process by which America's major film and TV suppliers began to experiment more and more with domestic production sites other than Los Angeles and New

---

[7] In the early 1970s, the U.S. Department of Justice filed separate antitrust suits against the three networks which complained of trade improprieties in violation of both Sections 1 and 2 of the Sherman Act. On November 17, 1976, NBC signed a settlement agreement which made concessions and freed itself from further litigation: *United States* v. *National Broadcasting Company,* No. 74-3601-RJK (C.D. Col. November 17, 1976). Later, CBS signed a similar consent decree on July 31, 1980, while ABC settled on November 14, 1980: *United States* v. *CBS, Inc.,* 74-3599-RJK (C.D. Col. July 31, 1980); and *United States* v. *American Broadcasting Companies,* 74-3600-RJK (C.D. Col. November 14, 1980).

York. In addition, this move towards on-location shooting has come to dominate movies and TV in the United States over the past fifteen years.

In a sense, the business of motion picture, television, and video production in America is now becoming nationalized as film bureau input from many major cities and all the states across the United States is a significant catalyst in ensuring this process. Local politicians have legislated more than ninety commissions nation-wide as a means of encouraging the glamour and high finance of Hollywood into their own backyards. These agencies in turn accommodate the needs and wishes of incoming media professionals, fostering valuable business ties, and bonding a mutually beneficial relationship which serves to localize motion picture and video work from coast to coast for the first time since the birth of the movies. Unquestionably, the film bureau phenomenon has grown into a vital and legitimate part of media production in the United States: guiding Hollywood through unfamiliar terrain; performing a lucrative service for the private sector; and simultaneously creating a public relations bonanza for both government officials as well as many of the more prominent members of the local citizenry.

Moreover, this interfacing between the commercial sphere and America's various state and municipal bureaucracies is a notable development simply because the relevant industry in this case is a mass communications medium. At least in peacetime, the United States has only infrequently mixed the affairs of state with the business of Hollywood on an overt level. Obviously, the dangers of appearing to politically compromise and co-opt content has always warranted this attitude. Still, the movies and the U.S. civil structure are today prominently intertwined in the only way that is suitable and logical under the American system: this union is motivated entirely by profit. In other words, the justification for the continued existence of each and every motion picture and television commission is exclusively economic development. It would be naive, however, not to next consider the related and apparent issue of how the film bureau phenomenon also affects the eventual shape of movie and video content in perhaps subtle and unintentional ways.

Thus, one question which remains to be answered is: to what extent will these business and economic changes in major American motion picture and television production affect the subsequent look and ideology of U.S. media content? The issue of mise-en-scene may be easier to deal with. ''Many directors are convinced that pictures such as 'Breaking Away,' photographed in Indiana, and 'Diner,' filmed in Baltimore, reflect the feeling of middle America outside of Hollywood to a degree that was seldom shown on the screen before'' (52, p. 65). Indeed, the number of offerings that exhibit an idiomatic flavor in their pictorial verisimilitude has been increasing annually ever since the early 1970s. Still, do these technical and aesthetic transformations in media production in the United States necessarily translate into a wide range of perspectives and interpretations of domestic life? Are the ideological concerns of our film and TV content gradually beginning to mirror the diversity and plurality of regional America and its various outlooks? Clearly, this second aspect of the original question dealing with the supposed potential for broader presentations of the dispositions and attitudes peculiar to certain U.S. subcultures is a far more subtle and complex matter; moreover, it undoubtedly cannot be adequately answered within the scope of this one essay.

Nevertheless, there are a number of starting points on which to begin further research and study. First of all, the above quote from Arthur Knight calls for and alludes to the apparent proliferations of indigenous filmmakers throughout the United States; specific examples include William Girdler in Detroit, John Hanson and Rob Nilsson in San Francisco and Minneapolis, Earl Owensby in North Carolina, George Romero in Pittsburgh, John Sayles in New Jersey, Charles Sellier, Jr. in Utah, and John Waters in Baltimore, to name just a few. Furthermore, many localized, smaller-budgeted moviemakers with talent and the requisite sensibilities have been able to enter the Hollywood arena over the last decade; this list includes such individuals as Martin Scorsese, Brian DePalma, David Lynch, John Carpenter, and John Landis.

Still, the question as to whether there has been any measurable ideological change in American film and TV content during this era of runaway production remains. What exactly is the contemporary relationship and interplay between the major U.S. commercial distributors and these independent film and TV producers? Are independent feature productions offering viable alternatives to mainstream media content? And is the American viewing public generally paying attention to regional productions and indigenous viewpoints?

Arthur Knight likewise refers to the preconceptions and biases of Hollywood's scriptwriters. In fact, a panel on this very issue was held during the 1978 annual cineposium for film and TV commissioners which met in Arizona. At that forum, Phil Oakley of the Louisiana Film Industry Office complained:

> I just want writers to go someplace one time and see the damn place they are writing about. They are ridiculing people and causing serious problems for their industry around the country. You hurt yourself very seriously when you write into a script only your idea of what people are like outside of Hollywood (55).

In turn, has this problem been remedied to any significant degree over the succeeding six years? Are there distinct differences in the kinds of movies and TV programs that are produced in each regional section of America? What is the history of film and television development in each of these geographical areas? In this way, film and TV bureaus are not only official liaisons functioning within the industrial structure of mass communications in America, they are also a resource for media historians who are interested in documenting and analyzing localized production activities. Important first steps have already been taken in exploring regionalism as a strategy in film historiography (25, 33, 34, 41). Still, much remains to be done in both cinema and television scholarship.

REFERENCES

1. Bennetts, Leslie. "Movie Making in New York Triples in 5 Years." *The New York Times*, October 6, 1982, p. C21.
2. *The Blade:* Toledo, Ohio. "North, South Carolina Fight Over DeLaurentis Studio." December, 8, 1983. P. P-2.
3. Bohn, Thomas W. and Richard L. Stromgren with Daniel H. Johnson. *Light and Shadows: A History of Motion Pictures* (2nd ed.). Sherman Oaks, CA: Alfred Publishing, 1978.
4. Conant, Michael. *Antitrust in the Motion Picture Industry.* Berkeley: University of California Press, 1960.
5. Crawford, Kay. "Press Release: Ah . . . Kansas!" *Travel and Tourism News.* November 12, 1982, p. 30.
6. *Daily Variety.* "Idaho Gov. Opens H'Wood Office to Woo Locationing in State." October 14, 1983, p. 4.
7. *Daily Variety.* "H'wood Film Council Joins Fight Against Runaway Prod'N." January 9, 1984, p. 6.
8. *Daily Variety.* Cineposium Ignores Issue: California Runaway Prod'n Drive No Sweat to State Film Panels." January 31, 1984, p. 16.
9. Dobbin, Ben. "Lights, Camera, Action: Movies Come Back to Illinois." *Illinois Issue,* February 1983, pp. 6-10.
10. Earll, Stephen (Ed.). *The Texas Production Manual: A Source Book for the Motion Picture and Video Industry,* (6th ed.). Austin: The Texas Film Commission, 1983.
11. Edgerton, Gary. *American Film Exhibition: An Analysis of the Motion Picture Industry's Market Structure, 1963-1980.* New York: Garland, 1983.
12. Film Clips: San Jose Film and Video Council Newsletter. "Association of Film Commissioners Cineposium '83, San Jose, California." May 1983. 10 pp.
13. Forsythe, Thomas M., State Film Coordinator, North Dakota Economic Development Commission. Letter to the author, May 27, 1983.
14. Georgia Department of Industry and Trade. "Profile: Georgia Film Industry, 1973-1982." 1983. 4 pp.
15. Guback, Thomas H. "Film as International Business: The Role of American Multinationals." Gorham Kindem (Ed.), *In The American Movie Industry: The Business of Motion Pictures,* pp. 336-350. Carbondale: Southern Illinois University Press, 1983.
16. Hoynes, Peggy. "Production Guide to Georgia." *Millimeter,* March, 1980, pp. 128-130.
17. Kleyweg, Hedy. "Special Report: Alabama." *The Hollywood Reporter,* June 26, 1981, pp. S1-S16.
18. Knight, Arthur. *The Liveliest Art: A Panoramic History of the Movies* (revised Ed.). New York: New American Library, 1978.
19. Lamson, Robert D. "Motion Picture Exhibition: An Economic Analysis of Quality, Output and Productivity." Unpublished Ph.D. dissertation. University of Washington, 1968.
20. Lander, Marylee, manager, Office of Film and Television Coordination, Dade County, Florida. Letter to the author, May 19, 1983.
21. Lapolla, Eve, assistant manager, Ohio Film Bureau. "Feature Filmmaking in Ohio." A presentation during Mass Communications Week, Bowling Green State University, Bowling Green, Ohio, March 10, 1983.
22. Littlefield, Nancy. "The Role of Film Commissioners." *American Premiere,* March 1982, pp. 11-16.
23. Livingston, Guy. "TV, Film Production Activities Flourishing in Massachusetts." *Daily Variety,* May 6, 1983, pp. 3, 8, 20.
24. Lorentz, Pare. "The Documentary Film." *McCall's,* August, 1939, in *Lorentz on Film: Movies 1927 to 1941.* New York: Hopkinson and Blake, Publishers, 1975. pp. 170-171.

25. Lyons, Timothy J. *The Silent Partner: The History of the American Film Manufacturing Company, 1910-1921*. New York: Arno, 1974.

26. McCarthy, Todd. "U.S. Productions in '81 Off by Only 2%." *Variety*, January 13, 1982, pp. 9, 52.

27. McCarthy, Todd. "H'Wood Prod'N Splurge in 1983." *Daily Variety*, January 3, 1984, pp. 1, 24, 26.

28. Maloney, Lane. "Jurow Advice: 'Break Out' of Hollywood—Avers Location Values Helpful." *Variety*, May 13, 1981, pp. 141, 146.

29. *Millimeter*. "Production Guide to New York: Dispelling Production Fears." June 1981, 10 pp.

30. Most, Bruce W. "Wooing Hollywood." *American Way*, July 1980, pp. 40-43.

31. Motion Picture and Television Bureau, Washington State Department of Commerce and Economic Development. "Location Information: History of Major Productions Filmed on Location in Washington State." 1983. 3 pp.

32. Myler, Kathleen. "Cameras Roll as Film Industry Speeds Up the Live Action Here." *Chicago Tribune*, Business sec., October 23, 1981, pp. 1, 3.

33. Nelson, Richard A. "A History of Latter-Day Saint Screen Portrayals in the AntiMormon Film Era, 1905-1936," Unpublished M.A. thesis, Brigham Young University, 1975.

34. Nelson, Richard A. *Florida and the American Motion Picture Industry, 1898-1980*, 2 volumes. New York: Garland, 1983.

35. *The New York Times*. "The Film Business Gains in New York." November 21, 1982, p. 54.

36. Papajohn, George. "It's Policeman's Job to See that City Gets the Picture." *Chicago Tribune*, Section 5, May 27, 1983, pp. 1, 6.

37. Powdermaker, Hortense. *Hollywood: The Dream Factory*. Boston: Little, Brown, 1950.

38. Schafer, Tom. "State Rolls Out Red Carpet for Filmmakers." *Sunday Magazine*, (Rockford, Illinois), October 18, 1981, pp. 4-5.

39. Segers, Frank. "Chicago Locations Boom, Casting Agents at Capacity." *Variety*, July 7, 1982, pp. 5, 24.

40. Smith, Karol W. and K. Sue Anderson. "Summary Report: Colorado Motion Picture and Television Advisory Commission, July 1969-June 1982." Division of Commerce and Development Department of Local Affairs. September 20, 1982. 22 pp.

41. Spehr, Paul C. *The Movies Begin: Making Movies in New Jersey, 1887-1920*. Newark: The Newark Museum, 1977.

42. Texas Film Commission. "Press Release: For Immediate Release." March 1, 1982, 1 p.

43. *Time*. "To the Heartland, with Cameras." September 19, 1977, pp. 71-74.

44. Toole, James M., director, Kentucky Film Office. Letter to the author, May 26, 1983.

45. Tusher, Will. "49 States in a Scramble to Lure Location Work Away from California." *Daily Variety*, October 13, 1983, pp. 1, 15.

46. Tusher, Will. "Runaway Post-Production Cited as Another Major Problem for California." *Daily Variety*, November 23, 1983, pp. 1, 25.

47. Tusher, Will. "Pair of Anti-Runaway Bills About to be Introduced in Current State Legislature." *Daily Variety*, January 12, 1984, pp. 1, 38.

48. Tusher, Will. "Runaway Prod'N Bill May Spawn State Film Commissioner Post." *Daily Variety*, January 19, 1984, pp. 3-4.

49. Ueckert, Sjon, director, New Mexico Film Commission. Letter to the author, May 23, 1983.

50. Ueckert, Sjon, director. New Mexico Film Commission. Letter to the author, July 18, 1983.

51. Umphrey, Don. "The Economic Impact of the 1980 Film/Tape Industry in Texas," Unpublished paper prepared for the Texas Film Commission. January 1982. 31 pp.

52. *U.S. News & World Report*. "Movies are Ranging the U.S. for Reality." May 31, 1982, pp. 64-67.

53. *Variety*. "Some Film Producers Mindless, Or Don't Care About Stereotypes." February 8, 1978, p. 24.

54. *Variety*. "Mass. Sees a 5-Year Upswing: TV is Outpacing Films." May 13, 1981, pp. 141-148.

55. *Variety*. "New Jersey as 'Location' Site; $12,000,000 Film Work in '81." May 12, 1982, pp. 180-182.

56. Wilson, Steve and Carol Wolfe (Eds.). *Picture Perfect Locations*. Boise: State of Idaho Film Bureau, 1983.

57. Wong, Henry L., Ph.D., director, Hawaii Film Office. Letter and 6 page report to the author, May 23, 1983.

58. Wunderwald, Garry L., Montana Motion Picture Coordinator, Department of Commerce, State of Montana. A prepared statement for prospective clients, 1983.

12

Ethical Issues in the Film Industry*

Clifford G. Christians and Kim B. Rotzoll

The news media frequently carry stories about immoral behavior in the film industry: "Movie Deals in Exchange for Hard Drugs," "Company Money for Personal Expense Accounts," "Tax Evasion," "Pirating Materials without Copyright Permission," "Forged Checks." The sensational headlines and lurid details seem natural and believable, in fact, for a glamour business of high finance. When David McClintick documented David Begelman's misappropriation of funds at Columbia Pictures, the malfeasance was nothing novel (12). Scandals have occurred in the motion picture business throughout its history.

Anyone concerned about the manner in which business operates in a capitalist society will wish to pursue such flagrant abuses. Actually, however, yellow journalism tends to divert attention away from the deeper structure within which the corruption occurs. The court cases, public charges, and spectacular news stories focus on individual actions without capturing the realities underneath which these events symptomize.

Therefore, in the opening phase of a major study funded by the McCormick Foundation, we attempted to capture the subterranean patterns. We sought to learn how the practitioners themselves perceive ethical decisions in their day-to-day work. The intent was to reach behind the externals and the exotic occurrences, and to examine how cinema executives decide, plan, and execute strategy. We came as no alien force with axes to grind, but wished to hear in their own language what film professionals define as ethical, how they interpret problematic events, and what actions they consider to overstep acceptable behavior.

* The authors thank their colleague at the University of Illinois, Professor Thomas Guback, for helpful criticisms of an earlier draft. This study was funded by the McCormick Foundation.

225

PROCEDURE

Since the days of Florian Znaniecki's *The Polish Peasant in Europe and America* and William F. Whyte's *Street Corner Society,* qualitative research has insisted on studying people in their natural environment. Social scientists contributing most to nonquantitative research use intact settings within which social life occurs as their primary resource—hospitals, prisons, residential neighborhoods, schools, regions of poverty and affluence, airplanes, parks, factories, streets, sidewalks, and ethnic enclaves.[1] Thus we also chose to question employees of the film industry in their actual workplace; in a paraphrase of Clifford Geertz, we pitched our tent among the natives to learn how those in other valleys guard their sheep (11).

We began by separating the cinema business into its typical functions—production, distribution, exhibition. Each of these categories we subdivided into local, regional, and national. Outside of that standard grid, we added educational film and the conglomerate/nonconglomerate factor. This strategy—approximating the organizational structure of the motion picture industry—allowed us to make important comparisons among the various subunits within the system. The values held by those in a conglomerate could now be studied in relation to nonconglomerates, those of a national chain with an independent, those in a small organization to large ones. Such analysis would have been impossible if we had chosen a random sample of the particular behaviors of members in the Academy of Motion Picture Arts and Sciences, for example.

Eight areas for study resulted, listed below along with company names to communicate what the categories mean. Since we agreed to keep the eight cooperating firms anonymous, the names included here are chosen for illustrative purposes only:

- Independent theater ownership (Sherman Brotman of Chicago, for example)
- Regional theater ownership (Kerasotes, Plitt, for example)
- National theater ownership (United Artists, General Cinema, for example)
- Major nonconglomerate film production/distribution (Fox, Warner, for example)
- Major conglomerate film production/distribution (Universal, Paramount, for example)
- Major independent film production/distribution (MTM, Disney, for example)
- Small independent film production (Clampett, Koch, for example)
- Educational film production (Coronet, Time-Life, for example)

With careful attention to geographical location, a reputable firm was selected for each category. Preference was given to the oldest company, for example. We excluded those recently involved in an executive scandal and those, to our knowledge, caught up in legal suits. We were concerned to map the ongoing culture of representative companies and to avoid embattled firms where immediate circum-

---

[1] For a summary and documentaion, see Christians and Carey (5).

stances might tend to distort replies. By telephone and personal contact, executives were located who agreed to distribute questionnaires to their personnel above the secretarial and bookkeeping levels.

The approach and research instrument were inductive. Rather than operating from a preconceived ethical paradigm or setting up a check list of "evil" actions, we deliberately allowed respondents maximum freedom to define their own perceptions of moral behavior.[2] In effect, we conducted a brief written interview. The questions were constructed almost as though we were conversing personally with the respondents and sought both detail and candor. In an effort to avoid imposing the researcher's frame of reference on the interviewees, we designed the following open-ended inquiries:

1. Do you feel that you encounter ethical decisions in the practice of your job?
2. If you *do*
   (a) Please indicate how frequently these decisions arise.
   (b) Please describe, in a paragraph or two, the *types of situations* in which you typically encounter the most important of these decisions.

In addition, respondents were requested to give their age, sex, length of employment, and nature of position held. Though distributed by the firm's management with a covering memo urging cooperation, completed forms were mailed directly to the researchers by the employees with anonymity assured.

Of the forms actually delivered to the company executives (750), more than one out of four were returned to us, totaling 212. Since we relied on distribution by others rather than direct mail, we consider this response rate to be completely satisfactory. In fact, in seven of the eight areas, 50 percent or more replied. The only softness occurred in the national theater exhibition category, where 325 questionnaires were sent to central headquarters. Of that number, 36 completed forms were mailed back to us—a small percentage due to the difficulty of distributing them effectively to employees located all over the United States. Incidentally, the small independent producer had three decision-making employees and two of them participated in our analysis. The largest number of returns (41) came from the nonconglomerate major. In effect, our strategy enabled a representative number of employees at eight companies to describe to us their perspective on ethics in cinema, 90 percent of them including concrete examples to accompany their description.

What we offer here is both description and analysis: delineation of what the 212 respondents told us; disclosure of the ethical system within which they appear to operate. Our sample proved to be as heterogeneous as the decision makers within

---

[2] The research was designed to avoid what Mills calls "abstracted empiricism" (13, ch. 2). The lack of definitional clarity concerning ethical terms and the complexities of moral choice pushed us toward the tradition of Weber's *verstehen* and away from a rigid and confining methodology (17, pp. 87-112). For a defense of the interpretive emphasis—by respondents themselves and in our assessing their readings—see (14).

the nine companies we investigated. The sample included small theater owners and managers (concerned with enforcing "R" ratings and patron conduct), as well as middle-level managers and several officials in the highest corporate ranks. It encompassed films for education, entertainment, and promotion, intended for theater, classrooms, and television audiences, films all touched along the way by a host of writers, directors, producers, lawyers, promotion personnel, and exhibitors.[3]

DOMINANT THEME: AN ETHICS OF "EFFICIENCY"

It would be impossible to detail adequately all the nuances of these unstructured responses in the limits of this article. What we offer is an overview of the dominant discoveries, with respondent comments representative of the major themes. And we know of no better way to encapsulate our general findings than through Jacques Ellul's concept *la technique*. Ellul argues that *la technique* or technical efficiency determines contemporary communications. He contends that in industrialized societies we are so beguiled by machines that machineness becomes the standard or model by which we make decisions. From his perspective, the media system is fundamentally impervious to all moral considerations, and such was our conclusion regarding cinema.

"As in ancient days men put out the eyes of nightingales in order to make them sing better," Ellul writes, so all moral considerations are eliminated in order to maximize profits, sales, and markets (8, p.75).[4] Administrative and accounting decisions replace moral oughts. Everything that succeeds is declared good; results become the criterion of all activity. Patience, social welfare, consideration, love, respect, and other such human goods are replaced in Ellul's description of our society by whatever best serves those in power, regardless of any rights of the people involved.

Ellul describes such matters in his dramatic book *Propaganda* (9). Whether he accurately represents mass communications as a whole, we do not wish to discuss here. It does seem obvious from the overall tone of our responses, however, that many of the practitioners find themselves participating in a system quite similar to that suggested by Ellul. The purpose of our study was not to test Ellul's hypothesis; rather, we used him only as a way of illuminating and synthesizing our findings. From examination of the responses, one conclusion is compelling—the film

---

[3] For an analysis of the epistemological assumptions involved, see Christians and Carey (5) and Fortner and Christians (10).

[4] He demonstrates how this notion works in contemporary society in *The Political Illusion* (7). Ellul's methodology is formally similar to his mentor, Max Weber (16), who did not analyze capitalism in terms of free enterprise, but as a frame of mind, a temperment, an ethos out of which events and institutions arise. Along these lines, what might be construed as simply a structure to provide order and continuity for the film arts must instead be seen as a set of impersonal forces which operate out of their own internal logic.

industry can, to a great extent, be characterized as dominated by *la technique*. Aesthetics and moral values do not hold sway in any meaningful sense, but economics and bureaucracy do instead.

Based on the responses, this medium can be interpreted as operating essentially on amoral criteria.[5] That is a stronger claim than accusing it merely of illegality and/or immorality. Already in 1948, when attempting to break the industry's vertical integration, the Supreme Court remarked on the "proclivity of the defendants [the eight major film companies] for illegal conduct."[6] Yet what the responses to the questionnaires suggest to us is not that the industry is legal with some illegalities here and there, nor that it operates essentially on the basis of moral principles with a few immoral actions on the side. Rather, the industry seems to be saturated by what Ellul calls a technicized amorality, devoid of all humane and principial elements, in which the good is replaced by big money, personal advantage, and cost-effective distribution. It seems to be a composite responsing to its own peculiar set of norms. A theater manager came close to this when he declared that no ethical problems exist in cinema because "nobody cares," and a sales director for a regional theater chain concluded: "Ethics simply are nonexistent in the theater business." An executive in educational film noted further that professional standards are a "bit vague in our industry in that they are not spelled out and are always in flux." What they mean, we think, is that the industry tends to be without explicit criteria by which right and wrong behavior can be judged. As the paragraphs below demonstrate, rather than following moral principals of right and wrong, the cinema industry has set up its own system for measuring conduct and achievement—guidelines arising from commercial success and organizational power.

Some of the nuances and qualifications of these general impressions will emerge as we proceed. However, it became obvious early in our research that we were confronting an unusual media system. Securing cooperation from representative companies was extraodinarily difficult, for example. We proceeded in this research project as a whole by obtaining approval from company presidents or directors for distributing the questionnaires to their personnel. In other areas (advertising and book publishing, for example) cooperation came much more easily and our objectives were rather quickly grasped (1, 15). In the film industry, however, we initially faced responses of cynicism and negativism: "What do stuffy academ-

---

[5] For details on amorality as a motif see Christians (4).

[6] The Supreme Court declared unanimously that the movie majors had illegally fixed prices, engaged in block booking, and discriminated in purchasing arrangements. Based on the Court's decision, the Justice Department ruled that theater ownership must be separated from production and distribution within the same company. The eight companies involved (commonly called the Big Five—Loew's, RKO, Paramount, Twentieth Century-Fox, Warner; and the Little Three—Columbia, United Artists, and Universal) monopolized 80 percent of all film business at the time. Cases argued Feb. 9-11, 1948 and decided May 3, 1948. Cf. *United States* v. *Griffith, Schine Chain Theatres* v. *United States, United States* v. *Paramount et al. Cases Argued and Decided in the Supreme Court of the United States*, vol. 92, pp. 1236-1305.

ics know about the film industry anyhow?'' ''Cinema is all crap; take our word for it and forget the survey.'' ''You say this study is sponsored by the McCormick Foundation; that's connected with the Chicago *Tribune*, isn't it? Are they investigating us?'' Those were some reactions when we approached film executives by telephone. In addition, many were completey mystified as to what our questions about ethics could possibly mean. This skepticism was overcome only by persistent follow-up, in three cases involving a mutually respected intermediary.

Taken together, these experiences alerted us to a peculiar situation. While sharing a few ethical features with the larger mass communications structure, motion pictures have a rather definite ethical identity separate from other media— an identity useful characterized in terms of Ellul's *la technique*. For none of the other media areas examined so far have we used *la technique* as a working pespective.

THREE MAJOR PROBLEM AREAS

In the 212 questionnaires returned, 525 situations involving ethical decisions were outlined by the respondents, more than two-thirds of them dealing either with financing, film content, or distribution. Here we offer what seem to represent typical responses from each of these three major categories, as well as some analysis of how they reflect the operating perspective.

Financing
Responses to our survey indicate clearly that management personnel in the motion picture industry are not generally perceived to handle money in an ethically defensible manner, but to operate instead within a network of bribery and kickbacks. Some representative responses, quoted verbatim, demonstrate the point:

- ''There are no ethical decisions in the movie business, just the decision of how far to go and get away with it. The media overflow with tales of embezzlement, perks, top-level mismanagement, intrigue and worse. Both the public and the stockholders be damned. In a word, the profit motive renders ethics irrelevant. The only counterbalance is that certain individuals—and precious few at that—live their personal and professional lives according to some reasonably high standard.'' [Vice-President of major producer/distributor with 24 years experience]
- ''In the movie business . . . there is lying, cheating, stealing, bribes, payoffs, kickbacks, and just plain old double dealing.'' [Advertising Manager of regional chain (133 theaters) with 35 years experience]
- ''In a seller's market, suppliers of film use various devices to bribe employees, such as individual pay-offs for information, bookings, etc. This is probably more prominent in this industry than others, because of the enormous egos of

producers and distributors, and the 'out-do' attitude among various individuals and companies.'' [President of regional theater chain with 28 years experience]

• ''The practice of kickbacks is rampant in all phases of production. Creative people have the dilemma of knowing that they are talented but understanding there is a large, significant percentage of work that will never come their way if they don't kick back. I'm not talking about the tiny few who are superstars. They make their own rules. But truly fine professionals, who earn top dollar and feel they shouldn't have to kick back, simply don't get employment from certain people. This situation is widespread, generally known and accepted in inner circles. Top management people in the biggest corporations get away with graft and nobody blows the whistle.'' [Producer/Director for major film company with 30 years experience]

• ''It is unhappily a common practice among suppliers (even of props) to offer kickbacks. This means the true prices are escalated which increases the production costs . . . . It frequently becomes necessary even to be on guard against your business manager or the designer to be sure *they* [emphasis his] are not receiving kickbacks.'' [Producer/Director for major film company with 35 years experience]

Other financial irregularities were also mentioned: padding budgets, keeping false records, exorbitant pricing, inadequate disclosure of financial data, lying about salaries, discriminatory hiring. All such money matters suggest that a particular financial style is endemic to the movie industry. One respondent summarized this area by wondering whether ''economics ever leaves off and morality begins.'' Another characterized the money situation in these terms, using a phrase almost identical to Ellul's terminology: ''In the name of competition and making a buck . . . results are more important than the methods.'' A 49-year-old executive of a major producer/distributor reflects accurately our own conclusions in studying the returned questionnaires: ''As long as success, personal gain, and competing with one's neighbor and corporations are the rules, ethics will never find a place.''

Finances in cinema, therefore, can be seen to operate predominantly by Ellul's principal of *la technique* and only to a lesser extent according to a deliberate moral perspective or even within legal boundaries. Rather than serving beneficent ends, money is often perceived to flow along the lines of self-serving power. As mentioned above, we are not speaking merely of an occasional abuse or a single flagrant violation of carefully articulated standards. ''The recent David Begelman scandal,'' warned a writer for a major independent studio, ''is merely the tip of the famous iceberg. . . . Hollywood is imbued with this sort of thing.'' ''In motion pictures,'' wrote a writer/producer with 12 years of experience, ''the name of the game is power. In terms of ethics, this translates into selling people out.''

Instead of explicit standards, the ''special deals and bonuses go . . . beyond stated policies.'' Written rules have been perceived to be replaced by a network of amoral forces, "a complexity of relationships and deal making," as one executive put it, "unattached to ethics." As the president of a regional theater chain wrote: "Granted the big guys push us around. . . . What worries me is that we push the little guys around; . . . the powerful take advantage of the lesser . . . not just in the name of profit but for the hell of it." "This business is not founded on ethics," concluded a director with 30 years of experience; "an open full-scale investigation would reveal much more than Watergate or politics." As one confidant apparently advised a young producer: "Never let morality interfere. You might call it the Vito-Genovese method of doing business—a kiss on the cheek and a baseball bat in the yard."

Production

Film production likewise can be seen as a complex pattern of arrangements among various functionaries in which aesthetic qualities have been replaced by the mechanical forces of *la technique*. Once more, a series of quotations from the survey forms are felt to do justice to the overall thrust of responses:

- "Every week we are wined and dined by salesmen, distributors, companies with new technologies. My biggest gripe is that this business is surrounded with vultures who don't know anything about the artistry involved, but who are busy padding their own pockets with all kinds of promotion schemes." [Artist with small independent for 15 years]
- "I would say without hesitation that the bulk of unethical behavior is conducted not by the men and women who actively produce the films, but by all the ancillary personnel who are *business* [emphasis his] oriented: lawyers, accountants, business agents, managers, unions, and others who conduct the business of film making but who do not themselves make films. Most artists are ethical by nature. . . . This business could use some patrolling—but get after the entrepeneurs, not the poor slobs who work on the sets where petty thievery is about the worst of it—or seducing a friend's girl." [Executive Production Supervisor of major film company with 19 years experience]
- "Ethical decisions in the film business are rarely simply questions of right and wrong, but rather constant dichotomies and ambiguity between commercialism and aesthetics of film. This commercialism is, furthermore, rarely on the level of pure money, rather a psychological investment by the individuals involved in the egotism which is, often falsely, allied with 'profit-making'; often these motivations are completely illogical. . . . The nature of the film business invites giving free reign to these motivations." [Manager of individually owned theater with seven years experience]
- "Get the lawyers in the film business as they are the problem. They are the worst since they can 'legally' play on one's desires, and so long as it's legal, what the hell are ethics? Business is business. It is not the letter of the law that is toyed with so much, but a lawyer's inept handling which can botch many

months, or years, of work, and because certain elements have been committed to paper, legally there is no redress. . . . The number of good lawyers are small; they often have as clients at least two parties who are on both sides of a potential deal.'' [Free Lance Writer/Producer with 40 years in film]

- ''Should I allow a scene to be played violently to please the audience who wants that type of fare or shall I take the guts out of it to please the sob sisters and do gooders? I must go with the action and the heck with the sob sisters. After all, we're in business, to make money and if bold action draws more business, that is the way our ethics must take us.'' [Film Director/Producer for major company with 25 years experience]

''Business dealings'' appeared on the majority of the survey forms as the locus of troubling problems—a phrase referring to the intertwined relationships between the product (the film) and all who lay claim to it, between a creative work and a commercial product. One respondent, for example, described four ethical problems on his questionnaire—all of them market-oriented. Thus someone concluded that all decisions eventually revolve around ''acceptable terms on program sales.''

Of course, there are always nuances. One writer indicated, for example, how troubled he was by the way the box office affected his work, yet vowed to take his audience ''someplace they've never been and show them something they've never seen and make them care.'' An executive producer felt he was able to keep his moral problems centered on artistic choices—the ''premise of each show,'' he asks himself each time, ''is it exploitative or constructive?'' A writer of children's shows apparently has found ways to incorporate human values and still provide a marketable product:

. . . our 'Fat Albert,' for example, deals with lying, stealing, drugs, death in the family, drinking, smoking, intolerance, sex, sibling rivalry, hearing and vision problems, retardation, brotherly love, television abuse, junk food, gambling, teacher rejection, and on and on. The network quivers a lot, but takes them.

Others realized that artistic authenticity and commercial viability continually confronted each other but that the latter did not always override the former.

However, as a general conclusion, it is patently obvious that writers and actors do not dominate film production. The legal and sales divisions do instead. Meaningful aesthetic work is seen to occur here and there, but not to dominate this aspect of the industry. Very clearly, content is perceived as determined not by recognizable moral or aesthetic standards, but by commercial viability. One writer, who left a major studio to form his own shop, wrote: ''The majors were always looking for crap to sell. Maybe it was only my artistic sense which was offended; but I think it's more than that when everybody just assumes that violence and explicit sexuality sell, therefore, they must be included in every story line. We had no freedom to be creative.'' An unmistakeable pattern emerges—large-grossing films parade as champions of the industry regardless of their morally offensive content or aesthetic triviality. ''Avoiding the commercially uncertain'' is another way of saying that a technics-saturated ethos characterizes film production.

Sales

Besides ethical questions in management and production, problems of distribution came up frequently in our study. Blind-bidding is the chief focus here and suggests how much the sales-distribution aspect functions by efficiency rather than by explicit moral principles. Typical responses are included below:

- ''We are forced to buy motion pictures without seeing them, pay exorbitant terms and bid 6–9 months in advance. Basically this is strictly a sellers' market. All pictures are blind bid and this is the most unethical part of all. We only have the benefit of 'superhype' and advertising people in making decisions on which pictures to bid.'' [Vice-President of small chain (23 theaters) with 20 years experience]
- ''Do we stick to our word? Most of our business agreements are oral. The sale of motion pictures is thus intangible, a potentially delicate situation which often leads to manipulation. You are advised in some fashion (presumably) what your opposition has offered so that you may raise your offer accordingly. This is a business of negotiation, not of a standard product. This is an industry of different type people. There are many whose word is not worth a lead nickel.'' [President of small chain (18 theaters) with 30 years experience]
- ''One situation is the ethics involved in changing deal points (deals are usually made in our business orally); thereafter, one party or the other may want to change an already negotiated point. The ethics of doing so are often not considered.'' [Vice-President for Business Affairs of major film company with six years experience]
- ''When you are in a very competitive market, and you plan to survive in this market, actions have to be taken that though they are not ethical, they become great business decisions. Any description of these situations would be unethical [emphasis his] on my part.'' [Film Buyer for regional theater chain with 14 years experience]
- ''Even customers of 16mm educational film base their decisions to purchase not just on lowest price/best quality. Favorite companies, favorite salesmen, better deals, what will you give me personally for the order—all these factors enter into approximately 50% of sales decisions.'' [Sales Director for educational film company with 12 years experience]

As explicit contractual arrangements are shunted aside in daily management and production, what emerges is an underlying pattern of secrecy and deal making which dominates distribution. Instead of open fairness to all potential buyers, each competing on equal terms, the seller/buyer relationship is characterized by forces of power. Thus questions about agreements cannot be settled judiciously in predictable ways, but are apparently caught up in a struggle where the haves oppress the have-nots. Transactions are not merely commercial in nature with all involved parties understanding the product and making judgments about its value with all the facts known. A minimal definition of fairness would suggest the equal application of policies to all competitors, large and small. In a world seen largely as devoid of moral qualities, such as the distribution of film where product is so fiercely sought, the words "equal" and "open" apparently do not apply with any consistency.

As with finance and production, a few individuals try to live by humane standards in distribution and exhibition. "Local level decisions," wrote one, "are usually ethical. Central office decisions are made without any thought or compassion." Thus an individual theater owner spoke valiantly of his "moral obligation" to keep the public informed (by honest advertising and personal recommendation) as to the suitability of his films, regardless of those he finally received for showing. But, once more, the overarching system makes such conscientious effort the proverbial exception which proves the rule.

CONCLUSION

It seems imperative to us that worthwhile analysis of cinema ethics must grasp the film industry as a system, a social structure. Simply referring to isolated improprieties—a gratutiously violent film or dishonest executive, for example—is only ephemeral. With the aid of the responses from practicioners, we have sought to think and probe more wholistically, using as our analog the heatness in red-hot metal; that is, following a cue from Ellul, we have been interested in the *Geist,* the connective patterns and deteminative style that permeate the film business.

Once the motion picture industry is viewed as an organism with specifiable boundaries, it is not surprising that one sees similar themes no matter how the various components are related and compared. Amoral efficiency appears with differing intensity, but all ways of organizing the data yield similar results. Film people apparently tend to react to questions concerning ethics with some predictability whether they have ten years of experience or 35, whether in production or distribution, whether working for a conglomerate or an independent, a firm of ten thousand employees or one hundred. Only in individually-owned theaters or studios, and in educational film, are the dynamics ameliorated somewhat. Certainly we are wary of overgeneralization and gross abstraction, but feel confident that the overall themes we have outlined in finance, production, and sales accurately lay hold of endemic patterns and are not artificially imposed from without.

This first round of research into cinema ethics prompts us to pursue kickbacks, marketing, and blind-bidding in the second phase. Consistent with the naturalistic form of step one, our aim is to locate representative cases in each of these three problem areas. Our objective at this next stage is to prepare some case histories which illuminate in depth how kickbacks, marketing, and blind-bidding operate in concrete settings. In terms of strategy, this entails participant-observation, examination of personal documents, and open-ended interviewing on site.[7] While the study outlined above is a first-level approximation, it serves the vital function of directing us to circumstances which are woven into the structural fabric of the cinema industry. We believe our study to date sweeps widely enough and speaks with sufficient nuance to permit our further examination of kickbacks, commercial certainty, and blind bidding as organizing concepts.[8] For anyone familiar with the standard ethical issues vis-à-vis motion pictures (pornography, violence, offensive language, drugs and alcohol among actors, stealing by executives and so forth) the significance and potential of our approach are self-evident.[9]

The overall impression from our sample's responses is of an industry that has spun itself into a certain form, that operates out of its own internal dynamics, and permits the ethos of cold, machine-like technics to go virtually unchallenged. Thus, should it wish to strengthen its influence as a powerful art form, reform must involve more than curbing violence and jailing bribers. The solution here apparently lies in seeing its entire ethos undergo a massive metamorphosis, in crushing *la technique*—a force so inherent in the industry now that its elimination virtually entails a new structure.

REFERENCES

1. Blum, Eleanor and Clifford Christians. "Ethical Problems in Book Publishing." *The Library Quarterly* 51 (2), April 1982, pp. 155-169.
2. Blumer, Herbert. "What is Wrong with Social Theory?" *American Sociological Review* 19, February 1954, pp. 3-10.
3. Bogdan, Robert and Steven J. Taylor. *Introduction to Qualitative Research Methods.* New York: John Wiley and Sons, 1975.
4. Christians, Clifford, "Jacques Ellul's Concerns with the Amorality of Contemporary Communications," *Communications: International Journal of Communication Research* 1, 1977, pp. 62-80.
5. Christians, Clifford and James Carey. "The Logic and Aims of Qualitative Research." In Guido H. Stempel and Bruce H. Westley (Eds.), pp. 342-362. *Research Methods in Mass Communication,* Englewood Cliffs, NJ: Prentice-Hall, 1981.
6. Christians, Clifford, Kim Rotzoll and Mark Fackler. *Media Ethics: Cases and Moral Reasoning.* New York: Longman, Inc. 1983.
7. Ellul, Jacques. *The Political Illusion.* New York: Alfred A. Knopf, 1967.
8. Ellul, Jacques. *Presence of the Kingdom.* New York: Seabury Press, 1967.
9. Ellul, Jacques. *Propaganda.* New York: Alfred A. Knopf, 1969.

---

[7] Bogdan and Taylor (3, chaps. 2-5) elaborate on these three mainstays of the qualitative approach.

[8] Pursuit of these three areas, we believe, will lead to what Herbert Blumer calls sensitizing concepts. Quantitative research constructs law-like abstractions through fixed procedures. In contrast to such definititve concepts, our interpretive model seeks to order empirical instances by discovering sensitized notions which distinctively convey the underlying meaning of the phenomena under study. For definitions of sensitizing and definitive concepts, see Blumer (2).

[9] For an overview of the traditional moral concerns regarding entertainment, see Christians, Rotzoll and Fackler (6, pp. 215-301).

10. Fortner, Robert and Clifford Christians. ''Separating Wheat from Chaff in Qualitative Studies.'' In Guido H. Stempel and Bruce H. Westley (Eds.), *Research Methods in Mass Communication*, pp. 363-374. Englewood Cliffs, NJ: Prentice-Hall, 1981.

11. Geertz, Clifford. ''Thick Description,'' in his *The Interpretation of Cultures*, pp. 3-30. New York: Basic Books, Inc., 1973.

12. McClintick, David. *Indecent Exposure: A True Story of Hollywood and Wall Street*. New York: William Morrow, 1982; Dell, 1983.

13. Mills, C. Wright. *The Sociological Imagination*, (chap. 2). London: Oxford University Press, 1967.

14. Rabinow, Paul and William M. Sullivan. ''The Interpretive Turn,'' in their *Interpretive Social Science*, pp. 1-21. Berkeley: University of California Press, 1979.

15. Rotzoll, Kim and Clifford Christians. ''Advertising Agency Practitioners' Perceptions of Ethical Decisions.'' *Journalism Quarterly* 57 (3) Autumn 1980, pp. 425-431.

16. Weber, Max. *The Protestant Ethic and the Spirit of Capitalism* (trans. Talcott Parsons.) New York: Scribner, 1930.

17. Weber, Max. *The Methodology of the Social Sciences*, Eds. Edward Shils and Henry Finch. New York: The Free Press, 1949.

13

A Case Study of Film Antitrust Legislation: *R.D. Goldberg* v. *Tri-States Theatre Corporation*

Cathy Schwichtenberg

The Supreme Court case, *United States* v. *Paramount Pictures, Inc., et al.* (38) was significant for both the motion picture industry and antitrust legislation. Although initially it may seem more profitable for film historians specializing in antitrust legislation to focus on the Paramount case, it is equally important to examine the smaller antitrust cases filed during that same time in district courts. These small cases should not be overlooked, for they served as the impetus behind the Paramount case. The Paramount case was not a sudden, inaugural historical event which stood alone. Rather, this landmark case was the culmination of many other film antitrust cases which involved theater monopolies on state and local levels. Thus, the argument advanced by the present article is that the smaller antitrust cases, involving affiliated and unaffiliated circuits, contributed to the necessity of the Paramount case.

Detailed case studies of the legal arguments and courtroom dramas between affiliated and unaffiliated exhibitors reveal, at the ''grass roots'' level, the specific types of legal battles which were fought over the control of property and first-run films. Examination of these local-level legal battles offer antitrust and motion picture historians an understanding of the characteristics of the entrepreneurial disputes which defined the historical, legal and economic milieu surrounding the Paramount case. Micro-social case studies, such as the one presented here, illustrate the range and types of disputes which occurred during the time of the Paramount decision.

In the 1930s the climate in small communities and towns was hostile to theater chains entering into active competition with local operators (12). Therefore, it is hardly surprising that the antitrust cases which were argued in state and local courts concerned allegations of block-booking, priorities over clearance for first-run films, and rental property agreements—all grievances which pertained to lack of competition, restraint of trade, and unfair business practices (1, 11, 18, 22, 40). Under such conditions, it is likely that the disputes between affiliated and unaffiliated circuits would take the form of extended legal battles—often spanning a number of years—over the territorial rights to a lucrative market.

Abraham H. Blank and Ralph D. Goldberg were two such exhibitors from the Midwest who became involved in a number of antitrust disputes over approximately ten years. While not all antitrust cases can be characterized as "personal vendettas," this is one discernable feature of the battles waged between Blank and Goldberg over theater territory in the Nebraska market. Beginning in the 1920s, the A.H. Blank circuit was affiliated with Paramount and incorporated as Tri-States and Central States Theatre Corporations which had substantial theater holdings in Iowa and Nebraska. From 1941 to 1951 one preliminary hearing and three cases were documented in Omaha, Nebraska involving Tri-States Theatre Corp. and a local exhibitor, the R.D. Goldberg Theatre Corp.

Blank and Goldberg's extended struggle for power may constitute a typical feature of small antitrust disputes; the generalizability of this feature is, at present, unknown but could be demonstrated by historians who investigate antitrust battles originating from other states and localities. Certainly the Paramount case is worthy of investigation itself as has been done (see, e.g., 7). But historians can often find equally important data in their own hometowns. Thus, the nature of the investigation reported here is perhaps best characterized as part of a local history, a specific antitrust case study of one preliminary hearing and three court cases involving Blank and Goldberg.

THE PARAMOUNT CASE AND THE BUSINESS ENVIRONMENT

In 1938 the Paramount case was filed against the eight largest U.S. film distributors. The defendants were the five fully integrated majors (Twentieth Century-Fox, RKO, Paramount, Warner Bros., and Loew's) and the three minors (Columbia, Universal and United Artists). After the Paramount case was filed in 1938, an Amended Supplemental Complaint was filed on November 14, 1940 outlining the eight distributors' numerous trade violations (2, 4, 7, 38). A week later on November 20, 1940 the government and the five majors were parties to the Consent Decree (2, 4, 7, 38), the industry's attempt at self-regulation. In the Consent Decree of 1940, the American Arbitration Association attempted to oversee the industry's self-regulation. However, while the Decree restricted minor trade practices, it left virtually unchanged the five majors' first-run theater monopolies. In 1944, the Paramount case was reopened, and then tried in 1945. The 1946 District Court decision held illegal horizontal and vertical agreements such as block-booking, pooling agreements, and distributors' uniform systems of runs and clearances, as practiced by the five majors and three minors (2, 4, 7, 38).

The lower court ordered competitive bidding for films and the Supreme Court affirmed the illegality of the trade practices noted above. *United States* v. *Paramount Pictures, Inc., et al.* was argued February 9-11, 1948 and decided May 3, 1948. All eight defendants were found to be in violation of the Sherman Antitrust Act which stated that both the "use" and "intent to use" monopoly power to exclude competitors is an illegal trade practice (2, 4, 7, 38). The District Court, while awaiting further proceedings, held further hearings and ordered the five majors to divorce themselves of their theater circuits and to divest themselves of one half of the theaters they owned (2, 4, 7, 38).

The time span from 1940 to 1942, within which is located the 1941 preliminary hearing of *Nebraska* v. *Goldberg* and the 1942 case *Goldberg et al.* v. *Tri-States Theatre Corp.* (16) was a time of unrest and panic for the motion picture industry. First, the District Court leveled its accusations, then the Decree modified them. Since the status of the five majors was in question, the circuits affiliated with them suddenly found that they had to fight in the courts to protect their holdings. At the same time, the independents, seeing that the majors' and their affiliates' power was no longer secured, attempted to acquire more theater holdings. Indeed, the independents were ready for the Decree which placed control "up for grabs" and reacted swiftly. A week after the Consent Decree, *Variety* reported the first antitrust suit to be filed by independents. Two independent owners from Pennsylvania requested triple damages amounting to $62,700 under the Clayton Antitrust Law and an injunction against distributors and the defendant-exhibitor (14).

1941 to 1942 saw a worsening of the overall exhibitor/distributor relationship, and the *Motion Picture Herald* reported that "during 1941, 'a black year' for exhibition, the Consent Decree proved a lamentable failure and independent exhibitors were assailed from both sides" (10). The Consent Decree failed to promote self-regulation since both independent exhibitors and affiliated exhibitors/distributors were dissatisfied with the Decree. On the one hand, the major distributors feared that smaller distributors such as Republic or Monogram might be exempt from the trade restrictions they were subject to; while the small, independent exhibitor had financial difficulties in obtaining legal counsel (4, p. 341). Overall, the Consent Decree further destabilized the industry. In 1942 the American Arbitration Association filed 167 complaints (24) and Abram F. Myers, chairman for Allied States Association (the exhibitor association) stated that "unless there is an abrupt change of policy by the distributors, this dizzy pace will be continued with disasterous results to all concerned" (10). Arbitration was near collapse (10) and this, among other things, created the conditions for cases such as those discussed here. In the wake of this frenetic activity on the part of independents and distributors alike, the 1941 hearing and the 1942 case between Goldberg and Blank serve as case studies at this historical juncture.

THE ANTITRUST DISPUTES BETWEEN GOLDBERG AND BLANK

In both the 1941 preliminary hearing (*Nebraska* v. *Goldberg*) and the 1942 case (*Golberg* v. *Tri-States*), Ralph D. Goldberg appears to have been A.H. Blank and Tri-States' nemesis and business competitor in Omaha, Nebraska. As a showman/ exhibitor, Goldberg had had considerable experience. As early as 1915, the three Goldberg brothers (3) had theater holdings in Nebraska. In October of 1915, S.H. Goldberg (one of Ralph's brothers), opened his new Omaha theater at 1410-14 Farnam Street (17); at the same time Blank opened his new Strand Theatre in Omaha (9). Significantly, in the 1942 *Goldberg* v. *Tri-States* case (16), the State Theatre building in dispute was located at 1410-1414 Farnam Street (16, p. 27). Goldberg is listed in the 1937 *Motion Picture Almanac* as manager of the Goldberg Theatre Corp. (25, p. 1024) and in the *Motion Picture Herald,* reference is made to "the Goldberg Circuit which has operated the Military [Theatre] since 1938" (5). In 1942 (apparently after the murder of his two brothers by an angered partner [37], Ralph D. Goldberg assumed the presidency of the then renamed R.D. Goldberg Theatre Corp. (26, p. 886). The trades referred to him as "a local circuit owner" (34) and in 1950 he completed a two-year remodeling project on his various houses (33).

At the time of litigation, Omaha could be characterized as Goldberg's "turf," with Blank and Tri-States entering into an open and competitive market comprised of subsequent-run independents; this was quite unlike the "closed" Iowa market which was dominated by Blank/Central States/Tri-States (31). Thus Ralph D. Goldberg was a reasonably ambitious, formidable competitor for A.H. Blank in the Omaha area as the following 1941 report on Goldberg's preliminary hearing would indicate.

The November 22, 1941 issue of the *Motion Picture Herald* reports that the date of a preliminary hearing was to be set in Omaha in an antitrust suit brought by Nebraska against the R.D. Goldberg circuit and nine distributors for trying to put out of business the Epstein Theatres Corp. and the A.H. Blank-Green Admiral Theatre. According to the *Motion Picture Herald,* the distributors had agreed to accept higher film rental terms from Goldberg which meant that the Epstein Theatre would be relegated to a playing position after the Goldberg theatres where previously the Epstein had played day and date with Goldberg's. Goldberg was also charged with raising admissions from 30 to 35 cents as part of the alleged conspiracy. The equity action attempted to obtain an injunction to restrain contemplated film deals and clearance revisions (19).

The Admiral Theatre, operated by the Blank Omaha interests, was reported as the first new house to be built in 15 years in Omaha. This is significant since the Omaha area was Goldberg's territory (31). Apparently Goldberg, as an independent, dealt with a number of distributors, one of which was Paramount. Thus, even though Blank was affiliated with Paramount, Paramount was one of the distributors charged by the state for conspiring with Goldberg against Blank's new Admiral Theatre (19). The Admiral Theatre threatened Goldberg's market and at the time of this hearing, Paramount seems to have dealt exclusively with Blank and occasionally with Goldberg (13). This type of dual business arrangement resulted in a territorial dispute (for a somewhat similar case, see, e.g., 7, p. 87 and 20).

The District Attorney's action against Goldberg was in conflict with an antitrust suit filed earlier by Goldberg charging that the major distributors were in a conspiracy with Blank against him (19). A total of more than 20 of Omaha's 32 theatres were involved in all of the actions (19). Thus, from the outset, it would appear that Goldberg and Tri-States/Blank were destined to go around in circles—one accusing the other of antitrust violations.

Goldberg v. Tri-States: a Territorial Dispute

On March 3, 1942 in an Omaha Nebraska District Court, Tri-States Theatre Corp., the Plaintiff, brought suit against Ralph D. Goldberg et al., the defendants, to prohibit the use of a certain building for theater purposes by the defendants. The ruling was in favor of Tri-States. Although Goldberg appealed their decision, the original ruling for Tri-States was affirmed (*Goldberg et al.* v. *Tri-States Theatre Corp.* [167]). The case was as follows: By 1933 or 1934 Ralph D. Goldberg operated eight subsequent-run theaters, with one in downtown Omaha, Nebraska (16, pp. 30-31). Goldberg wanted first-run films and, presumably, a first-run house. World Realty (of which Goldberg was director and officer, and his parents stockholders) had a 99-year lease on two theater buildings, the World and the State, which had previously been two first-run theaters located a block-and-a-half apart (with overlapping patronage [16, p. 30]). In Jaunary 1934, World Realty (Goldberg) subleased the World and State Theatres to Premier Theatre Company (a subsidiary of Tri-States) until 1950. Premier operated both theaters for awhile and then sank its money into the World Theatre because it had better accommodations. The State Theatre was closed and ceased operation as a theater; however, Premier continued to pay rent on the State Theatre and had the right to commercialize the building (16, p. 31).

Also in January 1934, World Realty (Goldberg) decided to dispose of the 99-year lease. The reason for this was not expressly indicated in the record, but supposedly Goldberg was in financial trouble since he needed to liquidate the indebtedness for which the Omaha National Bank was holding part of the capital stock as collateral (16, p. 31). World Realty approached A.H. Blank, then representing Tri-States through Premier and owning 50 percent of the capital stock in Tri-States, to purchase the lease. The Omaha National Bank attempted to influence Blank to make the deal. Blank replied that ''he was not interested in making a financial investment unless he could be certain that the State Theatre would be kept out of competition with the World'' (16, p. 31). Blank suggested that World Realty (Goldberg) take back the State Theatre building and agree to keep it out of competition as a theatre for 10 years. World Realty agreed to those terms, stating that plans were underway to convert the State Theatre building into a commercial garage (16, p. 31).

Blank then organized Commonwealth Theatres Corporation to purchase the 99-year lease on the world Theatre property. As part of this contractual transaction, World Realty canceled the previous subleases held by Premier on the World and State Theatres, and executed a new sublease on the World Theatre in favor of Premier, containing the restrictive agreement that World Realty would keep the State Theatre building out of competition with the World Theatre for 10 years (16, pp. 31-32). This restrictive agreement was the issue of dispute in Tri-States' action against Goldberg.

No sooner had Blank secured the sublease on the World Theatre for Premier, than Goldberg set out to acquire the title of the State Theatre building by purchasing the property from himself and reopening it. To do this, Goldberg organized the State Investment Company to secure two-thirds of the State Theatre property. Goldberg made an agreement with himself as State Investment and an officer from Omaha National Bank, on behalf of World Realty (himself) to cancel the 99-year lease (16, p. 27). Then, to reopen the State Theatre with himself as manager (after acquiring the other one-third of the State property), Goldberg, using State Investment as lessor, leased the theater building to himself by creating A.L. Kaplan Inc. (another corporation of which he was the sole stockholder) as lessee (16, p. 28). At this point Tri-States filed suit against Goldberg to prevent him from reopening the State as a theater, arguing that Goldberg was in violation of the restrictive clause in the World's sublease contract. The court decided in favor of Tri-States (16, p. 28).

Following the court's decision, Goldberg et al. appealed, accusing Tri-States of using the restrictive clause as "a part of a scheme and purpose to monopolize and to restrict the leasing and exhibition of first-run and other films in the Omaha area" (16, p. 30). This, it was asserted, was in violation of the Sherman Antitrust Act. Claiming "monopolistic conspiracy" (16, p. 31), Goldberg tried to prove that the restrictive clause was "unreasonable" and was being used to eliminate him as a competitor (16, p. 29). He accused Blank and Commonwealth of merging into one corporation—Tri-States (one of Goldberg's own business tactics)— because Tri-States bought all the stock in Commonwealth; but the court ruled that Commonwealth was a separate corporation from Tri-States (16, p. 32). Tri-States emphasized that Goldberg could open a theater in any location in the Omaha area except one block and a half from their World Theatre. Further, Tri-States argued that if Goldberg wanted to use the State Theatre building, he could transform it into anything he wished, except a theater (16, p. 30).

The court affirmed its previous decision in favor of Tri-States, denying Goldberg et al.'s appeal. On March 28, 1942, the case and ruling were reported in the *Motion Picture Herald*:

The State Theatre, Omaha, must remain closed until 1944 under terms of a lease made in 1934 by Tri-States Theatres, Inc., with Ralph D. Goldberg interests, according to a ruling by the U.S. Circuit Court at St. Louis. Tri-States claims that when it leased the Omaha theatre in 1934 a provision called for the closing of the State Theatre, located only a block and a half away. Mr. Goldberg, who claims he was "coerced" into the contract, is expected to appeal the decision (23).

Throughout the 1940s and into the early 1950s, Goldberg and Tri-States/Blank continued their struggle for power—one accusing the other of "monopoly," followed by appeals from either one or the other. On the national level, this trend also continued into the 1950s with antitrust suits reported as a common bill of fare in trade publications. For instance, *Variety* reported "United Par Named with Others in 450G Antitrust Action" (37), and in another issue, "322,000,000 in 94 Pending Suits vs. 8 Major Cos." (35); the *Motion Picture Herald* carried articles with such headlines as "U.S. Presses Action in Griffith Case" (39), "Time Extension Granted in Goldwyn Trust Suit" (36), and in another issue, "Five Trust Suits Filed; Name Distributor" (15).

Goldberg vs. Tri-States: The Examination of Documents
The 1940 Consent Decree, following fast upon the District Court's Amended Supplemental Complaint, was partly responsible for creating the initially suspended conditions that promoted "courtroom vendettas" between independent and affiliated circuits. Monopoly guidelines had not been drawn hard and fast by the government, therefore "monopoly" became a "catch word" used loosely in the attempt to acquire property or first-run films (4, p. 341). Independents watched for the momentary vulnerability of the five majors brought about by this period of transition, and they kept the courts and major distributors busy in their attempt to wrest power from the affiliated circuits. Whether through legal or illegal means, distributors responded to this crisis which placed their holdings in jeopardy (29) and the independents retaliated in kind. Thus, the 1940 Consent Decree defeated its purpose (8, p. 55). The Decree gave independents and affiliates the incentive to battle in the courts endlessly since both parties were unwilling to either relinquish control or compromise because the economic stakes were too high. Hence, in 1944, the government reactivated the Paramount case and petitioned the District Court to modify the Decree. The Justice Department wanted to remedy the Amended Supplemental Complaint by proposing the divorcement of the exhibition branches of the five majors from their production-distribution activities (8).

The reopening of the Paramount case necessitated reexamination of concrete evidence in the form of documents such as records, contracts, and accounting books in the possession of the distributors (4, p. 333). Early on, the distributors had feared having to disclose such information (6). A 1950 ruling in Salt Lake City, Utah was illustrative of a trend which resulted from the reopening of the Paramount case: "A U.S. District Court Judge in Salt Lake City has ruled that exhibitors have the right to inspect the distributors' books in a pending rental action filed by the latter'' (30, p. 20). Sometimes the examination of documents worked in an opposite direction with distributors examining exhibitors' records (21). The competing affiliated and unaffiliated theater corporations were only too eager to expose each others' devious monopolistic conspiracies and practices. Thus by ''reporting'' on each other, the corporations submitted to governmental pressure which, in the end, benefited neither side but rather worked in the service of the court, and ultimately led to the restructuring of the industry.

The following case can serve as an illustration of independent exhibitor Ralph D. Goldberg's use of the courts in his persistent attempt to challenge and defeat the Tri-States/Blank Theatre Corporation. On July 20, 1944, one month prior to the government's reopening of the Paramount case, in the Omaha Division of the Nebraska District Court, plaintiff Goldberg filed for a preliminary examination by the court of the records of the defendants, Tri-States Theatre Corporation et. al.;[1] see *R.D. Goldberg Theatre Corp.* v. *Tri-States Theatre Corp. et al.* (28).

The defendants joined in a motion to stay the court's order of July 1, 1944 requiring them to produce certain books, records, and contracts pending the disposition of their appeal to the United States Circuit Court of Appeals to fix the amount of the bond required to be filed (28, p. 522). The plaintiff, Goldberg Theatre Corp., objected to the allowance of the motion and the court denied the motion to stay the July 1 order as an unappealable interlocutory order (28, p. 521).

The May 3, 1948 ruling by the United States Supreme Court for divorcement and divestiture signaled, as in the order to reactivate the Paramount case in 1944, what was a massive investigation and examination of books, contracts, and records. Again competing theater corporations were only too willing to call attention to each others' trade practices, thus aiding the courts in obtaining the documents they needed to untangle the complex corporate networks.

On May 24, 1951 in the U.S. District Court of Nebraska, Omaha Division, the State Theatre Co., a copartnership, brought an action against Tri-States Theatre Corp. and Twentieth Century-Fox Film Corp.; see *State Theatre Co.* v. *Tri-States Theatre Corp., et al.* (32). At this time, the R.D. Goldberg Theatre Corp. operated the State Theatre in Omaha, Nebraska and Goldberg conducted his business out of the State Theatre building (27, p. 447). It is perhaps likely, considering the nature of this U.S. District Court case and the litigants involved, that between 1944 and 1951 Ralph D. Goldberg acquired the State Theatre with the help of a cosponsor, since the State Theatre in Omaha, Nebraska of the 1942 case was connected with Tri-States and the World Theatre dispute. Goldberg may have taken the opportunity offered him by the courts to ''settle an old score'' with Tri-States/Blank.

The court action filed by the State Theatre Co. involved an alleged combination and conspiracy on behalf of Tri-States and Fox to restrain trade. The State Theatre

---

[1] The defendants were Twentieth Century-Fox Film Corp., Loew's Inc., United Artists Corp., Universal Film Exchange Inc., Vitagraph Inc., RKO Film Booking Corp., RKO Radio Pictures Inc., Tri-State Theater Corp., Paramount Pictures Inc., and Paramount Film Distributing Corp.

Co. had the branch manager for Twentieth Century-Fox (one of the defendants) served with a subpoena requiring the production of the following items: "All books, papers, records, memoranda, correspondence and all other documents and papers relating to the leasing and/or releasing of motion picture films for exhibiton with the defendants Tri-States Theatre Corporation, Singer Omaha Corporation, and State Theatre Company of Omaha, Nebraska, for the period commencing October 1, 1944 to February 16, 1949" (32, p. 382).

The specific correspondence the State Theatre Co. wanted from Fox related to the State Theatre's request and demand for the leasing of films from Fox for exhibition in the State Theatre in Omaha, Nebraska. They also wanted all correspondence between the Omaha branch of Fox and the Fox Corporation in New York. In addition, the State Theatre Co. requested all correspondence, papers, records, and memoranda between the Omaha branch of Twentieth Century-Fox and Abraham H. Blank and/or his manager, Grace Ralph Branton, related to the leasing and/or releasing of films for exhibition in Tri-States Theatre Corp. in Omaha from October 1, 1944 to February 16, 1949 (32, p. 382).

The defendants, Twentieth Century-Fox Film Corp. and Tri-States Theatre Corp., filed motions to quash the subpoena. One reason offered by the defendants to quash the subpoena was the assertion that the State Theatre Corp. had failed to show "good cause" for the production of the documents. However, the court stated that a showing of "good cause" had been made by the plaintiff who claimed that the documents constituted relevant evidence (32, pp. 382-383). Then both defendants, Tri-States and Fox, argued that the subpoena was too broad and, as a result, they could not identify the documents in question. Fox also contended that the subpoena violated the Fourth Amendment which forbids unreasonable search and seizure (32, pp. 383-384). The court, however, denied the defendants' motion to quash the subpoena provided that the plaintiff pay for the cost of producing the large volume of papers, books, and documents which were many due to the plaintiff's broad subpoena (32, p. 384). While the District Court held that part of the subpoena did not sufficiently designate the documents requested, all motions to quash the subpoena were denied (32, p. 381).

CONCLUSION

Using the key dates of the Paramount case as a temporal framework, the legal milieu of the period offers a method by which to gauge some of the shifts and developments of smaller antitrust cases at state and local levels. This article offers an example of the struggle for power over real estate and first-run films, and the probable business double-dealing between Goldberg and Blank, thereby providing a specific example of an extended legal battle that may have been going on elsewhere between other exhibitors. In the end, Goldberg's probable retributory action against Tri-States/Blank, which took the form of exposing his rival to the courts for excluding him from the profits to be made, does not constitute "winning" in any significant and broader sense. As discussed here, the independents were not the "good guys"—the self-made men—against the "bad guys"—the evil monopolistic corporations. Both sides can be accurately characterized as equally shrewd businessmen who often went to great lengths to acquire more property and capital than they originally had.

The Paramount case, as a landmark case for antitrust legislation in the motion picture industry, cannot be divorced from the small antitrust cases which occurred simultaneously. The Paramount case can be most accurately conceived of as the legal culmination of widespread individual actions concerning property and capital which resulted in the ruling for divorcement and divestiture. By examining the "grass roots" level actions of such entrepreneurs as A.H. Blank and R.D. Goldberg, antitrust and film historians are better able to understand, in a more thorough fashion, this episode in film's legal history. From this perspective, the Paramount case can be seen and studied as not only an important historical event, but also as the result of individual struggles for power dramatized at state and local levels. Hence, data gathered from state and local motion picture antitrust cases serve to illuminate the actions and motives of individuals which created the conditions for the ruling which affected the entire industry. In a small, but nonetheless important way, Blank and Goldberg's legal battles contribute to our knowledge of a specific local history of antitrust legislation which, in turn, helps to illuminate the historical necessity of the Paramount decision.

REFERENCES

1. "Asks Divorce of Circuit from Detroit Theatre." *Motion Picture Herald,* May 26, 1945, p. 42.
2. Balio, Tino. "Retrenchment, Reappraisal, and Reorganization: 1948-." In Tino Balio (Ed.), *The American Film Industry,* pp. 315-320. Madison: University of Wisconsin Press, 1976.
3. Blank, Myron. Telephone interview, April 25, 1982.
4. Borneman, Ernest. "United States versus Hollywood: The Case Study of an Antitrust Suit." In Tino Balio (Ed.), *The American Film Industry,* pp. 332-345. Madison: University of Wisconsin Press, 1976.
5. "Buys Omaha Theatre." *Motion Picture Herald,* September 9, 1950, p. 18.
6. "Chi Distribs Feel That the Indies Restraint Suit Will Open Up Long Closed Books, Disclose Profits, etc." *Variety,* September 14, 1938, p. 3.
7. Conant, Michael. *Antitrust in the Motion Picture Industry.* Berkeley: University of California Press, 1960.
8. Crandall, Robert W. "The Postwas Performance of the Motion Picture Industry." *The Antitrust Bulletin* 20 (1), Spring 1975, pp. 49-56.
9. "Davenport's New $50,000 Theatre Opens Wednesday." *The Davenport Democrat and Leader,* September 19, 1915, p. 18.
10. "Decree Selling is Used to 'Jack Up' Rentals: Myers' Annual Report Charges Failure of Arbitration; Called 'Black Year.'" *Motion Picture Herald,* January 31, 1942, p. 16.
11. "Detroit Exhibitor Files Suit Against Majors." *Motion Picture Herald,* May 5, 1945, p. 48.
12. "Divorcement Legislation Grows Apace; Local Interests Manifest Little Sympathy to the Chains." *Variety,* August 17, 1938, p. 5.
13. Ellis, Dorsey. Interview, June 28, 1984.

14. "First Post-Consent Decree Suit Filed by Two Pennsy Indies." *Variety,* November 27, 1940, p. 7.

15. "Five Trust Suits Filed; Name Distributors." *Motion Picture Herald,* September 23, 1950, p. 30.

16. *Goldberg et al.* v. *Tri-States Theatre Corp.,* CCANeb, 126 F2d, 26 (1942).

17. "Goldberg's New Omaha House Aims at Comfort." *The Movie Picture World,* October 16, 1915, p. 486.

18. "Goldman Petitions Court on Theatre Divestiture." *Motion Picture Herald,* July 3, 1948, p. 24.

19. "Hearing on Nebraska Trust." *Motion Picture Herald,* November 22, 1941, p. 66.

20. *Interstate Circuit, Inc., et al.* v. *United States,* 306 U.S., 208 (1939).

21. "Judge Okays Distribs' O.O. of Volks' Books." *Variety,* January 11, 1950, p. 5.

22. "Majors Must Answer June 27 in Montana Trust Case." *Motion Picture Herald,* June 16, 1945, p. 40.

23. "Omaha House Ordered Closed." *Motion Picture Herald,* March 28, 1942, p. 44.

24. "167 AAA Complaints Filed: Clearance Biggest Issue." *Motion Picture Herald,* January 31, 1942, pp. 47-50.

25. Ramsaye, Terry (Ed.). *International Motion Picture Almanac 1937-38.* New York: Quigley Publishing Co., 1937.

26. Ramsaye, Terry (Ed.). *International Motion Picture Alamanc 1942-43.* New York: Quigley Publishing Co., 1942.

27. Ramsaye, Terry (Ed.). *International Motion Picture Almanac 1950-51.* New York: Quigley Publishing Co., 1950.

28. *R.D. Goldberg Theatre Corp.* v. *Tri-States Theatre Corp. et. al.,* DCNeb 119, F Supp, 521 (1944).

29. "Reserve Decision in Divorcement Appeal; Some Witnesses Not Called Due to "Retailiation Fear."" *Variety,* June 15, 1938, p. 6.

30. "Rule Exhibitor May See Distributor's Books." *Motion Picture Herald,* November 11, 1950, p. 20.

31. Schmidt, Jackson. Presentation: "Blank and His Competitors," Seminar in American Film History, University of Iowa, Iowa City, Iowa, April 23, 1982.

32. *State Theatre Co.* v. *Tri-States Theatre Corp. et al.,* DCNeb, 11 FRD, 381 (1951).

33. "The National Spotlight: Omaha." *Motion Picture Herald,* July 1, 1950, p. 35.

34. "The National Spotlight: Omaha." *Motion Picture Herald,* July 8, 1950, p. 25.

35. "322,000,000 in 94 Pending Suits vs. 8 Major Cos." *Variety,* February 1, 1950, pp. 5, 20.

36. "Time Extension Granted in Goldwyn Trust Suit." *Motion Picture Herald,* July 22, 1950, p. 30.

37. "United Par Named With Others in 450G Antitrust Action." *Variety,* January 25, 1950, p. 4.

38. *United States* v. *Paramount Pictures, Inc., et al.,* 334 U.S., 131 (1948).

39. "U.S. Presses Action in Griffith Case." *Motion Picture Herald,* July 22, 1950, p. 4.

40. "Will Query Major Pic Execs in N.Y. on Anti-Trust suit Brought by N.E. Group." *Variety,* July 13, 1938, p. 5.

AUTHOR INDEX

Italics indicate bibliographic citations.

SUBJECT INDEX